Endorsements

"In an era when incivility, bitter partisanship and dishonesty poison American politics, it's refreshing - indeed inspiring - to read a memoir by a man whose career, guided by a deep faith, epitomizes the opposite - charity, cheerfulness, moderation, and decency."

MORTON KONDRACKE,
FORMER EXECUTIVE EDITOR, ROLL CALL,
AND TELEVISION COMMENTATOR

A Higher Calling is also a tale about the pursuit of high personal values 'in the arena' - where politics and business, ambition and gain tangle, under the relentless glare of the media.

SHELBY COFFEY, III,
FORMER EDITOR, LOS ANGELES TIMES,
VICE CHAIRMAN, NEWSEUM

A fascinating story, charmingly told, and a shining contrast to the discordance and incivility of today's political culture.

OS GUINNESS,
AUTHOR OF 37 BOOKS ON FAITH
AND FREEDOM

"So inspired by A Higher Calling I decided to run for Congress in my home state of New Jersey!"

DAVID APPLEFIELD,
CEO, KIWAI MEDIA, SPECIAL PROJECTS
REPRESENTATIVE, FINANCIAL TIMES

"Don Bonker's deeply personal and insightful account — an exception to the all-too infrequent memoirs of those who served in Congress — is a story about integrity, faith and principles in serving as an elected official."

JOHN LAWRENCE,
AUTHOR OF THE CLASS OF '74

"*This Kennedyesque young county official defied all odds in his first election to Congress in 1974, the year of the so-called Watergate babies.* A Higher Calling *is about civility in the public square, needed now more than ever.*"

JOHN HUGHES,
AUTHOR & CHIEF HISTORIAN AT
WASHINGTON STATE BIOGRAPHIES

A HIGHER CALLING

How will long your commitment to public service as a U.S. Congressman and beyond has been — A Higher Calling Don Bonker
4/23/2023

A HIGHER CALLING

Faith & Politics in the Public Square

Don Bonker

David Applefield
Foreword by Shelby Coffey

ELM HILL

A Division of
HarperCollins Christian Publishing

www.elmhillbooks.com

A Higher Calling
Faith & Politics in the Public Square

Published in Nashville, Tennessee, by Elm Hill, an imprint of Thomas Nelson. Elm Hill and Thomas Nelson are registered trademarks of HarperCollins Christian Publishing, Inc.

Elm Hill titles may be purchased in bulk for educational, business, fund-raising, or sales promotional use. For information, please e-mail SpecialMarkets@ ThomasNelson.com.

Library of Congress Cataloging-in-Publication Data

Library of Congress Control Number: 2019914768

ARC ISBN: 978-1-400329137

ISBN: 978-1-400329052 (Paperback)
ISBN: 978-1-400329144 (Hardbound)
ISBN: 978-1-400329069 (eBook)

A Higher Calling
Don Bonker
Former US Congressman (D–WA)

Washington, DC

2019

Foreword

Shelby Coffey

"Choose your heroes wisely," says the legendary investor Warren Buffett.

One of the delights of Congressman Don Bonker's exuberant autobiography is that he shares the stories of his heroes and why they measured up.

This book is, in one sense, an adventure story of a life spent in pursuit of the best of public service from Capitol Hill to Moscow to America's Western wilderness. It is also a tale about the pursuit of high personal values "in the arena" where politics and business, ambition and gain tangle under the relentless glare of media.

Don Bonker starts with a wry take on his brief stint as a dance instructor, which gives the book its title—and its spirit. That spirit is quite evident among the legion of fans he has collected along the way that led to Congress, elected with the "Watergate Babies" Class of 1974...to two fascinating if disappointing runs for the Senate...and then to giving key counsel to Russian opponents of Vladimir Putin as the Kremlin strongman tightened his grip on power.

In person, the Bonker spirit is contagious.

He has a Kennedyesque shock of hair and an infectious toothy grin. (As one columnist wrote, whenever the Kennedys get together, "a tooth-stakes erupts.")

Bonker's conversation is ebullient, beginning often with a well-placed compliment, then off to commentary on the day's astonishing events in The Swamp, as Washington is nicknamed. Then he is on to business—quick, careful, and considerate—as he makes a request or points out the significance of an upcoming event.

He is a man of two Washingtons—the District of Columbia where he inspires smiles, and Washington State which always inspires him to smile.

He is a man of faith—often struggling with being both a Democrat and Christian—which is on display in this good book. He helped bring the National Prayer Breakfast to international prominence. And he has been a key, if quiet, force for others of faith who contend in public life.

Through this amusing and trenchant memoir, his wife, Carolyn, is ever gracious and insightful—a great and good woman who helps to steer the dancer through all the right moves.

By the end of the book, we appreciate Don Bonker's values—integrity, moral authority, principles—as well the virtues of humor, kindness, and going the extra mile and then some.

And just as he shines the light on his heroes, we see how, step-by-step, he became one. Though he would shy away from that characterization, it's an obvious call for those who have been lucky enough to know this eminent man.

With this fine book, more will be able to join that legion.

Shelby Coffey III
Vice Chairman, Newseum
Former Editor, *Los Angeles Times*

Contents

DANCING AROUND A MEMOIR

At first, I thought the time had come to write a memoir about my career in politics. I've always felt blessed and grateful for having had such a memorable public journey. Friends often ply me with flattery—"Don, you should write your memoirs." I usually nod along. Yes, they are right. It has been a career filled with stories that should be shared. I like reminding those who care to listen that I started out as a young and clueless dance instructor from Denver. I like the sound of that—a dance instructor from Denver who enters public life on a whim and emerges as a United States Congressman from the State of Washington. Chairing the Foreign Affairs subcommittee on international economic policy and trade, now that took some fancy choreography!

I seemed to have reached that strategic moment when it hit me. A memoir, sure, that's what retired public figures do. I better start recording what I've done before I run out of time. Although still active and vocal on topical issues—speaking at conferences, dashing off opinionated comments to newspapers, crisscrossing the country for meetings as a consultant—I began wondering and worrying how, in fact, I would be remembered and what I would do about it. What would my children and grandchildren and their children know about their father, grandfather, great-grandfather? I didn't exactly want to stop creating new achievements but it was time to start consolidating the memory of what I've already done. I contemplated how I would define my achievements. I imagined selecting a number of mental photographs from an inner gallery of memory, images that would make up an exhibition of a lifelong journey. How many images should I pick? Which ones would make the cut? What gets deleted or glossed over? I ran these questions through my head and contemplated the final one, the one we all come to ask at some vital moment late in life—have I made a difference? Have I made the difference that I wanted to make?

And so I began to write, to arrange that inner album of images and to put words to it, and a very strange thing happened. The act of remembrance began to ignite within me the same early energy that motivated me to seek public office and to serve my constituents in the first place. I revisited my life's work in memory and consulted the cartons of archives that cluttered my home office. I recreated many of the key conversations I had had over the years with some of the most spirited and highly principled public servants to have ever served our nation. I recalled and relived with both admiration and fondness the relationships that inspired me as a young congressman and wide-eyed lawmaker. The act of reliving one's past, I discovered, actually helped me understand who I was, and helped solidify the answer to the ultimate golden question—why am I here? That line of inquiry led me to a rather joyful epiphany—it wasn't so much a memoir that I was so eager to write, but a call to action. The chronology of my life may have some fleeting interest to the generations that follow or to the occasional researcher or student, but what I really want to be remembered are the things I'm still fighting for. I don't really want to lower my dupes to resignation as an elderly gentleman cataloging his own red-letter dates. I Reacknowledge the desire to raise them to the sky and let out a spirited yelp for a better republic. Walt Whitman wrote *Song of Myself*, not "The Life of a Brooklyn Poet."

Throughout my years in elective office, I dared not mention it. Who would vote for a dance instructor to be county auditor or US congressman? Well, that was before a Hollywood actor would be elected president of the United States.

Okay, I was a dance instructor. Dancing and politics, there is something of a correlation. It's not the dance steps that make the person a good dancer. It's not the mastery of technique that drives the spirit in your hips or lifts the feet of your dance partner. It's the energy and sense of purpose that hitches the trot to the fox, incites the bug to jitter. And the same is true in public office. For me, it has been service and commitment to the public good that has always beckoned and ignited me. And then, as I set out to pen my memoir, it struck me that this deep belief in service is what I needed to share with others.

As I observe the rapid erosion of public confidence that citizens demonstrate in our public servants and government at large, the urgency of putting voice to this mission of integrity and service builds like pressure in a volcano. My life and my work as a congressman, I realize, could be the inkwell that I dip my quill into as I share examples of the moral courage I have encountered across many decades as a Washington, DC insider.

As I reread the clippings and segments from the *Congressional Record* and copies of letters I had written to fellow representatives and senators and even presidents, a handful of diverse experiences across my political life emerge as having transformational power, the behavior and actions of select individuals which have helped me embrace higher standards and to be keenly conscious about how self-interest and political advantage can prevail over national interests and the common good. Memories that point to what is profoundly wrong and ones that direct me to what is so essentially right, that is what I'm inducting into this album.

As I was preparing to enter my first race for elective office in 1966, the need to reconcile my aspirations with a code of ethics or values had not occurred to me. I had been raised by a single mother who had struggled in the early years during the Great Depression with an absentee husband. Daily life was more about getting by day by day. While my mother made sure that discipline was the family norm, there was no dinner talk about ethical behavior or embracing principles that would make us better people. It was assumed. It was just embedded.

In June 1966, when I entered the county courthouse in Vancouver, Washington to file my candidacy for Clark County auditor—my debut into political life—all I had in hand was a flimsy belief that I was electable and a cheap leather briefcase. I didn't have a clue on how I would serve as a public servant. It was only a courthouse position, so, unlike being a legislator or county commissioner who would have to cope with the pressures of special interests and the complexity of political favors, I figured I could avoid what usually influenced a newcomer's public persona in elected office.

Upon election, I became the youngest elected official in the state and people across Washington State started to take notice. I was entering what was called constituency-based politics, with factional interests that could lead to typical selfish or ambitious goals rather than being focused solely on the common good. Elected just two years out of college, I had no clue of what lied ahead.

Deep in the collective consciousness of the American soul exists the conviction that public life and private morality are integrally related. Politics is a precursor to governance in a democracy—a sense of direction that needs a moral compass that can be trusted. But the moral factor at the heart of the public debate is often unrecognized or simply ignored; worse, it can be manipulated and twisted for politically self-serving and ideological agendas. In today's political environment, we have been anesthetized from the danger that this basis observation implies. We are used to blatant conflicts of interest in political life and are often unfazed by what should always be alarming. The baseline for moral conduct is often narrowly defined and can even be used to vilify candidates and elected officials as harboring overly traditional stances and conservative agendas, which, of course, has nothing to do with morality and everything to do with politics and power.

The traditional two political party system, which offered citizens diverse ideological and political choice as the bedrock of democracy, has been corroded quite simply by the amount of money that is injected in numerous ways into the decision making of candidates' priorities. Fellow lawmakers and citizens helplessly stand by as hundreds of millions of dollars of agenda-driven funds pour into congressional coffers and influence outcomes, application of laws, and the creation or blockage of new laws and rules, even when these outcomes are fundamentally contrary to our national interests. This is not about politics, as we often tell each other. This is about morality, or worse, immorality. Special interests are not national interests, and thus, as a congressman, I often had to remember to keep telling myself, "You work for the people who elected you."

In my last statewide race, I endured a number of interviews conducted by organizations and special interest groups whose purpose was to lock candidates into positions on a host of issues that were important to them. It was occurring on both sides of the political spectrum. For Democrats, it was environmentalist, pro-abortion, gay rights, labor unions. The same thing on the Republican side—being targeted by the NRA, the anti-abortion and anti-planned parenthood groups, those systematically opposed to any tax increases. These interviews were awkward for moderate candidates on both sides, not wanting to alienate potential supporters but recognizing that they were ultimately becoming beholden to these forces, which would compromise their ability to be true legislators. Unfortunately, such activity is chipping away at the ethical standards and values-based positions from which governance should find its authority.

So, as I had set out preparing the narrative of a memoir, I found myself on the stump again, ready to recite a soliloquy from this lifelong political op-ed of a career. The threads that have stitched the seams of a political journey hold me here in black tie for this last dance, a keynote speech on the floor of a much larger house, the American people, and readers from all walks of humanity. An unshakable belief in service to something bigger than myself, the importance of empathy and understanding in public policy, the role of collaboration in creating fair and durable policy, and the need to balance competing goals and imperatives to move society forward—these are the takeaways I want to offer, concerned citizens.

Looking back over my seven terms on Capitol Hill, the fundamentals of public discourse rarely change. Even when considering the days of the Founding Fathers, we see that they, too, had to cope with contentious issues: nationalism versus state rights, the balance between personal religious beliefs and public policy, the big divide between the Northern and Southern states, and ultimately dealing with the slavery issue.

Politics is the discourse of our public life, and its quality and pertinence can make a great difference, for good or for evil, coast to coast and across America's heartland and lands beyond. Political leaders can appeal to the people's best instincts or manipulate their worst impulses and fears. Every era's politicians are faced with the same question, and each man and woman in office must answer the moral test of his or her day. My soliloquy here quite simply comes down to this: public service must evoke in people a genuine desire to transcend our most selfish interests and respond to a larger vision that gives us all a sense of purpose in our lives and the belief that what is in the public good is in the private good.

In a nutshell, are our political leaders interested in *me* or *us*, *one* or *all*? I am reminded of that classical Latin phrase that is emblazoned across the scroll and clenched in the eagle's beak of the Great Seal of the United States. *E Pluribus Unum*. "Out of many, one" or "One out of many." The thirteen letters were symbolic of the Thirteen Colonies that emerged as a single nation.

I believe in the *us* and the *all* and have decided to highlight a select number of moments with political leaders with whom I have engaged over my career and who were known for their integrity and moral courage, and above all, their conscience. Actions for the common good over political or material self-interest showed me the right way, and when revisited now at a fragile moment in political life everywhere can serve as an anchor for a new, younger political class of leadership in the making, as they did for me.

—Don Bonker

I. Dance Studio to the Courthouse

CHAPTER 1

THE FORTUITOUS FISTFIGHT

I like telling people that my start in politics began with a fistfight on my first day of college. In a world that has grown so accustomed to violence and the oppressive dangers of firearms, a good 'ol fistfight actually sounds quaint. Considering this exchange of blows occurred at the Clark College "Get Acquainted Dance" only helps the story. But before I get to the guy who hit me—actually, the guy I knocked down in the Student Center in Vancouver, Washington in 1960—I need to go back a bit to my years in the US Coast Guard, my first chance to get away from home.

I had been assigned to the district headquarters in New Orleans, Louisiana, known for its exciting nightlife. For a young, single serviceman with a fairly parochial suburban upbringing, being stationed in New Orleans was like being sent to fantasyland. Being nineteen and free to wander the streets of the French Quarter in the evenings with all those enticing nightclubs, flashy neon signs, the jazzy sounds of brass, and the abundance of fun-loving gals and guys slinking along streets that didn't look like anything else I had ever seen in America kept me mighty alert. And admittedly intimidated. Notice that timid lives quietly inside that bigger word. I had a uniform which gave me a degree of confidence, but the boy inside those high-waisted, pleated pants was still a boy. I watched nightly the guys who seemed to maneuver best among the blondes and the brunettes, and they were the lean ones who could dance. It was too loud to talk in most of those clubs and bars, but the energy that came from letting the body follow the rhythm seemed like a sign from the heavens. Here in the French Quarter, as I watched the suave gestures of the dance instructors who nursed glasses of neat whiskey and waited for the girls, it struck me with envy that I wanted to dance. So little by little, I honed my dancing skills and the social skills seemed to follow. Coast Guard yeoman by day, dance instructor by night.

At the end of my four-year term in the Coast Guard, my degree in New Orleans nightlife was over and I returned to Denver with a vague plan to get an evening job somewhere and enroll at Denver University. There were several prominent dance studios in Denver at the time, including the illustrious chain Arthur Murray which slogan was, "If you can walk, we can teach you to dance." There was also the Fred Astaire Dance Studios, which were at the forefront of the rage of the day—dance lessons. No one wanted to be a wallflower, and social dancing was the equivalent of today's social media. If you could dance, you'd never feel quite so alone. I had no problem signing up as a dance instructor; in fact, I had my choice. Now with a secure evening job to help pay college tuition, and a constant flow of people who appreciated me, life was grand.

In a flash, I became exposed to a new social culture that was so captivating and easy to fold in to that, I regret to report, I never made it to the college enrollment office. I was in demand, and I was making a living, and having a ball. In the 1960s, before the popular wave of new dances—the Watusi, the Frug, the Boogaloo, the Tighten Up, the Monkey, the Jerk, and of course, the Twist—unleashed its rapid appeal to a new generation of young people, the dance studio that Murray and Astaire had capitalized on was attracting a rash of fiftyish and older women, many who were widowed, divorced, and otherwise lived lonely lives. There were ads everywhere, in the magazines and the back of city buses, that offered dance lessons, often the first one was free or at a big discount. This brought in flocks of mostly women and a few men in search of a new life, with attractive dance instructors in narrow-legged pants and open collared shirts greeting the newcomers at the entrances of the studios with broad smiles and slippery movements.

As I would soon discover, this was about much more than swirling around the dance floor and making people feel good. These dance studios had well-designed marketing schemes, which relied on deploying the likeable instructors to engage in conversations during the dance sessions to explore the personal needs and desires of their students. It was obvious that many were living lonely lives, some looking for another spouse and others just out to find a social life or reason to get out of the apartment. On the fourth lesson, the student was carefully ushered into a supervisor's office where the instructor's skills were tested in being able to achieve the ultimate promenade, close the deal on the costly longer-term commitment for continued dance lessons, or better, secure the pricey membership to the VIP Dance Club—the customer's ticket to a new and wonderful social life.

Slightly gullible at first, I quickly caught on. What stood out though for me was the time one older woman, clearly in her sixties, who had quickly embraced buying into a package of costly dance lessons and club membership prompted my supervisor to press further for an even larger amount. At about the same time, the Denver City district attorney had launched an investigation into dance studios that were using such scam operations to take advantage of vulnerable elderly women and men.

I saw what was happening and for me, this was a wake-up call. I reached out to my trophy dance student, the woman in her sixties, and pledged to support her if she sought to recover the tens of thousands of dollars in dance contracts that she had been coerced to commit to. I remember the words I spoke, verbatim: "I was part of making you the victim of the studio's exploits and I am prepared to testify on your behalf so you can recover some of the money."

Her response shocked me. She said, "These dance lessons and memberships brought me happiness I never had before and now you say it's all wrong. Please, I don't want to hear this!" The choreography of human feelings is so much harder to know than the fox-trot or even the emotionally complex tango.

That was the experience inside the dance studio. But this fantasy life had another dimension. Our little group of dance instructors were passionate about our profession but bored with guiding sixty-year-old bodies around the floor, and rather impatient each night to put our own dancing skills on full display. As soon as the studio shut down, we rushed to gather at one of several nightclubs in Denver that had live music, plenty to drink, dim lighting, and a full host of social opportunities. My fellow dance instructors had diverse backgrounds but two lovelies stand out in particular, one from Norway and the other from Germany. Attractive and fun to hang out with, we shared amusing anecdotes about daily attempts to teach ageing people to move, and then we'd pounce on the dance floor and do our thing until the club closed, sweaty and happy. Following four years in the highly disciplined environment of the US Coast Guard, suddenly, my life was something of a social bubble that was would not last forever.

These dance studios were set up to bring in older, lonely people with the means to buy into one of several pricey club-like programs. It was rare that someone young and attractive, without such means, would show up, but it happened one day when Carolyn Z. surprisingly became my student. This had me transcend from being an instructor to something much more. Previously, I did my share of dating but there hadn't been anything serious. I had quickly taken a liking to Carolyn Z. that had us coming together outside the dance studio.

But it wasn't until I met Carolyn Z., a much younger, attractive student with whom I had taken a liking, and another factor in my quick exit from the universe of the dance studio. In the Coast Guard days, I did my share of dating but there hadn't been anything serious. After going out with Carolyn Z. for a while, for the first time, I was feeling that this may be the right person. I introduced her to my mother, and eventually, we talked about our relationship. She shared openly that she had genuine affection for me but was reluctant about our future together. She had set high standards for herself, which did not include taking up with a dance instructor who showed little promise in life beyond the cha-cha-cha. In other words, she wanted to end the relationship, or worse, I felt I had been used. I had taken our closeness as an indication of possible long-term love, and I was wrong. To top it off, she humiliated me in front of my mother.

Rejection can be a heartbreaker for sure, but this time, it turned out to be a reality check if not a blessing. I had a wake-up call that the world of dance studios was mostly smoke and mirrors, dance steps, and illusions. I came to terms with a lifestyle that was garnished by fantasy, and in a heartbeat, I knew that I had to move from the dance floor to the college campus if I were to be serious about life. Somewhere in my gut, though, I swore I'd prove to Carolyn Z. and all those who didn't believe that I could be more than a dance instructor. That realization became a motivating force that got me through college and well beyond.

But what about that fistfight?

The challenge at the moment was college. Where would I go? Given my less than stellar high school record, could I even get accepted? Having abandoned my dance salary, how would I even pay tuition? Many questions and lots of uncertainty dominated the mood. I lived with my mother and needed a new path, and then I had remembered the letter that I hadn't answered.

Two months earlier, I had received a rare letter from my father, a man whom I barely knew. He had left our home at the beginning of WWII when I was only a child, leaving me to grow up with a foggy notion of who he was or why he left.

My mother remarried a handsome, decent man whose factory job gave us much needed financial security. But it was my grandfather on my mother's side who became my de facto father. He struggled during the Great Depression years, but nonetheless managed to maintain his stylish and socially savvy swagger. I recall, when I was on a date or hanging out with friends, he would discretely slip me a $5 bill, so I could impress those around me.

My biological father had no presence other than Mom's unfavorable references. Eventually, the question was raised about our last name. Was I still a Bonker? Our new stepfather's name was Lumsden, but my brother, Dan, and I had kept the name Bonker. I recall a dinner table conversation when Dan and I were asked, "Do you want to change your last name to Lumsden, so that we, as a family, would all have the same name?"

It was an awkward moment as we stared at one another, realizing across the table was our stepfather named Lumsden. Our real father had no presence at the table, yet Dan and I were in sync, comically blurting, "We want to keep Bonker."

As I was contemplating leaving Denver, I received a letter. It was addressed to me, and I left the envelop on my dresser in my bedroom, the four-cent US postage stamp for Camp Fire Girls pasted neatly in the right corner and his printed return address in Vancouver, Washington to the left.

The one-page letter stated that he wanted to help with my college education. There was a string attached, of course. To benefit from in-state tuition, I would have to relocate to where he and his second wife resided—Washington State. Having been snubbed by Carolyn Z. and disgusted by scam operations at the dance studio, I was ready to get out of Denver. I wanted to get serious, and this offer from Washington was the only option on the table. My mother reluctantly agreed, and I wrote back to the father I hardly knew and said, yes, I'd be coming.

Attending college was a must if I was ever to succeed, and now I had a way. My father resided in Vancouver, Washington across the Columbia River from Portland, Oregon, but at the travel agency where I purchased the airline ticket in those pre-online days, I only mentioned Vancouver and, of course, the ticket they issued was to the Canadian city of the same name in British Columbia. It was expected that I'd fly to the airport closest to Vancouver, Washington, that being Portland, Oregon. On my expected day of arrival, my estranged father eagerly awaited my arrival at PDX Portland International Airport while my flight was landing in Vancouver, Canada.

There is something painfully poetic about my showing up at the wrong airport, or his being absent from the arrivals terminal where I was standing alone with my suitcase. I am still thinking about what that really means some half a century later. Without cell phones, I am no longer sure how we sorted out this mix up, but I ended up getting a connection from Vancouver to Portland, an hour and a ten-minute flight, and when I finally walked off the gangway in the right airport, he was there. We recognized each other right away but that may be because we both had the look of people who were very focused on trying to find each other. My mother may have sent him recent photos of me, but again, this is something I never thought to ask. I had one suitcase, a wallet, a jacket, and a box of chocolates that my mother insisted I bring for the replacement wife. She always did the right things. He was in a brown suit, as if picking me up was a responsibility of great importance. He lifted my suitcase and we walked out to his car, a 1956 Buick Special with tan seats, and we drove mostly in silence to his house on Lieser Street in East Vancouver, where he and his second wife lived. In subsequent years, I have referred to that house as "my father's residence," ignorant of why even after having lived there for years I'd not call his house my home. We quickly agreed that I would enroll at the local Clark College, then return to Denver to organize my stuff, and come back by car in a few months to take up residence with him and my stepmother, Gladys. When I left Denver for good, it was especially tough for my mother given that I had already been away for four years serving in the military, and now I was departing to live with the man she once loved but who had abandoned her. She was used to being stoic, though, and knew that this was a pivotal moment for me if I were to get serious about college. On the 1250-mile journey to Vancouver, my mind was processing the multiple questions and doubts about this step. I was leaving behind my hometown, my devoted mother, the young woman I thought I loved but lost, those friends at the dance studio, and lots of memories. I also had to come to grips with what was ahead. Most of this doubt, though, was camouflage for the real fears. How would I relate to a father I did not know and with the lingering but unclear bitterness I must have been lugging around about his not being there as a father nor as a husband? I felt anxiety about everything, including starting college five years out of high school already with a dubious academic background and a quirky dance profession. Not least, how was I going to pay for college—a subject my father and I had not discussed, mostly because we struggled to find common ground to discuss anything.

The James Dean classic, *Rebel Without a Cause*, comes to mind although I never played chicken on a cliff with an old car.

The fistfight is coming.

Upon arriving at my father's residence in early September 1960, I had to quickly adapt to this new environment. Reconciling deep inner feelings that any child would have with an absentee father, fueled by my mother's negative stories about his abruptly abandoning us that made this all the more difficult. He had abandoned his family during difficult times, leaving us without support, and pushing us onto public assistance. And I never knew why.

The anger and resentment which had become deeply embedded over the years did not surface at first when I moved in to live with my father and his wife Gladys. It had obviously found its own place to live idly inside me, and now I kept our relationship at a distance, remaining most of the time in the bedroom he and his second wife had set up for me, coming out only to have dinner then quickly returning to study or dream. I was avoiding a normal father-son relationship, acting more like a student in a rented room.

This was debilitating to him, I am sure, carrying this guilt for so many years and now wanting to confront it but not being able to because the son wouldn't let him get close. At last, this surfaced when we were walking in silence around the block when suddenly, something sparked my deeply embedded anger as I began ranting. I even surprised myself with the ardor of my madness. He patiently listened or let the violence of my retaliatory words hit him without resistance, a quality I now thank him for a lifetime later. I suppose he expected this moment would occur one day and now it was here. When I came to stop having used up the verbal punches, he simply asked for my forgiveness.

From that day on the father-son relationship became a bit more normal. This would help me get through college and on to a new life. He was thrilled to have a son at his home, though I knew he felt some anxiety that I would not stay around, or I'd drop out of school or return to Denver. These early days were a test for both of us.

It was my father who had urged me to attend the Get Acquainted Dance on that first weekend at Clark College as a freshman. Going to the dance would be a good introduction for me to build a network of friends that would insure my staying for the long term. I agreed, got dressed, and made my way that Friday evening to the "get acquainted." Of course, the dance part would be the easy part, I thought. How many freshmen dance instructors are there? Especially ones who were pros at fox-trotting and the Viennese waltz.

I entered the student center and was unexpectedly accosted by the music and a dance called the Twist, a craze that had begun to infect teen-agers in the late 1950s. As a ballroom instructor training adults who were born around the turn of the century, I observed in shock these unchoreographed energetic bodies with hips, torsos, and legs rotating on the balls of their feet as a single unit, grinding back and forth on the floor at various speeds. It was a spectacle foreign to me. The couples didn't seem like couples, and they scarcely ever touched each other. Instead, their arms thrust in, out, up, and down, which someone once described as "piston-like motions of baffled bird keepers fighting off a flock of attack blue jays." You couldn't ever tell who was dancing with whom. The world of the dance studio with inspirational Latino rhythms like the rumba, tango, and cha-cha-cha was far from the campus jungle. The already embedded alienation just got worse as the one sphere of experience I was sure I was good at didn't buy me any kudos in this milieu.

I was not a good fit for this social event, which was supposed to be my getting acquainted party. Newly arrived students were to join in the spirit of celebration to their arrival at their new school. I don't recall being provocative, although I may have shaken my head at the scene. A male student approached me and started prodding at me. What was it that I didn't like? He wanted to know and challenged me to do something about it if I didn't like it. I acknowledged that this was not my kind of music, but backed away. He was relentless, though, and started poking at my chest as other students began to gather around to see how this was going to play out. I was cornered and was the obvious outsider. It became obvious to me that I had no choice, so I swung hard, punching him in the face once, and he went down.

Another student approached me like the ref in a boxing ring and warned me that the guy I had hit had some tough friends and I better scat, which I did and quickly headed back to my father's residence.

That was my fistfight. One punch.

My father and Gladys had been out walking the dog, obviously proud that I was at the school dance and enrolled in the local college, and that they now had a son. I approached my father with the news about what happened. He said we must to go back to the campus and be held accountable. He entered the student center with me and only a few people were still there, including Mrs. Marian Wood, Assistant Director of Student Affairs, who informed us that the other young man had been taken to the hospital. Apparently, my ring had sliced his face and he needed stitches.

She said both us had to report to the Dean of Student Affairs on Monday morning at 9:00 sharp.

Not the ideal way to begin my first week at college. What would the consequences be? Suspension for fighting? What was my father thinking? His son, whom he was just beginning to know, got into a fight and was summoned to meet the dean. Would I be kicked out of college? Would my father blame himself? Would I feel guilty? Why didn't I like the Twist, for goodness sakes?

On Monday morning, the other young man and I appeared before Mr. Manning Nelson, Director of Student Affairs, and were reprimanded for our inacceptable behavior. He came down hard on my new adversary because he had been drinking that evening, and he was placed on probation. Mr. Nelson then turned to me and firmly stated the one line that made all this worth repeating: "If you want to change the music, son, then march across the hallway and get involved in student government." If you want to change the music get involved in government. That was my personal invitation to channel strong opinions into public service. The fistfight turned me into a politician.

I followed Mr. Nelson's instructions and entered student government. Within three months, I was elected to run student activities, including the social events. At the next college dance, I had the style of the music changed from contemporary to ballroom, which is what I, of course, preferred, but not surprisingly, only a few people showed up on the night of the event, and the guys were mostly in bowties. Clearly, I had been out of step with contemporary student social life and I had learned the hard way, but I had also learned something crucial about myself, and about democracy as well. It's about all of us. And there are better ways of changing things. Curiously, there was also another upside to this meager tale. Word circulated that I had some mean dancing skills and could really cut a rug. Mrs. Marion Wood herself, the Assistant Director of Student Affairs, approached me asking if I would conduct a weekly dance class for her and several professors, which I agreed to do, and actually earned some pocket money. Not everyone was ready to convert to the Twist, fortunately.

My involvement in student government and campus politics then led me to various positions including the role of intercollegiate commissioner representing Clark College at statewide events, and finally, president of the International Club which positioned me to be head of the Clark College Delegation to the Pacific Northwest Model United Nations. Eventually, all this led to my becoming a candidate for student body president in my sophomore year. A primary election had narrowed the slate to two of us who would face off in the general election on May 1, 1961—me and John Decker. My early lessons were far from over.

The school newspaper, *The Penguin's Progress*, had published on the Friday before the runoff race photographs and a text on each of the candidates' platforms. John Decker's key phrase was "One man cannot achieve it alone, but, it only takes one man with a match to start the bonfire." The poetry of student politics continues to amaze and amuse. The outcome would likely be affected by *The Penguin's Progress* Friday edition, which in the end managed to cause some real confusion among student voters. The paper had managed to print my name under Decker's photo and his name under my mine. Our names and our pictures were inverted and thus no one knew if the text below each belonged to the photo or the real guy. One could not have invented a more symmetrical foul up!

John Decker won the race. If it had been a landslide, I could have said that I would have won by miles. If it had been close, well, it was likely that the wrong person won. Or, you could say that my photo won the race and they awarded it to a guy named Decker. My first shot at elected office had been marred by a weird twist that affected the outcome, which set a precedent for things to come. A good precedent. I had learned how things often turn out differently than you'd predict. The fistfight, a conflict, and a struggle led to creative resolution. An early challenge became the conduit to seeing that there was an enduring way of fighting back that was much more wholesome and fruitful than the rash impulse of the pugilist, although it felt good to give it to that guy. Politics. The political arena was one of dialog and consensus and perpetual evaluation of moral choices, even when the name doesn't match the photo. I'd have my get-back-at-Decker moment, but first, I had to figure out how to pay my tuition.

CHAPTER 2

"Go for It"

The relationship between one's personal ambition and the ability to pay for that vision is always complicated. The way we manage our wish to excel, to succeed, to shine, to achieve, to prove ourselves and the way we earn our living—and more, the way we define what it means to earn a good living—has been a stumbling block for many, many ambitious people. I knew I needed to get to college if I wanted to become something, and I also knew that college tuition, as it has always been for thousands and thousands of university students and wannabe students, a real challenge. The average college tuition in 1965 in the United States was $3,500. Today, it is $35,000. It behooves me now to think how fathers and mothers approach the massive hurdle of helping their children pay for college, and it haunts me to think of the ticking time bomb in America's packaging today of student loans, a tradable commodity and volatile debt product. Nonetheless, in 1965, I, too, was trying to figure out how a lower middle class kid with divorced parents —with dance instructor as my only marketable skill—would be able to pay for my education.

My father's offer to help was limited to housing and ground transportation. His commitment to financial support stopped there, and my pride—and perhaps residue of anger—held me back from pushing for more. It was not unusual in the 1960s for students to hold part-time jobs and a summer job. But it wasn't easy. Those days sensitized me for my career in politics, and I never forgot the sacrifice that students and families make to acquire education and earn degrees. This is one of the great acts of heroism that often goes unnoticed and understated. Where applicable, parents and grandparents should get diplomas too for the achievement of helping their kids through college. The stress that families live with while coming up with tens of thousands of dollars in annual fees is colossal. Between the large act of sacrifice and discipline involved in preserving savings, and the burden and anxiety of agreeing to loans, and the steep interest rates and harsh penalties that often haunt families for the rest of their lives, the payment of studies is a tremendous source of pain and pride.

Heading into the summer break that year in 1962, I desperately needed to find a job to keep my tuition payments going. I was told that the Washington State Highway Department was hiring students, and so I rushed to apply. Again, one detail in your life may lead you to another, which will set off a string of consequences which may alter the entire path in front of you. I like to keep this in mind and remind young people who tend to see one tedious request as a tedious task, and forget that the greatest asset we have as humans is our ability to remain open-minded. The human resource director at Google said in a recent article that his company looked for applicants who showed their ability to connect disparate things. Well, that is what happened to me. The State Highway Department required applicants to get a permit from a guy named Dr. Woodward, a local physician.

I figured a medical exam made sense as part of the process, so I made an appointment and showed up at the right time. Curiously, as this Dr. Woodward had me step on the scale and then pulled the ruler down onto my head, affirming that I was, in fact, five foot ten, he proceeded to ask me questions that were strangely unrelated to my health. "Are your parents Democrats or Republican?" he asked. I thought that was private, and you didn't ask people how they voted or how much money they make or which religion they belonged to. But I was a kid, and I answered. He then asked who I preferred as a presidential candidate. Dr. Woodward was not only a physician but also chairman of the Clark County Democratic Party, which in those days was a form of patronage. The governor of Washington was a Democrat, and the Highway Department and state liquor stores were rewarded the governing party with summer jobs. A fortuitous detail indeed.

Dr. Woodward signed off on the summer job permit but he doubled up to strongly urge me to be active in local party activities. Get in touch with Dan Marsh, he said. Dan was a young attorney running for the state legislature, and he needed help. I thanked the doc and called Mr. Marsh, a call which landed me the position of campaign manager. And this was my formal entry into state politics and the nation's political system. The

Highway Department health permit led me into grassroots politics, which was my trajectory into Washington State's Young Democrats, where I began as the editor of their monthly publication, *The Profile*, and rose to become one of the state's two National Committeeman, a position that catapulted me onto the national scene. And all I was after was a way to pay my college tuition, which I did.

As long as a Democrat was governor, I had summer time work at the State Highway Department and held other part-time jobs, which were sufficient to cover my tuition at Clark College—a state community college—as well as my last two years at the more pricey private Lewis & Clark College. In those days, the student loan option did not exist, so I was not burdened with a future debt and monthly payments. In the fall of 1962, I transferred from my two-year community college to Lewis & Clark, a private college "with a public conscience," that was run with in the pioneering spirit—as they like to say—located a few miles south of Portland, Oregon and within driving distance, so I was able to continue board at my father's residence and avoid the cost of housing or rent.

Though I did not live on campus, I maintained a strong interest in local politics, and the link it had with the national scene, and soon became head of the Young Democrats Club, which only had about fifteen to twenty members compared to our opposition, the Young Republican Club, which membership exceeded 300 students.

The limited experience I had in national issues helped contribute to my growing interest in international affairs and at Lewis & Clark, an institution which had been a founder and ongoing sponsor of the Model United Nations Security Council and represented thirteen universities and colleges in Oregon. As we conducted periodic meetings echoing the actual UN Security Council, I imagined becoming a Foreign Service Officer, but I self-deflated this pipe dream by contemplating my humdrum academic credentials and lack of any foreign language skills. Why would the State Department ever accept me for the diplomatic corps? The irony is amusing when I think that only twenty years later, I would be a US congressman and a senior member of the House Foreign Affairs Committee.

As a university student now with a connection at the national level, things began to change. I met and bonded with R. Spencer Oliver who served as the president of the national Young Democrats of America, and Steny Hoyer who was the first vice president of the Young Democrats. Steny went on to become a US congressman from Maryland in 1981 and ultimately the Majority Leader when Nancy Pelosi was Speaker of the

House. In 2017, Steny, whose nickname is "Boy Wonder" since he won a number of very close races, became the most senior member of the House of Representatives, having served for over thirty-seven years.

What is particularly mindful of those days was Spencer's mission to Mississippi to organize desegregated Young Democrat organizations on college campuses. Lyndon B. Johnson had become president in 1963, and it turned out to be a momentous time to be involved in the Democratic Party. Civil rights were a highly volatile issue in the Southern states at the time, and a great priority to President Johnson and his vision for a Great Society. I was originally scheduled to be on that trip with Spencer Oliver but had to back out, which turned out to be a blessing in that Spencer's car was involved in a tragic accident. One of his passengers had been killed and several others, including Spencer, were seriously injured.

Spencer was fortunate to recover and was able to continue his career in Washington, DC as a congressional staffer. Later, circumstances had it that he would come to enjoy a special footnote in history: the telephone that sat on his desk as the then director of the State Democratic Chairmen's Association was one of only two that had been bugged during the Watergate burglaries in 1973, and his is cited as the only one on which the calls were successfully intercepted and used as crucial evidence. Without Spencer Oliver and his phone, we can rightfully deduce Richard Nixon's dirty tricks would not have been uncovered. Woodward and Bernstein's exposé of Watergate, and the impeachment of the thirty-seventh president of the US would never have happened. Thank you, Spencer. He eventually became Executive Director of the Commission on Security Cooperation in Europe (CSCE) in Denmark, a position he held for twenty-five years.

Most people old enough to remember November 23, 1963 remember it well. Like the way people remember the circumstances of their day on September 11, 2001. And older folks recall December 6, 1941, the day the Japanese bombed Pearl Harbor. On November 23, 1963, I was seated in a Lewis & Clark classroom when Professor John Crampton plowed into the room in his typical defiant manner. A strange gleam were in his eyes, though, on this day, and he proceeded to pronounce, "I have an announcement to make." He was serious and we all looked at him and absorbed the news of his next words. "President John Kennedy was just assassinated," he hesitated, grinned strangely, and continued, "but the good news is he will no longer be president."

We were stunned. Each of us reacted in that personal moment with the array of shock and silence that the implications of the news commanded. There was the horrific news and then there was the oddly perverse comment that the professor had made. "You may leave," he told the class, but most of us just sat there. There was nowhere appropriate to go. John Kennedy had become an inspiration for many young people who were attracted to him and the idea of public service.

"Ask not...." Just t those two words evoke the man and his ethos, the message for a generation. I can hear them now and feel the tears welling up in my eyes. "Ask not what your country can do for you...." That was what called me to service. "Ask what you can do for your country." The 1961 Inauguration Address. Lyndon Johnson sitting behind him to his left, next to Richard Nixon whom he had defeated in the 1960 elections. President Eisenhower to his right, sitting next to his glamorous wife, Jacqueline. JFK had been my role model. He had set a high standard for not only elected officials but for all Americans. To be young and American was a source of pride. We stood for something. We would build a better future. My motivation was captured in that young articulate man with the Massachusetts accent. More than fifty-five years later, I still have all the magazines that featured John and Jackie Kennedy on their covers, *Time, Life, Newsweek*. I could never bear to discard them. They were a reminder of what I believed in.

I turned to the student seated next to me and asked, "Did I hear correctly that Professor Crampton said it was good news?"

He responded, "Yes, I think that's what he said."

We were practically crying, and students don't easily cry in front of each other. Walter Cronkite did on CBS News, and that meant that the news was tragic. The next day, sitting in the student lounge, still grieving, I noticed Professor Crampton enter, obviously looking for someone. He spotted me, his student, and came to my table. He stood there, paused, and then said, "I am truly sorry for what I said yesterday." He sat down next to me and started saying positive things about John Kennedy, adding that he disagreed with some of his policies which prompted his inexcusable statement that morning. Sharing that he genuinely regretted it, I noticed because his eyes were teary, and I knew then that people say things that they don't really mean when their emotions out-muscle their rational thinking and we displace our angers and frustrations. Politicians would do well to remember this when considering their constituents, their needs, their hopes, their fears....

I was scheduled to graduate in June 1964, and it was time to think about my next steps. Lewis & Clark had just acquired the Northwest School of Law, and thus law school was one idea. A master's degree in something—that, too, was on the table. I could simply look for a job like most kids. Then another professor, Dr. Donald Balmer, head of the Political Science Department, approached me. Sometimes you are looking for something which doesn't show up, and other times, as I've seen over and over, the very thing you need just appears. I wouldn't call this faith, but I have come to understand that a larger belief in the grander order of things is helpful for constructing the world that should be. Many strokes of luck have marked my life, and I am grateful for them while also humble by the way the greater order of the universe works despite our efforts to resist or to impose.

"Don, I have an exciting opportunity for you. Would you like to work for one of Oregon's US senators?" he asked, and began talking about an internship I knew nothing about.

I quickly learned that there was a highly competitive position as research intern in the Washington, DC office of Oregon Senator Maurine Neuberger. Initiated by her late husband ten years earlier, she continued the tradition of employing a talented intern chosen by a prestigious selection committee made up of the Dean of Faculty at Portland State University, the editor of a new publication, a circuit court judge, and the director of guidance from the Portland public schools. The committee would interview and choose a student candidate from fourteen Oregonian law schools and universities.

"Thanks, Dr. Balmer," I replied, but secretly, I was more than convinced that they'd never pick me. Dr. Balmer insisted I try, so I gathered the letters of recommendation they'd asked for, prepared the required 500-word statement which he helped to draft, and endured the two interviews. I was sure, it wouldn't be me, but I had promised my professor I'd give it a shot.

I can't say I remember the exact moment, but it was March 30, 1964 when I received a Western Union telegram from Senator Neuberger's office in Washington, DC. I remember those printed boxy letters marching across the page: "Committee has just notified me of your selection to serve as research intern in my Senate office in Washington for 1964. Congratulations! SEN. NEUBERGER."

Speechless, I was obviously thrilled and filled with disbelief. Chances and good luck happen in lots of forms. Don't look back. You work hard, you try, you pray, you study, you keep going, and the good things arrive. You never know for sure why or how or when, but the good things arrive. What I subsequently learned about the process and the choice of my great fortune continues to amuse me, although there was no looking back. I accepted that internship and never hesitated…"ask not" always close by.

The backstory of the Selection Committee's decision makes for a quirky read, and in retrospect, I understood that circumstances weighed in a lot more than merit. There had been a reaction to the previous year's research intern whose name I had learned had been Neil Goldschmidt, a young and confident guy from Eugene, Oregon, who would go on to become the forty-fifth mayor of Portland, the Secretary of Transportation under Jimmy Carter, and the governor of Oregon. Goldschmidt ultimately fell from great heights due to an extraordinarily painful scandal that revolved around a prolonged sexual relationship with a thirteen- or fourteen-year-old high school student when Goldschmidt had already been mayor. Thirty years after the abuse, the story was exposed by a local newspaper, Goldschmidt was disbarred, shamed, and ultimately published a public apology on the front page of *The Oregonian*.

As a young intern in Senator Neuberger's office, Goldschmidt ultimately had a falling out with the senator and never finished his one-year stint. Apparently, he got very involved with voter registration in Mississippi's 1964 Freedom Summer civil rights campaign and made multiple trips to the Southern states to advance this cause. I was told that, on numerous occasions, he would charge into the senator's office with prepared statements that he audaciously demanded she'd place in the Congressional Record.

The senator had no problem with the issue but refused to tolerate his disrespectful behavior and finally asked him to leave. The intern selection committee was notified that their next choice needed to be more mature, less agitating, and thus vetted for his or her personality. The preferred choice that year of the committee was a University of Oregon student who had impeccable credentials whose name, unfortunately, was similar to Goldschmidt, and so he was scratched from the top of the list. And I became the recommendation to the senator. Another fateful twist of personal history! Don't discount the things that happen for reasons beyond your control. I was happy to have applied, and being second in line meant that I got the chance to serve, and that was a keystroke of happenstance.

Maurine Neuberger was serving her first term, having succeeded her husband, Richard Neuberger, who had died in office the previous year, 1960. He had been a legendary figure before his election to the US Senate, notably as a columnist for the *New York Times* and author of many books, including *Adventures in Politics* and *The Lewis and Clark Expedition*. The sixties was a prominent era for Oregon in national politics led by Senator Wayne Morse, who politically covered the spectrum—having been elected as a Republican first, then as a Democrat, but also an independent. His passionate opposition to the Vietnam War was shared by Governor Mark Hatfield who, too, was a rising star in the Republican Party. At the 1968 Republican convention, Hatfield had been Richard Nixon's top choice for vice president, but was then sidelined precisely because of his adamant anti-war position. Nixon's second choice for the vice presidency was Spiro Agnew, governor of Maryland, who was indicted in 1973 on corruption charges and resigned in disgrace, leaving the position open to House Speaker Gerald Ford, who ascended to the presidency upon Richard Nixon's resignation following Watergate. Even the highest offices of the land often function like a game of Chutes and Ladders.

Replacing her husband the year after his death in 1959, Maurine Neuberger became the third woman to win an election to the US Senate. Mrs. Neuberger's commitment was to consumer issues, but her big mission was her aggressive attack on the tobacco industry. She was the primary sponsor of the first bill to mandate health warning labels on cigarette packages and authored a book highly critical of the tobacco interests, *Smoke Screen: Tobacco and the Public Welfare* (1963). During the Johnson era, the president championing his ambitious Great Society agenda on Capitol Hill made this a most interesting time for young staffers, even interns who made the grade by having a name like Bonker.

I showed up in Washington, DC with pride and honor as if the entire Pacific Northwest was counting on me. And I was ready to take on big tasks and tackle huge national issues as Senator Neuberger's new research intern. With this ardor for challenge, I was sent on my first ambitious task one day at the beginning of my mandate. "Don, you'll be conducting VIP tours of the US Capitol, mostly involving people with a close association to the senator," the administrative assistant, the AA, informed me. She spoke like this was a secret mission behind enemy lines and the safety of the nation was on my shoulders. Giving tours?

On one of my first tours, I was asked by an office secretary if I would take time to give her son's Boy Scout troop a tour of the capitol. This vital mission was somehow getting worse and I was feeling reluctant, but didn't want to become a Goldschmidt and complain. This was a waste of my precious research time and I secretly regretted agreeing to do it. The group of young fourteen-year-olds gathered in the senator's office, bedecked in their dark blue uniforms with emblems and rank stripes with yellow neckerchiefs bound with the official scout ring around their necks. I took on the air of civilian authority and proceeded to walk the group down the wide corridor of the congressional office building heading toward the capitol, planning to execute this tour quickly and get back to my cherished desk. I learned the importance of questioning your assumptions, and I continue to remind myself and others.

As we were strutting down the corridor, out of nowhere, the vice president of the United States, Herbert H. Humphrey, suddenly appeared. We all stopped in awe. I was as numb as the fourteen-year-olds. Mr. Humphrey graciously approached the flock of Cub Scouts with a big Minnesotan smile, lifted his hand in a salute, and asked what troop they belong to. Then, he cited the oath pledge and the whole group joined in unison. We were all part of the same regimen. There was instant joy and bonding. What a country! You come to the nation's capital and, without an appointment, you are chanting the scout pledge with the nation's number two!

"On my honor, I will do my best. To help all people at all times. To keep myself physically strong, mentally awake, and morally straight." Gosh, as I r-create this scene now, I'm struck by the simple wisdom of it. If we could only get our elected officials, from the president down to the county auditors, aligned with what we teach our scouts. That would be something.

The vice president then chimed in as if he had nothing better to do in the world, "You know what, let's go to the Senate Dining Room and have some ice cream." I doubt if you could seduce a bunch of fourteen-year-olds today with Chunky Monkey or Cherry Garcia, but for scouts in the early sixties, ice cream with the VP was a hoot. The young Cub Scouts excitedly gathered around tables in the empty dining room. They were served ice cream at the vice president's request as he visited each table with animated conversation.

As I was sitting there, about as low of a lower staffer as exists, I was trying to get the vice president's eye as if to say, "We have this one under control, isn't that so, Mr. Vice President?" We ended up spending an hour with Hubert Humphrey, and my wasted time on a dumb tour turned out to be a moment of great personal wealth, and my closest direct contact with political power accompanied by cub scouts and ice creame.

As my year as research intern came to a close, I was asked if I'd like to remain in Washington as the senator's legislative assistant. It was expected to be short term as Mrs. Neuberger had become engaged to a prominent Boston psychiatrist and it was expected that she would not seek reelection.

It is interesting to note the times in life you are faced with major decisions and must take a serious moment to consider options. I am reminded of the last three lines of the Robert Frost poem, *The Road Not*

Taken. "Two roads diverged in a wood, and I—I took the one less traveled by, And that has made all the difference." Do I try to find another position on the Hill? On the staff of a Senate committee where staffers could develop more specialized skills? Or maybe pursue another opportunity in Washington, DC? Or was the best possibility to return to Vancouver to seek an elective office and start building my own political career? It would be a moon shot. My time in Washington, DC gave me a taste of what I'd want to come back to, but with me as the one ready to help make laws and bring about change.

Timing is the key to most choices, and in politics, it is crucial. When I heard the surprise news that that Bruce Worthington, the incumbent county auditor in Clark County, Washington, had announced that he would not be seeking reelection and was relocating to San Francisco, I knew this was my moment. County auditor was the most political position in local government, a position that presided over a range of county services including Chief Electoral Officer. With the incumbent stepping aside, the door was open.

Of course, I had neither the proper credentials nor the political support to run for this or any office, but sometimes rare opportunities pull stronger on your desires than any rational argument. I was worried for a moment how the senator would respond if I declined her offer to stay on staff through the end of the year. Would there be a downside? As a lame-duck senator, I noticed that her staff had begun exiting the team, securing other positions, or simply moving on. Each time I heard that another staffer announced that he or she was leaving, it seemed even harder to add my decision to the heap. I wasn't a deserter. I was a team player, but I knew where my heart was, and so when I finally met with the senator and shared with her my idea of returning to Vancouver to run for county auditor, her largesse was overwhelming.

"That's why my husband started this intern program in the first place and I continued it, to inspire young people to go into public service," she said. And then added the icing to the cake. "Go for it!" she said, and I did.

CHAPTER 3

"Your Career Is Over
Before It Begins"

I drove back to Vancouver, a five-day road trip from Washington to Washington, which gave me plenty of time to let my mind question and ponder the doubts surrounding my decision to run for public office.

Pittsburgh, Cleveland, Chicago, Des Moines, Omaha, Cheyenne, Salt Lake City, Boise, and finally, Vancouver, Washington. Today, it is an easy drive mostly on I-80 with the last day and a half on I-84. The 2800-mile drive required around fifty hours behind the wheel. Traveling in my flashy red Thunderbird convertible, equipped with an 8-track tape deck and a cooler stocked with Fresca and Dr. Pepper, I felt like a weird mixture of Walt Whitman, Jack Kerouac, and Meriwether Lewis whose Corps of Discovery had traced the same route back in 1804. Lewis and his partner lent his name to my alma mater, Lewis & Clark, and of course, the very county that I was aiming to serve as auditor, Clark County. I am now following their trail 215 years later, but my convertible on I-80 was a bit different than the treacherous natural terrain they endured. The whole ethos of the Pacific Northwest is the pioneering spirit, and right through to this moment, that same spirit seems to drive innovation and exploration and individual ruggedness in carving out new ventures and transforming the local landscape.

Thumping to Johnny Cash's "Understand Your Man," which was on the charts that summer, my mind was calculating like crazy. Only eighteen months out of college with no experience except a senate internship, I was seeking a position that oversaw the budget and accounting system for an entire county government. The job included responsibility for recording of documents, issuing auto and marriage licenses, and conducting county elections. I had no political base, no financial support, and very little time to pull this together. A band of veteran insiders dominated Clark County courthouse and I'd have a dang of a time just being taken seriously. But I had days of driving to convince myself otherwise.

On the fifth day, I pulled into Vancouver—incorporated in 1857 by British Naval Officer George Vancouver, population 161791—and moved back in with my father and now soon-to-be stepmother, Gladys. They had a small house on Lieser Street, and my room was on the front side with a window that looked out onto the street. After a year living with three roommates in a townhouse in the SW quadrant of Washington, it was a bit odd now having as my new roommates my own father and the woman who would now be my stepmother. Quickly, I made contact with the chairman of the Clark County Democratic Party, David Lasher. Local party chairmen at the time had a lot of clout, so warming up to Lasher would be a necessity, a courtesy call to inform him that I would be a candidate for county auditor and to seek his blessing.

Mr. Lasher greeted me warmly and casually asked me about the political situation in the nation's capital. The tone grew serious when I told him outright, "Mr. Lasher, I am here to inform you of my decision to run for county auditor. I would very much appreciate your support." It was an awkward moment for both of us and I watched as he struggled to find the words to put me in my place.

"Don, sorry, but you will not be a candidate for county auditor." This response caught me at the back of my throat. Had he not heard what I said?

"Mr. Lasher, I have decided to be a candidate for the county auditor position."

He retorted without hesitation, "No, Don, you are not our candidate. We already have a person for this office, Richard Blaker. Why don't you take a run at county treasurer?"

I was savvy enough to know that that office was occupied by a Republican who would be impossible to defeat. Lasher was trying to diss the young whippersnapper standing in front of him.

I struggled to find a way to respond, finally coming up with a whiny plea. "Mr. Lasher, I respect that you have a preferred candidate but I have already committed to run for this office, and I intend to do it."

His impatience now turned to fury, and he warned me in no uncertain terms. "I will guarantee that your career will be over," he stated, "before it is started. Is that clear?"

I walked away stunned and a bit shaken. The Clark County Democratic Chairman had just threatened to ruin my start-up career if I ran against his candidate. The five days I had taken to cure myself of doubt just withered into the ether, and I was consumed by the panic of fresh doubt.

Lasher's preferred candidate, Richard Blaker, was a courthouse insider who had stepped down as Clark County Director of Civil Defense to devote full time to running for county auditor. In contemplating running for this office, I would not only have to go up against a strong Republican candidate who was highly qualified, I'd first have to take on the Democratic Party machine and battle in the primary against a well-seasoned Blaker. I wished I was back in the congressional cafeteria having ice cream with Hubert Humphrey and the scouts. It was time to reassess. The reasons were mounting against my filing for this office. I'd find a better moment to enter politics. I'd gain more experience first. I'd...I really didn't know what to do. Departing the courthouse, I headed back to my father's residence. I would inform him of my new decision that I would not be a candidate for county auditor—that I'd wait. I pulled my red car into the driveway, collected myself, and entered the house. I walked down the hall past the kitchen and spotted movement in the backyard. Out the backdoor, I continued and was stunned, overwhelmed, blown away to find him, my father, Mr. Bonker Sr., on the backyard lawn with paint brush in hand and a blue smock, painting signs: "Don Bonker for County Auditor." Spread all over the lawn were the same signs in various colors: "Don Bonker for County Auditor."

I was speechless. I looked at the signs. I looked at him. The hue of pride across his face. I was his candidate. I was his son. We shared the same name. This was stronger than anything I had felt before. I never said what it felt like nor ever really tried to put it in words what that moment meant to me, but I knew in a flash what I would do. All that doubt and second-guessing and fear and intimidation and wondering if the time was right and political posturing all flew out the window in the presence of those hand-painted signs.

My father had sealed the deal. I would run.

The following Monday, I showed up at the courthouse and officially filed as a candidate. While waiting in line to fill out the papers, I observed the other candidates were there too. They were in their fifties or sixties.

One stranger approached me, asking if I was standing in line for another candidate.

"My name is Don Bonker, and I am the candidate." From that moment on, when I heard myself say it, I became, for the first time, a candidate for public office, a phenomenon that I would repeat many times over the next decades. Running for political office is an existential experience where your private self and your public self meet each other, shake hands, and figure out how they'll coexist. For some, the relationship becomes complicated or even torturous. For others, the two selves fuse into one. For me, standing in line that morning, the two Dons got acquainted.

I began reaching out to college friends and people I had met at Democratic meetings in order to start building a campaign organization in what was mostly a Republican rural county. In the 1960s, candidates for county positions had traditional family roots in the nearby towns and their personas became recognizable around the courthouse and the local churches and schools and ball fields, and I quickly observed that both my Democrat and Republican opponents were already local fixtures. I was just a young tumbleweed who had blown into Vancouver in his red sports car and lived with his father.

The message and the issues were, of course, important, but with a county position, it wasn't the same as if I had been running for the legislature or city council where the issues were numerous and complex. County auditor was mostly administrative. Not a lot of fish to catch in the issues net. The local press quoted me making a lofty proclamation that "the need for centralizing of administration and mailing functions would result in increased savings, operational efficiency, and better services to the public." I look back and kind of cringe to think that I thought that campaign slogans about centralizing mailing functions would resonate with voters. You learn fast from the things you do. Or at least you better.

I was told too that a candidate's image played a huge part in the campaign. To think now in our age of hyper marketing and brand building and identity crafting that such self-evident truisms needed to even be said makes me marvel. My image in 1964 was absolutely a problem. Dance instructor in Denver cum county auditor via a stint in student government and a research internship in DC. Who was I? Those dancing days had impregnated me with a liking for stylish decor and a modish wardrobe, both traits inappropriate for the office I was seeking. I decided to change my rayon cardigan blazer and tone down my colorful and liberal appearance. I even bought a pair of plain framed black rimmed eyeglasses at the shop next to Sparks Home Furnishing store downtown to help me look more like a backroom accountant.

In Vancouver, both parties started to retain public relations firms for their campaigns, and the go-to Democratic PR guy was already signed up to work for another candidate, so I thought I'd have a chat with an alternative who was a Republican consultant. After a thirty-minute meeting with Mr. Gleason, he said "I have some advice if you want to win this race. You look like a Bobby Kennedy. Throw those glasses away. Let your hair grow out and be more natural." I was perplexed—a Republican PR guy was trying to help, or harm, my candidacy. Also, I was worried about my classy red Thunderbird convertible—would the automobile be a negative in the eyes of voters? When I would head out for meetings, unsure, I would park several blocks away so no one would see me get in and out of that vehicle. Who would vote for a young upstart in a fancy convertible to oversee the spending of local tax dollars.

Public speaking, of course, is always one of the most essential parts of public office, and every candidate has to get used to, and come to love, those minutes in front of a crowd. Every politician has his or her list of favorite moments as well as those they'd really like to forget—the duds, the disasters, the horror stories. Sometimes it is because no one showed up. Other times, the crowd is aggressive. And then of course we've all known the events that were plagued by microphones that didn't work, or amplifiers that distorted your voice, or rooms that were too small or too big or too hot, chairs that broke, signs that fell, and worse, the times you forgot your speech or butchered someone's name or were asked an embarrassing question. All politicians have to start somewhere, and I recall with vividness that first candidates' forum at the Saint Joseph Church north of Vancouver early in the primary election.

This was my opportunity to make an initial favorable impression on my future constituents, but it didn't exactly turn out the way I had imagined. It was my turn to speak. I had memorized my five-minute stump speech, but midway through, the words stopped flowing out of my mouth. It was like my voice had shut down. I suppose it was my nerves, my self-doubt, I'm not quite sure. Something spooked me and I simply forgot the rest of my lines. I don't recall if I saw my father in the audience, or if I did my best to avoid him, but I knew he was somewhere in the back. No one forgets the feeling of embarrassment quite like the feeling of being exposed in front of a crowd. The audience was stunned to see this young upstart in this embarrassing situation.

On the way home in my father's car, I sat in silence for a few minutes and then told him that I was not prepared to be a serious candidate. He listened to me but didn't say much, and as we were entering his driveway, he finally spoke. "I borrowed my friend's pickup truck, and he offered to help put up your campaign signs around the county." All that missed time growing up without a father started filling in. He was teaching me things now that I had never learned. Don't give up. Overcome one obstacle at time. The big picture does not get erased because of a detail. Courage is an ongoing quality. You learn from your mistakes. Self-improvement comes with experience. So you forgot your lines this time; next time, you won't, or better, you don't need to memorize your speeches. Just say what you know and what you care about. Be natural. Keep going. Love takes many forms and reaches out in many ways.

One day, I got a surprise call from the executive assistant of the local newspaper, *The Columbian*. Mr. Don Campbell, the publisher, wanted to meet with me. He was not a political reporter nor the editor. His family owned the newspaper and he was a very powerful man in Vancouver. When I entered his office, he was leaning back in his brown Naugahyde swivel chair, appearing skeptical in looking me over. So this was Don Bonker. He told me to take a seat and then blurted it out, "Are you a homosexual?"

"What?" This was in the early sixties and references to any sexual orientation was not openly discussed. Being labeled a homosexual, though, in those days would have inflicted fatal damage to anyone running for office.

Aghast by the question, I shyly replied, truthfully but embarrassed. "No, I am not." I do not know what I would have done had I been, in fact, gay. Today, the question asked like that would be far more damaging to the publisher than to the young candidate.

He paused for the better part of a minute, then explained. "I had to ask you directly because at the Royal Oaks Country Club, that's what everyone is talking about."

How did this happen? The Republican incumbent, Bruce Worthington, was homosexual, which was why he decided to, or was pressured to, leave Vancouver to live in San Francisco where there was a robust and free gay community and much greater tolerance for all forms of creative and libertine lifestyles. Because I was single and had a leaning for styling garb, a rumor had been circulating mostly in Republican circles that Don Bonker swayed the other way. Rumors in politics have often gone viral, and now, this one clearly had become an issue in my campaign. Had this smear been part of the threat I had received not to run? I never knew.

Still in Mr. Campbell's office, I could tell that he was contemplating the next steps.

"I'll tell you what, I'm going to confront those folks at the country club and warn them to stop making these false statements about you or deal with the consequences. But, as for you," he continued, "when you make campaign appearances, I strongly suggest you have a woman by your side."

I did not hesitate to seek someone to accompany me at public meetings. All campaigns have a pool of enthusiastic supporters, and in mine, I reached out to Joanne Z. who was director of the women's athletic program at Clark College. She was a few years older than me, had a robust personality, and I thought she was attractive. So she was ideally suited to follow the publisher's advice. For the next six months, I had Joanne Z. by my side, applauding my speeches, and helping with outreach to voters. After the election, I thanked Joanne for partnering on my campaign and finished with "see you around." What I had never realized was that she had assumed we had been dating and this campaigning was something more permanent. In other words, there was a love factor I had not contemplated and what, for me, was a campaign relationship became an agonizing breakup for her.

Gender in American politics has always been a gnarly mixture of sensitive issues, family values combined with religious advocacy, and confused with social mores and doused with all sorts of sex scandals, aberrations, deviance, affairs, consensual adultery, and outright abuse and harassment, not to mention legitimate and legal examples of pure and simple choice, which should not have any place in public scrutiny or determine the futures of political leaders who are no more or less human than anyone else. Scandal, though, is in the bloodstream of political and public life, and it always will be.

This latest episode of slander added more drama and another negative to my first experience at elective office. Threatened not to run by a party boss, and now told that I needed a woman by my side as an accoutrement for respectability, political life was cranking up to be a bit more warped than expected.

As we were getting closer to the primary election date, things were intensifying. My opponent had the party establishment support, but his campaign lacked momentum. My on-the-ground operations were doing well as my father and his friends were planting "Don Bonker for County Auditor" signs all over the county, and I was receiving favorable press coverage.

The primary election was scheduled for September 20, 1966 and voter turnout was expected to be very low, which generally worked against Democrats. The big day had arrived. I was still six months shy of turning thirty. That evening, after casting my vote, friends and supporters gathered in the family room at my father's home to observe the election results.

Gladys kept our glasses filled, and my father kept tinkering with the rabbit ears of the black-and-white TV as we watched the results come from the local station, but it was our volunteer at the Clark County Election Department who kept us posted on the precinct results throughout the evening. My father and Gladys were excited to welcome friends and supporters, having set up bulletin boards, listing all the county's precincts, so we could get the results and anticipate the outcome. Gladys prepared the tables of refreshments and drinks in anticipation of a victory celebration, which did finally occur.

It was around 11:15 p.m. and I tried to contain my excitement, but secretly, I was beside myself.

The final tally was Don Bonker at 5294 and Dick Blaker at 3221. I had obliterated the party's preferred choice and emerged victorious over the guy I had been threatened to stand down to.

I started to feel the sense of what elections were all about. Eight months of nonstop campaigning, raising money, rallying support, the speeches and endorsements, and finally, the nail-biting moment when the election numbers appeared on the bulletin board, and the cheers and hugs that accompany a big win. After midnight, everyone had departed, and exhausted, I headed for the bedroom with a smile on my bed. But it was impossible to fall asleep. My mind was processing so much about the election results, the campaign, and how I could defeat my Republican opponent who was so much more qualified.

Alone in my room, one thing stood out. My father. Those occasions when I felt it was a mistake to get into this race, and yet each time, it was he who remained hard at work to get me elected. He was the one who charged around the rural county with a borrowed pickup truck, putting up more "Vote for Bonker" signs. Via the election, he expressed himself; he was no longer the absentee father.

With the two Democrats, me and Blaker, totaling 8515 votes and the GOP's Fred Greenwood and his primary opponent weighing in at 8186, we had a slight advantage going into the general election. But with the Republicans outpolling us by about 500 votes, *The Columbian* predicted that it was "*not a big margin*" but would be "*enough to win.*"

If I were to come out on top in November, I needed to ensure that the Democratic Party was fully behind me, so I reached out to the same David Lasher, the party chairman who had promised to ruin my career, but this time, when I entered his musty office, he greeted me with a big smile and a hefty congratulations. I learned just then a fundamental about politics: if you win, everyone, including party leaders, wants to be on your side. Prove that you are a winner and those who were ready to throw you under the bus will rant, "He's a jolly good fellow!" and swear you have been best friends for decades.

During the primary elections, there were four candidates, now it was a one-on-one against Fred Greenwood. There was no question who was more qualified on paper to be the next Clark County auditor. Fred was the conventional candidate—lifelong resident of Clark County, active member of the St. James Church and many community organizations. Most importantly, his career in county government was established, notably having already spent eight years in the Clark County auditor's office. By contrast, there was young Don Bonker, still single although now occasionally spotted with a feminine side-kick by his flank to ward off any further malicious rumors, and still living with his father and stepmother. No experience and presently unemployed. The Greenwood campaign repeatedly ran newspaper advertisements highlighting the stark contrast between the two of us. It read like this: "COMPARE THE CANDIDATES."

FRED GREENWOOD	HIS OPPONENT
Age: 52	**Age:** 29
Marital Status: Married 28 years	**Marital Status:** Single
Twin sons, Jim and Jack, 23 years	
Residence: Lived in Vancouver, 45 years	**Residence:** Lives with parents
Employment: Vancouver Columbian, 8 years	**Employment:** Unemployed
Clark County Sheriff's Office, 7 years	
Part Owner Business, 7 years	
Clark County Auditor's Office, 8 years	
Auditor's Experience: 8 Years as Chief Elections Deputy	**Auditor Experience:** None

There was no contest. He was far more qualified and he tried to simply outmuscle his way to the polls. I decided to counter his attacks with my own. If I was young and inexperienced, I'd enlist elder and highly experienced political stars to step up to the plate for me. My newspaper ads included endorsements from Senator Henry M. Jackson who wrote, "Don Bonker represents the kind of young and vigorous talent we need in county government. Clark County cannot go wrong by electing him." Senator Maurine Neuberger who had told me to "go for it" now added praise claiming that my "mature and responsible judgment has made him one of the greatest aids I have ever had." The president of Lewis & Clark College, Dr. John Howard, added that "Don Bonker is motivated to a career in public service." Even Marian Wood, Director of Student Affairs at Clark College where I had had my fistfight and ended up giving dance classes to her and other staff members, chimed in, "Don Bonker is an outstanding leader...energetic and highly reliable." Remember, allies are forever. Howard Summers, the LCDR of my Coast Guard Reserve days, was pleased to pile on his word of support saying that I had served in an outstanding manner and had been an "excellent interpreter of our program." My inexperience was now covered over with lots of past experience, with testimony from prominent leaders who helped to boost my otherwise modest credentials.

The final weeks of the campaign had been invigorating thanks to the accumulation of supporters, traditional Democrats plus a new surge of young activists. Moving closer to the election date, other factors occurred including lively newspaper endorsements, which in local elections can affect the outcome. *The Columbian* rolled out its official candidate endorsements but stayed neutral in the Clark County race.

"Don Bonker, the Democratic candidate, is inexperienced in county government, but he has demonstrated during the election campaign an unusual capacity to learn about local government and the community, to which he has returned after an absence of several years. Bonker has favorably impressed many voters with young, aggressive leadership and new ideas which he has stressed during his campaign." I loved reading this out loud over and over, never tiring of "aggressive leadership and new ideas," although I also knew that I was in the presence of some form of double-speak since the local paper stopped short of endorsing me. Even now in my eighties, with a touch of hard hearing on my right, though, I find "aggressive leadership" highly pleasant in the ear.

Election day finally arrived on November 8, 1966, a midterm election that chose the 90th US Congress in the middle of Lyndon Johnson's four-year term. It had clearly shaped up as a victory for the Republicans on the whole, whose gain was captured in *The Columbian's* headline, "Joy for Republicans." From Florida to Washington, it stressed, "Republicans across the nation probably have more cause for joy after Tuesday's election than they have had since they reelected Eisenhower ten years ago." In local races, the coverage included a headline that screamed "Clark Caught in GOP Swing," but the opening paragraph noted that "Republicans apparently won all Clark County tested offices"—I pause here for emphasis—"but those of auditor and assessor. The exception was the county auditor's race where Democrat Don Bonker, in one of the most effective campaigns seen here in recent years, defeated Fred Greenwood."

Yes, I defied the odds. From the outset, my shortcomings and lack of experience plus a few negatives, had prompted me to consider withdrawing several times, but what pushed me forward, I later realized and am thrilled to voice today, was my father's relentless efforts to plaster the county with my campaign signs and the encouraging words I heard along the campaign trail. He had taught me, albeit later than he should have, to gain confidence in myself, to aim for what I knew was right, and to follow my convictions. I still think those signs helped a lot.

True, my father had had absolutely no presence in my early life, except for my mother's understandable remarks that revealed her angst and his negatives. His absence lined up with the Great Depression and the start of World War II, and my mother's—like many others—struggles to get by, even survive. Yet she and my grandfather provided a safe haven for me to grow up in, and thanks to that, I had what was otherwise a normal life.

Amazingly, there was reconciliation at the end of our journey. My mother and her third husband, Jules DuHamel, moved to Vancouver shortly after my first election in 1967. Now all of us were in the same community, even my brother who also moved his family to southwest Washington. Both sets of parents attended my graduation from Lewis & Clark College in 1964 and my marriage to Carolyn in 1971, as well as when I was sworn-in as a newly elected member of Congress back in the capital.

When my father's health deteriorated in the mid-1980s and he required assisted care, my mother and her husband, Jules, were there by his side offering full support. Yes, there were a lot of bumps in the road on that long journey, but finally, everyone came together at what we call "journey's end." The beloved English author and lay theologian C. S. Lewis wrote lines that I love to recall and share. "But for them it was only the beginning of the real story. All their life in this world and all their adventures in Narnia had only been the cover and the title page: now at last they were beginning Chapter One of the Great Story, which no one on earth has read: which goes on forever: in which every chapter is better than the one before."

CHAPTER 4

Upstart Shakes Up
Courthouse

Shaking up the courthouse was far from my mind as a twenty-nine-year-old, and in my first elected position to boot. Nor did I think of my agenda as being particularly ambitious. My experience with state and county services was practically nil—and my only real objective was to avoid messing up. The Seattle-based paper nonetheless dared to call me out only a year and half after the January 1966 election with this provocative affirmation, "Upstart shakes up courthouse."

Privately, I don't mind admitting I liked it. It is worth noting here just how much attention politicians pay to what is said about them in the press. It matters. You'd think they'd have thick skin and learn to take the punches with the praise, but the human ego is a funny thing, and even one comment, sometimes just one word—an adjective even—received at a vulnerable moment can be enough to push even a seasoned politico off his or her game. And likewise, one laudatory remark, a thumbs up or a well-timed "like," can make even the toughest bully gush or panic, or worse, say something that he or she comes to regret. We've come to see how hypersensitive even the holder of the highest office in the land can be when labeled or cited in a headline. Citizens and activists and advocates and lobbyists and plain old voters should not forget this. Public opinion matters. Eyeballs matter. We live in the age of the hyper viral. We used to have a moment to catch our breath or think out our next step. Not so anymore. It's all as fast as chemical reactions. And when it comes to press and media, there is always the straw that breaks the camel's back. There is always the drop that makes the glass overflow. The tipping point as a concept for influence and power is a phenomenon in reality. We only get to the tipping point, though when lots of people one at a time continue to add their tiny voice, make that call, send that email to their congressman or woman, attend that rally, or send in that letter to the editor. Somehow, I, the youngest elected county official in the state, was being called an upstart, or at least I was beginning to be perceived as one, when the *Argus*, our Pacific Northwest magazine, ran those words across its June 28, 1968 edition. I knew then that anyone could make the courthouse shake. Upstart was a tag I'd grow into, and even today as a former congressman and an active advocate for causes and clients, upstart is fitting.

The author Mike Layton, a prominent Seattle reporter for the Hearst-owned *Post-Intelligencer* newspaper, wrote soon after the June 1968 piece that "although Bonker, a quiet and thoughtful man, doesn't fit the usual clichés of the imaginative innovator—'whirlwind' and 'dynamo'—he is revolutionizing courthouse procedures here."

Layton went on to list the things apparently I had done in those first eighteen months in office: "...putting voter registrations on and preparing to computerize results of this fall's primary and general elections... embarked in a pilot program of modernizing courthouse accounting procedures (amazing that no county in Washington has yet adopted the double-entry bookkeeping system). A budget formula Bonker devised is enabling county commissioners to categorize programs by cost, to better set priorities (he is first in the state to put legal indexes on computer tape). He has made doing business with the county less confusing for the public (one example is a streamlined procedure for purchasing auto licenses with one-stop service and 'speed lines' for the January rush). He has assigned license renewal agencies to charitable organizations. No longer do applicants for marriage licenses in Clark County have to repeat the embarrassing oath that they are sound mentally and their blood untainted."

Upon taking office, I thought that my objectives had been modest. First, to select a first-rate team. That has been the most sensible priority in my career, and I strongly suggest the same to all newcomers in public office. Invest in your team first. People make the difference. Money, offices, tools, software, all that comes after. I had picked Dean Cole as my deputy county auditor who eventually became County Commissioner and later served in the governor's cabinet. I also picked Jim Gallagher, a staffer with the State Auditors Association who headed our efforts to advance election reforms. Jim went on to become the mayor of Vancouver.

Top priorities—pick top people and improve services for our constituents. The long lines and delays to get an auto license in those days were horrendous, and public frustration with this resonated throughout the campaign. I wanted to fix this problem quickly and I knew I had to tackle this head on. So one day, I showed up at the auto license section where six employees manned an extended counter and issued or renewed auto licenses all day. I announced I was there to address this problem and proceeded to the counter to assume one of the clerk's positions in order to show the team how it should be done with efficiency and cordiality. *Let the new county auditor himself show you,* I thought. I greeted my first and only engagement with a local resident, starting with "How can I help you, sir?" The man spoke and handed me some documents I had not seen before. He asked me several questions that were puzzling as my staff observed as their new boss fielded his first customer like a total rookie. I had to ask my clerks "What was this for?" "What do we do with that?" I shrugged my shoulders. I was stunned how much time these procedures took. More people were now in line, obviously upset with further delays. My first customer was getting impatient, bordering on anger. I was getting increasingly embarrassed. My ignorance reigned for a good twenty minutes before I turned in total despair to my dismayed clerk and acknowledged her excellent work, asked her to resume her tasks, and made a fast exit while masking my shame.

Yes, it was an embarrassing moment, trying to impress my employees and local residents. While I may have come across as naive, I was trying to fulfill a campaign pledge—my first priority as a newly elected official. In the past, the problems and frustrations were ignored. Now, my personal attention did convey to the auto-renewal staff that we had to address this matter. We had subsequent meetings to explore ways to make the system more efficient. Figuring out how to help people who are already doing the job do it better is one of the great management challenges we all face. Mission accomplished.

Later, I observed in the back of the building a huge stack of used auto license plates. I asked the supervisor, "How do we handle this backlog of old plates?" She said the Washington State Patrol people "pick them up every once in a while and I think they sell them, but don't know what they use the money for."

I made an appointment with the State Patrol's Southwest Washington Commander, a guy named Major Kermit Ekern, who confirmed the pickup and said the revenue became part of their contribution to a local charity and it also helped finance their annual Christmas Party. "This does not appear appropriate," I said and suggested it come to an end. One month later, my supervisor alerted me that the huge pile of license plates was now massive and they had no options for clearing the space behind the building. It was awkward if not embarrassing since this was my doing. I had to return and ask Major Ekern, sheepishly, if he would kindly resume picking up the license plates as before. He was a tall, strong, but gracious guy who politely responded in his typically amicable manner, "Okay, we'll resume picking 'em up; we roll with the punches around here." That's a line I learned to remember. I had so much to learn as the new head of this sprawling county office. Personalities, procedures, priorities, places, people. Rolling with punches.

Beyond the accomplishments listed by Mike Layton, what stood out now as I think back was the major breakthrough in our voting system and how I helped to revolutionize how ballots were counted. A new, innovative, but untested method on how votes were cast and counted began to take center stage, and this voting technology issue ultimately helped to propel my career beyond Clark County and afforded me statewide recognition. It was the voting machine phenomenon that propelled my candidacy for Washington Secretary of State.

In the 1970s, computerized voting was still at an experimental stage when IBM acquired the rights to supply the machinery for election modernization and poured millions into advancing the technology and securing the patent. The idea had come from a University of California professor, Joseph Harris, who had been working with an IBM representative, Robert Varni, at the time. Varni benefited from a court ruling that required IBM to divest itself from being involved in the election system, was able to take over ownership himself, and then changed the nomenclature from punch card to Votomatic.

Conducting elections using paper ballots has always been a sacred tradition in our democracy involving ordinary citizens as poll workers, who work late into the evening with selfless dedication and preside over the counting of ballots precinct by precinct. Normal people doing God's work in the name of the greater good. Ours has been a culture of volunteerism. While it was a trusted means to ensure safeguarding the integrity of vote counting, the mechanical tabulations overseen by poll workers implicated a slow count, delayed releasing of results, which sometimes took days and a considerable budget. This got my attention to be sure, but I had little idea of how it would propel my status statewide as a young upstart down in Vancouver. This, as county auditor, interested me and I did some research.

History buffs can attest that back in 1895, a guy named Samuel Shoup first pursued an alternative to paper ballots by putting his company, Republic Steel of Ohio, into the business of producing a mechanical method of vote tabulation. The so-called "lever machines" were touted as durable and efficient, and offered the necessary safeguards against rigging. By 1935, a sixth of all presidential ballots were being cast on mechanical voting machines, essentially all made by the same manufacturer. In 1968, I discovered that the lever-machine people had become a powerful lobbying force in state capitols around the country and had hired a sales force of influence peddlers to strongly oppose the alternative computerized voting system. If you look carefully, you'll always find some special interest pushing or pulling one way or another.

The haunting part of the problem of elections was the cost. These old hulking 874-pound machines came with a price tag in the mid-1950s that could bankrupt an election office up to $5,000 per machine. Beyond the huge price tag, there were enormous costs for storing these beasts and delivering them to and from the polling station in every election. Seeking a modern alternative made sense. To note, the last of these monstrous metal-lever voting machines rang up their last tallies in New York state during the 2010 midterm elections. With curious inattention to the environment, tugboats ultimately hauled them out into the Atlantic and sunk them to create artificial reefs supposedly needed to protect the coastlines.

The fish, of course, were never consented! But visual inspiration may lie here for a Disney film.

The traditional voting method back in my early days in office served to perpetuate antiquated and costly elections, which is why the Clark County Commissioners were receptive to a less costly computerized voting system. I presented the options and they were astounded by the cost comparison. Each lever voting machine cost five grand compared to the new Votomatic price tag of $185. The lever machines weighed close to a half ton each while the Votomatic device weighed only six pounds, and thus storage and transportation costs would represent more huge savings.

The commissioners encouraged me to go for it, so I reached out to Robert Varni, who was anxious to find a county jurisdiction interested in using his punch card Votomatic system, and he quickly arrived on the scene.

I assembled my deputy and the Chief Election Officer for an all-day meeting with Robert Varni, so that they could fully understand the concept and grasp the capability of this revolutionary new system for voting. We were at the cutting edge of changing the way democracy functioned. There was nothing more central to our form of government than the secret ballot, and we were at the brink of updating how the ballot and the voter interacted. Varni proceeded to describe the workings of the Votomatic system. The voter inserted a standardized IBM data processing card into a tablet-type device that had been programmed with pages listing the candidates and referendum questions. Each position on the cards was pre-scored so that the voter, using a "stylus," could punch out little circles of cardboard called "*chads*" on the ballot card. Candidate names were not printed on the cards but were printed on the pages of the ballot holder, and were aligned with the positions of the inserted card.

Varni went on to demonstrate how the voter slipped the ballot card into the holder and turned the pages exposing columns of ballot positions from left to right across the underlying card. After making his or her selection, the voter removed the ballot card and this is what would trigger the counted tabulation in a central location on card readers and attached computers.

I was impressed, although in retrospect, it was still pretty basic. The concept guaranteed the county huge savings, along with a more rapid and efficient means of counting ballots and reporting results. This jumped out at me as an innovative cause worthy of my advocating as a young county official, which was perfectly consistent with my young upstart image. When politicians can find good ways to prove that they are doing what they promised, they are happy. There is nothing more fundamental than people voting across America's heartland, and for over 200 years, we had been choosing our public leaders by paper ballot prior to the arrival of the lever machines in the late 1890s. Now we'd be using computers, and my county would be on the front lines of national innovation. Upstart indeed.

I informed Robert Varni we were prepared to move forward. Clark County would be the first in the State of Washington, perhaps nationally, to employ computers in our election system. This was something I now wanted to make happen.

He was pleased but responded with guarded enthusiasm. His recent attempts to try to have other counties buy into his Votomatic system were confronted by rigorous skepticism. Mr. Varni warned about the lever machine lobby, who, in the pre-false news days, would try to capitalize on fears that vote security and trust factor were untested and that technology was relatively new and posed risks of error and fraud. We have a lot more to be wary of today than in 1968, but still, at the time, the lobby was talented in instilling doubt.

Varni was spot on. The adoption of the Votomatic system would only happen if I were prepared to commit the time and energy to make repeated trips to Olympia, the state capitol, and make a compelling case to the state legislature. It would take the enactment of a law to authorize counties to introduce this new system. Ultimately, I would learn that it would take even much more than that; I'd have to educate the party leaders and the media on the reliability, the cost savings, and the safeguards if I hoped to introduce technical innovation to Clark County. And, I had to be prepared to go hard against the lever machine lobbyists. This turned out to be a great training ground for me as it is never an easy task for legislators or officials to take on well-funded and well-trained lobbyists. Had I not fought this fight, then I would probably not have had the guts and the fire power to take on the special interest groups that lined the halls of Congress and then took aim on the battlefields of legislative warfare throughout the congressional days that would begin only seven years later.

In Olympia, the state lawmakers had understandable concerns about a radically untested new voting system. The irony, of course, is all this happened a generation prior to the now historic "hanging chads" in Florida in the contested 2000 presidential elections between Al Gore and George W. Bush, which ended with the United States Supreme Court ruling 5–4 in Bush vs. Gore, 531 US 98 with Justice Rehnquist's tiebreaking vote essentially rewarding the US presidency to George W. Bush and altering the course of American and global history. America's previously admired electoral system had now shifted in the eyes of citizens around the world. Ah, the importance of election procedures.

Decades earlier back in Olympia, they knew that they would be held accountable if the system turned out be a disaster. All politicians everywhere are thinking about accountability. Where does the buck stop? Who gets caught holding the bag? How will I be perceived? Is it worth taking the risk of looking bad? On any issue, lawmakers must consider the proponents making their respective cases. In Olympia in 1968, I was the sole advocate for computerized voting—unknown, inexperienced, and young. I was challenging the tradition of how ballots were cast and counted that would have implications statewide, even nationally. The opponents were led by the machine-lever lobbyists and included most of the other county auditors around the state. Skeptics abound.

The battle to introduce change, I quickly learned, went far beyond persuading lawmakers to authorize punch card voting. State politicians were sizing me up as well. It's not only what you are proposing, it is often who you are, and who is behind you, and who sent you, and who will appreciate it when your proposal is accepted or rejected. Or ignored. Or delayed. Or gutted. I rolled out presentation after presentation before legislative committees and conducted individual meetings with legislators. I learned to be patient and relentless, ready to repeat myself as many times as necessary. I also learned that you could garner a lot of information by observing and fielding body language. The legislators were clearly cautious and hesitant with something this sensitive in the hands of a young, inexperienced county official. The Votomatic system wasn't the problem—I was. Gaining confidence in the political arena is a long-term process. But I came to see that it was my innocence that also served as an asset. And I didn't give up.

It took me over two years of lobbying in Olympia before the state legislature finally agreed to the authorization, and even then, they agreed to allow this in Clark County only. The limitation meant that if the change went well, they could reap the benefits, but if it went south I would take the bullet. Clark County would be the trial case to see if this were a viable voting system. If it wasn't, well, what did anyone expect from an inexperienced young official?

We were excited, though, and worked closely with Varni in our first Votomatic election, the September primary in 1970, so determined to guarantee success. Considerable statewide attention, lawmakers, media, other county auditors, the Secretary of State, party officials, and eager candidates were all leering in at what we were doing.

The media coverage would predictably be critical if there were serious flaws in this revolutionary voting technique. Fortunately, *The Columbian* newspaper described it as a "masterpiece of planning and administration," noting in an editorial, "One election result didn't appear in the tallies of the primary election in Clark County, and it wasn't even on the ballot. But the popularity vote may well have gone to Clark County's punch card voting system," I recall like it was yesterday. "Had there been a tally, it might have been the leading vote getter." Admittedly, there had been a few flaws on election night, but no serious setbacks and the success on the whole had been huge. Dr. Joseph Harris, a national authority on the elections and inventor of the Votomatic, gave the ultimate compliment and was quoted in the local newspaper: "I would say unequivocally that this is the best run election I've ever seen."

In the next legislative session, a bill was enacted to expand the use of punch card voting to all the state's counties, and the enthusiasm for its adoption spread quickly throughout the nation. By 1992, the Votomatic system was the dominant voting system in the United States, used by 27% more voters than those who used mechanical lever voting machines. This crescendoed of course until that notorious 2000 presidential election which catapulted the American electoral system into public scrutiny across the country and around the world. The technical flaw with the punch cards and the ultimate court decision that resulted changed the history of voting and the credibility of the American system. It also led to Congress passing the Help America Vote Act of 2002 that effectively banned pre-scored punch card ballots. I still think about the effect that our county innovation had on the entire system, and the role that one young county official can play in the bigger picture. Don't underestimate the importance of local law and reforms in local policy.

There are often great political dimensions to local reforms. They are almost never planned or expected but they simply evolve, as I witnessed during the voting machine adventure. My many appearances in the state capitol, testifying before committees, meeting with lawmakers, and hanging out in pubs with staffers, political operatives, and reporters resulted as well in my becoming much better known and more deeply connected.

The Seattle political columnist Joel Connelly cited me as a "rising star" in the Democratic Party and suddenly, I began receiving invitations from all parts of the state to give speeches and stage demonstrations on how this new voting system worked. The chairman of the State Democratic Committee asked me to do a tour of Washington's key counties to meet with party officials and hold precinct meetings as a display of new leadership and fresh direction in the Democrats.

As technology was taking hold in local government, what was emerging was my possible candidacy for the state office—Secretary of State. Rising to the state's chief election officer would have been a natural position for me given my recent identity with computerize voting.

The Office of Secretary of State had experienced a curious historical twist. In the 1950s, a certain local celebrity, Vic Meyers, a former bandleader, dominated the news. During the Great Depression, Meyers' popular night club band featured all around Seattle was shut down, leaving the guy frustrated and desperate and virtually unemployed. He journeyed to the state capitol to look for a job somewhere, and when he arrived at the Secretary of State's office, he announced to everyone's great surprise and amusement, "I am here to be a candidate for governor." Informed that the filing fee was more than what he had, he blurted, "I have forty bucks.

What office can I run for?" To everyone's surprise, the Italian nightclub entertainer ran for lieutenant governor and was elected! Throughout his public career, Vic Meyers was more about entertainment than politics. After three terms, he was defeated in 1964 by a young Seattle City councilman named A. Ludlow Kramer, better known as "Lud."

Lud Kramer was everything that Meyers wasn't. He became the youngest elected official statewide in 1964, known for his ambition and dedication to public causes. Serious and intensely political, he was a renegade Republican because of his championing of issues that were more in sync with the Democratic stance, including the rights of the poor and minorities, housing reforms, and the improvement of the prison and electoral systems. Indeed, Lud was known for taking trips to migrant farmworker camps in Yakima, join community protest movements in Seattle, and other hands-on public advocacy work. He found the standard Secretary of State job so boring that Governor Dan Evans was practically obliged to assign him to special commissions, which attracted a great deal of media attention.

By 1972, Lud Kramer was sending mixed signals about whether he would seek reelection. The word on the street was that the Nixon administration was considering Lud for the Under Secretary of Housing and Urban Affairs slot, and with that in sight, he flew off to Washington, DC to meet with secretary of HUD, George Romney. Kramer had typically generated a disproportionate amount of media attention due to his lively personality and visibility, but upon arrival, Secretary Romney refused to meet with him. A story leaked to the press that Kramer had checked into a hotel with a girlfriend—not his wife. Kramer's signature moment in national politics instantly crumbled into a pillow-talk scandal, and both the governor and the Republicans disavowed him. In defiance, Kramer kicked back and decided to run for mayor of Seattle, which resulted in his first election defeat. The double setbacks took a serious toll on his character and he started to act rather strangely in public. Everyone was startled when he was, soon after the election bid, spotted working at a Olympia gas station a few blocks from his Secretary of State office. A photograph of him holding a gas pump for a customer captured the media attention and went viral nationwide, even internationally. There is a sort of perverse delight that both the press and the public derive when politicians face humiliation. The politic ride that takes those in public office or those seeking public office is spiked with exaggerated peaks of delight and excruciating valleys of despairs. The politician's ego acts like a trampoline, and the rush to the top and the fall to the bottom is shot full of unhealthy doses of adrenaline.

Why—I asked myself and continue to contemplate as I've seen others with bright futures cave at the whim of poor judgment—why would the son of a wealthy family, a talented already elected Secretary of State and contender for a high-level federal office, and later candidate for mayor of a major American city, do this? When asked bluntly, he explained that the gas station gig was a part-time job to pay off his campaign debt since many Republican supporters withheld their contributions when the scandal hit, but I came to understand that Lud Kramer was actually sending another message—"feel sorry for me." He was begging or appealing to the public's ability to forgive and to have empathy. The life of the stumbled politician can evoke great pathos, and admittedly, I truly did feel sorry for him. There is always something tragic when a leader with great potential suddenly falters and is banished in humiliation. One wonders who and when one individual will succeed in climbing to greatness and who will ultimately fizzle and be briefly shamed and then forgotten. This existential consideration is not untrue of how many areas of activity function, but the political arena seems to stand out front in that it offers a hyper-volatility and velocity matched only perhaps by the world of entertainment, music, art, and cinema. What was the well-known edict shared by pop artist Andy Warhol and Campbell Soup on fame? "Famous for fifteen minutes."

With the bizarre shenanigans of Lud Kramer as backdrop and his third term bout as Secretary of State uncertain, I had to weigh an upcoming decision about next steps. These decisions were all about timing. In this case, my leadership on revolutionizing how ballots were tabulated positioned me ideally to run for the state's top election officer. Also, I was in the midterm of my second four-year-term as Clark County auditor, so I would not relinquish my elected office. Yet running statewide against a well-established incumbent was a moon shot.

CHAPTER 5

"Go Back and Marry That Guy"

E asily reelected in 1970, I was coasting along in my second term as county auditor when I received a call from Frank Foley, a highly regarded state senator.

"Hey, Don, need a favor."

Eager to please, I responded, "Whatever you want, Frank."

"Actually," he explained, "this is for Major Ekern of the State Patrol." He went on. "His daughter has just returned from someplace in Europe and needs a job." The major was concerned that if she didn't find a job, she'd head back to California, and he wanted her to stay home.

Carolyn was her name. A 1967 graduate of Seattle Pacific University, a member of the Theta Sigma Phi Honor Society, and the senior homecoming princess. Upon graduation, she had worked for a youth organization at USLA in California, then sojourned in Europe as had been the craze of the day. Everybody was buying the popular guide *Europe on $5 a Day.* Eventually, Major Ekern's daughter had settled at L'Abri, Switzerland, where she tutored the young children of an American couple and became absorbed into the Francis Schaeffer Fellowship Forum at L'Abri before returning to her parents' house in Vancouver. Frank needed me to keep her from wandering off again.

Carolyn's father had been the same State Patrol officer I had confronted four years earlier, I soon recalled. I assured the state senator, "Okay, have her come over and I'll see what I can do." So much about political office is about favors. You help someone, and they help you. Favors, alliances, exchanges, compromises, one big game of chess where you move your pieces in ways that are ultimately helpful. The key, of course, is to advance yourself while not losing track of where you are heading, and more importantly, who you are.

The minute Carolyn Ekern walked in the door, I was struck by my first impression. My God, she looks like Jaqueline Kennedy—wearing a coat dress, subtle plaid fabric, low heels, shoulder length brunette hair, sparkling brown eyes, and a contagious smile. I learned later that Carolyn was also surprised, expecting a county auditor to be a fiftyish, bespectacled, bald, and fat typical courthouse figure. Later that afternoon, Carolyn had tea with her mother and a friend, who asked how the interview went. Carolyn responded, "Interesting, but I think he is married."

The friend quickly responded, "Oh no, he is not. He's the most eligible bachelor in Vancouver."

My priority was to please the state senator, so I proceeded to set up a few appointments for Miss Ekern, including one at the local newspaper and another one at the local bank. And off she went. I made a few calls to follow up, hoping to be able to report back swiftly to Frank that the task was done. It became obvious after I talked to the editor and bank manager that this was going to be a bit more challenging. Her capabilities went beyond the secretarial assistant positions that were available. I rashly offered Carolyn a part-time position in the marriage license department in the county office, which, in retrospect, foreshadowed the ironic serendipity of our fate.

I had her meet Dean Cole, the deputy county auditor, to acquaint her with the responsibilities that came with the marriage license position. He later shared with me that conversation, mostly her experiences living in Switzerland, then paused and said to me, "Don, she may be the one for you." Obviously, she made a favorable impression on both of us. I remember thinking, *Forget the courthouse job, Don. How about a lifetime senior position as spouse? Partner? For better or worse?* I was secretly smitten.

In my day, they called this a crush. I had a crush on Carolyn.

Forty plus years later, as we were celebrating our forty-fifth anniversary, Carolyn amazingly retained her good looks and continued to draw compliments wherever she appeared. What continued to capture people's attention was her natural beauty and elegance, not cosmetics nor dyed hair, and yes, I was still smitten.

I hate to think of how I might have regretfully avoided the obvious had that fortuitous day occurred now and not in March 1970. I'm wholeheartedly supportive of the great and overdue advances we've made in leveling the gender playing field, especially in government and elected office and calling out and rectifying sexist attitudes and double standards, which I've witnessed and rebuked throughout my political life—even as a highly eligible bachelor. The #metoo movement continues and deepens in sensitizing an entire culture that has blindly tolerated wrongful treatment of many women and men too. And yet, as I think back at that glorious moment in my office when I was smitten by the presence of an amorous sentiment that would grace my existence forever, I somehow wish that we, in our culture, were driven too to launch a movement that also celebrated the magic of attraction and the glorious power of what our souls and our bodies seem to do so right. The old dance instructor in me gushes now as I recreate the lovely urge to place my right hand on young Carolyn's waist and lead her gleefully anywhere.

Although these were long before the days of articulated gender politics in the workplace, and there were no county regulations about office romance, as county auditor, I avoided, of course, dating any employee in the auditor's office—and they were almost all female. How would I be able to apply this sound rule if I started dating Major Ekern's daughter, Carolyn? Determined to invent an exception, since Cupid is sometimes stupid, I decided the rule didn't apply because this young woman was a temporary employee. Yes, the feeling was that strong, and what began as sharing the coworkers lunch table, I ventured across the line and asked her to join me for a real lunch.

She agreed. It happened in Portland at Jerry Gable's Restaurant, a romantic setting, and as we were in a booth with a music box that allowed choices, I asked for her preference while inserting quarters to pull up romantic tunes appropriate for a first date. But the music box malfunctioned and kept repeating the same song—the 1969 Burt Bacharach ditty, "Raindrops Keep Falling on My Head." It had a mesmerizing effect on that first evening together, and eventually, it would emerge as our theme song and played a sentimental role at our wedding one year later—and remains our favorite nearly fifty years later. After our second dinner date, I entered my office the next day with my deputy, Dean Cole, to find an unsettling scene: photos of me and another young woman whom I had previously dated (a reporter for *The Columbian*) that were taken by the newspaper's photographer, were now hanging upside down on their hooks. Carolyn had snuck into my office and cleverly made a point. I quickly removed those images and our relationship took on a new meaning from that moment on. Carolyn has been my pinup girl ever since. So much feeling and yet so timid with articulated words, as was typical of the era.

As Carolyn's temporary position was coming to an end, she had arranged interviews with the governor's office in Olympia. In talking with the experienced and savvy Dorothy Greeley, who held a supervisory position in the state legislature, Carolyn mentioned that she was dating this young county official in Vancouver. Curious, Ms. Greeley asked, "Who might that be?" When Carolyn responded, "The county auditor, Don Bonker," Ms. Greeley, a woman whose judgment she highly valued, shot back, "Carolyn, what are you doing here interviewing with the governor's office? Go back down there and marry that young man." Our best advice often comes from total strangers. She quickly abandoned her plans to work in Olympia and returned to Vancouver, taking a teaching position in a Clark County school district to be nearby and residing with her parents. Pleased that I had kept my promise to Frank Foley to keep Major Ekern's daughter from leaving, I marvel now at how political favors can prove to be mutually beneficial.

I found myself driving the eight miles to Major Ekern's residence regularly. On several occasions, I was pulled over by one particularly tall state patrolman for no particular reason and asked to show my driver's license, which was ridiculous since he knew who I was, and plus, my office issued the darn licenses in the first place. Later, I learned the tepid backstory that this patrolman shared an interest in Carolyn Ekern and just wanted to intimidate his competitor. Of course, there was no real competition.

I hoped to make Ms. Greeley's advice to Carolyn come true, and between June and December 1970, I proposed to Carolyn not once but on three separate occasions. Sheepishly, of course. Only two are worth sharing. The first was during a well-planned trip to Victoria with my father and stepmother where, ultimately, we would honeymoon, but not before a whole lot of Bonkeresque awkwardness. On that afternoon, I let my father in on the secret plan and he was thrilled. "When?" he asked, "and what can I do?" to which I responded it would be that evening, but I need to find a quiet and romantic restaurant to pull this off.

He offered gleefully to go to the front desk of our hotel and get a recommendation for me. And he said he'd also get reservations for a family style restaurant for himself and Gladys. Romantic for me, family style for him. He was happy to help and wanted to give me the space to be my own man. I wonder if he was somehow reliving what he had done with my mother or was trying to correct what he hadn't, but I never asked him. With time, I've learned that you have to ask the tough questions when you can. When Carolyn and I arrived at the suggested restaurant, it was obvious he had gotten things mixed up—we found ourselves at a noisy, crowded, children-friendly diner. Not a good setting for the big moment, and which stymied any attempt of getting sweet things to come from my mouth. My father ended up at a lovely restaurant at the end of a long pier with a fantastic view of the water, a setting that was intended for this young couple. My father later asked if I had popped the question and actually proposed to my beloved Carolyn.

"I don't know, I think so."

He looked puzzled. I was as well. "You think so?"

I'll never forget his look, as if we were in this together, which we weren't. That was my second failed attempt. It wouldn't be until nearly Christmas that I would make my third attempt. But this time, I would be better prepared, would have done my own research, would be equipped with an engagement ring I had purchased on my own, and would certainly be more convincing. The plan: we'd be at the Stanger House, my home at the time, to host our first Christmas Eve dinner, and I would have invited both sets of parents for the big announcement, thinking that marriage was a gift for everyone. I did my due diligence to find a ring I thought she would like, one with a center stone surrounded by a curved swell of diamonds on both sides. My idea was to present Carolyn with the ring before the guests arrived, and she would be all choked up and gushy and feeling so happy. The setting and script were good, but I was still lame with the timing. We were running late on the preparations and she was still scurrying about, chopping up some fruit for salad. I finally struggled to get the ring out of that little pillbox and held it behind my back, about to deliver the most important lines of my life when the doorbell rang. It was her parents, Major and Mrs. Ekern, arriving earlier than they were expected. It was their time to destabilize the son-in-law-to-be, poor Don. The scene was like living in one of those corny sitcom episodes of *I Love Lucy*, or for those who recall *The Honeymooners*, although a bit more upscale.

Soon, the small Stanger House was full of family and accompanying holiday spirit, with some expectation. This confirmed bachelor became faint and nauseous and retreated upstairs to my bedroom, leaving Carolyn be the solo life. She then graciously came to check on me, a pale soul lying down and still grasping the ring. I finally handed it to her accompanied with words I'm told were barely audible. It's hard to believe I was a politician. She looked at me lovingly, and looked down at the ring I had so tenderly selected. And it was now her turn to translate confidence into trepidation. Her response was not exactly a clear yes, certainly not a Hollywood yes, but she agreed that we would make an announcement of our engagement before our family members who were gathered downstairs. Suddenly, I started to feel better, even relieved, as Carolyn graciously put on the ring. Finally, it happened. And the mood filled with joy.

On Christmas Eve, I had a revealing epiphany as to why I did not hear a resounding yes from my future bride. Carefully, she explained in the presence of our Christmas tree that her hesitance to commit came with a clause in the margin. It was not by accident that she was sharing this on Christmas Day. She wanted to hear my personal commitment to a calling even higher than matrimony, to the Lord. I had recognized early on the importance of her faith and now realized it would definitely be a nonnegotiable part of our married life, our union. Obviously, I was being confronted with a decision that went beyond my multiple awkward attempts to propose. I had questions, real questions about faith, and so we hastily called on Howard Hart, pastor of the local Baptist church we were attending, who graciously took time from his family to meet with us that very evening, Christmas Day, considering this was an emergency, a spiritual 911 moment!

As we sat down, my head was swirling with what to ask him. I had been a faithful Presbyterian who had regularly attended church services, yet this was a leap from being a casual Christian to something deeper, a personal commitment that would be a life changer. How will this affect my daily life, my political career? If I fully commit, what do I give up? Does it mean future decisions and actions will be guided by my religious beliefs? Does this mean a new moral standard in my life? There will be no more sins, only redemption? The pastor listened carefully to my questions and replied in a manner expected of most pastors in similar settings, but for some reason, Carolyn detected that his comments were not exactly resonating with the county auditor. Although I started as a dance instructor, I had become a numbers guy and needed convincing. She patiently let the pastor wind down in his various responses then would weigh in with her own soft words which curiously but definitely found a faster and more direct way into my heart. Carolyn weighed in, saying, "Don, you have plans for sure; you're bright and ambitious. But know this, your Heavenly Father created and loves you more than you can imagine. You can trust Him and His son, Jesus, to be the guide and leader for your life."

It was not only her sharing but I felt the spirit in the room, a godliness which was awesome to the half-believer that I was. It was there in that pastor's dark office that I saw the light—the beauty of this young woman and her faith in God and her readiness to join me in body and spirit as husband and wife was what I had not seen before. God wasn't external. He was in her voice and in the sweet damp hands that were holding mine in the presence of the pastor, and convincing me to relax all those molecules of hesitation and fear. It was obvious that God's outreach to me was through Carolyn, not Pastor Hart. My decision not only affirmed my proposal to Carolyn, but it implanted a faith that became central in my life going forward. And my work. That faith is at the core of all decisions.

Six months later on July 10, 1971, we were married at the same historic Stanger House where I had been living at the time. The setting was ideal given the picturesque atmosphere with dazzling rolling hills in the background and a stunning view of the Columbia River and Mt. Hood. For the photographer, it was like an arboretum—six acres featuring a lovely pond, an elegant bridge over the creek that provided an idyllic background for our wedding album, with family and many cherished friends in attendance.

"The auditor issues his own marriage license," was the headline of a small article in *The Columbian* on July 8, 1971. It reported that Don Bonker had countless duties to keep him busy as Clark County auditor, but his most unique one has just been carried out. "He issued his own marriage license for his forthcoming wedding to Miss Carolyn Jo Ekern." It went on to report that it was the first time in Clark County that the auditor has had the "double responsibility of issuing a marriage license to himself, and playing the supporting role of bridegroom."

Traveling from California to serve as officiant was Reverend Hal Lindsey, a noted author at the time of *The Late Great Planet Earth*, who sported a blue blazer combined with a blue tie dotted with white stars and a white shirt with narrow red and blue stripes. Very patriotic. The wedding attracted many state and local officials, but our special guest was Oregon's US senator whom I had worked for a few years earlier. Maurine Neuberger, ever distinguished in a green and white silk suit, blessed us with a memorable gift, a silver salt and pepper shaker from her own wedding decades earlier.

As reported in *The Columbian*, Carolyn's veil was attached to a "Juliet headpiece of laced thread with blue ribbon, and her flowers were a nosegay of white roses, pale yellow daisies, and blue baby's breath." That's why she needed protection as she was about to walk down the grass aisle accompanied by her father as a drizzle developed. Her father, Kermit Ekern, quickly reached out to a guest and asked to borrow her white umbrella, a perfect match for the Victorian style white gown of silk organza with a short train that Carolyn was wearing. At the garden wedding were two sets of musicians. For the service, an ensemble composed of a harpsichord, viola and flute playing *Whither Thou Go'st*, followed by two violinists and a guitarist who played classic renditions at the reception, including, of course, our first date theme song, *Raindrops Keep Falling on My Head*, well-choreographed as the drizzle turned to rain outside the big white tents.

The Stanger House represented a generous slice of history that made our first year together all the more enriching. Constructed on the banks of the Columbia River, and listed on the National Register of Historic Places by John Stanger in 1867, it has been featured in the local press and was once described as "a simple two-room gabled structure built of milled cedar planks," "tucked away on the Image Road and partially hidden by roses and foliage as a picturesque house." Its historic meaning was even more enticing because of the creativity of its owners, Dr. Vince and Jane Weber. *The Columbian* devoted a full page of photos in its July 23, 1970 edition, describing the upstairs bedroom like this: "*...the bed in the loft, found in a barn next to the house is suspended from the ceiling by leather straps also discovered on the property as was the leather horse collar that graces the wall. White shag rugs were used on the walls. On the right is an antique iron crib.*"

It was Dr. Weber's vision and devotion to his beloved wife, Jane, the Stanger House and the six acres of the spectacular river-view property that led him to create the Jane Weber Arboretum on which board I've served as a trustee for over thirty years. The harmony between the sanctity of my vows to Carolyn and the holiness of that first home for us remains as a deep source of personal peace.

CHAPTER 6

"Keep It to Three Points"

N ow married and settling in at Stanger House, the young Bonkers faced another decision about the upcoming race for Secretary of State. My being a candidate for Secretary of State was a natural fit given its official duty was overseeing the state's election system, which I helped to transform to the computerized age. I now had the ideal set of credentials and statewide attention essential for building a political base in Olympia.

Defeating a two-term incumbent state official was, as far I as knew, unprecedented in Washington State. Ludlow Kramer, known as Lud, had become controversial and with his Republican support beginning to wane, he started to rethink how smart it would be to seek a third term. I was in a dilemma; if Lud went for the third term, I'd probably have to back off. If he decided not to stand, I would definitely run with the prospect of winning. Time was ticking and I was pressed to set an announcement date. The next week, Lud Kramer decided he would run for a third term. Now I was tormented.

Lud Kramer was the best-known state official, except for the governor, and I was the least known, so the odds appeared insurmountable. Back in the early 1970s, a statewide campaign rolled out in the old-time manner—lots of local speeches, volunteers handing out brochures, putting up signs, and building political contacts one by one in all the state's thirty-nine counties. Today, campaigns lace across counties and constituent bases by exploiting the digital tools and the demographics of heightened targeting, algorithms, and databases, tools that make even the websites, social media, tweets, and online advertising of yesterday seem slow and obsolete. In the 1970s, we just got out there and pounded the flesh, jumped into and out of cars, waved at cameras, tasted far too many locally baked pies, and looked like we recognized everyone.

Good 'ol campaigning.

My biggest challenge was being far removed from the vast number of voters who were densely located in and around Puget Sound. Democrats statewide had little or no knowledge about this young county official, Bonker. What should we do? I never had a problem asking the obvious question in the most simple way. I was open to suggestions. How would we get exposure quickly and gain on Lud?

Someone in the team had an idea. Let's send Christmas cards to party leaders and all the Democratic precinct committeemen and women. I liked it. I remembered that Carolyn and my wedding photo was exceptionally lovely, although I know I was particularly partial. People who saw that photo often said, "What a lovely couple." We were in traditional wedding attire, long white gown and tux with cummerbund with matching box tie. We bordered on classical design, and it was true, we were a handsome twosome. People like couples who look made for each other. Carolyn and Don were a hot item. The team jumped on this and we created a Christmas card with the photo. I personally signed them all with a good fountain pen, added a personal touch to the ones going to people I knew or at least knew a bit. Most I had never met nor had any idea who they were or what they cared about. We selected large and colorful stamps and mailed the lot out to 500 Democrats around the state.

Not surprisingly, reactions started filtering in. Many were puzzled and wrote back with obvious questions like "Who are you?" "How did I get on your Christmas list?" A few were forthcoming: "Which side of the family are you related to?" "Are you a former student? A classmate?" "How did we become acquainted?" Some were even more intriguing. One had on the return address, "Klickitat Drum & Bugle Corps, musing about who we were, Carolyn, looks too much classy for my crowd." Another real comment asked Carolyn if she was from Aunt Tilly's side of the family. In the name of clean politics, yes definitely. Aunt Tilly?

How is the ol' girl?

A letter from a woman named Lucille Myrick, dated December 28, 1971, resident of Auburn, Washington, conveyed true perplexity. Ms. Myrick candidly asked Carolyn, "Who are you?" *"I'm not really sure just who I am writing to, but am hoping you will tell me. Carolyn, if you sent the card to surprise me, you can bet it sure did. Thanks so much for sending it. But for the life of me, I haven't yet figured out just who you were before you married. I'm sure there must be some connection somewhere, so will you please write me the background from where you came. Ha, ha. You know how it is when you can't place someone."* These responses were like if we had sent out mass emails as targeted spam—yet they were beyond our expectations. You know, you get responses. At least I sent the cards to the group of Democrats that I knew I had to meet. Fortunately, my bride was standing next to me.

We also got calls from people still mystified who we were, carried in hand the Christmas card to family reunions. Our card became a conversation piece. Later, while traveling around the state, we repeatedly ran into people who had the card nearby or pinned up or sitting on their mantels. Mailing that wedding Christmas card definitely got people's attention and raised our profile around the state. One of the great, simple accidents of political campaigning of my career.

The Christmas card may have been a sassy start, but my statewide campaign still lacked both overarching strategy and efficient planning. The missteps seemed countless and each came with both pain and a tangible lesson. I'd sometimes accept invitations to give speeches, interviews, or agree to meet with party leaders in remote rural areas, painfully far from the population centers. On one occasion, Carolyn and I embarked on a five-hour journey in our beat-up 1964 Plymouth station wagon across the state with multiple stops to give speeches and collect donations at Democratic events. At one point, so overwhelmed by the absence of people, Carolyn rolled down the window and motioned like she wanted to throw our campaign brochures out into the wind as we passed through a rural town in eastern Washington. There were lots of lonely roads that seemed to go forever. Half of politics is just being willing to go down the lonely roads. It's hard to forget the bumper sticker someone had stuck on the car dashboard, "I'M A BONKER BACKER," which quickly became sun bleached and impossible to remove after the campaign.

Around the state, Democrats I recall were sponsoring traditional Jefferson-Jackson Day events, so this was a fine opportunity to make appearances and build support. Jefferson-Jackson Day has been a fundraising celebration often including dinner that lore contends began with Thomas Jefferson and Andrew Jackson. The Republicans do the same but call it Lincoln-Reagan Day Dinners. Strange bedfellows history makes. Today, a lot of states have dropped the Jefferson-Jackson name since Jefferson's relationship to slaves and Jackson's opinions on Native Americans have not helped democratic fundraising.

There was lots of ground travel around the state, which is why we welcomed the supporter who reached out to a friend with a private plane, a piper cub, and offered to fly Carolyn and me to these events in far-off parts of eastern Washington. He had been a Vietnam veteran and a novice pilot. Once we boarded the small prop plane, we nervously observed him tracing the lines on a gas station roadmap trying to locate a landing strip. We were up there under the clouds over a lot of trees and occasional road, a sparse hamlet, and we swirled around like a lost bird eyeing a strip that turned out to be an abandoned airfield. It was a scary landing, and the plane rolled to a stop just a few yards from a cliff that could have been a disaster. We climbed out of the craft, and I felt the bold and terrible feeling of abandonment as I searched the horizon for the crowd of supporters who supposedly ready to chant and scream with excitement and Don Bonker and his charming newlywed wife descended from the first-class section of a cramped piper cub. There was no one, other than that cliff which reminded me of the scary scene in *Rebel Without a Cause* when James Dean races a junker car across a field toward a cliff in a cruel game of chicken. Apparently, my supporters were patiently waiting at another airstrip. We got back into the vessel and retook the skies, eventually finding the right airstrip. I was already ninety minutes late with two meetings ahead, and the screams and whistles were more like some polite applause. The joys of the state political campaign! But in retrospect, I must admit I loved every minute of it. This is where the lives of our citizens meet the ambitions of our lawmakers. This is participatory democracy in action. Rural politicking....

It's good for the soul, and it's good for the character. It keeps you humble, and I wish more politicians in Washington spent more time in the most rural parts of their districts.

When we entered the Hunters Club, the few people remaining had endured far too many rounds of coffee and were brewing with impatience. I hate to think of what jokes they had time to invent with my last name. Here I was, now, and had to start from a negative position. Responsible government didn't begin with a late candidate. I did my best. Like I always do.

As I was speaking, Carolyn noticed unusual signs at the back of the building. There were two doors and one was marked with the sign "Pointers" and the other was "Setters." That became a favorite family joke, and we felt blessed that we were at least able to leave with amusement over how the Hunters Club directed its guests to the restrooms. Who were the pointers again? I tend to forget.

Rushing to the second event that evening, I was consumed by the contrast. It was in a local pub and those who were anxiously awaiting my appearance there had the good fortune of not having to go thirsty. There was no shortage of beer, and the mood here was festive and fun. It's true that beer can help a politician. It can also hurt him. It's a lot easier to enjoy beer than to listen to a boring stump speech. The most important thing here was that I was present. I had come to their pub, and that showed that I cared. If you care, you are more than halfway there. If you don't, you don't deserve to win.

On the whole, I was spending far too much time in rural areas, and I insisted that we make multiple visits to Spokane, the one city that had a sizable population in eastern Washington. Spokane is curiously known in America for its two ways of being pronounced. If you are anywhere other than Spokane you call the town "Spo-KAINE." If you hail from the place, it's "Spok-ANN." On one occasion, I was a guest speaker at an organization known as the 1930s Young Democrats, which dwindling membership was in their eighties. My so-called stump speech generated so much excitement that I could count the fillings in the back teeth of the yawning folks. I plodded through the Secretary of State's duties, trying to demonstrate some knowledge about the office I was seeking, and this was obviously too dull for the 1930s Young Dems. I didn't do that again.

When my wearisome thirty-minute talk came to an end, an elderly man in his late eighties, leaning on his cane, approached the podium. In his scratchy voice, he said "Young man, let me give you some advice. When you give a speech, keep it short. Make three points. That's it. That's all you need. Make three points." And he hobbled away, not even waiting for my response.

I turned to my Spokane campaign chairman and asked, "Who is that guy?"

"You didn't recognize him? That is Clarence C. Dill, the famous US senator from these parts. He'd been a heck of an orator back in his time."

Later, I learned that, in fact, Dill had been a colorful and controversial public figure in and out of elected office. He served in the House twice before serving two terms as US senator. Then he stepped down but ran again for governor, and then made a last ditch try for his old House seat, which he lost. I was pleased, of course, that a former US senator from eastern Washington had attended my rally, and his advice on public speaking, I never forgot, but I'm not too sure if associating with Clarence Cleveland Dill would have helped my campaign in any way. Today, in any case, guilt by association is a regular casualty in the political-media chopping block of public opinion. In fact, so many talented and accomplished individuals chose to stay clear of public service because of the insanely intrusive vetting tactics and the guillotine methods of fast and sharp-bladed media. A bit of easy research revealed that Dill was best known for his 1936 divorce two years after he had left the Senate, a divorce that was both colorful and messy by any era's standards. Somewhere, I read that the good senator's divorce from his New York wife, Rosalie Gardiner Jones, a celebrated feminist suffragist and author, included Dill's claims that Mrs. Dill had told his friends that he was a "political coward" for not seeking reelection. He added that she buried dogs and garbage in their backyard. Weirdly, the well-publicized divorce proceedings ended in his favor, and he got to keep their mansion in Spokane. I'm sure not too many people in the room also knew or cared that old Senator Dill was one of fifty members of the House to vote against declaring war against Germany back in 1917. The worst thing I had learned though about my now speech coach was that Dill had sponsored the Watson-Parker Railroad Labor Act in the mid-thirties because he thought that Pullman porters and maids on trains across America should be black, and the Act allowed black Americans to join the train unions without fear of being fired. Today's political suicide was yesterday's status quo. This was the same guy now who was advising me how to address supporters. With the senator's distilled advice, I set aside his tarnished past and began to wrap my speeches around three points—a speaking tip which has served me well throughout my career, although I rarely admit where I got the nod. Three points. No one is ready to absorb more than that at one time, as our current staccato of tweet messaging affirms. Dill finally died in 1978 at the age of ninety-three, but I had never seen him beyond that cameo performance at that pub along the campaign trail. What really happened to the family dog, well, Dill took that with him to his grave.

Early on, the party leaders in Seattle wanted to meet with me. For them, the Secretary of State was an important office since the official duties were mostly political, overseeing elections and party functions. Having their guy in the post was strategic. And I was young and impressionable, and they assumed I could be molded in their image. They were convinced I could win but only if I accepted their counsel. Start attacking the incumbent, Lud Kramer. I hesitated. This was not me. I was a golden retriever, not a Doberman. I'm not comfortable going on the attack, but they persisted and helped to arrange a press conference and scripted my new mantel as an attack dog. Kill Lud. Keep it simple. Lock 'er up! Make America Great Again. Sloganism. I wanted to please the party elders and, of course, I wanted to win, so I tried my Doberman costume.

They were spot on. The next day, Mr. Kramer held his own press event to respond. The journalists came back to me for more comments. The political arena thrived on conflict. For the first time, there was media attention on the otherwise dull Secretary of State race. This was an early example of how going negative on your opponent can pay dividends. The last four decades of American politics have been driven by toxic campaigns to maim and kill. Political campaigns have all but embraced chemical weaponry. I continued to feel discomfort taking this approach. But I did relish the new wave of attention.

The campaign strategy improved by visibility but I was still far behind and it seemed that there was no real way I could overcome the odds and win in 1972. The cards were stacked against me from the outset, and I doubted myself for taking on such a popular and well-established incumbent, and starting with a base so small that the huge disadvantage in a statewide campaign was insurmountable. Even a Doberman is still only a dog. Especially a retriever in Doberman's clothes.

The year 1972 was turning out to be a nightmare for all Democrats on ballots everywhere. The incumbent was the mean and lean Richard Nixon versus the highly principled but unpopular Democrat, George McGovern, who was destined to lose big time. McGovern, the country's most vocal anti-Vietnam War candidate, handed Richard Nixon the greatest landslide ever with only 23.2% of the vote. Nixon's winning every state except Massachusetts put perverse and cruel smiles on all the Republican candidates who were on the ballot in 1972. George McGovern was one of the finest men in twentieth century American politics, but the country was not ready for him and the Republican machine ate us for lunch.

While I had tallied a relatively strong showing against Lud Kramer, my campaign ended in a painful yet predictable defeat. In an editorial on November 10, 1972, *The Columbian* wrote: "Bonker, the youngest county auditor in the state when he took office six years ago, was up against formidable odds. Surveys have shown that the name of Lud Kramer was more familiar to the public than even the governor. Bonker started the campaign early. He built up a statewide organization, staffed mainly by eager and dedicated young men and women. He looked like the only new and forward-looking Democrat in a state where a team of progressive Republicans have turned party politics around. The top Democrats seemed to be the ones looking to the past. But Bonker's race demonstrated something that should be very dear to Clark County with its close connections to Oregon, where we have no political say-so at all. These conditions weren't right enough this time to turn the punch into a knockout, but that time will come…. Perhaps in 1976."

In defeat, I was also confronted with a hefty campaign debt. Financing campaigns, regardless of the office, is always a struggle, and in elections for offices where future policy decisions are key special interests tend to weigh in with strings-attached contributions. The Secretary of State office, fortunately, had no special interests sniffing around, so my campaign donations were modest and came mostly from party loyalists, family members, and friends. My indebtedness came with no forward-leaning obligations. In an interview after the election, I observed that candidates for Secretary of State have difficulty raising money because the office is not a dispenser of goods or of patronage. Potential contributors in King County said blatantly that there was no reason to contribute because the Secretary of State wouldn't be able to deliver favors.

My $21,000 debt of unpaid bills was a personal obligation. Carolyn rose to the occasion and accepted a position in Olympia, earning enough for us to pay off the debt while living with her folks and commuting home on the weekends. I'm humbled to report that my beloved Carolyn was the entirety of my "special interests."

When a politician loses an election, he or she is faced with an emotionally challenging moment, having to decide how to recover and what the next steps should be. It's an existential game of chess. There weren't many options in front on me at the time. A third term as county auditor would not have been a step up. There were greater things ahead, and I knew I had the energy and the ambition to keep going. Yet statewide offices would be out of play for another four years. The United States Congress did not seem like a viable option as long as the incumbent, Julia Butler Hansen, remained in office. I found myself seriously considering law school. I'd gain another degree and deepen my credentials while not seemingly lose ground or momentum. Lewis & Clark had recently acquired the Northwest School of Law, and a law degree was becoming my preferred choice.

That was where my mind was on the day I was quietly working at my desk at home, filling in the law school application, when I heard on KISM radio news at the top of the hour that Congresswoman Julia Butler Hansen had unexpectedly announced that she would be retiring at the end of her term. The news sent shock waves throughout the 3rd Congressional District and beyond—me. The seat would be open. The law school application would never be completed. Fate changed. Or more like fate took over. A light from Heaven shone down on me and I knew the path I'd follow.

Julia Butler Hansen would easily have been reelected. The first woman Democrat to be elected to congress from the state of Washington, she had chaired an Appropriations Subcommittee that enhanced her standing in the district and she was widely respected. But she was furious with how redistricting had changed the shape and constituency of the 3rd Congressional District. She said at the time, "With this new congressional map, my district is so large I might as well run for governor." Her decision to step down suddenly had us facing the most important decision of my political life, and undoubtedly the easiest.

At dinner that night, I looked Carolyn in the eyes as if proposing again, and she knew without my having said a single word. It was time to aim for the other Washington.

II. Courthouse to the Congress

CHAPTER 7

WHEN IS IT "MY TURN"

When an incumbent congressman or woman steps down, you can bet there are local legislators and others who have been eagerly waiting for years, even decades, to jump in, declaring "It's my turn." All newcomers jump into an already busy and complicated stream of hard-to-read currents, backwaters, and tricky rapids.

Washington State's 3rd Congressional District was no exception. The expectant heir apparent to Julia Butler Hansen's seat was State Senator Robert C. Bailey, better known as Bob, who had been Congresswoman Hansen's district assistant and also headed the Democratic Caucus in the state senate. Bailey was highly respected and well-known throughout the district, so few doubted that he would be the congresswoman's likely successor.

But there was also R. Ted Bottinger, the Democrat Majority Leader in the state senate from Tacoma, a lawyer who had already garnered the support of special interests and labor unions in Olympia which guaranteed him support for a strong campaign. As journalist and pundits were speculating which of the two would prevail, there was little mention of Don Bonker. Indeed, I had just lost a statewide election, and the odds were stacked against me in the primary election, so my candidacy was more about fantasy than reality. But the magic in life lies in the zone between fantasy and dreams. Fantasy is the disconnect between desire and truth, whereas dreams are ambitions that merit being pursued. In fact, they must be pursued or they'll haunt you for your whole life. Dreams should never be ignored. The whole persona of an individual is wrapped up there inside that dream.

The three of us would all be campaigning in the shadow of Congresswoman Julia Butler Hansen—known in both Washingtons as savvy, straightforward, and tough, which is an interesting characterization because she was also an accomplished writer of children's literature. She knew how to talk to kids. She even won an award for an obscure book called *Singing Paddles*, in which she tells the story of the Blair family's 1843 cross-country covered-wagon trip from Kentucky to Cathlamet, Washington where her people had settled. Maybe her rugged pioneering spirit came from that tradition. Wherever she appeared, the red carpet would roll out for a grand entrance. She was legendary even in her own time. When Julia Butler Hansen served in the state legislature in the 1940s, she once decked a state legislator over a disagreement. You didn't mess with Julia! Her successor would have to live up to her reputation.

In congress, Julia Butler Hansen chaired the House Appropriations Subcommittee on Interior and Related Agencies and presided over the federal funding of the Interior Department and other agencies, including the Arts and Humanities. The chairman of the full Appropriations Committee, George H. Mahon, an influential Texan who had served for twenty-two consecutive terms in congress, had been close to the House leadership from the age of FDR through the days of Gerald Ford. Known for his grand frugality, Chairman Mahon had once called together his subcommittee chairs and ordered them to reduce their respective budgets by ten percent. This is how the committee system worked. Julia resisted. "I understand, Julia, it's tough for all of us, it but must be done," the chairman responded, used to getting his way. As the story goes, they went back and forth, and finally, Chairman Mahon closed discussion. "Please, all of you report back next week with the reductions I've asked for."

When they came together the following week, Julia took the lead and announced, "Mr. Chairman, I've finally come up with the ten percent reductions you have respectfully requested." He looked pleased as if his authority had again reigned. She proceeded. "I've given you what you've asked for, Mr. Chairman," she said with a smirk. As it turned out, her recommended cuts targeted the federal agency projects in the chairman's own district of Lubbock County, Texas, where Mahon had advocated for the funding of Reese Air Force Base in Lubbock and Webb Air Force Base in Big Spring, as well as other public works project including the development of Interstate Highway 27, connecting Amarillo and his very own beloved Lubbock. Her cuts had come from his district. I wasn't in the room but can only imagine the rage that boiled within that man.

No one else would have dared to have said or done this to the chairman of the most powerful committee in the US House of Representatives. No, you didn't mess with Julia! She meant business, wasn't going to be bullied, and when she took aim, it was for the jugular. To succeed her would be no small task. Congressman Mahon finally retired in 1981, leaving the seat open to a young and wide-eyed George W. Bush, then thirty-one, to enter politics. His father, of course, George Sr., was already a US senator from Connecticut. Mahon died in 1985 but his reverence in Mitchell County, Texas was so profound it earned him a statue on the lawn in front of the Colorado City courthouse, and the federal courthouse and public library in Lubbock both take his name. He passed in 1985.

With Julia stepping down, my expectations were at a boiling point, but I was still pondering whether becoming a candidate for congress was the right thing to do since Bob Bailey had a huge advantage. I decided I would travel to Washington, DC and meet with the congresswoman herself to engage her directly. She'd help guide me. When a congressperson steps down, he or she cares about who the successor will be, knowing that his or her record and reputation will be honored or criticized. I made the call and she agreed to have lunch. Among Julia's DC sagas were her lengthy luncheons at the celebrated Monocle Restaurant on the Senate side of Capitol Hill on D Street. The "M," as it was popularly called, opened in 1960 with the election of John F. Kennedy, and built its reputation with the members of Congress and staffers as the "first tablecloth restaurant" in the capitol neighborhood, which, for decades, suffered from urban blight. It offered members the feeling of class without them having to motor over to the posh Georgetown.

It was not unusual for Congresswoman Julia Butler Hansen to enjoy two or three martinis over her sirloin steak, lean into her usual booth near the back, swizzle stick in hand, and contemplate the nuances of the conversation in progress.

We ordered our drinks and she welcomed my praise of her service and accomplishments in the 3rd District. She nodded in appreciation, goading me to come out with the guts of my message. Why was I there? I then told her that I was seriously considering entering the race to replace her. She took it in without much expression, and I was trying hard to read her inner thoughts. She was good at guarding them until it made sense to share them. I didn't think she had expected this. Our drinks came and that saved her from having to speak just yet. The waiter, in his white jacket and black tie, approached, and he knew what the congresswoman would be having—medium rare. She ordered the flatiron steak and I followed with the same. Ten ounces of beef was a heavy lunch, but I welcomed the extra protein. This was a big conversation. She obviously knew I was contemplating a race to replace her when she steered the discussion away and asked me about Carolyn. We ate our steaks and she ordered a second martini and smiled. "You know, Bob Bailey may be a candidate as well, so I'll give this some thought, Don, and get back to you," she added and we left it like that. I flew back to Seattle and sent her a note thanking her for her time and reminding her how important her input would be.

In a letter sent on February 13, 1974, she shared her thoughts with care and kindness. "As to yourself, Don, let me say that in 1960, Bob Bailey served as my chairman. He has always been a very faithful and loyal friend and dedicated employee. He has been a loyal and dedicated legislator, so dedicated and loyal to a job that paid in peanuts. In ten years, you will still be young and can serve with distinction. I may say that I love both you and Carolyn, but it would be completely inimical to all the things for which I stand if I came out merely for expediency and disavowed Bob. I believe that you, in the next few years, can develop a program that will enable you to fulfill a candidate's role as a 3rd District congressman and with great distinction, but I do believe if Bob were pushed aside for political expediency, you would reap a harvest of ill will. Finally, Don, both you and Bob are such fine people that it is very difficult to even respond to your letter with the depth of feeling which I have for both of you, but in my own mind, I feel that Bob, through his long and mostly unpaid service in the legislature, has earned the right to run. With my warmest personal regards to both you and Carolyn whom I love as if you were one of my own." And she signed it, "Julia."

It was a beautiful letter and one that I continue to cherish, although, of course, it had not conveyed the response I had hoped for.

No doubt, Bob Bailey had "earned the right to run" and deserved the congresswoman's unwavering support, but waiting ten years and then serving with "great distinction," well, that didn't sit well. I was respectful, but I was also a guy in a hurry. Her counsel made sense, of course, but a decade was like eternity. This was the children's book writer telling young ones to wait their turn, believe in the future, take your time.

I already had two strikes against me, I acknowledged, if I were to get into this race for congress: one was the Senate Majority leader who was endowed with a significant political leveraging campaign, and the other, also a state senator who was head of the Democrat Caucus and now had the incumbent's full blessings. It would take three strikes to send me back to the dugout, and for the moment, there were only two with me trying to figure out how to get on base. I was glad I had taken the time to properly inform Julia and had preserved my dignity and sense of protocol. But I was not going to give up that easily. I had already looked Carolyn in the eyes with the pledge that our holy dance had national legs.

My narrow home base would again come to haunt me. The redistricting that had upset Julia Butler Hansen was also working to my disadvantage. Every ten years, the Department of Commerce conducted a nationwide survey that included population shifts that had become the basis for state legislatures to redraw district borders, a process which is highly politicized and has increasingly gotten worse as the American congressional district system finds itself today in serious need of review and revision. The way today that data is collected, the depth of knowledge we now know about the demographics of communities, peoples' preferences, tendencies, choices, consumer trends, the association between our digital footprints and our ideologies, and our likeliness to act one way or another are all being drawn into complex and dangerously accurate analyses that have the capacity to color or flavor subtle shifts in numerous places, which collectively can and will change political outcomes in local, state, and federal elections. Redistricting was designed to regulate representational democracy, but these shift, when manipulated for partisan reasons, shake the foundations of our republic.

I recall in 1980 a political behemoth, Phil Burton, representing a San Francisco district in California, had taken charge of the highly politicized redrawing of congressional boundaries, thus creating a new district that resembled a snake crawling around Democrat villages and perfectly suited to guarantee the win of his brother, a certain John Burton, who would hold a press conference six years later to announce he was leaving Congress to deal with a drug and alcohol problem. The younger Burton eventually returned to politics and became head of the California State Senate, once described in a *San Francisco Chronicle* headline as "Pushy, Profane, Pugnacious and Powerful."

Examples like this are why we need to pay such close attention to the small things; they are part of the much larger thing indeed. Moving the boundaries of a congressional district by a couple blocks east or west, north or south is all it takes to disrupt voter turnout, voter behavior, established allegiances, and ultimately, the political balance that either enables or blocks political machines and the interests that support them to impose their will over citizens who passively report to the voting stations in the district attached to their home addresses.

In 1974, what had been done to the 3rd District had a riveting effect on the lay of the land. Ninety percent of the City of Vancouver, the district's largest base population, had been shipped off to a neighboring district. Our own home address fell outside the new boundary, however, fortuitously, Carolyn and I had moved the previous year from the historic Stanger House to Ridgefield, a small town that remained within the new confines of the 3rd District. This insured my legitimacy as a candidate, but my Vancouver voters would now be casting their ballots in the 4th Congressional District, more aligned with the politics of Eastern Washington. Many years later, I read in an interview that Bob Bailey had given with Dianne Bridgman of Washington State University's oral history program that he had claimed that Carolyn and I had moved *after* I had filed to run, which was not true. The transcripts goes on to cite him saying that "as soon as he (Bonker) was elected, he moved up to Olympia into a mobile, didn't even stay there but used it for mailing purposes until redistricting restored Vancouver when he left Olympia. He had a mobile home address across the alley from where my house is in Olympia. I went over one time to see if he was there, and they said, 'Oh no. He just rents this to use it for a mailing address."

This is where facts and fiction runs amok. Our Ridgefield residence was legitimate, but we had to spend lots of time in the Olympia area. Carolyn's parents were close to the Brodin family, and the shabby trailer home on their property often used by their parents was convenient for our overnight stays and also to store campaign material.

Despite Bob's errors of memory, all this is to say that the juggling of districts made it darn hard for local politicians who spent so much time and energy and money to establish bases of support to then accumulate and employ that support.

The newly shaped 3rd Congressional District was now larger than the entire state of Massachusetts, from Stockbridge to Boston, as Arlo Guthrie sang it, and now included vast tracks of sparsely populated land, encompassing what is known as Washington's Upper Peninsula near the Canadian border. Then it horseshoed around Seattle, absorbing parts of South Pierce and northeast King County. The remapping almost doubled the size of the 3rd District, while the city of Olympia, the state capital, and southwest Washington along the Pacific Ocean remained as the core population areas. The odds were worsening now for me and I needed to reassess the inner tensions between the personal dream and the political realities. Doubt was and continues to be an important litmus test in responsible action.

Keep questioning while neither abandoning nor allowing inner blindness to steer the ship. I needed more guidance.

I gathered plenty of advice from friends and supporters and decided the only intelligent next step was to make a trip around the district and get the feel of public opinion. In late February 1974, I visited the more traditional flag bearers of the district and checked in with party leaders, the labor unions, and others about my chances in a congressional race against two powerful state senators. What I learned in my weeklong trek through a vast rural area was that the Democratic Party leaders felt a strong obligation to support State Senator Bob Bailey. Well-known and respected, I heard it over and over. He had earned the right to replace Julia Butler Hansen.

I visited small Washington towns like Aberdeen, Elma, Shelton, and Raymond, which were all coping with economic hardship and needed federal help. That was the key to their automatic support for Bailey, and their hesitance to support an idealistic newcomer. There was a conservative desire to have someone more experienced to be their next congressman with existing political ties to the machinery, which might enable federal aid or bring into the district new projects and jobs and more money. I listened carefully and tried to hold off the feeling of despair. Like usual, though, providence arrives when it is supposed to, not before nor after.

My last stop was in the town of Montesano, population barely 3,000, situated in Grays Harbor County along the Wynoochee River bordered on the north by Lake Sylvia, and another community that depended on timber to sustain the local economy. The only other thing I knew about little Montesano was that the Nirvana lead singer, Kurt Cobain, spent part of his childhood in this town. In Montesano, I was to have dinner with a couple of residents in their mid-fifties, both of whom were professors at the local community college. They were not the typical party types, but I was told they were fully committed to supporting Democratic candidates, and if this dinner went well, they were likely to choose me as their preferred candidate for Congress. What I couldn't know in advance was that Montesano would become a game-changer for me, and that my political decision-making inner clock would be reset thanks to this visit. And timber would become our holy grail.

I was warmly greeted at my hosts' Victorian style home. As they escorted me into their living room for a brief chat before dinner, they seemed nervous. They both struggled to say what I thought they wanted to say to me. I was thinking that maybe they had already committed to Bob Bailey or even Senator Ted Bottinger and were reluctant to admit that they could not support my candidacy, and didn't have the heart to uninvite me for dinner. At least I'd be fed in Montesano. But no, that wasn't it at all. It was something else. The father and mother finally offered that their son, a college student in eastern Washington, was home during the quarter break and wanted to join us for dinner.

"Would that be a problem?" the father asked.

"That's fine, I'd like to meet him. I always like to discuss politics with students," I said. *Students vote too,* I thought.

"Well, there's something more. We just wanted to forewarn you," he uttered as he steered us to the dining room. Politicians get to see everything, and I was bracing myself for this mysterious undergraduate who appeared to be both polite and respectful and clean cut.

The dinner discussion was about politics, national and local. The Watergate scandal, for fellow Democrats, fed an appetite that could not be satisfied. Eventually, the conversation turned to Julia Butler Hansen's retirement and the prospects of my running to replace her. They realized it would be a challenge should I run, but encouraged me to follow my convictions. I buttered my dinner roll and wondered what the warning was all about.

Finally, the father looked to his son and gave a discrete nod. The son now had permission to speak. It was his moment.

"Mr. Bonker, my parents are not pleased with what I'm about to say, but I must be honest and do it." He paused and I gestured for him to carry on. "God has revealed to me that it is His will that you should not be a candidate this year, but at another time. I genuinely feel it's my responsibility to convey God's message to you, and you have to decide for yourself."

Although a part of me wanted to snuff out this little snot of a kid who was speaking like he was the angel Gabriel, delivering divine providence while being just a precocious sophomore at a state college. I was also mindful of another occasion where God's message came through another person, my wife. Be careful when dismissing messages. Hers had been in response to my questions about making a commitment to accepting Jesus. Carolyn, though, had not said that God was speaking through her; that was something that I had felt at the moment. And that made all the difference.

There was a slightly awkward silence. The parents, eyeing me, were anxious to hear my reaction. They did not share or even understand their son's faith, so having him convey this highly presumptuous spiritual message was embarrassing. I smiled. That always gives you an extra moment to collect your thoughts. I thanked him for traveling home across the state to meet with me and understood where he was coming from and why he felt the need to bring God's word directly to me. It was an honor receiving both the message and the messenger.

The conversation could have spiraled into something more ornate about religion, faith, and politics, or I could have taken offense. The father, obviously feeling both discomfort and relief that the son's discourse was over, announced, "It's getting late, and Mr. Bonker has a long drive to get home this evening." I looked at the boy to show him that I had heard him. I thanked the family and got up, the message from God bouncing around in my head.

As I got into the car that wintery evening, a harsh reality was settling in. While navigating through the narrow roads that would lead to the I-5, snow started blowing hard, softly crowding the windshield, obstructing my vision, and further cluttering my mind. Was it possible that the Lord had used this young student, someone I did not know, as a messenger to tell me something that I should know? Was this simply a confirmation of the political assessment I should have deduced myself from my travels around the district that week? That Bob Bailey was the likely successor and it would be best if I waited for another time? Ten years, as the charming Julia had suggested?

It was a lonely and agonizing trip back to Ridgefield. The narrow roads, my metaphor. I was weaving my way across my district, interpreting the narrow roads. Finding my way. It was late when I finally pulled down my driveway. Carolyn was well asleep. I had all but concluded that the signs and the information were all pointing one way, I should not be a candidate that year. I should resume work on my application to Lewis & Clark College Law School. I had time. The future was long and the road would be open.

The next morning, I shared the whole story of the week with Carolyn. "I don't want to lose again, it will end my political career," I avowed. Her perspective always brought value, and as she held her right hand up to my chest, I felt the message before it materialized into words.

She was cautioning me to hold off on a final decision. "Maybe you should consult with Pastor Bill before you decide?"

Bill Paris was the pastor at the Longview Community Church. He was also a Republican state legislator. Normally, I would not have consulted with a Republican about whether I should run for office, but we had a relationship of trust that superseded politics. Also, as a pastor, maybe he would enlighten me about the college student's transmittal of gospel as it related to my candidacy.

Two days later we met with Bill Paris at the Oak Tree Restaurant, located alongside I-5 between Ridgefield and Longview. Over a heaping dish of the Oak Tree's famous wings, I spoke and he listened as I laid out my situation. The pastor was measured in offering counsel. He said he was respectful of what the student had to say but ultimately, there weren't middlemen in these affairs of the soul. It was between God and me, my decision. "And when decisions are hard to come by, you need to commit to prayer," he suggested. "You'll know when the decision is clear to you. Often, God's plans for us," he reminded, "goes beyond what we know and can expect for ourselves."

Prayer it would be. Prayer had and has definitely helped to guide me in reaching pivotal decisions and navigating tumultuous paths and the narrow roads. This would be true again now, and in both the primary and general elections. The student had delivered what he thought was God's message to him; yet, the young man possibly had jumped to a conclusion that hadn't come from a divine place. The holy message was that I needed to contemplate and commit on my own, which is what I ultimately did. The answer came in prayer because, regardless of your degree of religious practice, the most private moments you have with yourself are sacred and these are the moments when what are true and real for you present themselves in their unfiltered, unadulterated, and fearless state. That is what I call prayer. And that is why I became a United States congressman.

Among the three Democratic contenders, there were few differences on national or local issues, and I was worried that I wouldn't be able to stand apart from these two highly experienced legislators. Yet unknown to me at the time was that local issue in Montesano and elsewhere in rural Washington that would prove critical in getting me to and through the primary, the real reason I had crisscrossed my district listening to the voters and had confronted the wrong conclusion from a boy claiming to be God's agent. He may have been, but the word of God was one that we did not pronounce over our meatloaf dinner in Montesano. But it was present. It was tangible and real and material. The word was timber. Wood. The boy's challenge, the pastor's direction, and my resignation to prayer all led to one conclusion. I'd run.

CHAPTER 8

Exporting Logs and Jobs

The primary campaign was driven by road trip through little places like Hoquiam, Shelton, Raymond, Centralia, Longview, and with each stop, what was becoming increasingly clear were the early signs that the local economies were not doing well. Southwest Washington had been traditionally a one industry economy. The region's abundant forest resources, which had helped sustain the local economy for a century, was starting to falter. The livelihoods of lumber mills and others who depended on timber appeared to be in jeopardy. The high employment levels and decent wages that the townspeople in the rural parts of my district had always relied on and which supported local businesses and the overall well-being of these small towns were at risk. I hadn't seen this coming because my patch had not been rural nor industrial up to now. Systems and administrations and local budgets were my topics. I loved trees but the economics of timber were off my charts.

Early in the campaign, the *Seattle Post-Intelligencer* was preparing a candidates' profile of the 3rd Congressional District race, and the reporter, Mike Layton, who interviewed each of us was eager to find an issue that separated the candidates. Mike had been a Korean War veteran and a tenacious journalist who'd go on to write a book about Ronald Reagan and the proxy war in Central America. His memoir was curiously called *My Very Worst Friend*. He had a good knack for asking questions in his way and learning things that others didn't yet know.

When he asked me, "What's your position on log exports?" I hesitated and went blank, not knowing anything about the issue. He quickly picked up on my ignorance and offered a few sentences to create context, leading me toward proclaiming a policy bias in favor of a ban on log exports, which seemed to make sense.

"Well," I said, "I probably would be against exporting logs," I blindly avowed. That's all he needed and proceeded with other questions.

When the *Post-Intelligencer*, two days later, published Layton's article prominently including photographs of all five candidates from both parties, including Republican Lud Kramer, the headline shouted: "New Issue in 3rd District Race." Mike Layton had highlighted that Don Bonker was the only candidate to oppose the export of logs. All the others expressed concerns that restrictions on the export of logs would hurt the economy and reduce revenue from state lands, which supported education and other state services.

It was obvious I had fallen into a trap. The other candidates had been better informed on the issue, clearly stating their positions while the young upstart appeared ignorant of the timber industry and the value it brought to the state economy. I could imagine the pundits and political elites shaking their heads with raised eyebrows as they read the article. Inexperienced Bonker had really stepped in it this time. Bob Bailey was probably wringing his hands with delight.

As it turned out, the so-called establishment rallied around exporting the raw logs to Japan because of the huge revenue log exports were bringing to the state coffers. A large portion of those funds were dedicated to building schools. Weyerhaeuser, one of the largest private owners of timberland in the United States with over twelve million acres of forest founded in Longview back around 1900, along with other big timber companies, relished the highest foreign bids on their timber. The longshoremen working on the docks in the ports around the 3rd District, Camas-Washougal, Port of Vancouver, Woodland, Longview, and Ilwaco also benefited by huge old-growth logs onto ships headed to Japan. There were other groups, including the Chambers of Commerce and the League of Women Voters, that were champions of free trade policies. Timber and forestry products have been at the core of the Pacific Northwest's economic life since the beginning of the republic, and now, I had weighed in with limited background to the topic that generated the most heated controversy. The pressure to maintain high prices for exported logs profited the sellers, but disadvantaged the local and independent mills that needed to buy local timber at reasonable prices. The cry to keep prices exorbitant was often made by those who claimed to advocate for fair open markets.

The higher priced timber from state-owned lands was a windfall to the state, the primary beneficiary being public schools. It also helped to fund other public entities including the University of Washington, building improvements on the capital campus, and providing services in timber-dependent counties. So, exports helped the wealthy powerhouse firms like Weyerhaeuser and the state, while hurting the independent mill owners and the workforce they hired to produce timber for domestic use. Who would dare question the tremendous value log export revenue was bringing to Washington citizens, except this naive congressional candidate, and, of course, the unemployed workers in Southwest Washington who had lost their jobs when mills closed due to the manipulated high prices maintained for export.

All the independent lumber mills, the plywood cooperatives, the small shingle-shake outlets, all those who depended on timber from both public and private lands to stay in business had few options. Historically, there had been ample timber supply to satisfy and sustain the export trade and the operations of these small lumber companies. But in the '70s, the export demand to Japan reached its highest level ever. The demand for our Douglas fir, Pacific silver, hemlock skyrocketed.

In 1962, the Columbus Day Storm, one of the most powerful extratropical cyclones recorded in the twentieth century, had devastated massive tracks of forest lands across Washington State, ripping down trees that would yield between eleven and seventeen billion board feet of timber. This prompted quick action by the federal government to provide funding of a salvage logging program to bring the wind-thrown timber to sawmills and plywood mills before it rotted. The State of Washington also awarded a tender for a salvage contract, which the Japanese eagerly accepted to help clean up the jackstrawed areas of fallen trees. But the Japanese's escalating dependence on Northwest Pacific timber served to spark a bidding war for the timber which sent prices even higher, pushing the local lumber mills and plywood co-ops even further out of reach. Only the Japanese were able to buy our wood. The ownership of forest lands (federal, state, and private) were reaping the benefits for sure, while the market conditions were also punishing the small mills and employers who simply could not compete against the Asian competition who had set up thousands of their own mills back home to process the imported raw logs from Washington State.

The Washington Department of National Resources, which managed forest lands, had one criterion—selling timber to the highest bidder, primarily Japan. About fifty-eight percent of its logs were loaded on huge transport trucks, headed for the various port districts, bypassing local lumber mills, which were either shutting down or on the brink of doing so.

The scene in 1974 was not unlike what happened a generation later in the American so-called Rust Belt. In the run-up to the 2016 presidential elections, the loss of manufacturing jobs was not caused by foreign imports but by the exporting of raw materials and thus jobs to foreign countries. As I traveled around the district talking with labor union leaders, local officials, and others, I could feel the depth of despair and hopelessness. As a candidate, I wanted to be responsive, but what was the solution? I didn't know. I did see the problem clearly, and that was a good place to start.

At one of my appearances in Vancouver, I was approached by a scrappy guy in a plaid shirt held together by a pair of tight suspenders. He had lumber mill worker written all over him. I braced myself as he spoke.

"I read in the newspaper that you are against log exports. Is that true?" he asked bluntly.

"Yes." I replied but didn't elaborate.

"Well, we're going to lose our jobs if we don't stop these log exports," he asserted. "What does it take to get you elected?"

Who was this guy and how should I respond? What I needed most was money since my Democratic opponents had tapped all the traditional Democratic sources. But how could this working class dude help me financially? I wondered.

"I need more funds to finance the campaign," I responded.

"How much do you need?" He got right to the matter.

"Well," I began, wondering if I should just talk turkey with a miller worker or if I should be more cautious. I proceeded, "At least fifty thousand dollars to get through the primary," I said.

"Okay, you're on. I will raise that amount for you. When can we get started?" His words obviously caught me by surprise. He was serious. An ally sent from a mill called Heaven.

His name was Larry Malloy. He was head of a plywood cooperative in Vancouver, an employee-owned company that depended on federal and state timber to produce their plywood products. It was one of multiple cooperatives that were spread around the 3rd District. The exports were killing them, and they were determined to keep their companies and save their jobs. We have the timber, we have the skills, we have the local demand for the wood. Why export logs? They understood all the basics, the very same basics that have been and continue to kill economies everywhere. Emerging markets and developing countries rich in raw materials, with ample work forces, and massive amounts of local need for both products and all the value added services are dying slowly as a few exporters or owners of the assets profit by sending the materials away and grinding the ability for their own towns to prosper along a value chain that has been sabotaged by greed. Selling at higher prices undercuts all the added value that sits idly in those logs or cotton or crude or uncut diamonds. Here, it was logs, and I was learning fast.

Larry Malloy and I met a few days later at his local plant.

"Here's what I'm going to do," he told me. "I'll call a meeting to bring together our 250 employees and will tell them to bring their check books," he said. "I'm thinking that'll get us about $6,000—not near the $50,000, but it'll be a good start. A house starts as a log." Then he reminded me that there were twelve more plywood co-ops in our district and we would make the pitch to each of them, he said with beaming confidence. We were here for each other. It made total sense, and I had my first real lessons in international trade and commerce within the grinding sounds of huge saw blades and the torrents of saw dust. This was the heart and soul of the 3rd District. Logs and millers.

Could he actually pull this off? I wondered. I am embarrassed that I event doubted Larry Malloy for a second. He exceeded my expectations. He delivered big time, starting at his own plant and then arranging similar meetings at all the other cooperative plants in Southwest Washington. Checks for twenty and thirty dollars came forward in the rough hands of men and women who worked the mills and planed the timber all day long. With bits of wood chips in their hair and along their arms, earplugs dangling around their necks, they stepped up and handed over paper committing the cash equivalent of an hour or two or a half day of wages for a guy who said he'd halt the exporting of their livelihoods. According to company rules, when the officers called a meeting, the workers were required to be there. So we knew the staff would show up, there were no assurances that these folks would pull out their checkbooks and kick in their much needed cash. That was my job—to prove to them that I was ready to advocate for the independent mills.

The meeting at the Hoquiam Plywood Cooperative had a riveting effect. It was a raucous turnout involving more than 100 local workers who were obviously disturbed and skeptical about the meeting. As we gathered, I was pleased that I had brought Carolyn with me this time. Her appearance, dignified in a lovely white floral dress, contrasted with the work gear and the orange hard hats and scuffed up boots around us. The president of the cooperative took the mic and announced playfully looking back over at Carolyn, "Hey, you guys, we have to behave and clean up our language." It was a different era. She waved and the workers cheered. One of those classic Audrey Hepburn moments.

During the meeting, one angry worker yelled, "No way I'm giving money to a politician I don't know!"

I wasn't surprised.

Larry Malloy instantly got up and shot back, "If you don't do a check, I'll drag you out of this building and throw a few a punches." Larry had a way of getting to the point. It was a tense moment, but his approach was just what was needed.

The worker responded, "Well, if he can save our jobs, then count me in as a Bonker Backer. I will even put his bumper sticker on the back of my ramshackle truck."

And not only did we get another small check, but that guy was the start of the campaign slogan that carried us to election day, "I'm a Bonker Backer."

Larry Malloy was a godsend. He reached the target and kept going, raising our campaign budget well above the fifty grand expectation. This was heavy duty grass roots politics. I owe a lot of my career to the trees of the 3rd District and those who turned them into plywood and roofs and floors of houses.

Continuing my campaign stops around the district, it became quickly obvious that the log export issue was gaining traction. People approached me at shopping malls, candidate meetings, pleased that "finally, someone is speaking out on this issue." In newspaper interviews, the log export issue was now in full play. And I spent a lot of time reading up on the history of both logging in Washington and the patterns of trade and exports and the impact they've had on Washingtonians. The environmentalists took notice and decided to go vocal since they were concerned about the huge amount of clear-cutting that was going on. And of course, the northern spotted owl, one of the great old-growth forest inhabitants, was gaining fame for being named in the Endangered Species Act of 1973, which Richard Nixon had signed into law. Our owls were now on our side too.

A noted conservationist from Florida and Pulitzer Prize winning author, Jack Emerson Davis, was quoted in the *Seattle Post-Intelligencer* saying, "Washington's ports are awash in logs waiting transport to the Far East. The feeding frenzy being conducted by log merchants is rapidly exhausting the state's stockpile, depriving the future of its economic base. Small independent mill operators are being forced out of business by soaring costs and reduced supply of saw logs. There is political risk to a candidate like Bonker who tries to intervene in such mass plunder. In trying to stop a mob lynching one is apt to be hanged along with the chicken thief."

Although I had begun by hiding behind this issue, fearing I may have taken the wrong position, now I was highlighting it in my speeches and sure I landed on the right side. Indeed, my strong position of banning log exports was featured in all my TV advertisements. The shooting of one ad took place at Tacoma, Washington's expansive port facility where acres of logs were awaiting shipment to Japan. The set could not have been more perfect. The PR guy directing the shoot had me standing in front of a huge stack of raw logs as I was filmed vowing "to end sending our logs and jobs to Japan." Suddenly, the port manager himself rushed over and confronted my PR guy about what was going on. Quick on his feet, the ad man, my own Don Draper, pulled the manager aside and whispered that we are filming a television ad about the great logging industry and the benefits of exporting of the state's logs. The man took on an air of pride and waved us to carry on. That Tacoma port manager must have been shocked when he saw the ad playing across the district the next night.

My two opponents started to feel discomfort with their earlier positions and now began to backtrack, trying to appear more sympathetic to the lumber mill workers in the 3rd District. It was a real log roll, and suddenly, the balance shifted and everything seemed to be working in my favor.

The primary election on September 18, 1974 was crucial. I had to win the primary. My home base was in Vancouver, but it was Olympia where the pundits and political journalists gathered at elections, and it was there where my family and supporters gathered to observe the election results that determined where I would be that evening. On election day, what do candidates do? It's a nerve-racking time. My mind was still focused on going after more votes, but the campaign was over, but it was obviously premature to consider next steps not knowing the outcome. What to do? We slept at Carolyn's parents' home outside Olympia and woke up to a delicious breakfast prepared by her mother while talking about the election and imminent outcome. Obviously, I couldn't focus on anything other than that, which prompted Carolyn's father, a veteran state patrolman. Ever savvy about people coping with angst, he got up, walked around the table, placed his hand on my shoulder, and made a bold suggestion, "Hey, Don, let's have a round of golf," knowing that this may have been the only way to get my mind off the election. For avid golfers, focusing on a drive or chip shot is the ideal distraction from the other realities in one's life. This became an election day tradition—my father-in-law and I playing golf and letting others worry about the election outcome.

Amy Bell, my campaign manager and Democrat activist, played host at her large Victorian home, a suitable setting for the most important moment in my public career. Wandering around the rooms, I could sense both excitement and some nail-biting, awaiting the poll results—anticipating the ups and downs, depending on which precincts and counties within the district were posting.

Around 10:30 p.m., there was a clear indication.

I was on the path to victory. Indeed, I heard that people at my Olympia campaign office were greeting callers with, "Hello, this is Congressman Bonker's headquarters," a sweet detail that definitely resonated with me and one that I would get accustomed to hearing.

The Associated Press then declared that I had won the election. Who could have imagined that I could overcome the odds that were stacked against me at the outset? Being in contention with the state's two most powerful senators, having no experience in lawmaking, running a district where ninety percent of my home base was in a neighboring district, how did I overcome these odds in the primary election? First, there was what I thought was a big blunder, taking a position on an issue that my opponents and pundits thought was naive, even foolish. Then, there was the quirky lumber mill guy always dressed in jeans and suspenders who would become my savior by raising campaign funds. Often in elections, it's the unexpected that determines the outcome. The turnout had not been heavy, but what mattered was who showed up at the polls. What made the difference were those who were motivated to stop our local logs from going overseas. When the final numbers were reported, it turned out that I had beat State Senator Bob Bailey in ten of the twelve counties, trailing only in Grays Harbor and Pacific, which was the Bailey home base. And in Pacific County, the prediction had been that he would gather sixty to seventy percent—he claimed he got 3500 to my 500 in his county—but Bob ended up with only forty-two percent. Bailey lost in his homeland solely because of the log export issue. He represented an area that was dependent on lumber mills—logs that were otherwise being shipped to Japan.

I compiled a surprising thirty-three percent overall. Bob Bailey, in that late in life interview with Dianne Bridgman for the oral history program, hadn't forgotten those logs that cost him his political career. "Our county depended on log exports," he said. "Actually, the logs would have rotted on the ground without exports. If the local buyers wanted cheap logs, they really wanted to do away with the bidding system, bid cheap, and let the low price win, which would raise havoc with our schools. These little mills were not designed to stay with us long, anyway. They close when the market gets bad, and it had nothing to do with log exports. They had a limited source of supply even before they invented the spotted owl." Reading that remembrance didn't please me, and I marveled at how memory tends to mend the weak spots where the pain was most intense. He accused me of plotting to use the logging issue as my bread and butter to make it to Congress since he was bothered that much of my campaign funding did line up with the defense of local mills. But he went on to vindicate his recollection by adding that his assessment was "sour grapes."

I raised a glass of Washington State Three Legged Red wine in his memory when I reached his touching tribute. He died at eighty-seven in 2005 in Olympia, representing a lost generation of dedicated fair playing public servants. "Don won it fair and square. No problem..." he said into the tape recorder. "Don Bonker was a good congressman and I'm probably alive and better off for not having won it."

CHAPTER 9

WATERGATE BABIES

I hadn't won it yet.

A convincing primary victory did give me a huge boost, though, going into the general elections in November 1973. Despite an intense campaign that touted the economic benefits of exporting logs, the anti-exporting sentiment was undeniably leaning in my favor. The Republican candidate, A. Ludlow Kramer, was struggling with an image problem and his ratings were slipping and his own party's lack of support didn't help. The denouement of the Watergate scandal, the most dramatic event in presidential history in decades, happened: Richard Nixon resigned as president of the United States, leaving former speaker of the house and recent VP, Gerald Ford, as the commander in chief. The Republican reputation haunted the party choices on ballots that year across the nation. Gerald Ford was known for his integrity but he had nearly no charisma at all and was incapable of inspiring any new excitement for the Republican Party. The Nixon stain was deep.

Democratic leaders were now beginning to show some excitement with my candidacy, and the rank and file were rallying behind the Bonker campaign. Larry Malloy, my robust plywood leader, was stilling raising money. Things were going well, but I still had to beat Lud who had defeated me two years earlier in a statewide race, which worked to his advantage. Rural and primarily Democratic Southwest Washington would be leaning my way.

Following the primary results, Kramer knew he was in trouble, but he was also unpredictable and was capable of doing me harm. I worried what would he do next. It didn't take long. Suddenly, he began appearing on national TV news almost every night for something that had nothing to do with his candidacy for Congress. The hyped news coverage of the Richard Nixon resignation left little space for anything else, but Lud found a way into the headlines—a young woman named Patty Hearst. The then nineteen-year-old granddaughter of American publishing magnate, William Randolph Hearst, blonde and wistful Patty became nationally known by being kidnapped on February 4, 1974 by a previously unknown terrorist group known as the Symbionese Liberation Army, the SLA. Americans were not too familiar with political kidnappings, and the scene of hooded and armed men holding the young and pretty Patty Hearst for ransom captured the American imagination the way that Bonnie and Clyde had. While isolated, abused, and threatened with death, Patty Hearst succumbed to what has become known as the Stockholm syndrome. She identified with her captors and reemerged as a converted supporter of their cause, making propaganda announcements for them against the "capitalist state," and even participating in bank robberies and other illegal activities. It was, as the FBI called it, one of the strangest cases in FBI history.

The Hearsts lived close to the SLA hideout and the group's intention was to leverage the family fortune and political influence in order to free two SLA members who had been arrested for the killing of Oakland, California's first black superintendent. Faced with their failure to free the imprisoned men, the SLA demanded that the captive's family to distribute $70 worth of food to every needy Californian, an operation that would cost Hearst an estimated $400 million. As a response, Patty Hearst's father, Randolf Hearst, organized a loan and arranged the immediate donation and distribution of $2 million worth of food to the poor in the San Francisco Bay Area. The distribution was hastily organized and the affair was chaotic, practically botched, resulting in the SLA refusing to honor the release of their hostage, who was now appearing on television adorned with an assault rifle and proclaiming slogans.

The Hearst family was in desperate need of someone who would take charge of the food distribution demands of the SLA and thus the saving of their daughter. That's where Lud Kramer stepped in. Kramer apparently had experienced once chairing a commission that involved food distribution to the needy, and thus he boastfully stepped up claiming he could do it, in an election year! He got the nod and took charge, staging press conferences daily.

I was dazzled. How the heck did Lud Kramer noodle his way into this one? Whenever I turned on the evening news, there was my opponent's face, playing hero and staging news conferences, pledging his support to help the poor, aiding the Hearst family, liberating the pretty granddaughter of America's richest man. That was my opponent in the 3rd District. I felt hopeless. I could barely get myself onto the local TV news programs one night a week and here was the Republican candidate going national every day. Timber couldn't hold a candle to Patty.

Kramer figured out that by abandoning his campaign for Congress in Washington State and spending weeks on end in San Francisco, he had created the greatest diversion. He had realized that he could not win unless something dramatic happened. He needed a game changer, and then came Patty. His Patty Hearst savior work cast him as a humanitarian, and the nightly news coverage was his big signing bonus. Going national superseded the local coverage.

As it turned out this would only work for a very short time before it began to backfire. In May 1974, the FBI raided an SLA safe house in Los Angeles and six SLA members were killed, including Donald DeFreeze, their criminal leader. Patty escaped out a back door and disappeared and would not be captured until September 18 in San Francisco. The story went cold and Lud lost his front-and-center role in the affair. Even better for me, 3rd District voters started to express scorn that the Republican Lud Kramer had shown more interest in feeding San Francisco's poor and garnering attention to himself than attending to those in his home district who were in economic duress—the very people he was hoping to represent in Congress. The journalists and pundits started calling Kramer an opportunist; they said he'd seize any emergency to get attention and praise. That style of campaigning had worked for him for years in elective office, they said, but now it was a liability. The Hearst story began to work to my advantage.

Beyond Lud Kramer, Patty Hearst, and the food distribution story, national election coverage started talking about a political tsunami spreading across America's heartland; there was a veritable backlash to the Watergate scandal and political sentiment was going against the Republican status quo. A surge of so-called "Watergate Babies" were now running for public office and were predicted to gain seats in Congress. A new wave of political youngsters rallying for a new style of governance following the seemingly unprecedented politically motivated break-in using gangsters, plumbers, as they were called, who'd do anything for political advantage. The Watergate baby candidates were, on the average, two decades younger than the average age of current members of

Congress. I was on my way to be one of these Watergate Babies, and the prospect made me proud.

What had begun as a bungled burglary at the Democratic Party HQ in the Watergate Hotel in Washington, DC had led to two years of investigations by journalists, the FBI, and Congress. The burglary was traced back to the campaign operations of President Richard M. Nixon, and the ensuing cover-up of the crimes led back to the Oval Office itself.

In the face of impending impeachment, Nixon resigned in August 1974, and three months later, his Republican Party would suffer a severe drubbing in the midterm elections. The GOP bore the brunt of high inflation and an oil embargo that sent gas prices to historic heights, a cruel reversal considering that only two years earlier, Nixon chalked up his landslide victory over Democrat George McGovern and the Republicans had savored their gains on Capitol Hill. This would not last.

The Class of '74 would induct seventy-five new Democrats to only seventeen new Republicans. The mammoth size of the '74 class that made it historic. Half of the freshly elected members in 1974 were young, under the age of forty, and relatively new to any public office. Tom Downey of New York was just twenty-five, the youngest member since the early 1800s. I was only thirty-seven and would fit perfectly the description of this new generation of Democrats going to Washington, DC for the first time.

And with this fresh blood, our generation of Democrats would go on to refurbish the image of the party. Beyond the incredulous Watergate scandal, the young class of elected congressmen viewed Congress as ossified, beholden to powerful interests, unresponsive to the people, and ripe for the taking.

Subsequently, populist undercurrents in national elections reemerged again in 1994 when Newt Gingrich cast his "Contract with America," a trend which swept for the Republicans fifty-four House and nine Senate seats on Capitol Hill. Twelve years later in the 2016 presidential elections, the wave surfaced with the help of digital social media and the surprising ascent of Donald Trump's "Make America Great Again," which gave him his surprise victory and solidified the GOP base in Congress.

The Democratic Watergate Babies of 1974, more than their senior colleagues in the House, captured the shifting public mood, and angst, in their respective districts. Considered more enlightened than the run-of-the-mill candidates of the past, most were college educated with good professional credentials. "We were the children of Vietnam, not World War II," Tim Wirth of Colorado reminded us. "We were products of television, not of print. We were products of computer politics, not court-house politics. And we were reflections of JFK as president, not FDR." And we were a departure from Richard Nixon, who was now America's villain.

Our legendary Watergate Class of '74 would ultimately bring with it a series of reforms that would change the way things were done in Washington, DC. And in retrospect, many of us were caught up in those lofty thoughts while on the campaign trail. I could hardly see that promising big picture of reform, of course, in those early pre-election days when still battling to get myself to the nation's capital.

Toby Moffet, who had captured a suburban Republican district in Connecticut, had been a street savvy organizer and former aid to Ralph Nader. Toby reminisced two decades later: "We were young, we looked weird. I can't even believe we got elected."

A thirty-one-year-old Methodist minister from the suburbs of Philadelphia named Bob Edgar had begun his campaign by looking up "Democratic" in the phone book to find the local headquarters. We were an eclectic bunch. Most of us had been caught up in the anti-Vietnam War movement, and were less dependent on the neither traditional Democrats nor organized labor. With time, the Class of '74 would leave a collective mark that changed the feel of Washington, DC.

Each of us had our own touch of originality. I, of course, had begun as the dance instructor and swirled through the local political terrain, stumbling on to the log export issue but also capturing the public demand for sweeping change in the nation's capital. At the outset, I had no idea that the hidden timber issue or the Watergate tsunami would be factors in my being elected to Congress.

On election night, friends, family, and supporters gathered at a local hotel in Olympia to view the voter count as they trickled in. When the final results reported that I had won with a margin of 62% to 38%—a landslide—it was Lud Kramer who openly admitted: "Let's face it, we were blown away," he said indicating that that defeat might bring an end to his colorful political career, which it did.

Capturing the Watergate spirit, *The Columbian* quoted me saying, "This campaign was truly a people's campaign. The traditional economic and political forces lined up in both the primary and general election behind my opponents have shown a candidate who can win without them." The Vancouver newspaper had limited coverage of the timber-log export issue since its distribution in Clark County was mostly a Portland,

Oregon suburb, yet *The Columbian* was proud to report that its own elected official would now be Southwest Washington's next US congressman.

Thinking back on that first day when I filed to run for office, I recall that I had no clue about the log export issue which motivated voters and propelled me through the primaries. Had I had any knowledge of the issue at the time I entered the race, I would have likely taken a pro-log export position, aligning with the other Democratic candidates on the issue. Again, I stumbled onto something. Then meeting this plaid shirted lumber miller with gifted fundraising capabilities made the difference in the primary election. There is serendipity, even in a political career.

Poor Patty Hearst served only two of the seven years she'd been sentenced to when the new president who accompanied us Watergate Babies to Washington—Jimmy Carter, the peanut farmer from Georgia—commuted her sentence. Two hours before leaving office in January 2001, then President Bill Clinton officially pardoned Hearst of her crimes. Lud Kramer created a foundation to provide grants to lower-income people, divorced his wife of seventeen years only to remarry her seventeen years later, and finally passed away from lung cancer in Liberty Lake in 2004.

As a freshman in the Class of '74, I'd be taking young Carolyn to the nation's capital. I had a whole lot of work to do, promises to keep, and "miles to go before I sleep, and miles to go before I sleep," to borrow from America's greatest poet, Robert Frost, who knew a few things about logs himself.

CHAPTER 10

The Class of '74 Rebels

The 1974 election was all about Richard Nixon. I should say Watergate, our greatest political scandal at the time. It was miraculous how courageous journalism and some daring whistleblowing, combined with a system that allows itself to keep itself in check, succeeded in toppling the president who was clearly guilty of malfeasance.

Nixon was sent packing but had orchestrated the least shameful scenario for his exit. His vice president, Gerald R. Ford, the former House Majority Leader, would succeed Tricky Dick and then would pardon his former boss, the ousted president, as a means of getting the country beyond the crisis and back to work.

The seventy-five newly elected members of the congressional Class of '74 ushered in a populist mood, which stretch across America's heartland and would have a stinging effect in the nation's capital. The political feel coming to Washington was undoubtedly contentious. The traditional norms inside the Beltway were being challenged head-on.

In early January 1975, the newly elected Democratic congressmen met for the first time in this elegant chamber room. As we were wondering around, getting acquainted—not unlike a college mixer—discussing the elections and expectations, the big questions were growing in intensity. Who would lead us?

What's our agenda? How would we make a difference?

What quickly emerged was a bold commitment to reform the way things were done in the House of Representatives. We were reformers, but what would we be reforming? Internal changes like how we handled amendments, committee procedures, legislative agendas needed changing, but these would not capture the spirit of the voters that had gotten us elected.

Before our Class of '74 arrived on the scene, the Democratic Study Group within Congress had considered a reform agenda, but the group did not have the votes to put the agenda into effect. As newcomers, we were convinced that our collective effort should be directed at the congressional committee system, the stacked deck syndrome, and the culprits who served as the chairmen. We'd wrangle the power away from the brokers and introduce fresh legislation. That was the idea.

The congressional committee system had been in place forever and it was set up in a way that kept power concentrated within the grip of those who controlled the committees and the subcommittees. Power corrupts, as we often repeat. The inevitable question was, "Who had the power?" According to congressional tradition, power resided with the Speaker of the House of Representatives, who had all the levers at his command to adjust votes, pressure members, facilitate the flow of cash or eliminate it, and thus assert his authority. The most notable and powerful speaker had been the legendary Sam Rayburn, a Democrat from Texas' 4th District, whose reign continued for twenty-one years in Congress, seventeen of which he served as the forty-third speaker. Rayburn, whose name is engraved over one of the three congressional office building blocks, was often referred to as "The Czar of Capitol Hill." Rayburn has been a mentor of Lyndon B. Johnson and history *aficionados* will be interested to note that in 1926, he was influential in the building of America's legendary Route 66, Will Rodgers Highway, or America's Main Street, which originally ran from Chicago to Santa Monica, California, and which had been a critical route in the migration to the west including during the Dust Bowl in the 1930s. Nat King Cole recorded Bobby Troup's popular blues ditty, *Get Your Kicks on Route 66*, followed by Bing Crosby, the Andrew Sisters, Chuck Berry, and finally, The Rolling Stones. Rayburn's Board of Education secret meetings in unidentified rooms in the capitol were reserved for poker games, bourbon drinking, and off-the-record discussions on politics. He died in 1961 of cancer and was awarded the Congressional Medal of Honor posthumously. The fumes of history were always circling my head as I walked the long corridors of the capitol in those early days.

At our swearing-in ceremony, we stood before another speaker in January 1975, a short man from Oklahoma named Carl Albert (D-OK), the forty-sixth speaker. Known as the "Little giant from Little Dixie"—he measured 5'4"—he was among the weakest speakers in modern times due in part to an alcohol problem that was well known by everyone. He had gained some national recognition during the Watergate hearings, and was visible as speaker during the Vietnam War, at the time of the JFK assassination, and during the tumultuous Democratic National Convention in Chicago in 1968. On the whole, Albert's reign was best characterized by a shift of institutional power from the speaker's chair to the committee chairmen known as the "committee barons."

He died in his hometown of McAlester, Oklahoma in 2000 after having published in 1990 a rather unremarkable autobiography called *Little Giant*. Albert did write that the "Class of '74 refused to be led. They wanted to build a record, not policy, and they had the votes to determine the outcome in Caucus meetings." Happily, we also had the votes to push him out as speaker in the next session, so he opted for retirement. His replacement, Tip O'Neil from Boston, who'd end up serving for five full sessions of Congress, brought back the gavel of leadership and a better functioning House of Representatives.

Those who ask whether committees are important may wish to call up former president and congressional scholar Woodrow Wilson's famous remark from the 1920s: "Congress in session is Congress in exhibition, whil'st Congress in the committee rooms was Congress at work."

As renegades in 1974, we thought we'd challenge the so-called seniority system. At that time, members became chairmen by simply outliving everyone else on their respective committees. Committee control had little or nothing to do with one's ability in the subject or leadership skills. If you were patient, sat back, and waited until your colleagues pass on, pass through, or pass out, you'd find yourself eventually gripping the gavel.

Officially, the party caucus had to approve committee chairmen when a newly elected Congress convened after the elections. While the Democratic Party Caucus had the final say, it was more of an ordination than selection or election. No one dared to challenge a sitting chairman. Yet, our Class of '74 was about to confront the system by targeting three of the more senior members who otherwise had maximum security holding on to their chairmanships.

Our first target was Chairman of the Agriculture Committee, Bob Poague, known to be cordial and approachable, but many of the House Democrats preferred Tom Foley who was next in line and whom I knew slightly from my Secretary of State campaign days in Washington State in 1972. When Tom Foley's name was put into nomination, it was an awkward moment for him. Known for his graciousness, Foley quickly took the podium and unselfishly expressed his strong support for Chairman

Poague. It was a nice gesture, but Poague had a lackluster track record and we continued to support Tom Foley and elected him as the next Chairman of the Agriculture Committee.

Our second conquest was the overthrow of Wright Patman, the powerful chairman of the House Banking, Currency, and Housing Committee. Targeting him at first came as a surprise because he had been considered a liberal and had few differences with the Class of '74. The root of all evil he had believed "was the concentration of economic power in the hands of a small number of bankers, business executives, and government officials," as the *New York Times* wrote in its 1976 obit. Patman's problem was his age, eighty-one at the time, with clear signs of early dementia. He would be the next to go. We didn't have a choice; we were committed to reform and he was no longer able to deliver. The *Times* also cited that, "When he was ousted from the chairmanship of the House Banking Committee at the beginning of the present Congress, *The New Yorker* magazine said of him: 'He's something of a crank, but he's an intelligent and knowledgeable crank. Those Young Turks who shoved the old Populist aside not only were being cruel, but were probably making a mistake. Ralph Nader, the consumer advocate, in an angry newspaper column at the same time, harked back to Mr. Patman's attempt in September 1972 to get the Banking Committee to investigate the route that Nixon campaign money traveled, from the original contributors, through the Nixon finance committees and various banks, into the pockets of the Watergate burglars.'" In Patman's heyday, he did some remarkable things like expose the way some tax-exempt foundations had been used to CIA money into politically motivated organizations. We hailed him, but he had to move over.

Finally, there was F. Edward Hébert, Chairman of the House Armed Services Committee, who was known to be "really painful." Eddie Hébert never hesitated to remind people about how powerful he was. Still holding the record as Louisiana's longest serving congressman, Hébert, who had started his career as the local *Times-Picayune* newspaper editor and had written about the illustrious Huey Long when he was elected governor, held the seat that was eventually taken over by the controversial firebrand Bobby Jindal. The day that Congressman Hébert appeared before the Class of '74 newly elected pioneers, he was defiant and boastful as he addressed us. I can hardly forget his opening words, "Well, boys and girls, what can I do for you?" This was not going to fly, and we booted him out as chairman.

Hébert, I must add, opposed school desegregation and signed the Southern Manifesto in opposition to the United States Supreme Court's

1954 Brown v. Board of Education decision. I am still happy to this day to report some forty years later that we gave him the axe.

No doubt, the ousting of three powerful chairmen was a shocker to the committee barons, and yet they continued to rule with authority, not consensus, not quite getting it yet that change was in the air. I confronted this arrogance early on, drawing on my earlier experience with the lumber giants in my state.

As we were ending the day to day challenges, commodities coming into the US market from Canada was a highly sensitive issue for us considering that Canadian lumber poured into the American Northwest despite loud cries from my district of unfair practices and ruinous pricing practices. This issue prompted me to seek a resolution by amending the Omnibus Trade Adjustment bill, which should have been a relatively routine procedure. Apparently, these amendments would have eased the economic pressure on the independent timber mills in the 3rd District, but curiously, they continued not to show up when the bill came up for amendment, a fact that provoked within me a growing frustration. What was going on? I wondered.

I consulted with a colleague who was savvy about the procedural matters of including amendments in bills. "Did you happen to sign that petition on social security demanding to bring it to the floor for a vote?" he asked.

Well, what the heck did that I have to do with it? I thought, recalling that, yes, I did.

"Well, that's the problem," he explained. "You better talk to Chairman Rostenkowski."

This, apparently, was his way of punishing members who signed such petitions, which could force a bill out of his Ways and Means Committee for a vote despite his objection. He had stripped my amendment out of the bill because I had signed that petition. Dan Rostenkowski from Chicago had been reared by the Cook County Democratic political machine run by the bigger-than-life Mayor Richard Daley. Known as the penultimate dealmaker and broker of compromises, now I began to understand why. Rostenkowski had brokered the 1966 Medicare legislation as well as law that kept the otherwise broke Social Security System solvent. He would have become speaker had he not been hurt by the Chicago violence during the 1968 Democratic convention.

I hesitated. This couldn't be the way how things should be done around here, I smirked. Chairman Rostenkowski was not easily approachable, I learned quickly. Classically Chicagoan, tough and authoritarian on committee matters, protected by a vigilant staff who made it difficult to even get an appointment with him. You had to earn it. Members were lining up to get his blessing on bills and amendments they wanted to get through his committee. He savored his power, and used it to teach you to get in line and not to oppose him.

One day, I recall he was on the House floor, managing a bill and was just sitting there as others were speaking. I got up my gumption and approached him.

"Mr. Chairman, our mutual friend, Marty Russo, said I should talk to you about the Omnibus Trade Adjustment bill."

He responded quickly, even in a friendly tone, saying, "You have. Problem solved." And he got up and walked away. The next Omnibus Trade bill included my amendment. I never signed another petition to bring legislation out of his committee. He was the "boss." I understood that there were ways to get things moving in your direction. Opposing Rostenkowski was not one of them.

It wasn't until 1992 that he finally met defeat when a federal grand jury investigated him over a weird scandal involving the purchase of $22,000 worth of postage stamps from the House post office using tax-payer money. The claim was that the congressman converted the stamps back into cash. Newt Gingrich went after Rostenkowski as a symbol of Democratic corruption, and Rostenkowski was then formally charged with abusing congressional payrolls and using public funds for his own vehicles. He ended up serving fifteen months in federal prison and paying a $100,000 fine, and in defending himself claimed that "bureaucracies all have a certain mindless logic." He had shown that to me himself.

The Class of '74 did manage to shake up things in Washington, DC, but I had always worried whether that disruption offered the nation a lasting positive effect. I have a hard time answering in the affirmative. Sure, we disposed of three powerful committee chairmen and made the selection process more open. But the so-called seniority system remained in place and continues to rule the House to this day, although when Newt Gingrich launched his populist Republican movement twenty years later in 1994, an initiative known as "Contract with America," a surge of newly elected Republicans instilled a type of reform that did have lasting effect. They adopted a new rule that ended lifetime chairmanships and replaced them with a six-year term limitation.

The House committee system includes twenty permanent committees and some thirty subcommittees. Although tedious to list, it's impor-tant that citizens know how the US House of Representatives divides up the work. The committees are: Agriculture (six subcommittees); Appropriations (twelve subcommittees); Armed Services (seven subcommittees); Budget, Education, and the Workforce (four subcommittees); Energy and Commerce (six subcommittees); Ethics, Financial Services (six subcommittees); Foreign Affairs (six subcommittees); Homeland Security (six subcommittees); House Administration, Judiciary (five subcommittees); Natural Resources (five subcommittees); Oversight and Government Reform (six subcommittees); Rules (two subcommittees); Science, Space, and Technology (five subcommittees); Small Business (five subcommittees); Transportation and Infrastructure (six subcommittees); Veterans' Affairs (four subcommittees); Ways and Means (six subcommittees); and one Permanent Select Committee on Intelligence with subcommittees on the CIA, the Department of Defense Intelligence, Emerging Threats, and the NSA and Cybersecurity, which, of course, did not exist in my day as a Watergate Baby.

Mastering the committee system has always been essential to the effectiveness of a new congressman. If you managed to get yourself onto a committee that helped you serve your district, it would be a boost on your chances of getting reelected. Simple survival tactics. My first choice in 1975 was obvious—the powerful House Appropriations Committee. My predecessor's clout came from her overseeing federal programs and funding that channeled huge benefits to our district. First-term members were not given much choice, though, and thus we resigned ourselves to the least influential committees of jurisdiction, the ones that were nudged in our direction. Even fourth-term members had to scramble to get onto the Appropriations Committee, so the prospect for a freshman like myself was practically nil. My backup choice was Government Operations, mostly oversight of federal programs, which I chose because I knew something about the work and thought I'd be good at it. I was pleased with my thinking, but that led some of my colleagues to suggest that such a choice was a bit odd. There was no way in the world that this could be of direct value to my district or help with my reelection. It was like working as the stock boy compared to being a floor manager in a big retail store. What was I thinking?

I quickly got a call from Tom Foley, the dean of our Washington delegation, the new Chairman of the Agriculture Committee, and of course, future Speaker of the House. He was ever so gracious as he mentioned, "Don, far be it from me to advise you on committee selections, but if you were to ask me and if I were so bold as to make a suggestion, I think you should go on the Foreign Affairs Committee." In our brief chat, he mentioned the importance of the Vietnam War and it would be wise to position myself on this important national issue.

"Okay, Tom, if you think so," I said. "But how would I go about getting on the House Foreign Affairs Committee?" He urged me to go talk to Congressman Morris "Mo" Udall, member of the Steering Committee for the western region of the country, himself from Arizona, and who made recommendations that carried weight on committee assignments.

The very next day, I made it my business to meet with Mo Udall, a nationally known Democrat with his own presidential ambitions, and I asked him for his help to get me on the House Foreign Affairs Committee. His response was guarded. "Don, I don't know if this is possible. Trying to make this change at the last minute is going to be difficult. Also, Foreign Affairs Committee is an important committee, so not sure I can make it happen. You are new." I understood, and thanked him anyway. As I turned to walk out of his office, the "Mo" blurted out, "Hold on, Don," he added. "Tom Foley, you know, is a close friend. Let me see what I can do to make it happen." I smiled, and thanked him.

Now I began fearing that I'd be stuck on the inconsequential Government Operations Committee, which I had foolishly volunteered to take. I waited impatiently for Udall's call, and finally, the call came.

He came off as straightforward in announcing how he got it done. "I went all out to get you on the committee. It was not easy. I had to use a lot of chits, but…" I could hear the good news coming. "I was able to pull it off. Congratulations! You are now a member of the House Foreign Affairs Committee." Yet the backstory was something different.

I was thrilled. In college, I had been involved with international student activities and had thought about the Foreign Service. Now I would be on the House Foreign Affairs Committee. I thanked Mo Udall, and as I return to this day in my mind's eye, I thank him again. This was a break that greatly changed the direction of my life's work. Udall would go on to run for the democratic nomination for the presidency in 1976 and nearly upset Jimmy Carter, but didn't. He did deliver the keynote at the convention, though, that year to great acclaim.

Nothing is ever quite the same as it appears, though, and the nuances of my new appointment on the Foreign Affairs Committee proved to be ridden with nuance. At the committee's first meeting, I glanced across the panel's seating, and I immediately noticed that there were three empty chairs. I subsequently learned that the Foreign Affairs Committee was not a preferred choice for the newly elected because it brought no value to one's home district. Additionally, Vietnam, a very heated political subject at the time, was filled with political risk and could prove highly distracting. That is why the House leadership had difficulty persuading members to be on the committee. I was the exception, of course. I did not rebuke Udall or Foley at all, nor did I feel set up. This was an opportunity to serve on an exceptionally important committee at an exceptionally difficult moment in our country's history. I was excited and also relieved that I would not be on the House Committee on Operations, among the most boring assignments in the House of Representatives. I would now be involved on international issues, which would be an adventure.

Yet, coming from the Northwest, there were also risks. Two renowned senators from the Northwest—Oregon's Senator Wayne Morse who had been one of the most outspoken politicians in opposition to the Vietnam War, and anti-war Frank Church from Idaho who chaired the Senate Foreign Relations Committee—had both lost their elections because of the perception in their respective states that they were preoccupied with world problems, more so than dealing with the concerns and needs that were being ignored. I had to remind myself to make my constituency a priority and downplay my work on the Foreign Affairs Committee. When the Foreign Affairs Committee met to make assignments to the various subcommittees, another bit of serendipity landed on my life. I'm not sure why, but I had arrived late, and the cherry-picking of the best subcommittees was already over. What remained was the subcommittee on Africa, not the best choice for me since my district had no relationship to the African continent at all, was the furthest from Africa, and had the fewest Americans with African origins or even African-Americans than any other district in the entire nation. So I'd ended up with the least relevant subcommittee in a committee that had few ways of helping the constituents of the 3rd District of Washington. *Well done, Don,* I chided myself.

I love the way that mishaps turn out to be blessings. Later that year, the chairman of the Africa subcommittee, Charles Diggs of Michigan, was indicted for mail fraud and for taking kickbacks on pay raises he had increased, and had to relinquish his chairmanship. He served fourteen months in jail. Diggs had been the first African-American to be elected to Congress and had been an active member of the civil rights movement and a strong advocate for the ending of South Africa's apartheid system. He had also been one of the founders of the Black Congressional Caucus and served as its first chairman. With Diggs gone, I was next in line, so I became chairman of a congressional subcommittee as a freshman, a rather unusual occurrence. In fact, this was outright rare, if not unprecedented, to become a subcommittee chairman in your first term. Africa was emerging as a geopolitical priority because of the sudden realignment of the continent's two most important countries, Ethiopia and Somalia. Both were switching their alliances on the East-West conundrum, as the two superpowers were jockeying to strategically secure their positions and influence in North Africa.

Fourteen years later, a candidate for the US Senate and heavily involved in fundraising, Congressman Tom Foley who was then Majority Leader, was a featured speaker at one of my fundraising events at a hotel ballroom near the capitol. He praised my leadership on international trade, and in his typical Foleyesque style, he referenced how I wisely positioned myself to obtain a seat on the Foreign Affairs Committee. "When Don Bonker came back to Washington as a newly elected congressman, he knew exactly what he wanted and how best to achieve it. Long before trade was an issue, he recognized its importance in the Puget Sound area and figured out that being on the Foreign Affairs Committee was a strategic move, since it had a subcommittee on trade. He knew this would be beneficial in his district and nationally. He wisely maneuvered to get a seat on the full committee and eventually became chairman of the subcommittee. Few people I know possessed that kind of savvy as a newly elected congressman." I was speechless. A collection of consequences and luck had steered me all along, and now the wide brush stroke of history had turned this simple dance instructor into a major choreographer. The crowd applauded, and I modestly nodded with gratitude.

Ah, politics.

III. Littered with Unknowns

CHAPTER 11

THE STAIRCASE STRIPPER

I thought that getting elected was the tough part. Little did I know that transitioning to a new life in a big and costly city on the East Coast would be a journey of its own. *The Columbian* reporter, Jim Van Nostrand, whom I ultimately hired as my press secretary, interviewed Carolyn and me on the eve of our departure from Washington State, calling our new life in the capital as "littered with unknowns." We were real neophytes, and all my statewide experience now funneled down into one belittling word—freshman. Van Nostrand asked in his column, "Can they find a suitable apartment renting for less than $500 or $600 a month or a desirable house costing less than $80,000 in Washington, DC? If the price is right, will it be in a neighborhood where crime and violence are not too widespread?" He went on to ask, "Will the high costs of living make even the $42,000 salary of a congressman inadequate? How much of their prized collection of antiques can they afford to ship east?"

It was true, we hadn't thought about how to make ends meet in our new home. We essentially had no money, but it was true that we had collected some fine old pieces that we were proud of. Van Nostrand also asked, "What problems lie ahead in shifting from the political career of an administrator to a life as a legislator?" Frankly, we had no idea. Carolyn was cited saying that we had already lived out of a suitcase for six months and had a long detailed list of things to do. It was just part of the "process of adjusting," true to all freshman experiences.

Carolyn's first task was, of course, to find a house. Our realtor agent was a woman named Terry Robinson, who had been closely knit to the Kennedy clan and was very savvy politically in her own right. In a short time, Terry found us a house on Yuma Street in Northwest Washington, near American University. As we were seated in her Cleveland Park home signing the closing documents, Terry leaned back on her sprawling white sofa, relaxed now that our purchase was a done deal, and I noticed that she was staring at Carolyn.

Finally, she spoke. "Carolyn, I can picture you one day in the White House." At age twenty-six, Carolyn did resemble a young Jacquelyn Kennedy. She then turned to me, looked hard, completing the comparison.

"As for you, Don? No, no, it's not going to happen." We all laughed.

In January 1975, we moved into our newly purchased 1940s brick colonial in the so-called American University district. It had been occupied by a Greek family who, having scaled down and moved to a neighborhood condo, gave us the option of purchasing as well their expansive living room Kashan rug and their mahogany dining room furniture. Carolyn later designed and stitched a needlepoint for the mahogany dining chairs, for which she received an honorable mention at the annual Woodlawn Needlework Exhibition.

Still early in our marriage, we had only a few housing items to ship to our new home in the nation's capital. One piece, though, was special and it was the start of a lifelong journey into the collecting of pieces of classical furniture. Shortly after our marriage, we had dinner at the home of the Washington State National Park Service's regional director. The meal was unusual, even a bit weird, but one detail caught our eye. We were attracted to an eighteenth century, slant top desk that had me musing that it may have once belonged to one of our nation's Founding Fathers. The host mentioned that it had been passed down through generations of his family and that they were about to be transferred to Utah. They felt that the desk was too fragile to endure the shipment, and considering our admiration of the piece, they offered to sell it to us. We did not hesitate, not realizing that a year later, we would be transporting it a much farther distance.

I remember vividly those first days. I would grab the *Washington Post* early each morning, anxious and hungry to be well-informed on "inside the beltway" current events. I recall reading those loud headlines all about a senior congressman, Wilbur Mills, who was chairman of the House Ways and Means Committee, and a possible contender for the Democratic nomination for president in 1972. As the *Post* reported, Mills had been out drinking with an Argentine woman. I read on feverishly. The woman was a local stripper whose stage name was "Fanny Fox." As Mills and Fox were driving in the congressman's car near the Tidal Basin waterfront at around 2:00 a.m., a Park police officer pulled over the vehicle and a scantily dressed Fox attempted to flee the scene by scurrying out of the car and jumping into the Tidal Basin.

The press gobbled this up and the incident attracted so much publicity that Wilbur Mills had to give up his chairmanship and eventually left Congress. Fanny Fox continued working as a stripper, but changed her stage name from "The Argentine Firecracker" to the "Tidal Basin Bombshell." I'm not sure if Carolyn was amused, but stories like this were contributing to our new on the job education. We had arrived in the nation's capital following the two dominant news stories of Watergate and the Nixon resignation. Now, there was the Wilbur Mills-Fanny Fox scandal and the congressman's departure from Congress. The political scene in DC was a raging soap opera.

On my first trip back to the southwest of Washington State, Carolyn stayed at our new home and started applying her keen eye for interior design on the rather sparsely furnished house. The house had a staircase bannister that had been painted over, and Carolyn's suspicion revealed that the authentic mahogany wood had been concealed by glossy white paint. We were from the timber state of Washington and couldn't be caught hiding our wooden bannister, but wishing to make it lovely again implied the arduous task of removing the old paint, which was an all-consuming and painstaking endeavor complete with bleeding fingertips from the toxic paint stripper and steel wool. When back in the district, I would call Carolyn, and on one occasion, I asked about the Wilber Mills-Fanny Fox scandal and other headlines. Then I asked, "What have you been doing this past week?"

She commented on the bannister project and her sore fingers, then suggested, "Don, if you don't come home soon, I may begin to call myself 'The Staircase Stripper,'" which is about as racy as we got in those Fanny Fox days, which were pale compared to the age of Stormy Daniels and the sitting president.

Of the seventy-five newly elected congressmen, Carolyn stood out among the wives in several respects. She was the youngest, being in her late twenties, and many would say the most attractive. One of our colleagues, Max Baucus, who became a prominent US senator and eventually US ambassador to China years later, pulled me aside when we were in Beijing and said, "Don, don't you remember? You should. Speaker Tip O'Neil used to banter around that Bonker's wife is the most beautiful of the congressional spouses." That would probably get him into the gender dog house these days, although I was proud to be Carolyn's husband.

Widely known for her natural appearance and grace, Carolyn became active in the International Club #1, which consisted of wives of prominent officials, and became involved with nonprofit organizations including World Vision, which meant she traveled to Africa during famines. She also co-chaired the CARE annual ball event. Indeed, my being on the House Foreign Affairs Committee was an entrée to many international events that made our experience in Washington all the more engaging for both of us.

One memorable moment worth sharing occurred at the Swedish Embassy. We had become friends with Ambassador Wachtmeister and his wife, Ulla, who invited us to a high profile dinner in honor of the king of Sweden. As we arrived, Countess Ulla pulled Carolyn aside to say, "Carolyn, I have you seated next to the king this evening. Enjoy." Carolyn was at table #1 while Congressman Bonker sat at table #27.

Carolyn reported later what transpired. The evening was organized around a Hawaiian theme and each table was displayed with a pineapple centerpiece shaped into a vase holding colorful orchid blossoms. At His Majesty's table sat Senator Dale Bumpers, who kept His Highness engaged with mostly friendly questions relating to farming. But then he asked, "Your Majesty, how many square miles are there in Sweden?"

He paused, then awkwardly replied, "Frankly, I don't know." Later, the Swedish king turned to Carolyn and teased, "Do you know, in Sweden, we produce pineapples?"

"Really? I did not know that," she responded. The king came back laughingly, "If you had done your homework, you would know we are a great producer of pineapples."

Carolyn graciously avowed, "Right, and if I had done my homework I'd perhaps also know how many square miles there are in Sweden."

He laughed, amused both by Carolyn's wit as well as the ease in which Americans can joke, even with royalty. As they were preparing to leave, he turned to Carolyn and asked, "My collar and tie, does it look right?"

She responded, "Yes, His Majesty, the king. Impeccable."

Even kings needed encouragement. From a distance I observed how nimble my wife was in her new role in the capital.

The Swedish event was exceptional, but only one of many during our early days in Washington, DC. Thanks to my being a member of the House Foreign Affairs Committee, there was a steady flow of embassy invitations into my office. Not having children, our evenings were mostly free and this made it possible to have an active social life and to travel overseas easily, which would have changed if we were to have a family.

Ignorantly, we kind of thought that having babies or deciding to get pregnant was going to be easy, like flipping a switch on the wall. Flick it and voila, Carolyn would be pregnant. So when we decided it was time, we had a wake-up call. Months of trying became years of yearning, waiting, and then several heartbreaking miscarriages.

We decided we'd explore the idea of adoption. How would we make that happen? Carolyn had the name of a doctor in Seattle who specialized in matching adoptable babies and eager parents. So she called and left our names with him in the case he could knew of a baby needing a loving home.

In November 1979, Carolyn and I flew off to a retreat in Bermuda with friends including our dear friend, Doug Coe. We always cherished our time with him and were comfortable sharing with him our needs and challenges. He was aware and sensitive to our desire of wanting to start a family and that we were now considering adoption.

Like usual, our Bermuda location was a delight—a spacious retreat with plenty of green lawn space, an adorable beach with fine white sand, and lovely weather, not overly hot with a cool breeze at night. And being among dear friends made our time in Bermuda special. One evening, Carolyn and I set off on a scenic stroll that led to a rocky point that had us standing on an alluring foot bridge. We chose to toss smooth stones into the crystal blue water below, and filled with inspiration and love for one another, our hands gripped together and we said to the Lord that we remained committed, whether or not we ever had children, while humbly offering our prayer request for a child, knowing it would be His blessing. An indelible moment.

Doug Coe also spent time praying with us, but his love didn't stop there. Shortly after we returned from the Bermuda retreat, Doug met with the same doctor Carolyn had contacted who confirmed to him that "Interestingly enough, a mother and her pregnant daughter just came in to see me." I came to understand that this was typical of Doug Coe's selfless humility—"let your good works be done in secret." He never claimed credit for making this happen. But we had our loving suspicions.

A few months later, Carolyn received a call from the doctor in Seattle who announced, "I think, perhaps, we have a baby for you coming in late June." Stunned, Carolyn jumped off the sofa and responded with multiple questions, wanting to know everything about this baby who would soon become our daughter.

We felt abundantly blessed and a sense of peace. We were preparing to travel on a congressional trip to China that would be fascinating.

This was still the era of the old Cultural Revolution, and the people all wore garments that were only gray and blue. They maneuvered around on bicycles. The old architecture was exquisite but deteriorated and held up by bamboo poles. The pollution was so bad that nearly everyone on the streets was wearing facemasks to filter the air.

China was mesmerizing to be sure, but our minds and hearts were centered on that special day when we would be picking up our baby whom we were so anxious to see. Back in Washington, DC, Carolyn had a regular checkup appointment with her doctor, and when asked how she was feeling, she shared, "Amazingly, I feel pregnant."

Dr. Cooper smiled. It was common phenomenon that women who were adopting would take on the physical sensation of pregnancy. The doctor graciously shook his finger, "You are absolutely going to adopt that baby!" He, as much as anyone, knew a relaxed heart would usher in a full term pregnancy.

Finally, the moment had arrived; our little daughter named Dawn Elyse was six days old when we were able to pick her up in Seattle. With sparkling brown eyes that spoke volumes to our hearts as we dressed her in a rosebud dress, we proceeded to catch the ferry back to Bainbridge Island.

Carolyn was three months pregnant with our son. Jonathan Todd would arrive safely, born close to Christmas, and join Dawn Elyse, giving the young Bonkers a "bumper crop" in 1980. Abundantly blessed!

Back to work.

During my first congressional recess as the newly elected congressman in late February 1975, I had set up town hall meetings around my district, seeing this as an opportunity for constituents to have one-on-one meetings with their congressman. Accompanied by Duke Murray, this debut event took place in the Upper Peninsula outside Port Angeles. Duke, a former vice president of Universal Studios—his wife, Kathleen, a former actress who'd picked Olympia for their retirement years—was the antithesis of the congressional district office manager. Duke was not the politically savvy type who transitions from the campaign to the official job. Duke Murray was completely different. We had come to know the Murrays thanks to our mutual interest in antiques and our shared faith. I could see the immense value Duke would add to my district office given his wisdom and business experience. So I hired him.

Upon arrival in Port Angeles, we hurriedly assembled tables and chairs to set the stage to meet constituents. As I extended my hand to welcome each man and woman, they sailed past me to shake hands with

Duke Murray. "Glad to meet you, Mr. Congressman." He pointed them to me. It is true, he was older and certainly looked more statesmanlike than I did, but admittedly, it wasn't fun being upstaged by my assistant.

Beyond Duke being part of my district office staff, he and his wife became dear friends. Their Olympia home had on display the most authentic antiques in the Northwest, a side business that certainly had Carolyn's attention. Indeed, out of her monthly allotment, she put aside an amount to make ongoing purchases from her "Papa Duke" for the next twenty years.

Around my district, these constituent sessions were revealing of the high, if not unrealistic, expectations that a freshman congressman could continue to maintain the same flow of federal dollars that his predecessor had. As chairman of the House Appropriations Subcommittee, former Congresswomen Julia Hansen generously spread government funding for projects all over the 3rd Congressional District.

My first awakening occurred at that Port Angeles meeting. Among the constituents waiting to see me was a seventeen-year-old lad who was accompanied by two younger girls. He was a Native American from the Makah tribe located at Neah Bay in the northwest corner of the district. He asked about funding of the Makah Police Academy.

I replied, "Tell me something about this academy." As it turned out, he was the director and the two teenage girls were the academy's only cadets.

His concern became obvious. "Mr. Congressman, we hope you can keep the federal funding of our academy."

It was clear early on that there was no way I'd ever be able to match my predecessor's Santa Claus performance, channeling so many federal dollars around the district, a talent that earned her a reputation as the Grand Madam of Funding. I became the *petit monsieur*.

We then traveled to Shelton near Olympia to meet with supporters, party activists, and labor officials who were eager to hear about my new experience in the nation's capital. They were the true Bonker Backers, and it was like meeting with family and having a candid discussion about the political landscape in both Washingtons. At one point, someone asked, "Why is our president, Jimmy Carter, getting so much negative media coverage?"

I shared my take, rambling on about how the national media was skeptical because of his policies, maybe also because of his religious beliefs. "The *Washington Post*," I added, "seems more interested in attacking political leaders than accurately reporting the news." Among us at that small gathering, I was unaware of a reporter in the room who was jotting down notes as I was speaking. The next day, his newspaper, *The Olympian*, had a front-page article with a headline that read: "Rep. Bonker attacks *The Washington Post.*"

A headline appearing in a local newspaper, I thought, was nothing to worry about. My naivete came to haunt me in record time. The headline arrived on the desk of *The Washington Post* editor, Ben Bradlee. This was, of course, the media icon and powerful editor who became a national figure after commanding the investigative reporting that led to the Watergate scandal, and ultimately, President Richard Nixon's resignation. Ben Bradlee, for personal reasons, also brought down the most powerful member of Congress, Wayne Hays, and forced him to resign by the sheer power of his pen and his journalistic special forces.

Holding his letter in my hand, did I have reason to fear he was coming after me next? His stifling words were nerve-racking. "If you are accurately reported in the *Daily Olympian*," in his agitating style, then, "You are full of it…you must know that." There was more. "If this is the quality of coverage, may God save the Republic." And he signed off with, "Yours in truth." I nervously drafted a conciliatory response and signed off, "Yours in truce."

Yes, I was hit hard by this legendary *Washington Post* editor, yet strangely, I felt honored. At Carolyn's request, the letter was duly framed and on display in my congressional bathroom.

From Shelton, I moved on to Hoquiam, a lumber-dependent community in Grays Harbor County that was besieged with economic hardship as logs and jobs were being shipped off to Japan. There I was, standing before thirty lumber mill workers who were fearful about losing their jobs and who expected that the person who represented them in Congress would fix the problem. That is what they sent me to Washington to do.

The federal government had initiated the so-called Trade Adjustment Act (TAA), a program that offered training for workers who were displaced because trade had caused them to lose their jobs. However well-intended, this program had little practical effect in places like Grays Harbor. These were local economies that had few alternatives for employment, so training for jobs that did not exist was not the solution. Keeping logs local was what they wanted and pretty much the only thing that would keep them gainfully employed.

As I was about to be introduced by Gig Johnston, president of the International Woodworkers of America union, a politically active man, I was thinking what could I say to relieve their fears and to give them some hope. Johnston's introduction got it right fortunately, "Don Bonker is the only one who had the guts to stand up to Weyerhaeuser and others who are prospering from shipping our logs to Japan." That's what had garnered the votes that got me elected. So my message would resonate, a freshman going up against the timber tycoons and establishment in both Washingtons. I knew what I had to say but I was concerned—could I really deliver on this campaign pledge? I would try, at least.

Before I could fulfill my promise, though, to Gig Johnston on timber, I'd intervene in an unexpected way, like so many twists and turns in my life. Gig had in tow his daughter, a young woman named Terri whom I met earlier at a town hall meeting in Grays Harbor County. She had an early interest in politics that had her traveling to Washington, DC in 1982, but something struck me as we were talking in the local labor hall. I wasn't sure what it was, but later on, while leaning against back in my aisle seat of the red eye flight—the same flight I'd come to know so well over the decades—from Washington State back to my Washington DC office, this young woman jumped back into my thought. *I got it, she was perfect for Dan,* I thought—Dan Evans my staff assistant, I was thinking. He was young, handsome, and personable. There was always a cluster of young women around his doorway just wanting to see him. When I got back to the capitol, I called Dan into my office and blurted with enthusiasm, "Dan, I just found your wife-to-be." I wasn't saving Washington's timber yet but matchmaking would be value added.

He was amused and maybe a bit embarrassed, but privately, he wondered how anyone could take this kind of Cupid premonition seriously. Nothing happened for a year until I hired Terri Johnston to come work for us in the DC office. I cornered Dan and informed him that he'd be picking the Terri I had told him about and that, on Wednesday, he'd need to fetch her at Dulles Airport. And, he should also find her a place to stay until she found an apartment. Admittedly, I put him in a tough position, my acting was like Yente in *Fiddler on the Roof.* It was an order from his boss, so he had little choice. With today's gender issues, encouraging amorous encounters would be ill-advised, but I had a strong feeling about this and just went with it.

On the day he was supposed to pick her up, he managed to have an accident. While on his bike, he hit a pothole near the National History Museum and was hurled through the air and crashed onto the curb. He sprained his thumb and had road rash over his hands, elbows, and knees. By the time he got bandaged, up he was late to leave for Dulles and poor Terri, with her oversized suitcases and washing-machine-sized box of "necessities," was impatiently waiting curbside in front of United Airlines. Dulles is nearly an hour from the capitol if there is not too much traffic, and my "Robert Redford" office guy finally zoomed up to the curb in his Honda hatchback, sporting bandages, and flashed a broad smile at Terri. "Hi, let's go!" He glanced at the massive cargo and was obliged to creatively tie her pyramid of "Shelton necessities" on top his gold hatchback, and they were off to her new digs, the home of Dan's parents, Pastor Louie and Coleen Evans—at least that was the story that was conveyed to Terri's parents. As they approached Capitol Hill, Dan clarified, "Oh, you will be staying with a fellow staffer, Chris Hedrick. Terri needed a place to sleep and seemed fine staying with another woman from the Bonker office. But when they arrived and the door opened, she was taken aback—Chris was a guy, not a girl. How was she going to tell her parents that she had just moved in with a strange man? Other than for the hippie-types of the day, times hadn't changed yet for most.

A congressional office is an intimate setting and my two young staffers could not ignore one another, I was pleased to observe, and yes, Dan and Terri eventually began dating. I was pleased that my prophecy was about to be fulfilled, at least I thought. But then, suddenly, they broke up, my prophecy was shelved, and secretly, I was heartbroken that my ancillary role as matchmaker was sidelined.

About the same time, as chairman of the Foreign Affairs Subcommittee on Human Rights and International Organizations, I got involved on a religious persecution issue in Nepal, a landlocked country in Southeast Asia. Hinduism was the state religion and there was little tolerance of other religions, which prompted the imprisonment of the son of a young man named Charles Mendies, whose mother was a Canadian Christian missionary and whose father was English-Burmese. Charles, who was born in Nepal, was reared as an evangelical Christian. At age thirty-four, he was arrested and found guilty of proselytizing by placing Bibles in Nepalese hotel rooms and imprisoned in Kathmandu's Central Jail along with seventeen cellmates.

The story bothered me and I was committed to doing something beyond passing a resolution to bring public attention to the situation, which would have been standard procedures. I asked Dan Evans to travel to Nepal to try to meet with Charles Mendies and to let him know that the US Congress was doing its upmost to get him released, which is what ultimately happened. And to jump ahead, Charles eventually became involved with the National Prayer Breakfast that became prominent in my life and work, as well as at other major Christian events worldwide.

There are always sub-plots to stories and consequences to the things we do, and often, the shortest distance to a destination is the long way around. Dan Evans had a very long return flight and had to change planes several times. On that long journey, he later told me that he had contemplated profoundly about his life. With a lot of time while traveling, he revisited his relationship with Terri, which had remained ambiguous and emotionally unresolved. While flying across the Atlantic through the night, his thoughts were deepening as he began to realize how he felt and what he knew. Upon landing at Dulles, he quickly exited the airport and grabbed a taxi directly to Terri's apartment. He rushed up to her door with his luggage direct from Nepal, paused, and when she opened it, proclaimed, "Terri, please marry me."

The marriage ceremony eventually took place in February 1986 in Terri's hometown, Shelton, Washington, where all this began with Dan's father, Reverend Louie Evans, proudly presiding over the wedding, and Terri's father, Gig Johnston, standing like a proud hemlock on his daughter's side. Attending the ceremony was a gratifying moment to be sure, way beyond having a bill signed into law.

Nine years later on February 12, 1995, my gift for bringing together dearly beloved couples was prominently featured in *The Seattle Times'* *Sunday Pacific Magazine*. It displayed a double-page spread with color photographs of two of the couples I introduced, Dan and Terri and Scott and Dana Jackson, sitting on a sofa with their five young children. I was positioned on the floor, horizontally, in front of the sofa. In the article, which appeared on Valentine's Day, Congressman Don Bonker's matchmaking talent was highlighted, claiming that I had taken "the sting out of dating and mating for six former singles." They called me a "low-key guy who doesn't excite easily, but matchmaking puts him in another gear." Citing the Evans matchup, they said I paced back and forth and "oozed confidence, chutzpah." The fact that "Evans already had a girlfriend…didn't stop Bonker from telling him he has just hired his future wife. The couple married three years later. Like other matchmakers, Bonker says introducing people is fun, joyous, something that comes naturally to certain people."

Dance instructor and matchmaker, two talents that bring joy and make me happy, but Congress was about hard work, nuanced subjects, details, egos, budgets, rules, systems, strategy, and above all, mobilizing a coordinated team to get things done. Dancing and matchmaking may have been my mantras, but my rule in staffing the DC office was to hire people who were smarter than me and strong enough to make me accountable for doing the right thing.

CHAPTER 12

FOXTROT ON THE
HOUSE FLOOR

The early days in a congressman's life are filled with neophyte moments. You are supposed to know what you are doing, but actually, everything is new; the system has its traditions and its legends, its traps, and its rules. Each member of Congress goes through his or her routine and learns along the way, making early errors and pretending to be a pro while still being a novice. My young team offered amazing support, and each came with his and her own story of cleverness. No politician could have ever made it to power and then served without the often faceless staff that both has his or her back at all moments and anticipate the needs and problems that are just around the corner. These selfless servants, sometimes, are inherited and sometimes just show up at the right time.

There was Scott Jackson who managed to get past the receptionist and enter my office to introduce himself. A recent graduate, he awkwardly said his name, then rambled on about his work ethic and some other forgettable lines. But what I recall and what landed him the job was one statement, "Congressman, if you hire me, there is no job too big or too small, and I will get it accomplished." I called in my chief of staff and asked him to find a way to hire this exceptional young man. On my daughter's birthday in late June, Scott volunteered to show up at her party as an authentic clown with full makeup and costume, but the high temperature and humidity in his forty-five-minute commute to our home caused the heavy makeup to melt, and by the time he arrived on the scene, his appearance looked scary to Dawn and her friends. Eventually, Scott became the finance chairman for my Senate campaign, then eventually held a number of high-level positions at World Vision, Path Foundation, and is today's president of the world's largest nonprofit organization.

Then there was Carol Grunberg. I had become chairman of the Foreign Affairs Subcommittee on International Economic Policy and Trade, a post which allowed me to hire five staffers. A coveted position to be sure for those anxious to paste their trademark on international trade, and so I found myself staring at a huge stack of applications, each screaming to be selected. Beyond being a graduate of Columbia University and mastering foreign language skills, Carol said the right thing to secure a job on my subcommittee. "Congressman, I may not get the position that was posted, but I'm here to offer my service for six months—without pay. After that, you can employ me, or I can depart, whatever works best for you and the subcommittee." Within two years, Carol had become the staff director of my subcommittee.

Service before everything else, that was what I heard and that was how she was hired.

I encouraged my staff to feel free to speak out, to question my motives on positions or votes, and to interrupt me if they saw that I was contemplating a decision that might get me in trouble. I often repeated that there was a blurred line as to right and wrong on Capitol Hill. A member of Congress may misstep or stumble into that gray zone, unaware and unconscious of a wrongdoing or violation. Every politician and probably every human being enters that gray zone. My staff always had my back and were never fearful about speaking up ahead of time.

"Congressman, you cannot purchase those paintings out of our office budget." That was Mark Murray, my staff director, who did not hesitate to enter my office and confront me directly, wagging the House Ethics Manual at me.

"Why not?" I replied in a slightly annoyed tone. "The paintings are for my new district office. It's official, for crying out loud, Mark."

He quickly pointed to the provision, which specified that office funds could not be used to purchase art work. The government was protecting the tax payers' money from being shot on Picassos and Andy Warhol!

I had purchased these paintings for my new district office in the historic Marshall House in Vancouver, Washington, and it had seemed appropriate to have a local artist's work grace the walls in this famous setting along the so-called "officer's row" built during the Civil War. It was a paltry $200-spend for a beautiful addition to the site. But Mark had made his point. I instructed my executive assistant, Linda Suter, to have my campaign budget, not the public funds, cover the cost of the paintings.

A few days later, Mark entered my office again. "Not a good idea, Congressman."

I shot back at him, "Is there anything in the House Ethics Manual that precludes me from using my own campaign funds to buy these paintings for our office?"

"Not really," he said.

"Then what's the deal?"

The next day, the loyal and totally meticulous Mark Murray reappeared with something other than the House Ethics Manual. It was a newspaper headline that he had designed to make his point. "Congressman Bonker abuses campaign funds for his personal pleasure." I got the point and wrote a personal check for two hundred dollars. When I left Congress, only one of the paintings stayed with me, the others went to my district staff.

Part of those first days was figuring out the perks that came with the job. My favorite was the unexpected privilege of having access to the Capitol Hill members' gym located in the Rayburn Building, which had been built in 1964. It was fully equipped with an exercise room, swimming pool, locker room, an indoor court for gymnastics, and other activities.

The upstart Class of '74 is credited for another advanced reform, one that is almost always overlooked as part of our collective achievement. We pushed through measures to install hoop baskets on both ends of the gym floor to accommodate our preferred but, until then, ignored sport—basketball. In the spirit of true bipartisanship, we had formed a congressional basketball team that competed against DC-based entities, including the White House, the Russian Embassy, the Department of Interior, and for the sake of not being overly embarrassed or injured, the George Washington University women's team. This predates the amazing outdoor courts that were built by converting the tennis court on the White House grounds in President's Park and which have subsequently staged ferocious games with such b-ball luminaries as Shaquille O'Neal, Kobe Bryant, and LeBron James.

We did have an occasional Democrat vs. Republican basketball game, usually played before the Baltimore Bullets team at their stadium. On one such occasion, after the game, we proceeded to the locker room to shower and change. As I was walking back to the stadium, I was struck by someone standing there who was obviously waiting to greet me. I could feel the buzz of his stare and I struggled to recognize him. As he smiled, I realized I knew him. Holy moly, it was my high school basketball coach, Jim

Hudson. My first thought was shame, I missed that layup at the end of the game, and I forgot to follow my shot at least twice! But what a delight to see Coach Hudson who had been my mentor, and who was now standing there in front of me twenty-three years later. In Washington, DC to coach a national high school game in the same complex, he realized that his former student was now a player on the floor, and a congressman.

For members, basketball was a welcome break from otherwise typically hectic days on Capitol Hill, although we were overly cautious about spending time on recreation. Often, when Carolyn or others would ask, "Where is the Congressman?" the scripted response was, "He's on the floor."

There is another congressional gym story that I like to tell. The Rayburn House gym allowed collegiality that was limited on Capitol Hill. There was no partisan distinction as members worked out in the exercise room or otherwise gathered around in the locker room. My locker neighbored the one of a political legend, and this proximity resulted in a very memorable incident. Someone had given me a twelve-ounce oversized bottle of shaving lotion, a classic brand called Clubman Pinaud Lilac Vegetal advertised for its old-fashion barber shop smell, which I placed on the top shelf of my open locker. The ads for this stuff called it a sweet creation with fragrant notes of lilac with a floral accord, softened with a warm musk scent. However, it did not settle well with me, and the clear yellowish bottle remained in the locker unused for maybe two or three years. Then oddly, I began to notice that the level of fluid in the bottle started going down. Someone was using the stuff on the sly when I wasn't around. Eventually, all of it was gone.

One day, between Christmas and New Year, I opened the locker door and found a brand new bottle of Lilac Vegetal that had replaced the old. Attached was a note that quickly caught my attention, "Vice President of the United States of America." There was a personal note and it was signed by George H. Bush, "Happy New Year, I want to start with a clear conscience so I can steal more of this stuff in 1982." A precious note from someone with the old-fashion barber shop smell who would be our next president. My original Lilac Vegetal was a twelve-ouncer, but the Honorable George H. Bush's replacement was only the six-ounce bottle. He was gracious but not generous that Christmas.

The real floor, of course, was in the capitol, and far more important than the Rayburn gym was the floor of the House. Members of the United States Congress cherish nothing more than the casting of votes in the House chamber. How you voted on any particular issue was important and significant because, as lawmakers, those votes became part of your permanent voting record, the legacy of your office, and the acts that would either be celebrated as part of your achievements or flagged as part of your failures, depending on who was doing the cheering or booing. Every newly elected congressman begins by vowing never to miss a vote, to be on full alert, and to rush over to the House floor to insert member's voting card which we would insert and press "yes" or "no" or just "present." The system of bells indicate when the votes are coming up. The voting of all members was displayed above the elevated press box in the chamber, allowing us to quickly glance to see how our colleagues were voting.

Well, incredible as it seems, I missed the very first vote. How did that happen? I had scheduled a luncheon meeting with the *Seattle Post-Intelligencer* reporter, Shelby Scates, who was enthusiastic about conducting an interview on my first day in Congress.

Embarrassed to be sure, I anticipated media coverage that would grill me for missing the first vote, but fortunately, nothing came of my false start and never-miss-a-vote mantra. Humiliating moments would crescendo, though. An upcoming vote was on a House bill to increase salaries for House members and senators snuck up quickly. As a newcomer, I had no intention of voting "yes" to give myself a higher paycheck. Heck, I just got here and hadn't done much to earn a raise. It would have been political suicide upping my pay after only a few months when my constituents were scraping by.

A pay hike in Congress is a rare instance of bipartisanship since everyone on both sides of the aisle wants to make more money. House leadership, though, must deal with the angst and public criticism of members who would certainly be portrayed as self-serving in the public square. The leadership gets itself in sync to devise strategies that ensure the vote passes. This is collective back scratching. Article 1, Section 6 of the Constitution requires that Congress shall determine its own pay. The Ethics Reform Act of 1989 created an automatic adjustment mechanism, removing some of the political embarrassment from the process. In 2018, the annual salary reached $208,000 per member, whereas when I started in 1974, it was $42,000. It was a tortuous exercise—balancing my personal needs, including taking on a second residence in Washington, DC, and dealing with the harsh media criticism and the predictable political fallout even from supporters when it came to getting more money. In 1974, the salary was far from lavish.

I could not ignore the fallout I feared with the Washington State delegation. A "no" vote for myself, though, would also be a no for everyone in the US Senate and House of Representatives. I thought about our two great senators, Scoop Jackson and Warren Magnuson, who were both chairmen of very important committees. Their respective value to the institution and indeed the nation was incalculable, certainly a hundred times greater than that of a freshman congressman. They deserved the few percentage points of extra pay, certainly. My casting a no vote would be seen as a great act of egoism and a personal slight to my revered colleagues, many of whom represented support that I would so desperately need as a young congressman.

When I arrived in the House chamber, I quickly inserted my voting card in the device that recorded that I was present and was voting and hit the "no" button. I did it. I was principled. I'd not give myself a raise. It would be interesting, I thought, to watch the tally on the panel above the Speaker of the House's chair, and I took a seat in a center row of the chamber like being in a theater or old movie house to view a good film.

Within a few minutes, the "Dean" of the Washington delegation, Representative Tom Foley, appeared out of nowhere and sat directly in front of me. After a first moment, he turned and addressed me, "Don, we need your vote." Looking at the panel that displayed each Member's vote, I observed that my vote wouldn't have been necessary since it looked like the vote was going to pass anyway. Tom Foley did not budge, and after a spell of awkward silence, he leaned in to me and repeated, "Don, we need your vote."

Now I was feeling uneasy. Why was he sitting this close to me? Didn't he have better things to do? On another occasion, I would have felt honored to have Representative Tom Foley sitting next to me, but at this moment, I was getting uncomfortable.

"Tom," I said, "the voting is going well, so why do you need me this time?" The heavy and early "yes" voting was part of the leadership's strategy to create the momentum to encourage more yes votes as if it were to pass nonetheless. Psychologically, it is easier to get votes for bills that pass than for bills that will be defeated.

It occurred to me that I had been targeted by the leadership. It was Tom Foley's task to make sure I voted "yes" on this measure. This was how it worked. Foley did not want to show that he did not have influence over even a freshman from his own state. Now I felt the panic. Looking up at the display panel, there was only a few minutes remaining, and the "yes" vote was quickly vanishing. Foley and the others knew it would be a cliffhanger. The entire United States Congress pay raise could come down to a single vote, and Tom Foley was saying to me, "We need your vote, Don."

Why on earth did I come over to the floor and set myself up this way, sitting conspicuously in the middle? If I had been smart, I would have come in at the last moment, cast my "no" vote, and quietly escaped. But there was no escaping Tom Foley now who turned to me again, this time like a drill sergeant.

"Don, your vote is needed!" Votes could be changed up to the moment that the voting closed.

With less than a minute to go, there was a one-vote margin that was going back and forth and the votes were registering on the clock. My one vote, I saw, could make a difference. Tom Foley's salary increase and other committee chairmen, indeed all the senators and House members would depend on my changing from "no" to "yes." I felt not only Tom's glare but others as well as time was running out. I kept repeating to myself, why did I come over here and put myself in the hottest seat in the nation? I looked up again and saw that the vote was frozen with one short of passing. I could, in fact, change my vote and make the difference for everyone.

What do I do? To flip my vote from "no" to a "yes" would please Tom Foley and the House leadership as well as my Senators Jackson and Magnuson, indeed, all those in the US Senate. But such a vote would now surely invite harsh media criticism and rail my constituency, especially now that the vote was coming down to the wire, and with one gesture, I would be tagged with the responsibility in both directions. Would I throw in the buzzer beater or be the guy who lost it in the final seconds? A newly elected guy who goes off to the capitol and votes to considerably increase his own income with taxpayer's money. I'd never live down either choice, I feared. Even my own mother had told me that she didn't think that the salary increase was justified. Facing a big scar on my badge of honor, Tom Foley was eyeing me as my hand moved to the button.

CHAPTER 13

NO TO GIFTS AND WOMEN

As I gained seniority on the House Foreign Relations Committee, I learned that Representative Donald Fraser, a Democrat from Minnesota, would be leaving the Foreign Affairs Committee in 1978 to run for the US Senate. Fraser had drawn national and international attention to himself as chairman of the international organizations and movements subcommittee, which held hearings on human rights violations by US allies. This subcommittee was key to reducing US aid to countries found guilty of gross human rights violators.

His highest profile case was, by far, the launching of an investigation against South Korea's influence peddling scheme directed at manipulating US foreign policy. The investigation targeted the charismatic religious cult leader and business broker, Sun Myung Moon, charging that Moon had dabbled in international espionage through his links to the Korean Central Intelligence Agency and its covert activities in the US. Of course, this now seems bland in the wake of what we've seen with in the indictments of Russian influence peddling and hacking into the US 2016 presidential elections, but for the day, it was a very big story.

The congressman had the full committee's blessing with a sizable budget and resources to conduct this year-long investigation. And the implications went far deeper than we, at first, could imagine. Sun Myung Moon had a sizeable cult following in the country known as "the Moonies," and they unleashed a furious personal assault on Fraser, which included multiple lawsuits and interference in his campaign. The group even organized smear attacks on Fraser's wife and daughter. Moon, who had spent five years in a labor camp in North Korea for spying for the South, escaped during the Korean War in 1950 when UN troops raided the camp. He emerged as a staunch anti-communist and a self-proclaimed messiah sent by Jesus to carry out his unfinished work. His book, *Divine Principle*, was translated into English in 1973, which his followers read as scripture. He oversaw mass blessing ceremonies and mass weddings, marrying 2,000 couples in Madison Square Garden and over 3,000 in Washington, DC. With Jesus' crucifixion before marriage, Moon believed that he would create perfect families and join the spiritual with the physical and liberate mankind from sin. The cult gained public attention, and in 1974, Moon's following prayed for Richard Nixon following the Watergate scandal in a group prayer called "Forgive, Love and Unite," and Nixon publicly thanked Moon's church and received Reverend Moon.

The "gifts of deceit" emerged as the theme of the investigation. At that time, I had my own experience with this nefarious activity. As a member of the House Foreign Affairs Committee, I agreed to meet the South Korean ambassador Hahm Pyong Choon. The ambassador had been his president's former chief of staff, and was thus well versed in international diplomacy. He was accompanied by a staffer whom we presumed was a military attaché considering we were discussing the bilateral relationship between our two nations. As the two were departing, the ambassador handed me a nicely wrapped gift, which I resisted for obvious reasons. He quickly responded, "I am familiar with the House ethics rules and can assure you this gift is valued less than twenty-five dollars." I thanked the ambassador, reluctantly taking the watch and handing it to my staff advisor, Mark Bisnow, who later gave it to Linda Suter, my administrative assistant. She reported back later and said it was obviously worth a lot more than $25.00, which prompted my quick instruction to return it to the Embassy of Korea. I thought that was the end of it.

But it did not end there. Mark escorted the ambassador and his military attaché to the elevator, and upon returning to our office, he reported with a slight smile that the military attaché pulled him aside and discretely said, "If the congressman wants, we can arrange a follow-up dinner meeting with a 'lovely' embassy specialist." Mark and I agreed, shaking our heads, this was possible or attempt to bribe and a strategy for potential blackmail.

Mark Bisnow, who had worked for Hubert Humphrey and then John Anderson's presidential campaign and went on to do talk radio and launch an e-letter company, always showed his multitalents. He later authored a book, *In the Shadow of the Dome: Chronicles of a Capitol Hill Aide*, in which he devoted a full chapter on what had happened with the

Koreans. "I attended a dinner party given by a gracious old friend, Norma Gilbert, at her Capitol Hill townhouse. I engaged in a conversation of Korean pandering, playfully noting the Koreans also presented gifts to my boss. As it turned out, the host was a friend of *Washington Post* gossip columnist Maxine Cheshire, which resulted in a call to Don Bonker about the incident. He confirmed, and when pressed repeatedly on the value of the watch, suggested it was worth perhaps $150 or $200. The reporter's article had all of Washington reading that Congressman Don Bonker had been recipient of a $2,000 watch—a premier status symbol, as she put it, favored by Hollywood celebrities. Whether the reporting was a typo error or a deliberate one, we never learned. Lost in the account was the fact that it had not been kept."

All of this occurred in the immediate aftermath of the Elizabeth Ray scandal when the press was on the prowl for news stories of congressional behavior or misbehavior. The lobbying activities of Korea were coming under particular suspicion, and the *Chicago Sun-Times* ran a banner headline across its front page: "Koreans Offer Congressman Watches, Women." The sub-headline ran, "But Freshman Don Bonker Is One Who Says, 'No Thanks.'" Other news publications picked up the story. The first round made me look heroic. I had, after all, rejected the proffered gifts.

By the time it reached local newspapers out west, it started to play differently. The various articles posed spicy questions, like, "Why hadn't he reported these matters sooner? Why was he dealing with the Koreans in the first place? Had they given him something before? Why did they think they could buy his influence?" *The Daily Olympian* wrote: "Congressman Bonker denies that he accepted gifts." The way a story plays out in national media versus how it plays in the local media is worthy of a study on its own.

Via World News Communications, Reverend Moon ended up buying UPI (United Press International), as well as the conservative *Washington Times* newspaper in 1982, which became the Republicans' go-to inside-the-Beltway source of daily news and the preferred paper of President Ronald Reagan. The same year, Moon was sentenced to an eighteen-month sentence for filing falsified federal income tax returns and for conspiracy, and the case became a key source of debate on the question of freedom of religion and freedom of speech. The renowned Harvard professor Lawrence Tribe argued that Moon had been subject to religious prejudice and Reverend Jerry Falwell of the Moral Majority defended Moon. I never met him personally, but recall vividly the Korean influence on the Hill and the watch they tried to buy me with.

CHAPTER 14

WRESTLING A SKUNK

In 1975, my debut on the House floor came by way of an amendment I offered to the State Department funding bill. It "authorized" various functions and policies at state and provided funding of its programs for a three-year period. I had been approached by the Foreign Affairs Officers Association to sponsor an amendment that would mandate an increase in the percentage of US ambassadors coming from the existing pool of Foreign Service Officers, which would lessen the growing trend to award these crucial functions to political appointees, whom had often been promised countries as rewards for campaign contributions. Diplomacy was at risk. We had businesspeople and fundraisers massaging the sore and stretched muscles of foreign relations instead of experienced professionals seasoned in cross-cultural field work and versed in local issues. Sponsoring this amendment seemed like the right thing to do, so I agreed to offer the amendment on the House floor, unaware that my own good-heartedness and smart thinking were rooted to a thick coat of foolish naivety.

I had no idea when I got up to explain my amendment that I'd be taking on, front and center, the mythically powerful legislator Wayne Hays, who chaired the Foreign Affairs subcommittee that oversaw the State Department's budget and programs. A rude awakening awaited me.

As I was explaining the amendment and the good reasons for offering it, Chairman Hays, who also chaired the House Administration Committee, seemed both amused and irritated that a freshman member would dare to offer an amendment without having cleared it with him and the floor manager beforehand. Others in the chamber grasped what was happening and settled in to see how the strong-willed chairman would crush his prey. I was a field mouse in the paws of a tomcat, and afternoon entertainment to the already initiated.

Hays was renowned for attacking anyone who dared to challenge him. If you crossed him, he would stoop so low as to cut off the air conditioning in your office in the middle of August. A July 24, 1972 *Wall Street Journal* article described the "acid-tongued" congressman "as being devastating in a debate—he is so genuinely mean and cantankerous that many colleagues shrink from confrontations with him. Quoting a congressman who said "getting into a debate with him is like wrestling a skunk, except the skunk doesn't smell."

As I concluded and sat down, initially content with myself, I had no idea who this "cantankerous" chairman was whom I dared to confront with my innocent little proposal. An annoyed Wayne Hays appeared like a huge grizzly bear about to emasculate both the amendment and its freshman sponsor. He ended in his typical haughty tone, "And finally, Mr. Speaker, I have another, more personal reason for opposing the amendment. I fully expect someday to be named ambassador to France, and I will not allow this amendment to get in my way!" There were chuckles in the audience.

The amendment was treated to a quick death, which sent its neophyte author into humiliating retreat.

A year later in 1976, Wayne Levere Hays himself was sent into his own humiliating retreat. Indeed, he was forced to resign amid a sassy sex scandal that brought this Capitol Hill titan to his knees. He would never make it to Paris, although more and more campaign contributors would continue to find themselves at the helm of American embassies around the world as compensation for their pecuniary support. Hays, rather, found himself embroiled in a national scandal that forced him out of office for good, thanks to one mistreated and apparently voluptuous female named Elizabeth Ray.

Hays had occupied two positions in Congress that had collectively given him the leverage of vise-grips over all of the whole tribe. As chairman of the Foreign Affairs subcommittee that presided over the State Department budget, he had undeniable clout with the administration. His travels abroad were not unlike those of a Head of State, thanks to the State Department catering to his every whim and his cozy relationship with then Secretary Henry Kissinger.

But it was the House Administration Committee that gave him the levers of power that he used capriciously to reward and punish his colleagues. Only a few members wanted to be on the Administration Committee, intimidated by the chairman's absolute power. He acted like he was the mayor of the capitol since he presided over Members' budgets, their parking spaces, and a random array of perks that members savored, needed, lived by....

Wayne Hays was also known for using this position to bully members and staff, dispensing both favors and punishment as he saw fit. He was the most feared person on Capitol Hill, with power that rivaled even the Speaker Carl Albert.

It's a wonder how Congressman Hays held on to his chairmanship during the '74 revolt. I attribute this to his being good at strategy and at manipulative schmoozing. With calculated coyness, he hosted a series of luncheons, inviting the newly elected members to come and discuss their aspirations as hopeful first termers. He quickly agreed to give them more discretion on budgets, unlimited trips to their districts, funds for sending out newsletters, and other admin knickknacks. He won them over. Some of us.

Chairing the House Administration Committee came with crude authority over colleagues to be sure, but the position also carried some risks. Wayne Hays finally stepped in a honey trap of his own making and merited the humiliation that awaited him. He would ultimately be forced to resign, as were two of his predecessors who also crossed the line and were thrown in the clink. Maybe the job lent itself to the abuse that it enticed, but in any case, Hays was the granddaddy of abuse.

Wayne Hays didn't only delight in settling personal scores with Members, he also had a habit of employing young women who had blatantly limited office abilities beyond satisfying his personal needs. In today's gender climate, one would assume that Hays would have been strung up much sooner than he was in the less vigilant '70s. Eventually, one of his employed prey, Ms. Elizabeth Ray, settled a score with him that shattered his dominant position on Capitol Hill.

If you are wondering what he actually did and why she was so upset, let me tell you. There is satisfaction in naming the perpetrators of cruelty. Despite their two-year secret affair where Ms. Rey was paid with public funds to bed the slimy Ohioan, Wayne Hays had recently divorced his wife and was preparing a full-blown wedding reception to none other than his replacement woman, his district assistant, whom he had been taking up with at the same time he was seeing Ms. Rey on the sly. It was actually a bit hard to know who was the legitimate mistress. He seemed to have been cheating on everyone. The wedding was to be held in the US

Capitol, which in itself was unusual, and Hays had his new hometown honey flown in for the big shindig. As a precaution, he instructed the Capitol Police to make sure that they prevented a certain Elizabeth Ray from entering the gala room should she happen to show up. Ray, it was known, had claimed to be okay with the nuptials, but not being allowed to attend the wedding party and having the police alerted to block her sent her anger spiraling into an uncontrollable tornado, and her desire for public revenge rose to an F5!

Bad press has always been a good way to avenge wrongdoing in Washington, and Ms. Ray gave no pause before being contacted by the all-powerful *Washington Post*. Their investigating team was eager to offer her an extensive interview, and Ms. Ray gleefully dangled quotes that she knew would be delightfully damaging to the congressman with the warped libido.

"I can't type, I can't file, I can't even answer the phone," she told the reporter, although she was collecting a staff salary. "I was good enough to be his mistress for two years, but not good enough to be invited to his wedding. I'm on the Oversight Committee, but I call it the Out-of-Sight Committee," she continued.

When asked if she hated Congressman Hays, she replied, "I don't hate him. I'm a nervous wreck; I'm afraid of him. There are ten or fifteen other offices on the Hill where I know girls who have had to do this to get a job. Only mine is so cruel; the other congressmen, at least, treat them like a date."

She offered plenty of fodder, but it was not Elizabeth Ray who finally brought down Wayne Hays. It was Ben Bradlee, the iconic managing editor of the *Washington Post*, who commandeered the death blow. Hays had made some disparaging comments directed at Ben Bradlee, and the award-winning editor of Watergate fame assigned a team of *Post* reporters to continue interviewing the vulnerable Elizabeth Ray as she continued to let out office secrets that went beyond pillow talk.

Ever since the day that Wayne Hays had shot down my amendment, whenever I saw him in the corridors of the capitol and House office buildings, I would try to avoid crossing his path, fearing even more reprisal. He was that intimidating. I wasn't alone in feeling such disdain. Representative Phillip Burton from California was quoted in the *Washington Post* as portraying Hays as "the meanest man in Congress. He's also the most powerful. Everyone is afraid of him."

In the midst of the Hays scandal, I was seated in an empty House chamber one day, pondering over an upcoming vote when suddenly, out of nowhere, Wayne Hays in the flesh sits down right next to me. There are over 500 seats in the chamber, and although members are free to wander around at will, chat with colleagues, or rush in and out before and after votes, Hays chose to settle down right next to me.

My God, I was thinking. *Why is he doing this?* Was this more intimidation? I was puzzled. Although shamed, Wayne Hays was still in charge and reigned supreme while denying the embroiled embarrassment of his sex scandal.

There was a prolonged silence as we both looked out over the floor. I was asking myself, *What should I do? Do I start talking to him? Maybe I could graciously move away? Was there a way to escape graciously?* Obviously, he had intentions or he would not be sitting there next to me. There are 420 empty seats. I nervously sat, waiting for him to act. The silence was deafening.

Finally, he broke, "Do you go to a church in this area?"

I replied plainly, "Yes, the National Presbyterian Church."

Two more minutes passed, then he continued. "Does it have a good pastor?"

"In fact, it does. Louie Evans is his name. He is highly regarded and a good friend."

Surprised, I had no idea where this was going. He did not come across as mean-spirited. He seemed reflective, even humble. More silence, then he began to unwind a story about an experience he had had a few days earlier in his district in Ohio.

"For the first time ever, I attended a Catholic Church service in Columbus. As I was leaving, the priest said to me, 'Congressman, we've been praying for you, please know that our thoughts and hearts are with you during this difficult time.' Can you believe that?" he went on. "Someone I don't know. Now I'm in this horrible situation, and he is praying for me." He shook his head, like he had encountered an act of grace for the first time in his life, like he couldn't understand why someone he did not know would care about his well-being. Like he expected to be judged, and he wasn't.

I didn't have many words to say in return, but I did say this, "That's what faith is about, loving and supporting others, especially during difficult times."

He sat there a few more minutes in silence, then said, "Thanks," and got up and left. As he walked away, I sat there stunned that this guy whom I had avoided and feared had now revealed a touch of humility that was rarely shown on Capitol Hill. I felt his pain, and although I had good reason to have no empathy for this abusive individual, I did feel his pain.

For the next month, before he relinquished his chairmanship of the House Administration Committee, I was surprised that Wayne Hays called me on the phone several times late in the evening at my residence. Mostly, I listened. There was so much going on in his life, no letting up on the ugly controversy. He was tortured about whether to leave Congress or not and struggled with how his life had turned upside down.

On September 1, 1976, he resigned on the floor of the House, a broken man.

A few months later, Carolyn and I happened to be at a fellowship retreat in Ohio not far from Wayne Hays' district residence, and we decided we'd stop by as a courtesy. We made contact and he and his wife invited us spend the rest of the weekend with them. Although hesitant, we agreed.

I got to know more about him personally, and our talk led to a shared interest in antiques. We visited a few shops in a nearby town and eyed a few nice things but bought nothing. Several months later, a walnut end table with a mahogany drawer was delivered to our DC residence. It was the same piece of furniture that we had admired at an antique store on that weekend but had not purchased. Hays somehow found out that we'd admired it, bought it, and had it delivered with a kind note of appreciation. This was not the same Wayne Hayes I had first encountered when naively offering an amendment to his bill in the House chamber. He was good at logistics, although not his own.

As I reflect now on the Wayne Hays episode, what stands out first to me is how a thirty-three-year-old escort ruined the career and life of the most powerful, albeit heedless, member of Congress at the time. The tale demonstrates to me how vulnerable we all are regardless of the positions we hold. And how tables can and will turn. Secondly, I ask myself why would this fallen man turn to me, not his friends or supporters or family, during a moment of severe personal crisis? Why me whom he had chosen to humiliate only months earlier? Being so dominant and feared, there were few he could turn to. Is that why he chose me? The clarity that I saw too was that it takes a personal tragedy to unthrone the powerful and render the mean king into a simple and humble man. It took the pain of public defeat and the plunge of being exposed and shamed for him to begin to understand the greater meaning of his life. I'm not sure he was ever redeemed, but there was a religious message here in the story of Wayne Hays. There was a form of divine justice that was served in the end.

Wayne Hays quietly remained involved in local Ohio politics until he died relatively forgotten on February 10, 1989.

IV. Faith in the Public Square

CHAPTER 15

BIPARTISAN SOULMATES

"How is it possible you can be both a Democrat and a Christian?" That was the first question I was asked in the Q and A session following a speech I delivered at a faith-based organization's event in Seattle over forty years ago. I remember the question better than my response, but I should have reminded the gentleman who asked to consider that Jesus rode into Jerusalem on a donkey, not an elephant!

Once you enter the public square as an elected official, the spotlight is on you, and your faith matters to others. Whether it is your adversaries, the skeptical media, or even supporters, there will be plenty of scrutiny, even distrust. Your character is called into question nonstop. Your moral fiber is always on the line, although some political figures manage to twist and slide and escape the judgment that they merit. And others get squarely called out and dragged before the court of public scrutiny and sometimes the court of law.

In contemporary American life, it is often said that people, even friends and family members, who want to stay on good terms should avoid two topics: politics and religion. Both are capable of sparking a lively discussion, but to mix them will likely prove contentious. I've had to deal with this over the years because of my faith and involvement in politics and the inseparable nature of both.

How do we reconcile faith and politics in the public square? When we speak of religion, we are talking about absolutes and when we speak of politics, we focus on the art of compromise. So how can you compromise absolutes? It is difficult to be sure, which is why our Founding Fathers wisely put some distance between church and state. To bring either religious certitude to the political arena or an overriding political agenda to religion—as some televangelists have done–can be divisive and destructive.

Indeed, religion shapes our view of the world and our notion of right and wrong. Politics is a process by which we translate this notion into public policy. Even in a pluralistic society, religion and politics are inseparable.

The question is always present—how does one's faith shape his or her views in a political context? For some citizens, it is easy to dismiss or ignore as they proceed to weigh the other factors on taking positions or preparing to vote. For others, having values rooted in faith is essential in defining who they are and how they deal with the issues. However, any public statement on how one's religious beliefs determined a particular vote, even on social issues, must be made with caution. Most members of Congress face issues where they are conflicted but are still expected to give a full explanation on how or why they voted in a particular way.

I am comforted in these situations by the words of Isaiah, who gave us a perspective that is insightful, a reminder that "God's ways are not your ways; neither are his thoughts your thoughts." So, if you want to be exalted, you must humble yourself. To become rich, you must become poor. To be a great leader, you must be a servant. This is a useful guide for leadership.

Any Democrat who professes to have faith must cope with skepticism and questions. Among liberal supporters, many believe such a holistic approach will distort how one thinks and votes. Those in the Christian community have doubts as well, believing if they are God's chosen ones, why aren't they Republican?

Do we measure a person's faith by party affiliation? Do we judge a person solely on the basis of voting or taking stands on particular issues? Or is it more about a person's character and integrity that radiates beyond a voting record? Unfortunately, the American public is more inclined to cast votes based on a politician's political affiliation and voting record than on the personal qualities of character and integrity of the individual. As we are voting in the chambers on the floor of the House, I've often looked across the aisle at many Republicans whom I respect despite our differences, and wondered about the souls within the women and men about to vote.

Congress is a representative of American diversity—geographic, political, ethnic, cultural, ideological, sources of both strengths and potential threats to our democracy. Our challenge, in the halls of Congress and beyond, is to achieve consensus while ensuring the protection of minority rights. The strength of our democracy, we must remember, is not the protection of the masses, it's the protection of the smallest minority, the least popular idea. The chain is only as strong as the weakest link.

There is unity for those of us who share a common faith, not necessarily a common religion. We know God is sovereign. We know our deity causes "all things to work together for good for those who love him." We are confident that there is a plan for each of us, as individuals and as members of Congress. We have each been placed here for a purpose, regardless if we are Democrats or Republicans, conservatives or liberals. Having differences is central to being alive—family, workplace, public service—and differences often lead to arguments and conflict, but they also lead to understanding and consensus and richer solutions. Is there an alternative? Is it possible to resolve our differences with a loving and forgiving spirit? With respect for one another? With prayer? Is there a higher calling beyond our party and political leaders, our campaign funders, and lobbyists seeking favor?

"He speaks of hands and arms, each having different functions and that in this diversity you still have unity." That was Paul in the New Testament. Why is it not possible for us to have that viewpoint in our political system? Good question.

From the chronological moment of void following my senatorial loss, there is particular poignancy in telling the tale of our sacred foursome of friends. Four politicians. Four friends. We all lost. And thus set off on a new definition of winning. My conclusion was actually my beginning.

A precious moment in Congress occurred early in my second term in 1977 when I was approached by Doug Coe, head of the National Prayer Breakfast, who asked if I would consider meeting with three other newly elected fellow congressmen on a regular basis. I questioned, "Why is this necessary?" but I respected Doug and quickly consented. Of course, it was not about any issue or policy, and I had no clue about the other three he wanted to include.

I learned later that Doug Coe had been thinking about this since his arrival in Washington, DC four years earlier. The idea was to set up small prayer groups of congressmen who would set aside their political differences in a setting to encourage some bonding in their faith and friendship. It was not an easy task as Doug learned when he began approaching several members to commit to taking time from their hectic and busy schedules. Indeed, convincing a congressman's scheduler to confirm a meeting for such a purpose was highly unlikely. Doug then opted for his only alternative, catching up with a member heading to the House chamber to vote, frantically explaining why being part of a small group would matter.

Finally, he got four House members to commit to coming together once a week, which they did faithfully for several years. Then they all headed for other destinations. One, Gerald Ford, became president of the United States and tapped his friend, Melvin Laird, to be his Secretary of Defense. Of the remaining two, Al Quie was elected governor of Minnesota and Charles Goodell was appointed to serve in the US Senate. Our small group would be Doug Coe's second attempt to faithfully meet every week, which we did for twelve years.

As we were taking seats around the table, it became obvious that the four of us represented the gamut of political diversity, which was Doug's intent in bringing us together. Get people whose politics were different to not only sit together, but to eat together, talk, and to ultimately realize that even when we were driven by opposing points of view, we could also be unified in our love for each other and for what just might be best for the world. Among the four of us, our ideas covered the full political spectrum: one on the right, the other on the left, and two distinctly different moderates. Two of us were from the north, the other two from the south.

There was Paul Trible, a Republican, elected in 1976 to represent Virginia's 1st Congressional District, an area that included historic Williamsburg. His wife, Rosemary, was a former Miss Junior America and she stayed close to his side throughout his time in public office. Paul later served in the US Senate for one term from 1983–1989, until he opted to run for governor where he was clearly the early favorite to capture the GOP nomination, but ultimately, he lost to another Republican and returned to the private sector. Paul became president of Christopher Newport University, transforming it into a world-class institution, widely recognized as his legendary achievement.

Bill Nelson was a Floridian from the 9th Congressional District, which included Orlando. A moderate Democrat, Nelson had a promising career from the outset, believing he had a shot for the governorship of the Sunshine State in 1990, but he was unsuccessful. He held a statewide office until he was finally elected to the US Senate in 2000. Bill also became the second sitting member of Congress to become an astronaut. Our group attended the Space Shuttle Columbia's launching on January 12, 1986.

The third of our group, Tom Evans, served in the US House from 1977 to 1983, and once chaired the National Republican Party. Tom had close ties to President Ronald Reagan and other high-ranking Republicans, but was defeated in his attempt at a fourth term in 1982, due in part to false allegations that were heavily covered by hostile local media. His wife, Mary Page, was a renowned artist on the East Coast.

And then, of course, there was me. That was our sacred fearless foursome, which Doug Coe coerced into having lunch together for no apparent reason.

The luncheon, of course, was simply to get us acquainted. More importantly Doug wanted us to commit to meeting every week in order to build close ties among ourselves and to include, by extension, our respective families. Doug believed that the godliness of being together would suffice in our overcoming the political differences that otherwise would divide us. And this he'd be able to hold up as an example for others. We agreed. We met, we ate, and we agreed to keep meeting.

The more complicated issue was scheduling space in congressional offices, which was a formidable challenge. The demands led by committee hearings and mark-up sessions, relentless voting on the House floor, multiple visits from our congressional district, and public appearances made it hard for the four of us to settle on a fixed time and place to get together. We were convinced though that we needed to commit to making our weekly meeting a priority or we'd not do it. None of us wanted to disappoint Doug Coe. We informed our staff that these get-togethers were an urgent necessity. Oregon's Senator Mark Hatfield, who chaired the powerful Senate Appropriations Committee, came to the rescue and offered us his personal office in the US capitol for our weekly gatherings, and that helped a great deal.

His personal office in the capitol was one of the crown jewels on the Senate side, an entitlement if you were chairman of the powerful Senate Appropriations Committee. As we set aside our political and policy differences at the door step, entering the senator's office was not unlike being in an elegant living room in a classic colonial home, with a marble fireplace, treasured artwork, an iconic Persian rug, and a magnificent view of the Washington Monument. Once we arrived, nobody wanted to leave.

Over the next twelve years, we fulfilled that commitment, not merely meeting every Wednesday but also by building close relationships that we came to cherish. None of us had any idea about the profound effect this would have on our lives. It was clear we were coming together as close friends now, leaving outside the door whatever issues, politics, and votes that would otherwise have us disagreeing or arguing. We learned not to judge.

Comically, when a vote was called in the House chamber, we would rush over to the House floor to cast our votes, almost always taking opposite sides, then rush back to the Hatfield room with no disruption on the spirit of our coming together. We were equally amazed how our differences never seemed to have mattered much. We even prayed for each other. As our bonding became increasingly evident among our colleagues in the House, we delighted in watching their surprise in observing how our friendships were transcending the political reasons that we were supposed to be at odds with each other. This definitely sent a message, one that has greatly dissipated in today's Congress, which may be one of the great understatements of all time. Doug Coe knew what he was doing, and there are moments when I pray that another Doug Coe may bless the halls of our government.

Our bonding as individual members of Congress spilled over to our families. Indeed, our spouses and children would meet for dinners and other occasions, and as families, we celebrated events as our children grew up. Throughout the twelve years, not one single moment was compromised by political differences. Coe's prophesy that love was stronger than division was proving to work.

The four of us made a joint appearance before the National Association of Evangelicals Seminar in April 1980, which Paul Trible wrote about. "Whatever our differences—philosophy, geography, party—they don't mean quite as much as they did in the past," he stated. "We are there to encourage and support one another, to help each other through the very difficult times in our private and our public lives. My good friend, Don Bonker, and I cancel each other out almost every time that we vote. As to political identity, I am considered a conservative Republican and he is a liberal Democrat. I have come to know and love him as a brother in Christ."

The April 28, 1980 *Congressional Record* included a presentation of our group.

By 1988, each of us had reached inevitable crossroads in our political careers. We were still young with attractive families, and, of course, we were not lacking in ambition. Having a seat in the House of Representatives often served as a launching pad for higher office, be it US senator or a state governorship. Each of us was conscious of this as we expanded our political and financial support, wanting to be prepared for the right opportunity. For the three of us, 1988–1990 appeared to be a timely time to "go for it." It's a rare opportunity when there is no incumbent, yet the stakes are extremely high because we were giving up our current elected offices, attempting to gain a higher one. These were the most important decisions in our respective careers.

For a year or so, when we came together at Hatfield's capitol office, these decisions were foremost in our minds. As we shared the challenges of new statewide campaigns, it was like we were on the same team, although the elections were unrelated and party politics had nothing to do with our allegiance. It was unbelievable that a small group of Republicans and Democrats would meet weekly to offer encouragement and prayers for one another, even when the outcome might affect who controlled the US Senate. This is what we treasured about our special relationship. And we knew our model of brotherhood was one that needed to be shared.

When election day arrived and the votes were tallied and results posted in our respective states, the outcome was in no uncertain terms shocking.

It was a stunning low for each of us.

In one fell swoop, our public careers appeared to be over, and suddenly, we had to face the certainty of uncertainty. In the void of our newly gained positions as defeated members of Congress, we decided to take a post-campaign break. We needed to take emotional inventory, set our sights straight, and invent new futures. One of us suggested we get outside the parameters of our normal cultural comfort zone, and that resonated as smart. Collectively, we agreed to spend a week together in the independent island nation, which was not far, English-speaking, with good hotels, and minimal risk of our getting Montezuma's revenge—an ideal location for meditation over our unexpected losses and uncertainty in each of our lives. The charming island, with its mild climate and white sands, would serve us well as a backdrop to discuss and better understand the outcome of the election and how our political experiment and love feast had now left us unemployed and out of power...and confused.

As believers, foremost, we wanted to try to understand the role of God's will. We expected the Lord's blessing would be in victory, not defeat. We thought we deserved to win because we were driven by public service. Our decision to run and our respective campaigns had been wrapped around prayer, seeking God's direction and support. We were faithful and had good intentions, believing we could better serve the Lord at a higher level. What had gone wrong?

The flight to Hamilton, Bermuda was only two hours and ten minutes, but the island country was an entire reality away. This is where we'd contemplate the deeper meaning of defeat. How could we better serve humanity as losers? This led us to the conclusion that divine purpose lay with something beyond winning an election. We also were consciences of what we had individually and collectively known for years. His ways were often opposite our ways. There was greater meaning in the events life served us than the events themselves.

It was that victory which merited celebration. All candidates emerged with pride and confidence and embraced the power and influence that came with the higher office. But what about the office that was even higher than the higher office? The true corner office with the view over the whole? The Senate of the big picture?

We sat at a wrought iron table on the greenest of grass in the garden near our hotel and ordered the best tall glasses of iced tea I had ever had. Here, we talked about pride and humility, the prime tenants of the Holy Book, and how that shaped who we were. But the theme that we could not ignore was our coping with defeat. Were we actually able to build more character and greater depth from experiencing defeat? Would defeat make us stronger and better people? I watched four white egrets as they walked across the tenth green of the golf course our hotel was located on. I identified with them, so much in harmony with the green and yet not at all golfers.

Our long commitment to these two precious groups was a testimony of brotherly love that transcended our political differences. But was it enough? Could we have done more? At the time, I had been reading several books about England's legendary William Wilberforce, whose small prayer group had shaken the country far beyond what his close friend, Prime Minister William Pitt, could have ever imagined accomplishing.

William Wilberforce was only twenty-one years of age when he was first elected to parliament. A conservative from a prominent family, he was known for his jovial personality and quick wit. Once he arrived in London, Wilberforce was cheerfully welcomed in the elite private clubs and societies as he quickly embraced the pleasure of political networking. He spent evenings with friends, consuming sumptuous dinners accompanied by multiple bottles of wine followed by a theatrical performance, dancing, or a night of gambling.

London in the 1770s was the apex of political and economic power, but it was also a time of social and moral decadence. Charles Dickens' opening lines of *A Tale of Two Cities*, "It was the best of times; it was the worst of times," captured the mood of London. While Wilberforce was enjoying the best of times, for most of the population, life could not have been worse.

As Wilberforce was pursuing his political career, his mother invited him on a tour of the continent. Wilberforce agreed and asked his old school master from Hull, Isaac Milner, to join on the trip. As their discussion shifted from politics to religion Wilberforce agreed to Miller's request that he read the Scriptures daily. That is what planted the seed in Wilberforce. His frivolous nature changed and he decided to make tough choices about his personal and political life.

Chuck Colson penned in an article in *Christianity Today* on September 6, 1985. Chuck Colson captured that moment of epiphany. "On this foggy Sunday morning in 1787, as Wilberforce sat at his desk, he thought about his conversion: Had God seen fit to save him only for the eternal rescue of his own soul, or also to bring His light to the world around him? True Christianity must go deeper. It must not only save but serve. It must bring God's compassion to the oppressed, as well as oppose the oppressors."

Wilberforce's mind clicked, and he dipped his pen in the inkwell. "Almighty God has set before me two great objectives," he wrote, his heart suddenly pumping with passion, "the abolition of the slave trade and the reformation of manners."

That moment led to one of the epic struggles of modern history. William Wilberforce felt he was called to stand against the entrenched evils of his day—the self-indulgent hedonism of a society, moral decadence, and the slave trade that underwrote those excesses. As he noted, "this barbaric practice of trafficking in human flesh for private gain."

Ending the slave trade would be a lifetime commitment, but it was a daunting task. Suddenly, in February 1788, Wilberforce fell gravely ill and he asked his close friend from his college days to promptly introduce the issue of abolition in Parliament on his behalf. William Pitt, who became prime minister at age twenty-four, was reluctant to take on the economic powers but agreed to do so out of the warmth of their friendship.

After twenty-five years of repeated attempts and contentious debates, on July 26, 1833, the bill for the abolition of slavery finally passed its second reading in the House of Commons.

Wilberforce's triumph over slave trafficking and his other notable accomplishments were not done solo. He resided in a fashionable villa in southwest of London near where other prominent and wealthy evangelical Anglicans lived, who shared Wilberforce's political agenda. Known as the Clapham Sect, mostly conservatives, five of them served as members of parliament and were prepared to commit their wealth and power to confront social injustice and to reach out to the underprivileged.

They met in the evenings and on weekends to discuss slave trade, penal reform, education for an illiterate populace, especially children employed in factories. They worked on parliamentary reform, wrote publications, and spoke to the needy. Wilberforce and his group gave away most of their wealth to support programs which included the Education of Africans, the Society for Bettering the Condition of the Poor, and even the Society for the Relief of Debtors, which helped those imprisoned for debt.

Colson shared the details of his visit to London and visiting the site where the Clapham Sect had been located. But he was surprised by the lack of acknowledgement of their ministry and notable deeds. Colson then recounted a deep spiritual moment when he "stopped and stared across the green. In my mind's eye," he wrote, "I began to see row upon row of black men and women walking right across the soft grass. I could hear the clanging of the chains as they fell from arms and legs." Upon rereading this, my convictions were affirmed. We need to be conscious all the time of the lessons of history, of the moral choices we make every day. We cannot be content with passive acceptance of things that are ethically wrong even when it is expedient to remain silent.

My mind just flashed on the portrait of Abraham Lincoln that I have hanging on my wall at home. Printed on the reverse side is a list of Lincoln's twenty-six failures and defeats, including the nine elections he lost before being elected the sixteenth president of the United States; the poor boy known for his honesty, Honest Abe who also was deeply reflective and submerged in long and dark moods of melancholy. The most respected and beloved president in our history, yet Lincoln's career was more about defeat than victory. More grade schools across America are called Lincoln School than the name of any other. There are 205 American towns named after Abraham Lincoln. It was his character and humble leadership that got us through the Civil War and the most traumatic national crisis in our national history. The conviction of Wilberforce and Lincoln, this was the principled axis and personal courage that I have returned to for strength and inspiration. Now, I'd be going to a neutral place to contemplate our moral compass with three men whose lives and work I aligned with and who continued to affirm what I believed about humanity.

Bermuda gave us a better perspective going forward. Losing an election introduced us to another purpose or higher calling as we were reminded. "Many are the plans in a man's heart," Paul the Apostle, Saul of Tarsus, took up the baton and finished Proverbs 19:21 with "But it is the Lord's purpose that prevails." Our key was to contemplate that purpose, to decide what we were placed on this earth to do.

As we were enjoying our post-campaign break in Bermuda, it was time to contemplate God's purpose in each of our lives going forward. At that moment, no clue about the future. We could only commit to prayer, which we did. Upon return and closing down our congressional offices and preparing for the next steps, God's purpose was starting to unfold in each of our lives. Bill Nelson was elected to a statewide office, then on to serve in the US Senate for eighteen years. Paul Trible became president of Christopher University in Virginia, a position far more rewarding than had he been elected governor of Virginia. And I continued my work internationally, joining APCO Worldwide where I remained for thirty years. I also served as president of the International Management Development Institute (IMDI) and was chairman of the International Human Rights Foundation.

Thirty-five years later, as we came together on the northern neck of Virginia, an estate that Paul Trible had inherited, it became immensely clear that, in retrospect, we all felt abundantly blessed by that fateful election. Loss was only loss when you learned nothing more and better about yourself. Defeat was only defeat if it diminished the person you were or allowed bitterness to cancel the positive that you were always able to give form to. That was a narrative so familiar for anyone reading the Old Testament. It's not always about victory, but God's purpose.

CHAPTER 16

To Thine Own Self Be True

A half century after John F. Kennedy wrote *Profiles in Courage* for which he won a Pulitzer Prize—a work which portrays eight individuals who served in the US Senate and who had the courage and integrity to take great political and personal risk to make right decisions—I found myself witnessing the erosion of courage among our elected ones. Powerful economic forces have become routinely toxic in the influencing of how votes are being cast by our elected officials. The very integrity of the legislative branch, the sanctity of public trust of our government is what is being compromised. Homeland Security may be looking in all the wrong places.

Neatly, we call this silent hand of decay special interests. It is one thing for an industry or corporation to wish to defend and protect its core businesses and share prices. It is quite another thing when its method of defense rubs against or jeopardizes the larger interests or safety of American citizens and the security and well-being of the nation. And significantly when those efforts are extended to include the moral appropriation of the individuals to whom the public trust had been granted.

When I worked for Senator Maureen Neuberger in the mid-1960s, the political parties and their pillars of support—mostly organized labor for Democrats, mostly corporate business interests for the Republicans—were the flavor of the day when it came to attempting to sway legislators. Today, the political landscape has been wildly disfigured from those less perverse days. Very big money and super PACs—political action committees—operating mostly within the permissive guidelines of law, now dominate the engine house of our political system. Accordingly, the cost of staging an electoral campaign, primaries included, has soared. The higher the cost of running a campaign, and the more cash an election effort requires to secure victory, the greater the advantage is to incumbents and others who have secured the backing of one or several special interests. Members of Congress were all vulnerable to the high pressure applied by the leadership of their parties, sometimes at the county level and sometimes at the national level, to raise tens and often hundreds of thousands of dollars needed to sustain a campaign or the PAC, which nourishes selected candidates. Candidates are often reluctant to comply because they know the compromises that await them down the line, but they also know that supporting the PAC in question is a must if they want to win or survive. Further down the line, chairing a committee is the real way of ensuring that one's work in Congress is impactful and will be ornately tied to this communion with the PAC leaders and their agenda.

Where does the money come from? We've often called out Wall Street, lobbying firms, and law firms representing special interests, corporations, trade and commodity organizations, and innocuous looking committees and organizations which backers have specific, targeted agendas. To draw from Donald Trump's 1987 book penned by Tony Schwartz, *The Art of the Deal*, consider this standard scenario: A lobbyist shows up at a small reception to whisper something in a congressman's ear, with a big check already prepared in an envelope. An expected deliverable is articulated, intimated, and expected. For many individuals in Congress, this is disconcerting. But the check is a necessary evil, and there are always gray zones in which deliverables can be contextualized, defended, and explained. Political survival is the elephant in the room. You want to remain in office, you'll learn to cope with the reality of our political system. The open mind is perversely mixed with the political compromise. The sharp line that defines integrity is now blurry and thick. Integrity slips from the zone of moral absolute into a bloated zone of comfort. "What do I believe in?" becomes "What can I live with?"

I have often been asked what I've considered to be the most important thing about being a congressman. My response has always been and continues to be summed up in one word—integrity. And I often find myself thinking about a passage that guides my own behavior, found in Psalms 15, "He who walks with integrity, and works righteousness, and speaks the truth in his heart. He does not slander with his tongue, nor does evil to his neighbor. He who does these things will never be shaken." I noticed long ago that the word there is "shaken," not fallen or defeated. The moral corruption that has leaked into the soul of the political system is about shaking up the clarity, rendering integrity into a blurred discussion or a negotiation. A shakedown is extortion. All a special interest needs to do is to shake you. If you shake, you'll accommodate those who wish to appropriate a slice of your independent thinking in exchange for a slice of your assured survival. This is the perverse side of win-win. This is a narcissistic arrangement, and yet one that has come to dominate so many relationships—Republican and Democrat, right wing and left wing, young and old.

I like to draw on the legendary Mohandas K. Gandhi who defined integrity by warning against what he called the seven social sins: politics without principle, wealth without work, commerce without morality, pleasure without conscience, education without character, science without humanity, and worship without sacrifice. He pointed to the essential relationship between our public life and our ethical stance. We should print Gandhi's guiding points and tape them to our bathroom mirrors, to our refrigerator doors, inside our lockers, on the dashboards of our vehicles, and adopt them as screensavers on our computers and devices.

What once made the American political system different than others, China's or Russia's for example, is that moral character of the elected official had been embedded into our political ethos. Morality was related to the spiritual values of the republic. There were well thought out reasons why institutional religion and the state were designed to remain separate, while the moral values and the baseline of common good were inscribed into the bedrock of our written political doctrines.

Moral issues must be at the starting point for all public debate. In today's political coverage and the endless polling of voters, moral issues tend to be narrowly defined and often become the basis for conflict and judgment instead of acting as our higher ground, our perpetual search for the overarching common good.

As a candidate once forty years ago speaking at a faith-based organization in Seattle, I remember I was asked, "Is it possible to be both a Democrat and a Christian?" Jesus rode into Jerusalem on a donkey, not an elephant, I shared and the room glowed with laughter. I have come to be worried about both the donkey and the elephant today, but the story still brings a smile.

The Old Testament has many narratives about the most unlikely figures being chosen leaders. Like Joseph and Moses, whose responses were "Why me? No, I stutter, I can't speak well. I've been in prison." Becoming a leader is not about self-promotion or being driven by pure ambition. The best example in our times has been South Africa's Nelson Mandela, a man of conscience who endured twenty-seven years in prison before being asked by his captors to lead the same country that imprisoned him and to shepherd South Africa through a tumultuous transition from white rule under a racist apartheid system to a truly democratically elected government, representing a predominantly black majority.

When I was a county official, I recall aspiring political wannabes would often come to my office seeking my support. I would inquire each time about their motives and ask them why they wanted to be a legislator. What was their purposes for wanting to serve others? What did they hope to accomplish? For many, they struggled to explain their purpose or mission. I could sense their motivation was more often about personal ambition than about standing in the public arena. How could one hope to help define a nation if he or she could not properly define himself or herself?

We didn't always have blue states and red states. The division of America came with the Gulf War and the Bush years. The country took on a deep fracture following 9/11 and the world took cover behind the large schism of "us and them." Friends and families were faced with two options in order to remain on good terms and avoid venom at dinner tables and around Thanksgiving turkeys—avoid politics and religion. Either would spark discussions that would prove contentious. As a man of faith and a politician, my whole existence lives in this now avoided zone.

We are now living in an era when ideological forces and the partisan divide are slowly replacing civility and integrity in what has become a flawed political system. Without leaders of moral conviction, our nation will continue on the path of deterioration, as has been the case with all other nations in previous times.

How do we reconcile faith and politics in the public square? Religiosity is about moral absolutes while politics is about compromise. So how can you compromise absolutes? With difficulty. The Founding Fathers wisely put distance between church and state. But religion shapes our view of the world and our notion of right and wrong. Politics is a process by which we translate this notion into public policy. Even in a pluralistic society, religion and politics are inseparable.

Is it possible to resolve our differences by a loving and forgiving spirit, respect for one another, and by prayer? Is there a higher calling beyond our party and political leaders, our campaign funders, and lobbyists seeking favor? Isn't it possible for diverse viewpoints to feed the whole?

My suggestion to our leaders is to take note of the wisdom that William Shakespeare wrote into the celebrated speech of Polonius in the third scene of Act 1 of *Hamlet*: "This above all, to thine own self be true/ And it must follow, as the night the day/Thou canst not then be false to any man...."

CHAPTER 17

THE WAY TO RECONCILIATION

In October 1943, a man named Abraham Vereide was riding on the upper deck of the ferry *Chippewa*, crossing Seattle's Puget Sound on a lovely evening, when a stranger offered what was on his mind, "What a contrast this is to the war-torn world about us. There must be a way out of this mess." Vereide, a man of God, reminded him of what Jesus had said about the way. "Lord, we do not know where You are going, how can we know the way?" Citing John 14:1–6, Vereide added what Jesus said, "I am the way, and the truth and the life: no one comes to the father but by me."

I researched Vereide further and his comments on "the way," and stumbled on an essay he published in *The Seattle Times* in 1943 in the midst of World War II. He reminds us that the original Greek word for "way" as found in the *New Testament* is pronounced "*hodos*." Literally, it means "*road*," a route to a destination. In the figurative sense, it implies "a means toward something," a vehicle to a destination. "Testimonies from history came to mind of times when the people of 'the Way' had given a lead in national and international affairs," he wrote, adding that today, "parts of the human race had turned everyone to his own way— in self-will, rebellion, and disobedience, which is reflected in the present world conflict." Interested in this curious fellow, and especially in ways to help resolve moral conflict with political action, I kept reading. Abraham Vereide had arrived by boat in New York in 1905 as a nineteen-year-old Norwegian immigrant, a sheep farmer, a shepherd in search of something, perhaps his own way in the world. He moved west like a pilgrim, continuing all the way to Butte, Montana where he became an itinerant horseback circuit-riding pastor working throughout the state. In 1917, as a young man of thirty-one, he moved to Seattle and took up residence as a pastor at the Norwegian Danish Methodist Lutheran Episcopal Church. His zeal for preaching and his care for the poor inspired the city labor unions to set up an enterprise which combined industrial relief for workers with a training program for the handicapped.

That was the founding of Goodwill Industries of Seattle, Portland, and San Francisco. As head of Goodwill Industries, Vereide traveled throughout the United States championing for the down and out, the poor, handicapped, and depressed. Vereide came to the realization that as long as the leadership of the business, industrial, professional, and political communities ignored the plight of the poor, the underclass would never be addressed. Fellow Methodist clergyman, Edgar J. Helms, simultaneously opened an immigrants ministry in Boston, serving New England which emerged as the national headquarters for Goodwill Industries of America, and the two centers collectively become the core of one of the first and foremost charities for the needy in the world. It is unclear who or how this collaborative effort unfolded, and some sources cite Vereide as the initial founder, while others name Helms. The ambiguity of history is less important than that the will to help the disadvantaged had found resonance in the creation of a structure that had policy and vision at its core. From 1931 onwards, Vereide joined Helms on the East Coast and they ran the organization from Boston. Vereide also had befriended Arthur B. Langlie, who later became mayor of Seattle and governor of Washington State, and the association of these two men led to the beginning of the Prayer Breakfast, an idea that quickly spread to Oregon, San Francisco, Chicago, and finally, New York. Ten years later in 1941, Vereide met with a group of business and political friends who began to informally convene at the historic Willard Hotel near the White House in Washington, DC. Aside from being the place where Julia Ward Howe wrote *The Battle Hymn of the Republic* and where Abraham Lincoln was secretly lodged for more than a month until his inauguration day on March 4, 1861 due to imminent threat of assassination attempts, it is believed that the Willard Hotel lobby was the original source of the term lobbyist since Ulysses S. Grant liked to drink whiskey and smoke cigars there and opportunists corner him in the lobby and attempt to curry favor.

Vereide's business meetings at the Willard thus had real historical context. Following impassioned debate, the group managed to reach the consensus that "a leadership led by God" was the best way to cultivate, encourage, and inspire leaders at every level of society. A commitment to the will of God, His plan, empowered by His Spirit, was in the best overall interest of the nation and its citizens. In God we trust, we recall, is inscribed on our money. In America, our politics, our economic vitality, and our spiritual life are joined by a cohesive unity of belief. The group discussed many topics before embracing the edict that the Quaker William Penn had shared in inspiring the framers of the constitution: "Men must either be governed by God or ruled by tyrants."

Encouraged by that common thread, on January 22, 1943, Abraham Vereide met Vice President Henry Wallace at the University Club in Washington, DC following a game of squash. There is no historical account of who had won the game. The vice president, who had flirted with pursuits of spirituality, invited Abraham to ride back to the capital with him, and on their way, they discussed the idea of a small, off-the-record, private leadership group among members of the Senate. That initiative eventually became known as the Senate Breakfast Group, which also met at the Willard Hotel.

Whenever the group convened and began discussing political and personal matters, a variety of pastors and religious people would show up, offering quotations and little sermonettes, which was not always welcomed. The men talked privately and decided to move to the capitol and meet in a private room on the Senate side hoping to limit the involvement of pastors and others and ensuring greater discretion for senators only.

As the precursor to prayer on the Hill, organized private chat sessions remained like this until December 1952 when Senator Frank Carlson, a Republican from Kansas who would go on to become both a senator from Kansas and the governor of Kansas, had a meeting at campaign headquarters in New York with WWII hero, General Dwight D. Eisenhower, who had just won the presidential elections but had not yet taken office. Carlson had run Eisenhower's campaign efforts in Kansas and had no problem approaching the president-elect. Eisenhower hailed from Kansas himself and thus the men shared that source of common identity.

"General, I'd love to have you attend one of the Senate Prayer Breakfast meetings after your inauguration in January." Eisenhower's response, "I'd be delighted to," stunned him with pleasure, and he knew he was onto something much bigger. There was a place for spiritual pursuit within political life. This was the start of the Presidential Prayer Breakfast.

The House of Representatives had also begun to host its own weekly prayer group, and they came along to meet with the newly elected president. Open discussion included the organization of a National Prayer Breakfast that would bring together business and political leaders in a spirit of faith and unity. But the stumbling block was how to make this happen, and how to budget the undertaking. We were obliged to avoid using taxpayer dollars to fund such events. That was precisely when Senator Carlson recalled and recounted a discussion he had had with the illustrious Conrad Hilton, the owner of America's most prestigious hotel chain, the previous year during the 1952 National Republican Convention in Chicago. The Republicans came together to nominate Eisenhower, nicknamed Ike, and his running mate, Richard Nixon. The platform was to end the unpopular Korean War, develop nuclear weapons as our strongest message for deterrence, and to stop enemies of religious discrimination, which was part of the perceived threat of Communist infiltrators within the United States.

Senator Carlson's personal account of his dialogue with the hotel magnate Conrad Hilton went like this: "Upon his visit with General Eisenhower, I mentioned the next man to see was Dr. Billy Graham. Mr. Hilton said, 'You know, I'm a devout Catholic, and I've contributed to his work for years, and I've never met him. I want to meet him.' I got them together. As they were leaving, Mr. Hilton made this comment to me, 'Senator, any time I can be of help in a religious or a Christian cause, you call on me.' A year later, I called him in Beverly Hills and said, 'Conrad, you made a commitment last June.' 'What was it?' he asked. 'We want to have a prayer breakfast with the president of the United States. I want you to let us use the ballroom of the Hilton Hotel, and I want you to cover the expense of the breakfast.'"

Conrad Hilton complied.

The first National Prayer Breakfast (NPB) occurred in February 1953, and for the next sixty-five years, every NPB had taken place at the Hilton Hotel in Washington, DC. And every president since then has participated. That is how the National Prayer Breakfast got started and grew into a three-day event which would include 4,000 attendees. Eventually, the event took on an international dimension with over 1,500 leaders of all sorts from around the world wishing to attend the event, maneuvering in various ways to get onto the guest list. The Senate and House weekly prayer groups continued to function as the official hosts, but the NPB would soon need to be organized as a nonprofit organization and involve hundreds of volunteers for the annual occasion which began on the second Thursday of every February.

Although Abraham Vereide was the historic inspiration and founder of the National Prayer Breakfast, there was a young man he was mentoring, also from the Pacific Northwest, who would become his successor in the late 1960s, an extraordinary fellow named Doug Coe. For the next fifty years, Coe came to reign the NPB through his organization, the Fellowship Foundation, and emerged as something of an evangelist godfather to this high profile event. Influential and well-known, Coe curiously never became a household name, although US presidents, congressional leaders, foreign dignitaries, and others followed Doug Coe's vision of "the way" as their influence for how faith would fold into their public lives.

I first met Doug Coe in 1976, about one year after my arrival in Washington, DC. His mission was to bring together leaders in a spirit of faith and love by forming on Capitol Hill a small prayer group of congressmen with different political beliefs to meet weekly and to pray and support one another. That's how I connected with two Republicans and a fellow Democrat weekly for the next twelve years, and developed close personal relationships despite quite differing political orientation.

Doug's character and unwavering integrity, humility, affection, and genuine caring for others were obviously embedded deeply in his faith. Over my fourteen years as congressman, I worked closely with Doug Coe and the National Prayer Breakfast, speaking about my faith in the political arena and moderating many of the three-day sessions. What Doug appreciated about me was my ability to bring foreign guests to this annual event, many from Russia and the former Soviet republics. Thus, I helped to broaden the boundaries and scope of the net.

This level of participation spilled beyond the NPB. There were activities close to home in Seattle that I spoke at as well. Thanks to Wes Anderson's leadership, I would often serve as moderator or featured speaker at Wednesday dinner events or host breakfasts with Washington State congressmen. To me, these gatherings symbolized what the faith movement was all about, the gathering of lawmakers regardless of political beliefs to partake in a moment of deep sharing personal stories and faith and demonstrating what Doug Coe committed his life to—Republicans and Democrats coming together in a spirit of love, forgiveness, and reconciliation, placing our human concerns and character above all else. This is what I labeled our higher calling.

Describing any richly complex human being is a challenge, but Doug Coe was particularly exceptional. My heart and mind are full of strong memories of him. The September 13, 2010 article "Frat House for Jesus" by Peter J. Boyer in the *New Yorker* is a worthy glimpse of Doug Coe. "His admirers describe him in terms that suggest a near-mystical visionary with a powerful personal magnetism," Boyer notes. Having known Doug well, I feel compelled to add to the memory since Doug Coe died two weeks after the 65th National Prayer Breakfast in 2017, leaving a powerful legacy of faith within the buildings and mindset of Washington, DC and indeed in places around the world. As a political culture, our deep-rooted belief that a woman or man's character must be at the core of our political choice may be one of the most distinct aspects of the American system, and Doug Coe's soul is testimony of the public and private avenues of our elected servants.

It is interesting to note that Doug avoided terms like Christian or evangelical. When he talked about his personal faith, it was always "I am a follower of Jesus," or "I am not a Christian, but a believer."

He did not attend church. Yet, among the political elite in Washington, DC, he would oversee the National Prayer Breakfast and the prayer groups on the Hill, at the Defense Department, and even at the White House. Doug focused on the principles and teachings of Jesus Christ, whose words he studied as if he were studying theology or philosophy. In his personal journal, he wrote, "Peace between nations depends on goodwill between individuals." It was important for political leaders to remember that.

Tall and good-looking, Doug was photogenic and gracious, yet he avoided interviews and photographers. Nothing that he did or believed was about himself. When *Time* magazine named Doug Coe as one of the nation's most influential evangelicals, he tried to persuade the writer not to include him on the list, and failing that, he declined to provide a photograph of himself.

Although NPB speakers, including presidents, wanted to acknowledge and thank the revered Doug Coe, he chose not to be seated at the head table. His low-key demeanor had the skeptical media convinced that Coe and his Fellowship Foundation were secretive or even disguised as a religious cult. That was definitely not the case.

As highly politicized as Washington, DC gets, Doug Coe managed to maintain the respect and trust from the full political spectrum. He was the only external person allowed to join the weekly Senate prayer breakfast meetings, and his time with senators and congressmen, and even the president, was always about prayer. Even during the decades that the Moral Majority and insider evangelicals advanced their political agendas with elected officials and the American public, the trend neither tarnished nor enticed this man. His own politics were neutral, or better described as living in a holier realm above all smallness and partisan thinking. The one issue he cared about unwaveringly was how we outreached to the poor.

Even his Fellowship organization maintained a purely nondoctrinal approach to all things, eschewing the term Christian and nonecclesiastical denominations which tended to be divisive. Baptists may not feel close to Methodists let alone Catholics or Jews or Muslims, but the Scripture was the written word, and the message on how to live and love within those words he felt had the power to unite humanity. The core figures within the Fellowship included evangelicals, but they did not engage in proselytizing. Doug even resisted the organization becoming overly formal in structure. There would be no chief executive, and even the name Fellowship was unofficial. The group's affiliated ministries varied widely in their missions.

One operated a secondary school in Uganda, another funded programs for inner city youth in Washington, DC. The heart of the mission, though, was the Fellowship's interpersonal ministry, the bridging of the political divide among national and world leaders. That was it, pure and simple, and Coe was a rock.

A graduate of Rice University and a physics major, Doug arrived in Washington, DC in 1967 with a rather unambitious agenda. For him, it was all about fellowship and adhering to the principles and teachings of Jesus, but soon, that vision carried him way beyond what he had expected. He saw that those teachings were "the most significant spiritual force in the lives of leaders, especially in Washington, of any entity that I know of," he once said. "There is nothing comparable."

While Doug Coe was fully devoted to political and business leaders in the United States, his commitment embraced the whole world. About 1,500 of the 4,000 who participated in the three-day prayer breakfasts were international participants and foreign leaders. Over the years, he would end up visiting more than 160 countries, often traveling with an accompanying congressman, and in most cases, he'd succeed in meeting with heads of state whether they were democratically elected or self-imposed dictators or tyrants. A leader had to lead, and a leader had a soul. There was always something to connect with, a human place where hearts could touch.

In 1983, Doug asked Senator Charles Grassley, a newly elected Republican from Iowa, to join him on a trip to Africa, which would include a meeting with Somalia's dictator Siad Barre, the same Siad that Paul Tsongas and I sat with in 1975. Grassley asked Doug, "What do you want me to do when I get there?"

"Just talk about the Senate group that you're part of and how they came together to talk about personal life and words of Jesus that helped them work out their differences." For Doug, it was never about partisanship or politics. Scripture cultivated faith and faith was the plasma of reconciliation or "the way."

Every United States president since 1953 has attended and spoken at the National Prayer Breakfast. Each has left a few words behind to reinforce the mission of the metaphoric house of worship. **Dwight D. Eisenhower** began with: "In the company of fellow believers united in faith and hope, there is strength for renewed effort to serve our God and neighbor—the obstacles to their accomplishment becomes less and less formidable."

John F. Kennedy added to the canon: "Every president has taken comfort and courage when told, as we are told today, that the Lord will be with thee. He will not fail thee nor forsake thee. Fear not, neither be thou dismayed—that in times such as these we must reach beyond ourselves if we are to seek ultimate courage and infinite wisdom."

Lyndon B. Johnson told us: "This private unity of public men and their God is an enduring source of strength for our nation and for our cause. It is a source of reassurance for the people of America to know that those entrusted with public office are never too powerful and never too proud to pray, for while history has shown that nations can be powerful without being godly, history has also demonstrated that people do not prosper where the rulers of their nation are godless."

Jimmy Carter proclaimed: "I have a sense of confidence that if we emphasize and reinforce those ties of mutual faith, our subservience an humility before God, and our acquiescence in His deeply sought guidance, we can prevail—we need to cling to things that don't change, to truth and justice, to fairness, to brotherhood, to love and to faith."

Ronald Reagan added: "There are such diversities in the world, such terrible and passionate divisions between men, but prayer and fellowship among the great universe of God's believers are the beginning of reconciliation—we all have souls and we all have the same problems. Man finds liberation only when he binds himself to God and commits himself to his fellow man."

George H. W. Bush remarked: "Let us pray today that as a people, we will continue to bring the power of prayer to bear on all the challenges we confront. Let us pray that we will strengthen the values that this great land was founded on, that we will reverse any threat of moral decline, and that we will dedicate ourselves to the ethic of service to someone else in need."

Bill Clinton preached: "The scriptures tell us we need faith as a source of strength, the assurance of things hoped for, and the conviction of things unseen. We need our faith as a source of hope—faith teaches us that each of us is capable of redemption and, therefore, that progress is possible."

George W. Bush stated: "By surrendering our will to God's will, we learn to serve His eternal purpose. Through prayer, our faith is strengthened, our hearts are humbled, and our lives are transformed. Prayer encourages us to go out into the world and serve."

Barack Obama shared: "We know too that whatever our differences, there is one law that binds all great religions together. Jesus told us to "love thy neighbor as thyself." It is, of course, the Golden Rule. It is an ancient rule, a simple rule, but also perhaps the most challenging. It asks us to reconcile with bitter enemies or resolve ancient hatreds, and that requires a living, breathing act of faith."

At the sixty-sixth prayer meeting in 2018, **Donald Trump** reminded the attendees to be true to the example of America's great founders. What resonated most, though, was the memory of Doug Coe who left this world on February 21, 2017 at the age of eighty-nine, and who had done so much over forty years to bring to national and global leaders the constant need for spiritual awareness.

CHAPTER 18

THE WALL OF SEPARATION

The most perplexing issue in past centuries and modern time is the coexistence of religion and state, which is also referred to as church and state. By extension, we can talk about soul and body, the spiritual and the material or nature and civilization. By which authority do we organize our lives? The divine or the profane? This dichotomy plagued European nations during the monarchical era with royal leaders either exploiting or abusing religion to justify authoritarian political rule. When kings or queens or czars or emperors were seen to be anointed by God or having divine blessings, then the people or subjects were obliged to blindly accept God's authority as administered by His Royal Majesty.

America's Founding Fathers avoided this well-beaten path by incorporating the Bill of Rights in the very original and revolutionary constitution, with the First Amendment worthy of particular note.

The content of the First Amendment was a divisive issue at historic moment it was being drafted for the first time, but the Founding Fathers finally reached a compromise, which had turned out to be a literary act of brilliance. In just sixteen words, effectively, the authors of the constitution addressed the most contentious issue of the age: "Congress shall make no law respecting an establishment of religion, or prohibiting the free exercise thereof." Without abandoning the spiritual and ethical concerns of the republic and its citizens, the constitution separated in no uncertain terms the entangled relationship between religion and government.

Greatly condensed by Congress, the language passed the House and Senate with almost no recorded debate, which, although ensuring immediate clarity, also complicated future discussion and debate over the original intent of the First Amendment. The architect of this portion of the First Amendment, Thomas Jefferson, fortunately left a trail of comments and opinions that have guided court rulings over the years, most notably his 1802 letter to the Danbury Baptists (a religious minority concerned about the dominant position of the Congregational Church of Connecticut). Although much has been written about the origins of the First Amendment, we often forget to reexamine the origins of our separation of church and state when considering contemporary issues that need to be politically and legally sorted with respect to our nation's baseline, the constitution. Jefferson wrote: "Believing with you that religion is a matter which lies solely between Man & God, that he owes account to none other for his faith or his worship, that the legitimate powers of government reach actions only, & not opinions, I contemplate with sovereign reverence that act of the whole American people which declared that their legislature should 'make no law respecting an establishment of religion, or prohibiting the free exercise thereof,' thus building a wall of separation between Church & State."

Jefferson's goal was not his alone. It is fascinating to consider that Jefferson's fight for religious freedom along with John Adams and others, supported by the devout Evangelical Presbyterians and Baptists who were adamant for political and theological reasons, contended that mixing church and state corrupted both. Jefferson once assured a Jewish correspondent that in the case of religious freedom, "divided we stand, united we fall." So being pro-freedom of religion meant implied a fierce stance for a separation of church and state.

Jefferson's ideals spread far beyond America. When serving as ambassador to France, he learned about the statute's adoption in 1786 and had it translated into French and Italian. Jeffersonian position on religious freedom became an emblem of the nation, with the statute reprinted in brochures encouraging emigration to America. He was equally clear that while religious belief was fully protected, that protection could never justify illegal actions in the name of religion, including acts of terrorism or bigotry.

Jefferson's "wall of separation" was straightforward, but the Founding Fathers were unable to imagine how "the wall of separation" would one day become so complex and even contentious. Indeed, the US Supreme Court has worked to protect the wall against a succession of highly politicized issues such as school prayer, abortion, gay rights. Today, the constant internal battle is less about church and state as it is about religion and politics. The distinctions between state and political issues, I'll reserve for another time.

In the early 1980s, a movement of growing proportion emerged in the American scene. It was called the Moral Majority, and it challenged the traditional Baptist principle of separating religion and politics. It was sparked by Reverend Jerry Falwell's loud and media-driven concern about the decay of the nation's morality. As founder of Liberty University in Virginia and a legendary TV pastor with a national following, Jerry Falwell in 1979 teamed up with Republican political strategists, Paul Weyrich and Richard Viguerie, to mobilize a new force on the conservative American spectrum, the New Christian Right, with particularly strong outreach in the South and the so-called Bible Belt states. The New Christian Right gained momentum and quickly spread to other states. It was based on an old polemic, but it had a new face, and it was energized by feisty leadership and widespread, grassroot funding.

The Moral Majority became a political phenomenon in the 1980s with a large membership that reached the deep pockets needed to finance national media campaigns and grassroots organizations. It took bold and effective political stances and charged head first at politicians and candidates that it opposed. Its message of restoring moral authority, known as "the social agenda," resonated with core Republicans and even traditional Democrats. Presidential and congressional candidates could not ignore the mounting influence of the Moral Majority throughout campaigns and within the halls of Congress.

The Moral Majority was more political than religious, as evidenced in how the organization aligned itself in presidential elections. Jimmy Carter, as president of the United States and a self-professed evangelical Christian and a Democrat, heightened the national awareness of a faith-based agenda and was a milestone in American history. Yet, the Moral Majority was quick to endorse his opponent, Ronald Reagan, in the 1980 election. Carter stated that "a group headed by Jerry Falwell purchased $10 million in commercials on Southern radio and TV to brand me as a traitor to the South and no longer a Christian." He had reason to feel betrayed by fellow believers in that one-fifth of the Moral Majority voters that had supported Carter in 1976 switched to Reagan in 1980.

Falwell's movement tilted the election toward Reagan along with convincing churchgoers to be more politically active in federal and state campaigns and to engage in lobbying Congress against abortion and other issues. While the Moral Majority finally ran out of steam and was dissolved in 1989, it had a measurable and lasting effect on our political system. "The social agenda" became an integral part of congressional campaigns and dominant on the Republican Party's agenda. The Democrats took advantage of the other side, galvanizing support among the pro-abortion organizations and LGBT community.

Although the two most touted populist issues in federal elections have almost always been the economy (jobs, jobs, jobs) and national security, there has never been a more divisive and contentious issue in America than abortion. Both the pro- and anti-abortion movements were well effective nationally and locally, and both sides were exuberant with passion. The Moral Majority fundamentalists who genuinely believe abortion was a murderous crime and subject to capital punishment, thus pro-life, stood off against Planned Parenthood which advocated that abortion was a fundamental right for all women, pro-choice. There was no room for compromise.

The public battle began with a landmark decision by the United States Supreme Court in 1973, when it declared that a right to privacy under the Due Process Clause of the Fourteenth Amendment extended to a woman's decision to have an abortion. Prior to this historic decision, the abortion issue transcended political boundaries. All sorts of political anomalies appeared relating to abortion. In 1971, Senator Ted Kennedy, a liberal from a traditional Catholic family, once declared that "wanted or unwanted, I believe that human life, even at its earliest stages, has certain rights which must be recognized—the right to be born, the right to love, the right to grow old." On the other side, in the late 1960s, conservative Southern states like Mississippi, Georgia, and Kansas passed laws legalizing abortion.

Indeed, the historic Roe v. Wade decision of the Supreme Court 410 US 113 in 1973 was pivotal. Chief Justice Warren Burger wrote, "The court today rejects any claim that the Constitution requires abortion on demand." The ruling was directed at the states that had taken various actions on the course of a pregnancy by attempting to resolve this delicate test, thus tying state regulation of abortion to the third trimester of pregnancy. In blocking many states and federal restrictions on abortion in the United States, *Roe v. Wade* prompted a national debate that continues today about the issue, including whether and to what extent abortion should be legal, who should decide the legality of abortion, what methods the Supreme Court should use in constitutional adjudication, and what the role should be of religious and moral views in the political sphere.

The abortion issue quickly became polarizing, prompting the pro-life movements on the right with Republicans ensuring that an anti-abortion plank be embedded in their platform at the National Convention in 1976. Millions of Americans became single-issue voters. The pro-life movement tilted the 1976 presidential election in favor of Ronald Reagan. The Democrat liberals and women organizations started to play catch-up to ensure debate to the public course on this prickly issue.

While the Supreme Court intended to strike a balance and bring resolution among the states, Congress could not ignore the consequences, notably how to deal with economic disparity as it affected the Supreme Court judgment. Middle-class and wealthy Americans could legally have abortions within the Supreme Court's guidelines, while those who could not afford or otherwise did not have access to early abortions were condemned to limited choices.

That gave rise to the so-called 1976 Hyde Amendment. The author, Congressman Henry Hyde, was a staunch conservative Republican congressman from Illinois, who sat on the House Judiciary Committee and became the symbol of the anti-abortionist activists who demanded a ban on the use of federal funds to pay for or subsidize abortions. His zeal to defeat federal abortion funding included partial birth abortion and other conservative causes such as doctor-assisted suicide, same sex marriage, flag burning, and later, on he directed his energy to have President Bill Clinton removed from office after he perjured himself on his sexual relations with Monika Lewinsky. The Hyde Amendment's intent was to prohibit the use of Medicaid funds for abortion. Only since 1994 have there been several narrow exceptions on federal funding for abortion, namely when continuing the pregnancy will endanger the woman's life, or when the pregnancy results from rape or incest.

By far, the question of abortion and legislation was the most difficult issue I faced in my fourteen years in the House of Representatives. As a progressive Democrat, voting in favor of the Hyde Amendment was viewed as treasonous. How could Don Bonker not support abortion rights? The position I took shattered my political base? The issues at hand were complicated because a clear stance required a nuanced understanding of the difference between abortion and the funding of abortion with public money. There was also the question of fairness and access to the same services. For certain, ethical and religious beliefs were key, but there was a lot of need for careful discussion.

The Hyde Amendment put to test my religious beliefs and political ideology. I'm reminded of the father and husband character, Tevia, in the Broadway show *Fiddler on the Roof*, who agonizes over his family's moral dilemmas. Contemplating the arguments in favor and against his daughter's marriage plans, he repeatedly states, "On the one hand…" only to follow with "On the other hand." I, too, agonized over the abortion issue.

On the one hand, abortion was a legal option available to most American women who choose for their own personal or health reasons to end their pregnancy—if they had access and could afford it. The Hyde Amendment would ban the use of federal funding for abortions by restricting women who received their health care through the federal government (Medicaid, Native Americans, US servicewomen, federal employees).

Studies gave evidence that low-income women, women of color, young women, and immigrants disproportionately relied on Medicaid coverage. Economic inequalities in the US were perpetuating racial and gender inequality. Women of color made up the majority of Medicare recipients. About forty-two percent of women who were opting for abortions lived below the poverty line.

However discriminatory this appeared, the Hyde Amendment was clearly about the government's role, the federal funding of abortions, not about the legality or morality of abortion itself. The Moral Majority would chastise anyone who voted for allowing tax dollars to be paid for abortions. There was a distinction between being pro-choice and who was paying for your choice. They also felt abortion was morally wrong –a human life should be preserved at all costs.

I recall countless meetings with party leaders and women activists in Olympia, the state capital, who pressed me hard on the Hyde Amendment. They grilled me: "Are you going embrace the evangelical position on all social issues, which is contrary to our party's beliefs?" I was helpless in trying to explain my vote. Beyond Psalms 139, there is recognition that God gives life throughout the Scripture, but such arguments would fall deft to these liberal activists. The argument of opposing the use of taxpayers' money in ways that violated the moral beliefs of other taxpayers did resonate with me, although I did abide by the belief that all women had a fundamental right to choose their own course of action and moral stance.

The evangelicals were mostly skeptical and showed little appreciation for my voting for the Hyde Amendment because they weren't able to identify with the sheer fact that the issue had two sides and was complex. Indeed, had they publicly supported or praised my stance on abortion, that attention would have undoubtedly done me more harm within the Democratic Party. The issue was sensitive on all fronts.

How I became directly involved in the Hyde Amendment remains a mystery to me. A. Robert Smith, a journalist from the Northwest, described the situation in his December 22, 1977 column, "Bonker solves abortion impasse." His opening paragraph captured the political drama of the moment. "Power isn't everything in Washington, as two of the most powerful men in Congress, Sen. Warren G. Magnuson, D-WA, and Rep. George Mahon, D-TX, demonstrated during the five-month deadlock over whether Congress would allow Medicaid to pay for abortions. Occasionally an agile-minded newcomer, with no visible trappings of influences steps in, as Rep. Don Bonker, D-WA, did on the abortion impasse to rescue his elders from paralysis."

In June 1977, the Senate was in gridlock over the controversial Hyde Amendment, which was attached to the Health, Education, and Welfare Appropriation bill. The House bill banned the use of federal funds to "pay for abortions or to promote or encourage abortions." Senator Magnuson from my state of Washington, who chaired the Senate Appropriations Committee, turned to Senator Edward Brooke, a Republican from Massachusetts, who was the only black member in the Senate and who supported abortion rights. Both recognized they had to adapt language that would restrict funding to only certain categories of women's circumstances if they expected the House to agree to it. Senator Brooke proposed allowing federal payment when the mother's life was endangered or in cases of rape or incest or when a doctor considered the procedure to be "medically necessary."

The anti-abortion forces on the House side felt that latter phrase was too open-ended. They demanded that any amendment have a provision to narrowly limit where the mother's life was in peril. The Senate would not sign off one way or the other, and the deadlock settled in.

From June through October 1977, there were ten efforts to break the deadlock, prompting House Speaker Tip O'Neill, the Democrat from Massachusetts and from a heavily Catholic district, to pass the buck to others to try to resolve the abortion issue, which was so politically dangerous to all elected officials. I have a tendency to feel implicated in the most difficult issues where morality and politics lock horns. This may be my calling, and I asked myself what role was there for me to play here?

Faced with a blank, I saw no way forward. My place in this national battle was inconsequential in every respect. I was not an expert in abortion issues, nor did I serve on any of the committees of jurisdiction, and I specifically had no influence with the Conference Committee which had final say on reconciling differences that the Senate and House experienced. I feared that weighing in would only lead to another Wayne Hays mistake; a junior House member foolishly getting in over his head, trying to usurp the congressional chieftains who presided over this contentious issue. The wisest way to proceed would be to remain as quiet and inconsequential as possible. But was that me? Our Washington delegation included the two most respected men in the Senate, including Magnuson, along with Congressman Tom Foley, who was in line to be speaker, and Brock Adams, who had served in President Carter's cabinet and would later be elected to the US Senate. So, we were well represented. Would my upstart nature be stepping out of bounds once again?

Probably. But I became focused on a curious truth. I was in a unique position. There were not a whole lot of progressive Democrats who were supporting the Hyde Amendment. Did my hybrid situation being both pro-choice and pro-Hyde Amendment make me increasingly credible? Was this an opportunity that would help shape my early tenure in the House of Representatives and show that, on delicate issues where morality and political policy interacted, I would be a go-to representative?

I called a staff meeting to discuss both strategy and to craft language that might be acceptable to both sides. We came up with talking points, and I started phoning a select number of Republican Hyde Amendment backers to talk through ways of achieving a possible compromise. I was on their side, but they had to yield in places that would provide a breakthrough. Access to abortion was connected to equality issues, and women's choices had to be respected. I was known around the halls of Congress as a Democrat who had genuine faith, and that gave me enough credibility to approach a few of my Republican colleagues on this difficult issue. Had I categorically opposed the Hyde Amendment, I would have had zero credibility in making these calls to Republicans. Being a reformer while sharing solidarity was the key, and always has been for me.

I connected with about thirty Republican colleagues who were open to considering alternative language, but they also feared that provisions allowing abortion in rape cases would invite women to fraudulently claim they had been raped. My mantra was to listen, not to judge. I asked for their ideas, what would be and what would not be acceptable. How would they vote if any of the following specific changes were included? That is how I prepared the field and leveled out the most obstructive cases, with wording and details.

These discussions and series of careful questions led me to the insertion of phrases that conditioned eligibility for abortion payments, required that recipients of the abortion assistance had reported the sexual aggression to the police or public health agencies. I also added the word "force" in front of rape to disqualify underage women who had engaged in consensual sex but because of their status as minors, were legally considered victims of statutory rape. I knew that the opposition had strong feelings about funding abortion to underage women and that without the language that clarified the criminal violation, this would not pass. The Senate still balked, but they were getting closer. One step at a time I learned that lawmaking required both patience and resilience.

The amendment I drafted essentially allowed Medicaid funding of abortions only when the life of the mother was endangered, for rape or incest victims who had reported the crime or where "severe and long-lasting physical damage" to the mother—it could not just be emotional since that was too subjective to have approved—would result from pregnancy, as verified by two physicians.

I presented the language to Senator Magnuson who conferred with Senator Brooke, and they were "reluctant" but they agreed to go along with this restrictive language, deliberately allowing that they had given much ground in order to make it easier for anti-abortion members of Congress to go along with the reformed version. It went to a vote and the House approved it 181 to 167.

My role had been significant but I did not want to publicize or promote what I had done to break the deadlock, fearing the political fallout on both sides would have consequences. A junior congressman stepping in to broker a deal between Republicans and Democrats—that landed on the desk of the conference committee that was stalled on this contentious issue. Yes, a major accomplishment that would have me rushing to do a press conference and boasting about my political and legislative skills. Not this time. If anything, I was rushing to avoid any press attention and get a few acknowledgements from my colleagues on both sides of the aisle.

There is the work and there is the attention you draw to yourself for that work. Sometimes the attention is detrimental, whereby the work was crucial. Often, we see lots of attention where there was essentially no work. And occasionally, there is groundbreaking work balanced with legitimate attention that is merited and the political dividend is deserved. The same reporter, A. Robert Smith, noted in his next column, "Rep. Mahon, chairman of House Appropriations Committee, considered a powerhouse on Capitol Hill, dropped Bonker a thank-you note, saying 'without your help, we would not have succeeded. You did a great job.'" I was gratified while hoping very few readers would have picked up on this. We needed pro-choice legislation that was as economically inclusive as possible, where those with deep moral or religious objections could also breathe. Mahon, who was a close friend of Jimmy Carter's, was a strict Methodist who didn't drink or smoke. He continued to serve in Congress for forty-four years, and was the longest ranking chairman of the House Appropriations Committee, although in an interview before his death at age eighty-five, he said that when elected in 1934, he had only planned on remaining in Congress for two terms so not to be seen as "a political accident."

The language embedded in the Hyde Amendment has continued to be approved every year for the last four decades. While the funding restrictions on abortion are generally accepted, they continue to be controversial but lean in various ways toward policy that favors Republicans. As writer Emma Green penned in *The Atlantic*, scientific advances "fundamentally shift the moral intuition around abortion," hinting at the emotional complication related to improved imagery enabling biological parents-to-be to see the faces of unborn babies earlier and earlier. There is new pressure on Democrats to check their vulnerability on their right to choose legislation that applies through the first forty weeks of pregnancy. Science and technology will continue to pressure the way legislators respond to the moral and religious resistance to aborting unborn children, while the movement toward much greater gender equality and inclusiveness in our society will push for increasingly liberal understandings of choice. A recent article in *The Oklahoman* captured the new Democratic sentiment: "In 2016, the party included repeal of the Hyde Amendment in its presidential platform. 'We believe unequivocally, like the majority of Americans, that every woman should have access to quality reproductive health care services, including safe and legal abortion—regardless of where she lives, how much money she makes, or how she is insured,' the platform said." This was in line with what we heard from Hillary Clinton on the stump and saw during the Obama administration, which sought to force even religiously affiliated groups to provide free birth control, including abortifacients, as part of their health care plans. This mindset is evident in California where the Democrat-dominated legislature passed a law, now before the US Supreme Court, requiring pregnancy centers that don't offer abortions to advertise where women can get state-subsidized abortions, and in deep blue New York State where Democrats want to decriminalize late-term abortions.

While the Hyde Amendment may continue to reside in safe harbor, it continues to be painstakingly complex for many in Congress who cannot dodge the stinging effect that abortion has and will continue to have in our country. Morality, advertising and video, gender, technology, and the genetic understanding of life itself are converging into a culture in rapid reinvention. Both Democrats and Republicans and every new political movement in every election year going forward will react to the termination of life and the way government legislates and funds it as an unpredictable disturbance in the minds and hearts of voters. The contradictory political echo that abortion provokes reflects the widening diversity in the demographics within both our country's staunch religious beliefs and America's insatiable thirst for openness and personal freedom.

CHAPTER 19

EQUAL ACCESS FOR ALL

In early 1984, I received an unexpected call from friend and mentor, Senator Hatfield. After an exchange of our usual pleasantries, he asked if I would take the lead on the House side on legislation he was introducing in the US Senate. "I will send you the Senate resolution and some background material," he offered.

But I quickly responded, "Mark, if it is something you want, I'd be glad to do it." I put the phone down and paused for a minute, then called in my chief of staff, Mark Murray, and told him that I just got a call from Senator Hatfield about some new legislation.

He replied, "Really, that's impressive. What did he want?"

"He wants me to introduce a House resolution similar to what he just filed in the Senate."

Mark asked, "What's it about?"

"Not sure, but I think it has to do with students having the right to hold religious meetings in high schools."

The background materials arrived by congressional page and I quickly ripped into the thick envelope. I could see what Senator Hatfield was getting at. During the 1980s, high schools were dealing with a sensitive church-state issue. At the time, a few organizations were encouraging students to come together in prayer groups, Bible studies, and fellowship meetings. Most schools already allowed various service clubs, chess, scuba diving, skiing, and the like to meet on school campuses. So why couldn't Bible study groups meet as well? The ACLU and other organizations vigorously challenged school districts that permitted religious-related activity based on the separation of church and state clauses in the constitution.

In their various rulings, the courts supported the right of school districts to prohibit student-led religious clubs on campuses. Many school administrators complied with these decisions feeling that they were simply following what Thomas Jefferson had called the "wall of separation" between church and state. The separation was sacred to our system. But so was the protection of religious rights. In 1981, the US Supreme Court ruled in Widmar v. Vincent that public universities which allowed political, student-led groups to use campus buildings for their meetings could not deny equal privileges to a Christian student groups on campus. The court reasoned that university students are mature individuals and that the university was acting in a neutral manner. The court felt that universities should not be viewed as promoting religion simply because of their equal treatment to all student groups.

Obviously, there were two separate court decisions—one allowing religious groups to have such meetings on public university campuses, and the other prohibiting such activity at the high school level. Senator Mark Hatfield's staff crafted legislation in a manner that would apply the *Widmar v. Vincent* court decision to public high schools nationally, thus bringing resolution to this contentious issue. Back in my office, my assistant asked if I wanted to sign up cosponsors of the legislation. I responded that it may be difficult and would take too much time. I was anxious to get the bill filed so I could call the senator and say, "It's done." Mark and I agreed this legislation was probably going nowhere. The fact is about 18,000 bills are introduced in each session of Congress, but only a small fraction ever make their way to the president's desk. Often, it's more about symbolism than serious legislating.

The bill would go to the House Education and Labor Committee, which Mark and I felt would likely encounter resistance, at least from the Democrats. The most liberal-minded House members sought to serve on this committee and had aligned with teacher associations and unions. They would definitely be turned off by legislation that mandates that public schools cater to religious and Bible groups, especially if its advocates were the Moral Majority and evangelical types.

Our conclusion was that this bill would go nowhere, at least in the House of Representatives.

A few weeks later, my secretary rushed in and said, "Congressman, the chairman of the Education and Labor Committee is on the phone."

I had no clue as to why he would be calling me, but I quickly got on line. Before I could even say hello, he blurted, "Young man, come to my office as soon as you can because we need to talk about your resolution."

"Okay, I can come now if it works for you," and that ended the conversation.

As I walked into his office, Chairman Carl Perkins stood up and greeted me graciously.

"Thanks for coming over and I appreciate you for introducing the Equal Access bill." He was in his seventies, likeable, a Southern Democrat with a positive attitude. He went on to say, "This is what I've been looking for and we'll get it out of my committee and on to the House floor. Now, let's go over and see Tip O'Neill, put him on the alert so we can get floor action soon."

I was awestruck. So this was how things worked in the capitol? A few days earlier, I concluded the Hatfield bill was going nowhere, would never get on the committee agenda, my Democratic colleagues would oppose it, and ultimately, it'd be among the 17,000 bills destined for the trash bin. Suddenly, the chairman of the Committee on Education and Labor is fully supportive, a guarantee that it'd be reported out of his committee, and now we were walking over to the capitol to see Speaker Tip O'Neill for his blessings and support. Incredulous.

Upon reflection, I wondered why Chairman Perkins, a Kentucky congressman who'd served since 1949 and whose work helped create the Head Start program, would have been so excited about the Hatfield-Bonker Equal Access legislation. I never asked him, but I concluded that he was a person of faith and had made a pledge to someone in his district, a supporter or contributor or family member that he would get this bill enacted. Perkins cared deeply about most matters that touched schools, and it is not surprising that his legacy has been noted by the creation of the federal student loan program called the Perkins Loan. I was thrilled to call Mark Hatfield and give him the good news. This was fun.

The original Hatfield-Bonker legislation was drafted in a simple, straightforward way. It read, "It shall be unlawful for any public secondary school which receives federal financial assistance and which has a limited open forum to deny equal access or a fair opportunity to, or discriminate against, any students who wish to conduct a meeting within that limited open forum on the basis of the religious, political, philosophical, or other content of the speech at such meetings."

Essentially, if a public secondary school allows for the existence of one or more extracurricular student groups on school property during noninstructional time, then it must grant equal opportunity to all non-curricular student groups.

Chairman Perkins proceeded with committee hearings, presided over a markup of the legislation, preparing to move it on to the House floor. My staff closely monitored the committee proceedings, providing me with daily reports. The bill was being more favorably considered than ever expected, due in part to Chairman Perkins' support, but there was something else that puzzled my staff and myself. Congressman Barney Frank, a respected liberal Democrat from Massachusetts who was also openly gay, appeared to be supportive. This got the attention of the other Democratic committee members. That was encouraging.

My staff kept reporting about a rash of amendments that seemed to complicate, and even weaken, what the original intent of the legislation had been. Members almost always have a bucket of amendments (that's what they are called—bucket amendments) offered often on behalf of lobbyists and special interests, that which helped congressmen prove that they were being proactive in a particular way to satisfy a particular supporter or advocacy group. Bucket amendments didn't surprise me, and sometimes they were relatively harmless and often conceding to help shape your core content or add significant details, but with this bill, I was slightly disturbed that the intent of the bill was being chipped away at for reasons that were not yet evident.

One such bucket amendment included language that permitted faith-based clubs of all religions, but excluded groups which dealt with atheism, Goth culture, heavy metal music, Satanism, Wicca, and other neo-pagan religions. School districts would be able to opt out of the act by prohibiting all noncurriculum clubs or by giving up federal funding. Neither option was acceptable in my thinking. Prohibiting all clubs would create a lot of frustration and anger among the students, but creating restrictive language would run against the grain of the freedom of religious expression that the bill was fostering.

The final draft absorbed newly added provisions, including 1) attendance would be voluntary; 2) the group would have to be student-initiated; 3) the group could not be sponsored by the school itself, by teachers, by other school employees, or by the government. This meant that such employees could not promote, lead, or participate in a meeting. However, a teacher or other school employee could be assigned to a group for "custodial purposes."

The final also stipulated that persons from the community may not "direct, conduct, control, or regularly attend activities of student groups." This was to ensure that activities on school premises were not manipulated by outside groups. The act also directed schools to treat all of their student-led noncurriculum clubs equally.

Senator Hatfield, like any legislator who acts as principal author of a resolution or bill, expected to be consulted or involved if amendments were offered. That was the statesmanlike tradition in the US Senate. Always consult the author. But that is not what happened in the House Education and Labor Committee, which proceeded to incorporate language that went far beyond and distorted Senator Hatfield's original draft.

I was sitting with Senator Hatfield when he reviewed the final House version. He was upset. He looked up at me and said, "I think we should consider withdrawing our support if this is what it's going to look like."

My immediate feeling was disappointment. I felt I had let him down since all this mischief took place on my bill, on my watch. He was not blaming me, but finally added, "Let me think about it and I will get back to you." I nodded in consent, wondering what I could have done to have better protected our bill.

Ultimately, he decided to go forward and the Equal Access Act passed in the Senate with a vote of 88–11. On the House side, it was approved 337–77. It became law on August 11, 1984. Predictably, it has been the subject of multiple court decisions, ultimately reaching the Supreme Court, which ruled in favor of the law. There are always bits of contrition hidden inside even victories.

Several years after I left Congress, I was at my home getting dressed for work when Carolyn rushed in and said, "Don, you've got to come and watch this on TV." I grabbed my tie and hurried into our family room. The *Today's Show* was on and the commentator was reporting on the Equal Access Act. It was about a controversy over whether after-school gay and lesbian clubs would be protected by the Equal Access Act.

Many school districts were again caught up in a dilemma and legal battles over this. Did a federal law originally intended to allow Christian groups the right to assemble on school property extend to gay and lesbian students? The choice was clear. Schools would have to allow the so-called GSAs (gay-straight alliance) to assemble with all the same EAA protections or ban all noncurricular clubs from after-school activities on school property. If school districts opted to prohibit all such activity to avoid granting protections to GSAs, they would likely face more lawsuits on discrimination and risked even being liable for damages and attorney fees.

I was shocked watching national television now reporting on the Equal Access Act. The Hatfield-Bonker legislation was all about allowing student Bible and prayer groups to get together so not to be in violation of legalities on the church and state separation issue. And now the EAA was primarily about the applicability of LGBT groups under the Act. It wasn't until that moment that I realized why Congressman Barney Frank had been so supportive of the legislation. He obviously saw far beyond what Senator Hatfield and I were thinking about at the time. And he was right. The Act protects all types of student groups and helps ensure that our schools are open and tolerant of every type of diversity that Americans identify with.

Now I believe the bill should have been called the Barney Frank Equal Access Act. Barney retired from the US Congress in 2013. One of these days, I'm going to call him up in Massachusetts and revisit this piece of US legislative history. Stuart E. Weisberg's 2009 book, *Barney Frank: The Story of America's Only Left-Handed, Gay, Jewish Congressman*, lends an excellent context to the Equal Access Act.

The controversy with EAA did not stop there. The issue would come up again in 1988 when I was a candidate for the US Senate. The real test would be in the primary, so it was important to solidify my base and, of course, raise huge amounts of campaign funds. Aspiring to serve in the US Senate, the key to the door was financing, and it was unlikely that any candidate could reach funding goals without the support of Jewish leaders, especially within their state.

Meeting with Jewish leaders in Washington and other states was a must, and for incumbents, the key was their voting records. This was especially true for me given that I was a senior member of the House Foreign Affairs Committee that dealt with Middle East issues. While I had a favorable voting record and enjoyed support among Jewish leaders—mostly Democratic—in the Seattle area, now running for the Senate put me under greater scrutiny. Surprisingly, it was a domestic issue that had me on the defensive as I met with Jewish groups and pitched for donations. The word had circulated that I was the principal sponsor of the Equal Access Act.

At fundraising gatherings, I was increasingly pressed about the EAA law that raised alarms among many local Jews who were concerned that Christian organizations would proselytize and their students would loop in their Jewish friends and convert them to the Christian faith.

Now that I was in a statewide race, scrutiny about my faith and how it influenced my political actions as a future congressmen and future US Senator was being closely scrutinized. The Moral Majority was actively shaping the public view of all Christians as conservative and evangelical. It was a perception that began to haunt my candidacy while I needed to maintain the support of my Christian base while not being perceived as a conservative evangelist. The women's groups and party leaders were asking the similar questions about me. It was time for me to address this concern clearly and convincingly. I had to find a way to close this gap between morality and the Moral Majority.

That's when I turned to my dear friend, Os Guinness, to help guide me through what had emerged as a troubling issue. Os was a renowned author of thirty-seven books and a lecturer-in-demand worldwide, whose message was about "faith in the public square." Carolyn first met Os Guinness and his wife, Jenny, when she was at L'Abri, Switzerland in 1970. Jenny, a former model, had appeared on the cover of *Vogue Magazine* six times, and we had later met as couples in Oxford, England and have remained close friends ever since. While Os was popular and valued intellectually for his writings and speeches about the Christian faith, he avoided being dragged into the Moral Majority camp, so he was ideally suited to counsel me at that critical moment.

Os Guinness helped me to craft an article that was prominently featured in *The Seattle Times* on May 26, 1988. The article began like this. "Tell me where you come from, and I will tell you what you are." I went on to say that "the tendency to stereotype people on the basis of their background, so poignantly expressed by Nobel laureate Saul Bellow, is nowhere so evident as in the debate over church-state relations. Emotions run high on both sides, and labels polarize issues and participants."

I reminded readers that "during my fourteen years in Congress, I have been called both a 'secular humanist' and a fanatical fundamentalist.' I am neither. I am a progressive Democrat and a Presbyterian who takes his faith seriously. I am one congressman who believes strongly in both religious freedom and the separation of church and state."

Our challenge, I continued, is to build on our diversity as a source of strength under the First Amendment by reaffirming religious liberty for citizens of all faiths and no faith. I gave three basic principles which guided my view.

First, religious liberty or freedom of conscience was a fundamental and inalienable human right. America is only as just and free as it is respectful of this right, especially toward the beliefs of the smallest minorities and least popular communities. This right must be universal. As chairman of the Foreign Affairs Subcommittee on Human Rights, I conducted extensive hearings on religious persecution around the world, including the Jewish community in the Soviet Union, the Baha'i in Iran, Coptics in Egypt, and the Falashas in Ethiopia. I sponsored amendments that added religious persecution to the list of human rights violations to be considered in our foreign aid decisions.

Secondly, the constitution provides the most nearly perfect basis for ordering the delicate relationship of religion and public life. The constitution requires a policy of state impartiality toward religion, a policy that, in the words of the 1963 Supreme Court decision prohibiting school prayer, neither advances nor inhibits religion. This is one of the reasons I opposed any form of state-sponsored prayer. The constitutional requirement of government impartiality toward religion was lucidly presented by a liberal constitutional scholar and Harvard professor, Laurence H. Tribe, at a congressional hearing in which he testified in support of the Equal Access Act in 1984. Tribe stated that "the ultimate aims of the establishment clause of the First Amendment are two—to assure that the church not be armed with the government powers of sword or purse, and that government not be wrapped in the mantle of infallibility that comes from identification with the Divine, a mantle that makes it possible for government to denounce its critics as enemies of the Almighty."

Lastly, I argued that we needed to get beyond the labels to forge a national consensus for religious freedom and the separation of church and state. The church-state debate was polarized. The "removers" dominated one side of the argument. They were the ones who wanted to eradicate religion from every aspect of public life. On the other hand, there were the "reimposers" who wanted to force their views on everyone in disregard of the rights and beliefs of others. These two extremes render what is an interesting and engaging debate in perpetual risk of ignited conflict instead of peaceful disagreement and consensus.

I doubt whether the publication of *The Seattle Times* article had much effect on my campaign for the US Senate, but it did allow me to explain or rationalize how my religious beliefs led to my involvement with the Equal Access Act, which, half a century later, continues to play a lively role in daily American discourse and after-school activities in schools across the country.

V. Profiles of Character

CHAPTER 20

CONVICTION ABOVE AMBITION

Courage, as in the type that John Kennedy portrayed in *Profiles in Courage*, continues to be considered just about the most admirable of human virtues. Think of the Lion in *The Wizard of Oz*. It's what we revere most. I would place it just behind kindness.

"Grace under pressure" was how Ernest Hemingway defined courage, and I've always liked that. If JFK had written *Profiles in Courage* fifty years after he had, I have always thought that he could have added another chapter on a great man who is often forgotten, Oregon Senator Mark Hatfield, my Republican hero. Though a member of the Grand Old Party, Hatfield became my role model both as a political moderate and a man of great faith. On many occasions, his moral courage put him at odds with political advantage on highly contentious issues, which became the hallmark of his distinguished career. In his book, *Against the Grain: Reflections of a Rebel Republican*, Hatfield described his faith in the public square like this: "In my life, religion is a powerful matter. It offers peace of mind, a sense of destiny, on understanding of my role as part of humanity, all beautifully exemplified by the life of Jesus. I strive not to wear my religion on my sleeve. Instead, I try to let me actions, attitudes, deeds, even my body language reflect those ideals that attracted me to the Gospel in the first place."

Mark Hatfield knew that labels were never important in a spiritual context. He contended that labels were divisive, particularly in politics where tension and debates over issues ensued, and "labels," he wrote, "such as conservative, moderate, liberal, or right wing are thrown about as if they were swords." This insight has never been truer than today when a word, a reference, or a label not only can ruin a good candidate but can travel and unravel out of hand with cruelty using the boundless abilities of social medial and digital communications. What can take years to construct can be ruined in minutes.

Senator Hatfield, although deeply connected to a politic of morality, did not fully embrace the political agenda of the Moral Majority and other ultra-right Christian entities. Unpopular was his standing with many conservatives Christians. He stated that he was "gravely concerned about the message they communicate relating to Christianity, as if acceptance of their political agenda automatically defines a true Christian. That's simply spurious, because true Christianity means walking one's life in line with the teachings of Jesus. Love, reconciliation, forgiveness are all primary." There was nothing in the Gospel that stated that one must accept school prayer or support war. To identify any political agenda with Christianity is a miscommunication of the Gospel, plain and simple.

The titles of his two prominent books capture the essence of his stature. One, *Against the Grain: Reflections of a Rebel Republican* and the other, *Between a Rock and Hard Place*, both illustrated how he personally coped with difficult issues. "Christians reaching out in deed as well as word to touch the lives of the poor, the lonely, and the frightened, are the only expression in the flesh of the living Christ that many people are going to know. If social justice is to be true, it needs a biblical base," he wrote.

What has always stood out to me was his opposition to the Vietnam War. The senator had been a critic to this American misadventure dating back to his days as governor, which alarmed both the Republican establishment and the evangelicals. He unveiled this in *Against the Grain* where he noted that, "Vietnam was the issue that called me to the Senate, and Vietnam would haunt me for a long, long time to come."

Senator Hatfield's anti-war stance was highlighted at the 1968 Republican Convention now that his name suddenly appeared on Richard Nixon's short list as his vice presidential running mate. A rising star within the Republican Party, Hatfield was selected to give one of the seconding speeches for Nixon's nomination. As the political elites attempt to package a presidential ticket that brought an appeal beyond the party doctrine, Hatfield's moderate views on civil rights, social justice, and resource preservation would be a good choice, but his anti-Vietnam position had him more aligned with the Democratic Party. His Christian faith had set him apart from other contenders, he became an asset as the evangelical vote had become a viable constituency that would give the party a sizeable boost at the ballot box.

While Nixon personally favored Hatfield, the president also realized this would be difficult to reconcile in a hotly contested bout. The party convention operatives felt they had to persuade Hatfield to rally behind Nixon's more hawkish policies to prevail militarily in Southeast Asia. On the day before the final VP announcement, Mark Hatfield had lunch with the publisher of the *Miami Herald* newspaper. As they were wrapping up, someone rushed to the table and handed the publisher a fresh edition of the next day's paper. The headline screamed, "Nixon-Hatfield Ticket." It was a speculative mock-up of the paper should the news story break that way. It seemed to have made an impression on Hatfield because right after lunch, he proceeded to a VIP room for a scheduled meeting with Nixon's top advisors and party leaders who were pitching for the young Oregonian. They had to convince Hatfield to reverse his position or at least tone down his rhetoric on Vietnam if he wanted to be on the ticket.

It was an agonizing choice for this young, aspiring Republican, a rare opportunity to become vice president of the United States, and one day perhaps, president, which is what would have happened had he joined the ticket since Nixon ended up resigning, and Spiro Agnew had been forced from office, ushered in the way for House Speaker Gerald Ford to become the thirty-eighth president in 1974. Just "tone it down" or desert his convictions on this highly contentious issue, which almost anyone else would have done to have been elevated to the second highest position in the United States. Political self-interest? Or maintain deep convictions?

Richard Nixon was admittedly in a quandary. He liked Hatfield and was smitten to have him as a running mate, but had to balance that with his senior advisors who were questioning whether he would help or hinder the right formula for winning the election. The choice came down to Hatfield or Spiro Agnew, governor of Maryland, whose state had more electoral votes than Hatfield's Oregon.

A nail-biting evening for the Hatfields as they were given updates by Nixon's inner circle, including Billy Graham, about whether he would ultimately be the chosen one. He turned to his wife, Antoinette, and remarked that "they likely have it." When they awoke the next morning, the Hatfields learned that Nixon's hawkish advisors prevailed and that Spiro Agnew would be the anointed one. Agnew ultimately turned out to be an awful choice as he was forced to resign over corruption charges following arrogant statement that helped divide an already fragmented nation.

The imminent Watergate episode ultimately pushed Nixon out of the White House. Had Hatfield been the choice, he would have indeed become president of the United States—a huge loss for America to be sure, but a shining example of a national leader who chose principle over political ambition. An unfortunate rarity in American history.

That was the legendary Senator Mark Hatfield. There was also the personal side I saw up close. My personal knowledge of Hatfield dated back to my college days when he served as governor of Oregon. At Lewis & Clark College, I was president of the Young Democrats but chose not to support anyone running against him. I also interned for the US senator in 1965 whom he eventually replaced, Maurine Neuberger.

Shortly after I was elected to Congress in 1974, Carolyn and I were invited to join a small group of faith-led friends, which included the Hatfields. All those traits that Hatfield displayed on the national state, I witnessed up close. He possessed the traits I wanted for my own personal and public life. Our small group of six couples remained close for thirty years, getting together regularly, embarking on trips, celebrating birthdays and anniversaries.

As I often state, God's ways are often opposite man's ways. The Old Testament has many narratives about the most unlikely figures being the chosen leaders. Like Joseph and Moses, their responses: "Why me? No, I stutter, I can't speak well, I've been in prison." What is going on here? It was not someone being self-promotional or driven by ambition and success. We forget Moses had no degree from divinity school.

Asking yourself "Why me?" is a great start to initiate positive and courageous acts in our society.

Other examples of courage include the cases of incredible suffering that people endure before they were finally able to become leaders. No one fits this description better than South African Nelson Mandela, a man who endured twenty-seven years in prison on Robben Island before being asked by his captors to lead the country. This was during a tumultuous transition from racist apartheid to a truly democratically elected government, representing the predominantly black majority.

When I was a county official, some aspiring political wannabe would come to seek my support. I would inquire about his or her motives: "Why do you want to be a legislator? What is your purpose for serving others? What do you hope to accomplish?" When they struggled to respond, I sensed immediately that the ambition was more about ambition than the devotion to stand in the public arena to serve. If you want to help define a nation, define your time, define the way the world should be, you must be able to properly define yourself.

We are now living in an era when the ideological forces and the partisan divide have overcome civility and integrity in a deeply flawed political culture. God is on the side of truth, or moral behavior, or social justice, not the narrow interpretation of such; God is not all about ambition and success. Without leaders of moral conviction like Mark Hatfield, our nation will continue to limp down the unfortunate path of deterioration.

CHAPTER 21

ODDITY IS PRESIDENTIAL

P aul Tsongas, who was the son of a Greek immigrant, portrayed few of the characteristics usually associated with a political career. He was dispassionate and anything but flamboyant, yet within four years, he rose to the rank of US senator and became the only member of the Class of '74 to become a serious candidate for presidency of the United States. He was morally determined and straight as an arrow to serve and serve well.

Paul's career was spiraling upwards without hesitation until one day, as he stepped out of the shower, he detected something that was wrong. He was eventually diagnosed with non-Hodgkin's lymphoma and without much delay had to endure a bone marrow transplant. His health emergency gave him no choice but to retire from the Senate and abruptly end his career. Then in 1991, there was a sudden turnaround. His cancer was in remission and he received a clean bill of health from the doctors. He decided to resume his political career.

He called me and invited me to join him at the National Press Club. He would make an announcement. He would be announcing his candidacy for president. I was stunned. Following life-threatening cancer, fearlessly, he now would be running for the most powerful position in the world and the most demanding of all jobs. His bill of health would obviously be an issue which is why he had a notable physician on hand at the Press Club to pronounce that he was fit to be president.

Paul Tsongas was a theorist when it came to national issues within the Democratic Party and in the presidential campaign. From the 1950s through the 1980s, Democrats aligned with organized labor, and rank-and-file Democrats remained rooted in the New Deal era of thinking.

Viewed as a social liberal and moderate on most issues, Tsongas carved a new path on economic issues.

Some Democrats were alarmed by his embracing the Republican economic doctrine known as Reaganomics. *The Boston Herald* on his home turf editorialized that his political philosophy had "far more in common with Republican Mitt Romney," who would end up voting for Paul Tsongas in the 1992 presidential primary, than his Massachusetts seatmate, Senator Ted Kennedy, who was the national champion of liberal causes.

Paul's economic message resonated with independents and some Republicans who were eagerly awaiting a voice that echoes their views, being pro-business while also supporting social and environmental issues. His outreach to voters went beyond traditional party boundaries, which made him original and refreshing. He believed in people and doing the right thing. He wanted citizens to feel empowered and motivated to take initiatives, create value, and build futures without the weight of government holding them back, while he was also opposed to vulgar and disproportionate greed and social inequality. The two were not contradictory. His message had a popular appeal with working class Americans who wanted a fair change but didn't want to be underwriting freeloaders. The popularity of the Donald Trump campaign in 2016 rode somewhat on the aftermath of this same swing, and which ultimately allowed an unpredictable inexperienced rogue politician like Trump to be propelled into the White House. Tsongas' movement came too early to gain the legs it would have needed to have gained real momentum.

There were multiple Democrats running for president in 1992 and Paul did manage to make it into the final cut. It was him and the well-funded Governor Bill Clinton of Arkansas. I had announced that I'd be running for the US Senate that year in Washington State. Clinton was the featured speaker at a rally in Seattle, and during the reception, he was conversing with political leaders about organizing his campaign in Washington State. He approached me and asked point blank if I'd chair his Washington State campaign, which was an honor and which, in retrospect, I see would have given my career a major boost. My excuse was that I would be running my own campaign and couldn't take on the task, but of course, my deeper hesitation was that I was already firmly committed to Paul Tsongas.

As pundits and political journalist recognized, Tsongas was not a typical politician nor presidential candidate. He was deeply unconventional both in his style and message. Candidates tend to master one-liners, pear down their stump speeches to memorable slogans, and often say as little as possible. They minimize risk, play to the heart and soul of the voters, and whenever possible, dodge the realities that may prove to be controversial or dangerous. Avoid the potholes in the road, watch out for traps, smile for the cameras, and wave a lot. Paul was different. He was known for his candor and his straightforwardness.

Short answers that didn't mean much were not his thing. I remember how he was with the Ethiopian dictator. Getting serious was not how you drew cheers and excitement at campaign rallies.

The *Independent Online* once described Paul as "a political oddity." I saw what they meant as we made joint appearances around Washington State. At a campaign rally one afternoon in Seattle, nearly 3,000 people showed up at a public square. I made the opening comments and introduced Senator Paul Tsongas to the crowd. He opened with a startling statement: "This is Friday, a work day. Why are you people here? You should go back and do your jobs!" It made me jittery, but the crowd loved it. They didn't want staged political rhetoric.

Shortly before my introduction, a University of Washington Huskie football star approached me, holding a football that he came to present to Paul Tsongas. I hesitated, not knowing the young man and concerned that the unscripted football presentation would be a distraction. I yielded, though, and Paul graciously took the football, then tossed a perfect spiral out into the crowd. Someone caught it and threw it back to Paul. Presidential candidate Paul Tsongas was throwing the football with the crowd! This went on a number of times, until he caught it and said okay, it was time to talk about important matters. There was an obvious connection between him and the people and a rare moment of silence at a robust campaign rally. This moment affirmed for me what I had suspected and what they already knew about Paul Tsongas. He was a presidential candidate with a special character.

While his campaign was unconventional, it was also a struggle. The political polls were not leaning in his direction, but for Paul Tsongas, his candidacy was more about his economic message than getting elected. He didn't just want to win, he wanted to share a vision for the growth of the American economy.

The *New York Times* described the Tsongas message as a "bitter economic medicine which played well among educated, affluent, suburbanites, but seemed to fall flat among core Democratic constituencies like blacks and labor." Bill Clinton, his rival, had a superior campaign organization which had been in preparation for decades. Clinton had charisma, compared to what one reporter said about Paul Tsongas, "On a personal charisma scale of one to ten, he rated minus three." Clinton, though, was struggling with his own problems, his marital infidelity and his avoidance of the military draft during Vietnam.

Having lost to Tsongas in the pivotal and early New Hampshire primary, Clinton's sly campaign manager, James Carville, tagged Clinton with the label "the Comeback Kid" and pushed out the invented news that the Clinton's campaign was back on track.

As we approached the so-called Super Tuesday for primary elections, Paul Tsongas continued to rack up wins in key primary states, including Delaware, Maryland, Arizona, Washington, Utah, and Massachusetts. However, Clinton went on to win in the more populous and delegate-rich states.

Content-driven, Tsongas did not possess Clinton's fundraising skills nor machine and ran out of cash in March 1992, obliging him to suspend the campaign on March 20, 1992. "Without adequate money to win, the alternative is to play the role of spoiler," he said to the *New York Times*. "That is not worthy," he explained, unwilling to create damage.

In a presidential election that is in full gear, it is never an easy decision to drop out. Paul Tsongas was a serious contender in the final stretch that had the candidates frantically competing for endorsements and voters in two vital states, for the Democrats at least, Illinois and Michigan. Paul invited me to join him in Chicago and I obliged. In his hotel suite one morning, I got an inside view of how things were playing out. The intensity in the room was palpable with his key strategists and advisors gathered and debating a time-sensitive issue. Paul's free trade position was proving difficult as he was taking his campaign to the country's most unionized state— Michigan. Bill Clinton had his own problem with unions since his home state, Arkansas, was considered a "worker's right" and thus anti-union state. The endorsement and support of labor unions would be crucial.

It could have been a typical scene in any presidential candidate's schedule. Paul's advisors were jockeying to make their respective cases, but I observed that they were also positioning to make a favorable impression on the man they hoped would be the future president of the United States. Proving yourself in the campaign was the best way to position yourself for a White House position. As the discussion ratcheted up, Tsongas, getting impatient with the rambling disagreement among his advisors, weighed in with a "time out" sign, saying enough. "I'm going to my room, and when I return, please give me a recommendation I can live with." As Paul exited, I could see he was exhausted. Of course, residential campaigns are exhausting, but I sensed maybe something more and feared that his cancer was returning. I wasn't wrong.

Shortly thereafter, Paul announced his withdrawal from the race while offering few specifics, which surprised his supporters. Bill Clinton had gained the momentum, boastfully claiming that he was the "Comeback Kid" and was running a series of nasty TV ads against Paul. There was also a potential controversy involving Paul's finance director's mishandling of campaign funds, which had the potential of escalating into a real problem. Most likely, it was a combination of all these factors that led Paul Tsongas to shut down his campaign before the Michigan primary. A number of his advisors predictably jumped onto the Clinton bandwagon, still aspiring to a future in the White House.

Bill Clinton went on to become the forty-sixth president of the United States.

Tsongas transformed his vision into a new activity. He cofounded the Concord Coalition, which worked for responsible financial policy and a balanced budget, and led the effort to establish a third party. He went on to author three books. In his 1981 book, *The Road from Here*, Tsongas outlined his revitalized agenda for liberals covering subjects ranging from the Soviet Union to the environment. In his 1984 book, *Heading Home*, he told the story of combating cancer and his decision to withdraw from politics. In 1995, he published *Journey of Purpose* in which he argued for social inclusion and fiscal responsibility while attaining economic growth. Two years after the publication of *Journey of Purpose*, it was confirmed, the non-Hodgkin's lymphoma cancer had sadly returned. Paul Tsongas passed away on January 18, 1997, a month before his fifty-seventh birthday.

It is hard to settle with a few lines of text to capture the strength and beauty of a great person. I yield to the elegant words of an obit in the *Independent* on January 20, 1997: "His voice was lispy and nasal, his speaking style leaden, albeit occasionally leavened by some self-deprecating aside. His message was less Periclean than puritan. At his worst, he could come across as insufferably pious and sanctimonious—a 'holier-than-thou' moralizer who, in the 1992 campaign, visibly irritated a Bill Clinton under constant fire on the 'character' front. At his best, however, he was one of the country's most impressive politicians, straightforward, farsighted and utterly honest. He set an unparalleled example of integrity, candor and commitment."

Aside from the perpetual sense of loss I feel having lost a friend and a mentor, I feel a parallel gratitude for the ongoing strength I have drawn from Paul's example. Our relationship has continued to be something I cherish—dating back to the Class of '74, the fact-finding trip to the Horn of Africa a few years later, and, of course, his campaign for the presidency in 1992. The nation, its leaders, and especially our voting public continues to need to remember that Paul Tsongas represented America's collective best, and if purpose is forever part of our collective journey, then we, as citizens of a nation of values, should anticipate a thriving future.

CHAPTER 22

A BEACON LIGHT FOR
HUMAN RIGHTS

In the fall of 1980, Carolyn and I received an invitation to a Washington "insiders" reception at a historic Georgetown mansion, and we were both excited to be on their exclusive guest list. Roger and Christine Stevens were icons in both New York and Washington, DC. The best one-line description of Roger appeared in his obituary in the *New York Times* on February 4, 1998. "Roger L. Stevens, the real estate magnate, legendary Broadway producer, and bravura fundraiser who enriched Washington's cultural life by creating the John F. Kennedy Center for the Performing Arts."

But it was not for Roger Stevens that we received the invitation; it was his wife Christine's doing. She was a fervent advocate of animal protection. Once described in the local press as "a giant voice for animal welfare...passionate yet always reasoned, Christine Stevens took up one cause after another and she never gave up."

Her passion of the moment was the curtailing of commercial whaling. I became the one congressman who became critical to her strategy to persuade the International Whaling Commission (IWC) to impose an indefinite moratorium on commercial whaling. Her persistence succeeded in getting me to attend IWC meetings in England, sponsor legislation, author op-eds, and work closely with the Animal Welfare Institute, which she, of course, founded. I also agreed wholeheartedly that whales, our largest mammals, needed protection. Many of the practices of the day were abusive and outright cruel.

Carolyn and I dressed as smartly as possible and drove over to the mansion on the Stevens Estate in Georgetown.

Upon our arrival, Christine Stevens graciously introduced us to her friends, introducing me modestly as the "savior of whales." Later in the evening, we were seated in their lovely library, next to a woman, and having one of those typical "How are you? Why are you in DC? What do you do?" exchanges, and the woman in her evening dress pronounced her name. Dollie Cole. Ms. Cole had once been described in a Detroit newspaper as a colorful, outspoken widow, highly respected as an entrepreneur, actress, community leader, and philanthropist. Her husband had been the former head of General Motors, and he had died in a plane crash in Michigan in 1977.

Dollie Cole asked what I did. "I'm in Congress," I replied, "and am involved in human rights issues." She was interested and we chatted for a few more minutes.

As the conversation was ending, she said, "Tomorrow, I am having lunch with a friend from Sweden. Is it possible you could join us?"

I accepted, pleased to deepen my network of influential Washingtonians. The party was filled with exceptional hor d'oeuvres and good wines, and I was pleased both to have been helpful in battling the slaughter of whales and now befriending a group of people who had the ability to make differences in various fields of concern. Carolyn enjoyed the evening, and I was proud as ever to have her clinging on my arm as we departed.

The luncheon was at the Four Seasons and it was an intimate setting—just the three of us. Dollie Cole's Swedish friend turned out to be Peter Wallenberg, who was described by the *Financial Times* as "the Swedish industrialist who was long at the helm of one of Europe's most powerful corporate dynasties." When the *New York Times* ultimately ran his obit, I recall they portrayed Wallenberg as head "of a dynasty that was often referred to as a Swedish version of the Rockefellers."

Why had Dollie Cole, whom I had just met, arrange this meeting? This Swedish business tycoon was already well connected at the highest level with business leaders and politicians, while I was a mere junior member of the US House of Representatives. As Peter Wallenberg began talking about why he was in Washington, DC, it began to become clear why I was at his table.

It was all about a family member, Raoul Wallenberg, who had served as a diplomat in Budapest, Hungary during World War II and whose involvement in using his diplomatic immunity to save Jews and political prisoners from the Nazis became legendary. At the end of the war when Europe was being carved up, Russia had asserted its control over the eastern European countries, and Raoul mysteriously disappeared. As the Swedish tycoon explained, his country did not have the standing or muscle to confront the Russian authorities about Raoul's disappearance or whereabouts. "Only America can do this," he added.

"I need your help, Congressman. The State Department is sympathetic, but they tell me they are limited in how they can intervene. This is Sweden's problem and the US-Russia relationship is complicated enough," he shared. I listened. He went on, "But they informed me, if Congress were to get involved, it would be helpful."

I quickly picked up on what he was asking and hinted that I could look into the possibility of a congressional hearing or even explore the idea of introducing a House resolution. But I needed more information. He was thrilled.

He reached into his vest pocket and produced a very elegant calling card with his name embossed in script. He wrote down a name and a phone number in blue-black ink with his Mont Blanc fountain pen. "Could I indulge you to please call this person in California? Her name is Annette Lantos. She is head of an organization dedicated to helping Raoul." He let the ink dry, and passed the card to me and I slipped it into my shirt pocket.

The next day, I dialed Mrs. Lantos from my house in Northwest Washington. She was pleased to get a call from a House committee chairman, especially one who seemed prepared to conduct a hearing on the disappearance of Raoul Wallenberg. Peter Wallenberg had briefed her.

"What—if I may ask, Mrs. Lantos—is your interest in this?" I asked.

She explained, "We are the victims of the Holocaust in Hungary. Raoul helped with my husband's escape." She didn't need to say more, but at the end, she mentioned, "Incidentally, my husband, Tom, is running for Congress." Tom Lantos had been head of the Department of Economics at San Francisco University, had previously been on Senator Joe Biden's staff, and had traveled extensively worldwide. He was not lacking in aspiration, but there were only a few options to a possible run for office. In November 1979, the circumstances shifted. The incumbent Democrat from the 11th District of California, the courageous Congressman Leo Ryan, had been shot and killed on the Port Kaituma airstrip in northern Guyana by Jim Jones' operatives while on a mission to investigate claims and help free Americans, mostly Californians, who were being held against their will by the People's Temple at a settlement that came to be known as Jonestown. A total of 909 Americans died on the same day in what the US House of

Representatives labeled a "mass suicide, murder ritual." A special election in Ryan's district followed and a Republican, William Royer, took office. Tom Lantos decided to oppose Royer in the 1980 general election and won. The district he would represent included Silicon Valley.

Annette Lantos had more than peaked my curiosity. I began to read the records on Raoul Wallenberg. During World War II, Raoul Wallenberg had been a Swedish diplomat, and was responsible for saving tens of thousands of Jews in Nazi-occupied Hungary during the Holocaust from German Nazis and Hungarian fascists. As a special envoy in Budapest, Wallenberg had apparently issued protective passports and sheltered Jews in buildings designated as Swedish territory. On January 17, 1945, during the Siege of Budapest by the Russian Red Army, Wallenberg was detained on suspicion of espionage and was never seen again. He just disappeared and there were no official records beyond this.

The motives behind Raoul Wallenberg's arrest and imprisonment by the Soviet government, along with questions about his disappearance and possible death, obviously raised multiple questions. Indeed, it remained a disturbing mystery, one that began to torment me too.

Between 1945 and the early '70s, the Wallenberg family failed at gaining any tangible news about the circumstances of Raoul's disappearance. The Wallenberg family, led by Peter whom I had met with Dollie Cole, was now adamant about getting a response from the Kremlin. Was Raoul still alive? If not, how did he die and where was the body? The Swedish government's relentless efforts to get answers from Russia proved ineffective. Peter Wallenberg was convinced that only the United States could confront the Russians on this matter, and now I was his ticket in.

This soon became a high priority. As chairman of the subcommittee on human rights, I moved ahead with hearings on the disappearance of Raoul Wallenberg. Rather abruptly, people were coming out of the woodwork and lining up to testify, including US officials, senior members of Congress, and a number of human rights organizations. Raoul Wallenberg's disappearance was emerging as a means of leveraging US-Russia relations, while the opposite was also true. US-Russia relations were shedding greater attention on Raoul Wallenberg. We would either negotiate his release or obtain an explanation for his disappearance.

In the meantime, Tom Lantos succeeded in being elected to Congress.

All I was able to manage was elevating the issue to center stage. The star performer was the newly elected congressman from California, Tom Lantos. Lantos' passion to honor Wallenberg was relentless, and he championed initiatives to recognize Wallenberg's courageous humanitarianism, having saved thousands of Hungarian Jews from the death camps. Tom Lantos obtained for the Wallenberg legacy the status of Honorary Citizen of the United States, which only Winston Churchill had been granted. Tom had introduced H. Res. 220, titled "Proclaiming Raoul Wallenberg to be an Honorary Citizen of the United States," which was assigned to my subcommittee hearing on June 4, 1981.

It went further.

A portion of 15th Street, SW in Washington, DC, on which the US Holocaust Memorial Museum is located, was renamed Raoul Wallenberg Place by Act of Congress 11985. The US Postal Service issued a stamp in his honor supported by Representative Tom Lantos, who said at the time, "In this age devoid of heroes, Wallenberg is the archetype of a hero who risked his life to save the lives of tens of thousands of people whose religion he did not share." In Manhattan, a monument honoring him was installed on Raoul Wallenberg Walk, named in his honor. And on July 2012, Wallenberg was posthumously awarded a Congressional Gold Medal by the United States Congress.

It was not until October 2016, seventy-one years after his disappearance, that Raoul Wallenberg was formally declared dead by the Swedish Tax Agency.

That initial phone call to Mrs. Lantos and the Wallenberg case that followed brought me into a close thirty-year relationship with Tom and Annette Lantos. Early on, it was the subcommittee hearing on granting Wallenberg honorary US citizenship that was central in our exchanges. Hearing records note that I acknowledged Annette Lantos as my inspiration for taking official action on behalf of Raoul Wallenberg.

Her official reply in the hearing moved me. "I will never forget that day when a person unknown to you had the audacity to pick up the telephone and make a personal call and responded to my pleas about this man who saved my husband's life and my life, and my request that this man not be forgotten. Chairman Bonker was listening not only with his ears, but more significantly his heart. I am sure that is why he perceived the significance of this story."

Tom Lantos' interaction with Raoul Wallenberg dates back to World War II and deserves a note of its own. Lantos was sixteen when he was sent to a labor camp in Szob, north of Budapest. He and his fellow inmates were forced to maintain a key bridge on the Budapest-Vienna rail line. Lantos escaped, was captured and beaten, then escaped a second time and returned to Budapest and lived with an aunt where he met Wallenberg for the first time.

Tom joined the Hungarian resistance, secretly delivering

life-saving food and medicine to Jews in various safe houses, and also assisted Wallenberg in issuing fake documents for Jewish Hungarians, and secretly ushering them out of the country. His experiences during the Holocaust and afterwards were highlighted in the Academy Award-winning documentary, *The Last Days* (1998), which was produced by Steven Spielberg's Shoah Foundation.

Tom Lantos and I bonded from the start, a chemistry we attributed to our mutual commitment to human rights. I had the official position as chairman of the committee of jurisdiction on human rights issues, but his voice and advocacy went well beyond. Shortly after coming to the House of Representatives, he set up the Human Rights Caucus, involving over 100 members who collectively became advocates for the greater cause of human rights.

It was not only Tom's moral authority that commanded attention and was legendary, but also his Hungarian accent and courtly demeanor that set him apart from others. He often sparked controversy over points of conviction or made cutting comments in the committee room if a witness did not testify to his liking. In 2006, he was one of five members of Congress arrested in a protest march outside the Sudanese Embassy over the genocide in Darfur. He eventually became chairman of the House Foreign Affairs Committee.

The Bonkers and Lantoses ultimately traveled together many times during our years in Congress, and then over fifteen years after I left Congress. It is when you travel together that you really get to see someone up close. The various circumstances that travelers confront end up revealing much of your character, and it was this way that I really got to know Tom and observe his profound statesmanship. In 1995, I became president of the International Management and Development Institute (IMDI), a transatlantic organization that sponsored congressional trips to Europe to meet with corporate and official leaders. As a member of the House Foreign Affairs Committee, Lantos had unlimited travel rights internationally, but he preferred IMDI because the trips were not paid by tax dollars. As chairman of the subcommittee on human rights, I moved ahead with hearings on the disappearance of Raoul Wallenberg, and I was able to observe how Tom naturally commanded respect. He never catered for admiration but did insist on the importance of morality in public policy.

I have vivid memories across a gamut of trips, but there is one that jumps out. It was 1985 and a US Congress-European Parliamentarian annual meeting was taking place in Athens, Greece. A foreign affairs sanctioned trip would have us traveling in a VIP Air Force aircraft with half a dozen congressmen and spouses, State Department officials, and an onboard doctor. It was a comfortable and practical way to travel. Although our destination was Athens, it made sense and was customary for the delegation to make multiple visits to other countries more or less along the way. This was cost-effective and efficient. This journey had us going to Russia and Romania. Tom was the designated chairman of the "codels," which we called them—congressional delegations.

We stopped first though in Helsinki, Finland before proceeding to Moscow. Upon landing, we were unexpectedly informed by local State Department officials that the Russian authorities had withdrawn Tom Lantos' visa. The obvious question was whether we should proceed to Russia without him or should be hold back. We deliberated and decided to remain in Helsinki as he worked through official channels. After about three days in Helsinki, Tom had mounted enough pressure and was cleared. His visa was reinstated and we set off for Moscow.

From Moscow, we continued to an entirely intriguing destination, Ceausescu's Romania. Lantos was determined to confront the strong-armed communist leader, Nicolae Ceausescu, head on. US-Romanian relations were, to say the least, complicated. We were at a perilous juncture. Ceausescu's rule, likened to Stalin's, was clearly the most severely repressive and authoritarian in Eastern Europe. However, the fact that the Romanian dictator distanced himself from Moscow led the US administration to look more favorably at Romania than other Soviet republics.

Our foreign relations with the region came down to the Jackson-Vanik Amendment, a law which granted trade and economic benefits to Eastern Bloc countries, which allowed Jewish and other ethnic families to leave the country. Romania was one of three countries with Poland and Hungary that was granted the J-V waiver, as we called it. We were landing in Bucharest to make a courtesy call and to do some maintenance on the J-V waiver.

Carolyn and I were seated next to Tom and Annette as our military airplane had begun its descent. Approaching Bucharest's Otopeni airfield, we looked out the window and were instantly shocked. There was near-zero visibility as we were nearing the landing strip. Then suddenly, the plane jolted upward, a brusk movement that frightened us. The pilot motioned to Tom. "Conditions have worsened. For safety reasons, we should not attempt landing."

Tom nodded, apparently in agreement, but added to the pilot, "Thank you, Captain, but we absolutely have to be in Bucharest. Can you try again?"

Those of us seated up front looked at each other a bit shocked by what he had just asked. But we sat silently as the pilot circled back around and was prepping for another attempted landing. This time, we came perilously close to the runway, then at the last second, the pilot pulled back again and the plane lurched upward. At that moment, we were thinking, *Thank God, we were still safe and would now abort Bucharest and carry on to Athens.*

The pilot turned to Tom and this time was more adamant. "Too risky to land in Bucharest."

We all nervously watched Tom as he was pondering what to do. Then he shot back, "Can you find another airport nearby?"

We were aghast as the pilot reluctantly agreed to check. Horrible weather conditions in an unfriendly Communist country. If delayed we'd possibly miss our meeting in Athens. What was he thinking? The aircraft climbed and headed east. An hour later, we started our descent to Constanza, a coastal city on the Black Sea formerly named Tomis. As we taxied to the one building terminal, I could see the look of surprise on the faces of the ground crew as they observed the American government airplane approach. Romanian soldiers greeted us nervously, machine guns in hands, as we climbed down the gangway. We were escorted to a room in the airport and for the next four hours, we sat anxiously on standby. Tom was on the phone with the US ambassador, trying to work out arrangements that could get us back to Bucharest. It would require a five-hour bus ride across a mountainous area in severe weather conditions. That was obviously not going to happen, and Tom and the ambassador agreed. We'd reboard the aircraft and head to Athens. The meeting with Ceausescu would have to wait for another occasion.

We were pleased that we were Athens-bound. Our hosts there would roll out the red carpet, the conditions would be lavish, Greek food was great, and, of course, we'd be meeting to discuss Transatlantic issues. The ride was smooth and I could taste the *moussaka* and *retsina* as we approached the Greek capital. With the copilot at the wheel, the pilot stepped back into the cabin with information for Mr. Lantos. Landing conditions in Bucharest had improved.

Oh no, we all thought. *We are not going back there!* We landed in Athens and Tom asked who is going back to Romania with me? Most of the codel members, including Carolyn, disembarked for a swell evening in Athens, and only a few of us stayed on the airplane. I was staying with Tom to do our work. We taxied down the runway and headed back to Bucharest. Our scaled-down delegation included Congressman Tom Lantos, myself, and the two top congressmen on the House Ways and Means Committee—Bill

Frenzel and Sam Gibbons, high ranking on the House Ways and Means Committee who had final say on Romania's Jackson-Vanik waiver.

Stepping off the plane and driving through the streets of Bucharest, one could feel what suppression was like in the Cold War era. The country's rich heritage, its culture, even the historic architecture, and now everyday life, lacked the vibrancy that had once attracted visitors to this city. Not anymore. People lived in fear. You could feel it.

Once we arrived at President Ceausescu's palace—he had many of them—we were escorted into the grand chamber and asked to await the president's arrival. Whether intentional or not, the Romanian president had us waiting thirty minutes—that led to a rocky beginning. I saw photos of him but was struck when he walked into this statutory room looking more like a Presbyterian minister than a dictator. He was short, bespectacled, with facial expressions that were grim and far from welcoming.

When Ceausescu addressed this group of influential congressmen, it was more like a lecture. He didn't hesitate to blatantly criticize the United States for its hypocrisy, reacting to our repealing of the J-V waiver. It was not just the content of his diatribe, but the wordiness, the lecturing tone. I was thinking to myself, all the effort to get there to hear this relentless attack on the US. Not one ounce of consideration for what we might have to say.

Tom was patient and gracious. Finally, it was his moment to respond, and he did so without mincing words. He warned President Ceausescu that continued human rights violations would jeopardize the trade benefits of the Jackson-Vanik waiver, which his country needed. Ceausescu abruptly stood, turned, and departed. He was an authentic dictator, asserting his authority and dismissive of us being there. He would not be spoken to in this tone. We looked at each other, understanding perfectly well the character of this man. We returned to our embassy vehicle and were ushered directly back to the airplane that would bring us back to Athens.

Many years later, I met a couple, through my brother, who had resided in Cluj-Napoca, Romania for a period of time. The husband, Iuliu Bucur, had worked for the Romanian army as a crane operator, so he had knowledge about many government secrets. Mr. Bucur and his wife, Elvira, were devout Christians, which put them at high risk in the public square. They longed for the freedom of worship they were denied in Communist Romania. Iuliu was exhausted by the regime that punished everyone who dared to say anything about the government in public. And should anyone talk about God while at work or in a store, the label "instigator" would be tagged to you and you'd be considered a political dissident, with harsh consequences deemed appropriate by a heartless regime. Iuliu learned it was best to say nothing and do whatever the government required. On a Monday morning, August 7, 1983, Iuliu Bucur had enough. Enough of the hunger. Enough of the secrets. Enough of Ceausescu's Romania. He convinced his brother-in-law to join him in what would be a dangerous attempt to secretly make their way to the Yugoslavian border. Julie Cox, a writer for the *Worldwide Challenge* magazine, wrote the story of the couple's "desperate run toward the final two fences. Leaping over a second vibrating fence, they raced on to the final barrier. This last fence appeared to be straight from Nazi Germany: Standing about thirty feet high, it was covered with coiled barbed wire, and the top curved forward to prevent anyone from scaling it. Literally climbing for their lives, they scrambled up the barb-covered fence, knowing that they could be shot in the back at any moment. Blood covered their bodies; their clothes and shoes were torn to shreds…but they made it over. As their bloodied, bare feet sank into the soft ground on the other side, they knew they'd reached the neutral zone. They had successfully passed the border. They were free!"

Eventually, they arrived in America and, in time, became US citizens. The story continues to serve as a reminder for me.

In December 1989, a public uprising sent Ceausescu and his wife, Elena, a partner in the authoritarian rule, fleeing the capitol by helicopter. They were apprehended, turned over to the army, which organized a quick show trial, sentenced them to death, and promptly executed the dictator and his wife.

Tom Lantos

Beyond Romania, Tom Lantos had a profound influence internationally. Born and raised in Hungary during the Holocaust, he felt some trepidation that many of America's allies gave scant attention to human rights abuses. During the Carter and Reagan presidencies, human rights had become a major factor in conducting foreign policy. Not so with European nations.

Upon his arrival on Capitol Hill, Tom Lantos created the Congressional Human Rights Caucus that quickly signed up over 100 Congressmen as members, definitely got the Speaker's attention and leveraging human rights to a higher priority in U.S. foreign policy. He also set up the Congressional Human Rights Foundation to secure funding and outreach beyond the Halls of Congress that eventually became the Parliamentary Human Rights Foundation (PHRF).

His purpose was to get more countries, through their parliamentarians, to be equally committed to advancing the cause of human rights and the rule of law, working closely with other parliamentarians to create institutions and develop policies that would be at the vanguard of the human rights struggle and to respond rapidly to the human rights crises.

Now in the private sector, we stayed in touch and one day he asked if I would be Chairman of the PHRF Board of Directors, which I accepted and eventually became president. For me, it was a privilege to stay involved with Tom Lantos and continue working on this important issue.

In December, 2007, Congressman Lantos announced he would not seek re-election and two months later died of esophageal cancer. At a ceremonial service in the U.S. Capitol, House Speaker Nancy Pelosi stated that "He used his powerful voice to stir the consciousness of world leaders" and U2 lead singer Bono called him a "prizefighter." whose stamina would make him go "any amount of rounds, with anyone, anywhere, to protect human rights and common decency."

The Lantos legacy of moral conviction and commitment to advancing the cause of human rights led to the formation of the Lantos Foundation for Human Rights and Justice in 2008. To us his own words, the noble banner of human rights to every corner of the earth" is the Foundation's mission. For the past ten years it has focused on the free exercise of religion, the rule of law, giving voice to those living unde brutal regimes and corporate responsibility.

The Foundation's president is Katrina Lantos Swett, who has faithfully continued her father's incredible legacy, and presides over the Foundation's annual presentation of the Human Rights Prize in Washington, D. C. Among those who have been recipients of this special award include His Holiness the Dalai Lama, Professor Elie Wiesel, the Hong Kong Democracy activist Joshua Wong, and Bill Browder.

The Lantos beacon light for Human Rights continues to radiate worldwide thanks to his family's on-going commitment to a legacy of promoting the fundamental rights that all people deserve.

To this day, I hail the moral courage of Tom Lantos, who showed me up close during that tax supported perk to the parliamentary gathering in Athens, that he had a serious mission to serve—to confront this nefarious dictator and leverage US policy to end Romania's violation of human rights. For him, the down time in Athens was an afterthought. That's what set Tom Lantos apart from the others. The *retsina* had to wait, but when we finally raised our glasses that evening in the Plaka, steps from the birthplace of democracy, we knew we had done a full day's work.

CHAPTER 23

COWBOY IN THE CABINET

Trade in the '70s was a boring subject, and the geopolitical intrigue of trade wars as our papers broadcast now just wasn't part of the ethos of the moment. As chairman of the subcommittee on International Economic and Policy, I did conduct dozens of hearings, not all newsworthy but significant nonetheless, covering export control programs, economic sanctions, the Foreign Corrupt Practices Act, nuclear nonproliferation, anti-terrorism. Following one of the hearings, a Commerce Department deputy assistant approached me after having testified himself. Apparently, the newly appointed Secretary of Commerce, Malcolm Baldrige, tasked his deputy assistant to invite me to his office for a tête-à-tête breakfast meeting.

My memory of Malcolm Baldrige prompts one of Warren Buffet's signature quotes: "This country doesn't avoid problems, it just solves them." Secretaries of Commerce come and go. They are highly politicized appointees that may or may not have business experience, but few have any real impact serving in that position. The Department of Commerce has traditionally been far more bureaucratic than entrepreneurial. Commerce was primarily in the hands of the private sector in America. Government regulated and did some overseeing, but real business was driven by businesspeople. Malcolm Baldrige, President Ronald Reagan's appointee, was different from his predecessors.

The appointment was set, and I headed one morning to meet Reagan's choice to head the Department of Commerce, Malcolm Baldrige.

I entered his office and was immediately impressed. This was an office worthy of a cabinet secretary—large, classic interior, spacious with several places to sit for meetings, not counting the secretary's large oak desk and the two chairs that sat squarely in front. This was a place that made you feel important simply for finding yourself invited to be there. What was particularly extraordinary was the display of memorabilia that Secretary Baldrige had brought with him. Not your typical cutesy artwork or political nostalgia, Baldrige's assortment included a centerpiece that captivated the scene and set the stage. The large western leather saddle perched on a stand could not be ignored. Aside from a successful business career followed by a cabinet position, Secretary Baldrige was known for his passion—competing in rodeos around the country. He rode wild horses even at his age of sixty-five. The cover of a *Mac Baldrige* biography displayed a photo of him and Ronald Reagan riding horses. The subtitle read "The Cowboy in Ronald Reagan's Cabinet."

A very cordial and engaging person, Baldrige's purpose for bringing me to his office was to enlist my help on legislation to upgrade the commercial attaches who served as consultants in our embassies to help American businesses wishing to conduct business or invest in the local country. They were ranked below the State Department's Economic Officers, he reported, and "we need to upgrade the position." Point blank, he asked, "Can you help?"

"Mr. Secretary, it makes sense and I can add language on the next authorization bill." He was pleased with my quick and positive response. As I was departing, he added, "Congressman, we have common interest and much to do, so I suggest we do these breakfast meetings at least once a month." I was a bit awed that a cabinet secretary, who was in much demand and close to the president, would make this suggestion. My response was obvious. A monthly breakfast meeting it would be.

Over the next year, we had breakfast sessions and discussed many trade-related topics, but our focus was clearly on the export side. We wanted to help American businesses sell more US-made goods overseas. Secretary Baldrige shared his concern about the huge trade deficit stating, "We can either limit imports or promote exports." He said his department estimated that 20,000 American companies could be competitive internationally, but they were small and medium size and boosting exports was not yet cost efficient.

We discussed how Japan and most European countries had sophisticated full-scale trading companies that supplied financing and necessary export services. Indeed, Japan's eight thousand trading companies made them dominant globally, especially in America, which alarmed many in Washington, DC at the time. I, of course, saw this playing out in my own district where my local lumber mills were on the front lines, victims of the Japanese seizing federal and state timber, shipping the logs and jobs back to their own mills. I reiterated how Canada's subsidizing of their lumber companies gave them an advantage in the US market. This was not fair trade. He shook his head.

We agreed to work together on legislation that would allow America's small and medium size companies to form export trading companies, recognizing that a single company is not prepared to deal with the intermediary functions: collecting information on foreign markets, providing financial services, completing paperwork associated with export transactions, coping with customs requirements, and providing warehousing and transportation services. It was unlikely that individual companies could be active in foreign markets unless they joined others in forming an export trading company. On March 18, 1981, I introduced the Export Trading Act, which included two key provisions. One was to establish an antitrust "safe harbor" for export activities, which would insure that companies who put together ETCs would not be in violation of antitrust laws. The other involved the banking sector, which was met with skepticism at the Federal Reserve Board. Our efforts to amend the banking laws to provide for "meaningful and effective" bank participation in the financing and development of ETCs were met by opposition in the House Banking Committee. They reported it was a significant breach in the wall that had separated banking and commerce since the 1930s. By gutting the banking provision, it took the wind out of the sail in achieving the full potential of ETCs. Financing is critical to international trade, which is why we have the Export-Import Bank set up to help Boeing, General Electric, and other large corporation in exporting their goods and services.

Nonetheless, our bill was hailed as a major legislative achievement, and the Reagan White House staged a highly publicized signing ceremony at a port facility in Long Beach, California. I was invited to participate and stood alongside Secretary Malcolm Baldrige as President Ronald Reagan signed the bill on October 2, 1982. The Department of Commerce produced a video on the economic trading company that was distributed around the country. The idea was groundbreaking but the ETC concept never reached its full potential, mostly because the law limited bank participation, which was needed for the financing part of the concept. Indeed, I met with the state's small and medium size lumber mill companies in Seattle to pitch the ETC idea and how it could make these companies more competitive in international markets. They liked the idea but were reluctant to move forward because there was no financial mechanism, which was so essential if it were to happen.

At an oversight hearing that I chaired on June 22, 1984, I noted this shortcoming in my opening statement. "Many of us who supported the export ETC legislation had hoped that it would revolutionize trade for America and make available new export opportunities for small and medium size companies who, in the past, did not have access to world markets. These businesses have not moved in forming trading companies as we would had anticipated in the early stages. I think this is due to business caution and the lack of what I thought would be a pioneering spirit in getting small and medium size companies to rush to the Department of Commerce with their certification requests. That hasn't really happened."

Later, Malcom Baldrige approached me on what would become his greatest initiative as Secretary of Commerce. He had a bold plan to reorganize the federal government by creating a new Department of International Trade and Industry. Recognizing that the Democrats controlled both the Senate and House, it could not happen without Democrat sponsorship. Given our working relationship and my standing as the Democrats lead on trade, he asked if I would introduce his proposed legislation.

This put me in something of a bind. Yes, I'd like to partner with the secretary on this major initiative, recognizing that reorganizing the government's trade functions was crucial if we were to get our act together. But upon review of the proposal, it was clear that the scope was beyond what would be acceptable by Senate and House committees. Secondly, I was concerned that my sponsorship of a Republican administration's trade proposal would put me at odds with the Democratic leadership. I did not want to tarnish my leadership role and the reality that I was beginning to be recognized as an authority on trade policy.

What was politically toxic in the secretary's proposal was the creation of a new position, the US Trade Representative, which, as an independent agency, he would place under the proposed Department of International Trade and Industry. The House Ways and Means Committee would never ever accept this because their jurisdiction on trade would flip over to the House Energy and Commerce Committee.

The secretary understood my concerns but it was obvious he was not backing off the idea of folding the US Trade Representative into the new cabinet position. Opposition was mounting, notably in the agricultural sector, the country's single biggest exporter, which would be left out if the new department had final say on trade issues. Former Assistant Treasury

Secretary C. Fred Bergsten told the *Washington Post* on July 17, 1983, "I don't think the Secretary of Commerce, even if he were God, could pull this together. There are too many heavy hitters." Yet President Ronald Reagan endorsed the plan and it was sent up to Capitol Hill, recognizing it would be dead on arrival on Capitol Hill.

This put me in a dilemma. I did not want to oppose Secretary Baldrige, but neither could I be silent. On November 16, 1983, I came up with a compromise solution, which I introduced as the Democrats' alternative trade reorganization plan. This is how the *Washington Post's* Stuart Auerbach described the two proposals at the time: "Rep. Don L. Bonker (D-Wash.) plans to introduce today a Democratic alternative to the Reagan administration's trade reorganization proposal that includes a strong emphasis on industrial policy within a new Department of Commerce and Trade. Thus the new bill further complicates the administration efforts, ushered by Commerce Secretary Malcolm Baldrige, to streamline the government's multi-headed organization to make trade policy and implement it. The Bonker bill would replace the DITI secretary as the government's chief trade official with an assistant to the president for international trade, modeled on the national security adviser.

"Although the USTR has the responsibility to be the president's chief trade adviser, the Bonker proposal says, Trade Representative William Brock has often been left out of key trade policy decisions.

"'Today there is no clear leader in the administration on international trade,' said Bonker, chairman of the House Foreign Affairs subcommittee on international economics and trade."

While the two proposals sparked a lot of discussion and positioning in the trade community and on Capitol Hill, neither made it out of their respective committees. It was Malcolm Baldrige's biggest setback as the star performer in the Reagan administration. He handled rodeos but this bronco threw him off. I felt badly for him on a personal level, but such was politics.

Malcolm Baldrige was truly an extraordinary chap. As the *New York Times* once described him as "known for his droll wit and frequently pithy manners of expression. His hobby of steer roping set him apart from the more sedentary members of the Reagan Cabinet and he was proficient enough at the sport to occasionally win prize money." He was elected to the Cowboy Hall of Fame in 1984. With his somber pinstripe suits, he often wore a hand-tooled western belt. It's interesting to note that his father also served one term in Congress.

Not since the days of Herbert Hoover had a Secretary of Commerce accomplished so much. Management skills were part of his legacy, resulting in Congress establishing the Malcolm Baldrige National Quality Award in his honor.

President Reagan also designated him to take the lead in crafting a national trade policy. And it was that which brought us together on a regular basis. As a Republican cabinet member, it was expected he would reach out to Republican leaders in Congress to rally support in his trade initiatives. Instead, he opted to work with a Democrat on what was becoming a partisan issue. This, for him, was an achieved success. For me, it was a privilege to work with this legendary person. While we had contrasting views on trade reorganization, it did not alter our working cooperatively on many issues.

If the way you die says something about the way you lived, I tip my cap to Malcolm Baldrige who succumbed to internal injuries from a rodeo accident on July 25, 1987. He was participating in a calf roping competition and wouldn't have wanted it any other way.

As international trade was emerging as a major issue between the Reagan White House and the Democrats on Capitol Hill, over the next several years, I conducted numerous hearings, delivered a few hundred speeches, and published a litany of articles and op-eds on the subject. Democrats were leaning toward protectionism, while I was more aligned with the other party's free trade positions. All this was playing out as the Democratic leadership asked me to take the lead on crafting the party's trade policy. It would be something of a cha-cha-cha dance, and fortunately, I liked to dance.

The Democrats held their annual retreat at the Greenbrier resort in bucolic White Sulfur Springs, West Virginia, which I, of course, attended. Somewhere along that three-hour train ride across Virginia, House Majority Leader Jim Wright approached me. He wanted to chat about trade policy. "Don, we got to do something about trade to counter Reagan's championing of the issue. What do you think we should do?" he asked. I shared my thoughts and we talked about forming a task force to come up with some additional ideas and a game plan. "Okay, let's do that," he left me and placed a hand squarely on my shoulder. I understood he was serious about this.

The Greenbrier was breathtaking. A national landmark, the inn was serving Washingtonians since 1778 including twenty-seven US presidents. Some say that the natural springs and the Allegheny Mountains is what attracted the international guests; others swear by the natural spa, the traditional estate homes, and the golf. A perfect place to brainstorm away from the DC humidity.

Upon returning to the capital, Jim Wright promptly arranged a meeting with Speaker Tip O'Neill, who quickly agreed to set up the Speaker's Trade and Competitiveness Task Force. He said I would be chairman and added a line I won't forget: "Be sure to coordinate with the committee chairmen so we don't get into spicy jurisdiction issues." Eleven other Democratic colleagues were selected to be on the task force, and we proceeded to draft a bill that would be an alternative to Ronald Reagan's trade record. On October 18, 1985, Speaker O'Neill convened a press conference to announce the introduction of the Trade and Competitiveness Act, a piece of legislation that was covered extensively by the Washington media. Indeed, it was highlighted with a half-page photo in the *Washington Post*. Reporter Stuart Auerbach noted, "'We are happy, as Democrats, that we have made the president stop sitting still and got him to do something on trade,' said Speaker Thomas (Tip) O'Neill Jr. (D-Mass.) as he unveiled a Democrats Program on Trade. Rep. Don Bonker (D-Wash.) chairman of the special Democratic trade task force appointed by O'Neill and House Majority Leader Jim Wright (D-Tex.), called his party's initiative 'far more detailed and compressive' than trade packages put forward by either the White House or House Republicans. The White House is dealing with the politics of the problem, not the substance." The article went on to grab something else I said at the time. "'There's something about America's sense of fairness that makes this a political imperative even though unfair trade practices account for a small proportion of the US trade deficit,' Bonker said."

Following Ronald Reagan's national radio commentary on which he spoke about trade policies, Speaker O'Neill asked me to give the Democrat's response to draw the contrast to the Democrat's new trade initiative, which I did. At this point, I had emerged as a national leader on international trade, chairing the Subcommittee on International Economic Policy and Trade, heading the Speaker's Task Force on Trade, authoring the Trade and Competitiveness Act and other trade bills, along with sitting as a member of the President's Export Trade Council. Suddenly, I had more speaking requests than I could handle, but I said yes to a great many of them, which helped me hone my message covering the spectrum of trade issues. My constituents saw that I had taken on the very essence of trade that they had sent me to Washington to tackle. The culmination of this work and these speeches led me to write the 1988 book on trade, which, although never a bestseller, was and is often referred to and cited.

The trade speeches seeded the chapters and the act of collecting materials to comprehensively cover trade helped me assemble a highly competent staff and full access to the resources of the Library of Congress. You wouldn't imagine to what extent the regular five-hour commute between my two Washingtons helped, but it was precisely these long back and forth journeys that allowed the necessary time for the book to be completed. Having it published would be the next obstacle, and I learned how writing and publishing were two distinct animals.

Speaker Tip O'Neill had just published his own book, *Man of the House: The Life and Political Memoirs of Speaker Tip O'Neill*, which led me to ask the speaker if I could contact his literary agent, Lance Ermatinger, noted in John Parker's book on the Kennedys as "the world's most ineffective literary agent." He said yes and I retained him to help secure a publisher. Ermatinger was obviously not all that impressed with my manuscript and forwarded the manuscript to a number of third tier publishers. I was pleased with the book as was O'Neill since it weighed in heavily against the Reagan vision for trade, but the effort to get the pages into print was going nowhere. I had dinner one evening with Paul Tsongas while on a trip to Boston. Paul appreciated my knowledge and work on trade and even avowed once that I would be his choice for US Trade Representative if he were elected president. Over clam chowder, he told me he knew someone who might be interested in the book.

A few weeks later, I got a call from a senior editor at Houghton Mifflin, the prominent Boston publisher, who asked straight out, "Have you signed up with a publisher yet?"

I said, "No, but I do have an agent working on it."

He said Houghton Mifflin was prepared to offer a $20,000 advance for the property. I tried not to sound overly impressed, but secretly, I was jumping out of my socks. This was fantastic news. And Houghton Mifflin was about as good as it got in the American publishing scene. Amazingly, nothing had moved on the book front until that fortuitous dinner with Paul Tsongas.

For the sake of context, the top ten bestselling authors in nonfiction in 1988 were *A Brief History of Time* by Stephen W. Hawking; *Trump* by Donald J. Trump with Tony Schwartz; *All I Really Need to Know I Learned in Kindergarten* by Robert Fulghum; *Talking Straight* by Lee Iacocca with Sonny Kleinfield; *Gracie* by George Burns; *The Rise and Fall of the Great Powers* by Paul Kennedy; *For the Record* by Donald T. Regan; *Thriving on*

Chaos by Tom Peters; *Love, Medicine and Miracles* by Bernie S. Siegel; and *Child Star* by Shirley Temple Black who'd go on to be our ambassador to Czechoslavakia.

Curiously, Bill Cosby's *Time Flies* was also on the list that year, as was L. Ron Hubbard's *Dianetics*. I signed with Houghton Mifflin and was told that they had the mechanism for a marketing strategy that included organizing a book signing tour around the country. They wanted to delay the release date for six months to coincide with the 1988 Democrat National Convention at the Omni in Atlanta. The House Democrat leader, Richard Gephart, was running for president on the trade issue and my publisher felt it would be a major platform in the presidential campaign, and thus good for book sales. But as it turned out, trade took a backseat and was mostly ignored as other issues loomed over the convention. The convention was chaired by Jim Wright, and Texas Senator Lloyd Bentsen nominated Governor Michael Dukakis of Massachusetts to be the presidential candidate. Bill Clinton's speech was a dud, Anne Richards made the memorable statement that George Bush was born with a silver foot in his mouth, and fellow Texan, Jim Hightower, labeled President Bush as a "toothache of a man." Lots of colorful stuff, but trade wasn't front row and the book which had come out on July 1, two weeks prior to the convention, took a backseat.

Houghton Mifflin did not profit from publishing my book despite the twenty grand advance which indicated that they did see sales potential from the start. The title did get some favorable reviews, and the publication was timely in my own race for the US Senate in November of that year. *America's Trade Crisis* by Don Bonker, of course, predates the invention of both the Internet and Amazon.com, but I was amused to observe that readers can pick up a used copy online at $3.95 and, to date, you can still be the first person to "review this item." Better yet, *America's Trade Crisis* is ranked 13,052,767 in the Amazon Best Sellers Rank. What I enjoy most about this bit of dated memorabilia is that the book description states "Bonker's prescription is to encourage the promotion of American exports abroad rather than to restrict imports. His book provides a useful summary and history of a difficult problem likely to be under discussion in this election year," which still sounds pretty spot on for a topical title thirty years later. It may be time for a new edition!

VI. Patches of
U.S. Foreign Policy

CHAPTER 24

A Reign of Terror

Among our congressional Class of '74, there was a remarkable Democrat of exceptional intelligence and great moral fiber from the 5th District of Massachusetts with a funny Greek name, Paul Efthemios Tsongas. We were both stunned to get a call from the White House, notifying us that President Jimmy Carter personally asked that the two of us embark on a fact-finding trip to the Horn of Africa. The president wanted us to explore the two most important countries in the region, Ethiopia and Somalia, considering that the recent bloody coups in both nations were a challenge to local stability and America's strategic interest in the region.

As chairman of the Foreign Affairs subcommittee on Africa, I was an obvious choice. Paul Tsongas had served in the Peace Corps for six years, two of which were in Ethiopia between 1962–1964. I welcomed this rare opportunity to join my colleague from Massachusetts to make this trip together. He eventually became one of the six members from the Class of '74 to go on to the US Senate and the only one to run for president.

When Paul and I came to Washington in January 1975, the Horn of Africa was in turmoil. America's longtime ally, Haile Selassie, known as the Emperor of Ethiopia, had been overthrown by a revolutionary junta known as the "Derg." Its leader, Colonel Mengistu Haile Mariam, sent some sixty senior officials of the emperor's government to the firing squad. Haile Selassie and the patriarch of the dominant Ethiopian Orthodox Church had both been secretly killed. Mengistu emerged as the undisputed leader after orchestrating the physical elimination of most of his rivals around the country. For the Department of State, this was a shock. For many years, Ethiopia had been our staunch ally thanks to Emperor Haile Selassie, the undisputed leader of the region in the early twentieth century. His legendary speech at the League of Nations placed him on the world stage. In 1935, his photo appeared on the cover of *Time* magazine as Man of the Year. In those days, there was no greater recognition in media than that. This idiosyncratic, American-backed leader had now been replaced by a violent pro-Soviet military regime that was quickly pivoting the country toward full-blown Marxism-Leninism and a one-party communist state. Although many Americans didn't seem to care, on the geopolitical scale of 1 to 10, this was about a 9.5, with 10 being the most serious.

The Horn of Africa's other star, Somalia, was undergoing a similar tumultuous transition. Its president, Ali Shermarke, had also been assassinated by a military major general, Siad Barre, who led a military coup d'etat in October 1969. While this new regime advanced significant reforms including an improved literacy rate, in 1976, it changed course, radicalizing the official state orthodoxy and traditional religion and imposing Marxist precepts—the communist label. For that short period, Somalia fell squarely into the Russian corner. And President Carter wanted us to check out what was really going on.

The increasingly Soviet-dependent Somalia began to shift in the mid-1970s, triggered by a dispute it had with neighboring Ethiopia over the vast Ogaden region which bordered Somalia and, of course, the region of Eritrea which finally broke away from Ethiopia in one of the longest and bloodiest wars of the century. Ethiopia's Mengistu Halie Mariam convinced Russia to take his side, which unleashed a massive Soviet intervention which included 20,000 Cuban forces and several thousand Soviet experts dispatched to support Ethiopia's claim over this contested area. An angry Mohamed Siad Barre denounced Russia and kicked them out of the country.

America witnessed this bizarre turn of events, not unpleased with Somalia's new rejection of Moscow, but we had no plan to deal with it. Both superpowers, America and Russia, recognized that their respective strategic interests in the region were at stake. Russia's geopolitical strategy was always about being dominate in developing countries, while the US was poised to counter or block Soviet advances in the Horn of Africa and elsewhere.

The State Department was not pleased that the newly elected president Jimmy Carter would pick two young, inexperienced congressmen to take on this delicate mission. Carter's Secretary of State was Cyrus Vance, who had been Secretary of the Army under President Kennedy, and had been closely involved in the Paris Peace Accords in the late '60s. Carter had given him the role of negotiating the Panama Canal Treaty, the peace talks in Rhodesia, as well as others in Namibia and South Africa. Vance would go on to work on the historic Camp David Accords, the SALT II agreement, and argued for strong condemnation of Soviet activities in Africa. Keen on strategic negotiations as a means of deescalating conflict, Vance, who would finally resign over the handling of Iran and the botched military intervention that led to the 444-day hostage crisis and the loss of our embassy in Tehran, had his own ideas about Ethiopia and Somalia. And they did not include Don Bonker and Paul Tsongas.

Just as Paul and I arrived in Addis Ababa, the US ambassador, Arthur Hummel, who had been the former director of Voice of America, and other top US officials were forced to leave the country. Fortunately, a few State Department people still remained in country and were able to assist us with our mission. Although with the death of Haile Selassie the previous year, we were in the first days of the end of the Solomonic dynasty, which had been in power since the thirteenth century; few back in Washington quite understood the depth of the problem we were there to report on. Something huge was happening and Paul and I were sent to collect facts. It sounds pretty lightweight now when I rethink about this. We should have been accompanied by academic experts, linguists, cultural anthropologists, and a pack of Marines.

As we were driving from the airport to the US Embassy, we observed firsthand that this pro-West nation in Africa was experiencing a brutal reign of terror and suppression. It was not unlike the scenes one observed in the Soviet Republic countries where people were fearful of walking on the streets or being seen in market hubs. In Addis Ababa, Mafia-type thugs, we learned, had roamed various neighborhoods, armed with weapons, and had a mandate to kill at their own discretion.

Haile Mengistu, who had begun as a simple soldier, emerged as the chairman of the Derg military junta, and earned his nickname "the Butcher of Addis Ababa" by murdering an estimated 150,000 Ethiopians to ensure total control of the country. The fear in the streets was palpable.

On that first evening in Addis, an embassy person escorted us around the embassy compound and we could sense the fear that others were feeling. We had been warned to be cautious of snipers and others who had license to kill and there was no guarantee of our safety. I was from Washington State—how does one be cautious of snipers? Duck?

Over the next two mornings, an embassy driver drove us around

Addis Ababa, and what we witnessed was horrifying. Dozens of young men and women were lying dead on the streets. The regime had set up neighborhood watch committees known as the "*kebeles*," and given license to kill anyone and everyone thought to question or oppose the new regime. It got worse. Families, we learned, had to pay the *kebeles* a tax known as the "wasted bullet" to claim the bodies of their loved ones. This was a dire warning to the local citizens to comply.

The Swedish General Secretary of Save the Children Fund testified that "1,000 children have been killed, and their bodies were left lying in the gutter as you drive out of Addis Ababa." Amnesty International estimated that up to 500,000 people were killed during the Ethiopian Red Terror, as the Derg offensive came to be known.

In the evening, Paul Tsongas attempted to reach out to friends and contacts from his Peace Corps days who resided in a village about forty miles south of Addis. I remember him telling me that he had tried everything to get in touch with all the people he knew, but he'd not managed to get even one response. On the third day of our visit, he finally had a breakthrough. An old friend of his had seen Paul on local television and called the embassy. They spoke and discretely set up a time to meet. Paul met with him first, alone, thinking that it was important not to make his old acquaintance from the Peace Corps days feel as if he were being used by the US government. That would scare him. The friend opened up and shared unthinkable details to Paul. Firsthand accounts of terrifying situations that had driven them underground to avoid becoming victims themselves.

The embassy's foreign-hire staffer left to hold the fort informed us that he got word that Colonel Mengistu himself wanted to meet with the two US congressmen who were currently in Addis. We were the only US government officials in the country at the time. We cabled the State Department in Washington. There were obvious concerns given Mengistu's unpredictability—would it be prudent to set ourselves up to be captured or held as prisoners to extract concessions from the US? Could we even be shot as a clear message to President Carter and the American people that Mengistu wasn't messing around? Paul and I decided that we must do this. We were there, and we were the only means who would understand what this despot wanted and was capable of. The rendezvous was set. The fact that the colonel wanted to meet at 2:00 a.m. was a bit disconcerting. This was a fresh form of diplomacy for both of us, maybe even more for me since Tsongas had at least been in the Peace Corps while I was doing the cha-cha-cha in New Orleans. I never cease to forget to remind myself how choreography is key to all movement.

Paul and I recognized the risks but never doubted we should meet this dictator. That was why President Carter sent us to Ethiopia in the first place. That was our mandate; this was public service—to get the facts. We needed to meet the source. Two in the morning it would be.

Upon arrival at Haile Selassie's palace-style manor, now occupied by Colonel Mengistu, it was scary as we entered the guarded gate, which was marked by two statuesque lions. They were eyecatchers to be sure, but it was the sound of lions roaring in the basement that had us fretfully glancing at one another as we were escorted to Mengistu's office. It was thought that the lions had been Selassie's pets. The tradition for meeting Emperor Selassie in his marble office was to stand erect, like a soldier about to salute, awaiting his nod to approach the seating area. Upon departure, the script had people graciously backing toward the main door, again with attention and respect aimed toward the emperor. Such protocol norms did not apply to Ethiopia's new despot, whose attire and behavior resembled a revolutionary now fully in control of the country.

We were now face to face with the so-called "Butcher of Addis Ababa." Paul did not hesitate to confront Mengistu about the dead bodies all over the streets of Addis Ababa. I got nervous as he was lecturing our host about human rights. I was thinking, *Paul, tone it down, let's not anger this guy.* Paul was unrelenting, hitting him hard for human rights abuses, which was a key factor of Jimmy Carter's foreign policy. I was staring at Mengistu's face, trying to anticipate how he would respond.

It was obvious Mengistu could understand English but chose to speak through an interpreter. He ignored Paul's questions and went on the offensive. He said, "It was Haile Selassie who was the chief violator of human rights." He was referring to the 1972 drought and famine in the Wollo province where 150,000 people had died from the harsh conditions. He claimed that the catastrophe was covered up by Selassie. "He even withheld emergency food supplies to the region." He called it "a big cover-up." We listened. "America refused to do anything about it."

It was a feisty exchange, both sides making their respective cases. Later, Paul and I conferred about our reporting back to President Carter about the content of our conversation and the things we observed, including the terrorism and killings that we witnessed here in Addis Ababa. We attempted to find the right balance between diplomacy without prodding the lion, while also making it clear that we were intimidated and that we were there to gather the facts, the whole truth. We could not express fear in any way while we could not project arrogance or moral superiority. We were sitting in his palace and it was his country, and the historical context was embedded in his past. We were envoys of the United States president. We would observe, listen, and peacefully leave to report back to our chief.

There was little doubt that Emperor Selassie had mishandled the Wollo drought crisis. He had other surging problems that also helped to radicalized Mengistu and his supporters. The emperor had been styling himself as a god on earth and doled out favors and resources to a select group of nobles without weighing his own political vulnerabilities. Deities have a hard time with seeing their own weaknesses or admitting error. Well before Selassie's reign, Ethiopia had known the plague of periodic droughts. Nearly all the land was owned by nobles, while peasants toiled on these estates, a form of local slavery, which could not be sustained forever. Radical change often comes when more than one circumstance occurs at once. It is the combination of forces that ruptures the status quo, and sometimes this takes decades or centuries. This was Ethiopia's time to erupt.

We had no idea on what was being reported outside of Addis Ababa since local media was controlled and limited. I thought I better call Carolyn to tell her not to worry. But my late night, or early morning, call on the one secure embassy line with the garbled connection had the opposite effect. My details of the dictator and the lions freaked her out and caused her to be even more alarmed. She remembered what the Romans had done to the Christians in the Forum. "It's not like that," I tried to comfort her.

Paul and I departed safely the next morning, traveling by conventional commercial carrier, but with ghastly memories of our brief experience. This was only the first leg of our mission. We would continue on to Somalia to complete our assessment of the situation in the Horn of Africa. I remember taking off from Bole Airport in Addis, and the feeling of relief as the wheels lifted off the tarmac. Paul and I exchanged a glance of solidarity. This was an important job we were committed to.

The flight was less than two hours. It's only 600 miles from Addis to the Somalian capital Mogadishu, but the local situation had its own unique reality. We touched down behind enemy lines and were greeted with signs of the emerging Ogaden War that ensnarled Somalia and Ethiopia. The war was enabling Mohamed Siad Barre to solidify his authority by playing the national unity card and establishing a one-party government. The scene was far different than what we had just experienced in Addis Ababa.

In our meeting with Siad Barre, the attention was not so much on how he came to power and his authoritarian rule as it was how Somalia could align with the United States. Siad had gone on record as saying, "I support any political entity that represents our interest...."

This was the key to the message that we would take back to President Jimmy Carter. Siad had been born into the nation that was called Italian Somaliland in 1919 and had worked his way up the ranks from local policeman during the period when the British took control of the country. When Italy regained control, Siad was sent to the military academy in Rome. By 1966, he had climbed to the rank of major general and then seized power as commander in chief in 1969. Convinced of his elite power, he imposed the harsh enforcement of an ideology he called scientific socialism. Supported by the Soviet Union, he abolished the traditional clans that had governed the rural fiefdoms for centuries. When the clans fought back against the military, and the Russians did not help as he demanded, he pivoted his pleas toward US aid, promising in exchange to introduce reforms and free elections. It's fascinating to observe objectively how quickly US foreign policy can shift when free elections and an articulated willingness for reform are simply on the table. If they talk the talk, we usually agree to a mountain of help, even before they walk the walk, which often does not come. Here comes Paul Tsongas and Don Bonker, freshmen congressmen, committed to change, driven by faith, and sent by our new president, a man most of the world knew had been a peanut farmer from Georgia.

As we were about to depart, Paul and I discussed preparing a report that we would hand-deliver to President Carter immediately upon our return. He agreed and we committed to spend the long flight back to Washington to get it done. This was pre-laptop days and no heavy typewriters on airplanes, so we both divided up portions and frantically scribbled our various experiences and perceptions that would make for a credible report.

One week later, we personally delivered our Horn of Africa report to the president in the Oval Office.

Surprisingly, he was not surrounded with State Department and National Security officials, but just several White House aides who took notes and, of course, received our report, which we assumed would be widely circulated within the administration. President Carter obviously had both strategic and human rights interests that were critical to his foreign policy as a newly elected president. America's big rival, Russia, had recently overtaken Africa's most prominent, pro-western country, which would have significant consequences in that continent. He also had earlier reports about human rights abuses in Ethiopia, which was a major concern and could not be ignored. While it was a formal meeting, it was clear he was personally interested in what we had to say.

We also presented our report to several organizations in New York and Washington. The press coverage of our life-threatening trip had been limited, except for a cartoon in Paul's local newspaper, depicting our trip as a "congressional junket," a description I continue to chuckle at. It was undoubtedly amusing to Paul's constituents in Massachusetts. The cartoonist had portrayed me as a Tip O'Neil lookalike, and characterizing the trip as one of lavish pleasures and extravagant perks.

Mengistu Haile Mariam and his Derg militia would continue to rule for eleven years before an uprising forced the dictator to flee the country in 1991 in an agreement which had been brokered by the United States. The Ethiopian people who had suffered mightily could now find refuge in hope and healing, I thought, calling upon Psalms 14, "Terror shall grip them, for God is with those who love him. He is the refuge of the poor and humble when evildoers are oppressing them, that God would come now to save his people."

Siad Barre was ultimately forced out of office in January 1991 saying, "When I leave Somalia, I will leave buildings, not people." He first fled in 1992 to Nairobi, but his presence provoked discontent quickly, and within two weeks, he left for Lagos, Nigeria, which was under the military rule of General Ibrahim Badamasi Babangida, or IBB. I wondered if the choice of Nigeria had to do with the Nigerian military being part of his brokered departure, or if it was his own personal recollection of having been honored as a great African statesman in 1980 with a twenty-one-gun salute and honor guard welcome at the airport a decade earlier by the civilian president of Nigeria at the time, Shehu Shagari, who ironically would then be deposed in a 1983 coup led by none other than Major General Muhammadu Buhari, who'd go on to become Nigeria's elected president in 2015. Ironically, Siad would also witness the wizardry of Sani Abacha who had orchestrated his own dance step of coups d'etat, human rights abuses, and money laundering, including the coup that installed Major General Buhari the first time in1983 and another which had him overthrown in 1985.

Siad died in 1995 in Lagos. Whereas Ethiopia has emerged as one of Africa's fastest growing economies and best governed African nations, Somalia continues to suffer from lawlessness and political instability compounded by constant threats by the Al-Qaeda aligned terrorist organization, Al-Shabaab.

That early journey for two idealistic legislators continues to replay itself in my memory as I continue to observe the way the United States deals with troubled nations and the host of figures who lead them. Our mission to the Horn of Africa was rare, if not unprecedented, for first-term congressmen. It was another example of missteps and the awkward moments that shaped my earlier career. The president picked me because I chaired the Foreign Affairs subcommittee. It was happenstance that I ended up on the full committee and assigned to the Africa subcommittee. I had missed the committee assignment meeting, which was not a preferred choice for members of the House, and thus became chairman only because the existing chairman was forced to resign due to an indictment. It is not always about strategy and smart decisions that shape who we are and the paths of our public careers. But sometimes, this works out quick well.

Perhaps, even more powerful than the drama of negotiating war zones and tangling with despots was the experience of bonding with Paul Tsongas who, following that mission to the Horn of Africa, became one of my closest friends and sources of inspiration.

CHAPTER 25

THE SOUL OF OUR
FOREIGN POLICY

It is a bit rewarding going back and rereading what you wrote nearly forty years earlier. Most of the time, I'm impressed with what I had to say, and am pleased to acknowledge that I'd say it again today if asked to. On December 22, 1980, the *New York Times* published an op-ed I had submitted in which I stated that "the advocacy of human rights is the moral imperative in our foreign policy that sets us apart from the Soviet Union. As the beacon of liberty around the world, our nation must pursue policies that help to shape a more decent world. Dare we do less?"

Back at the Foreign Affairs Committee, reorganizing meeting, Congressman Fraser's departure was an opening for me to be the new subcommittee chairman. In the 97th Congress, beginning in 1981, I recommended that the subcommittee title be changed to Subcommittee on Human Rights and International Organizations.

In his 1979 inaugural address, President Jimmy Carter stated that "our commitment to human rights must be absolute." It was his intent to make human rights integral to the nation's foreign policy, however, this would encounter resistance from the remnants of the State Department's more dogged Cold War mentality.

A State Department spokesman stated at the time, "Human rights is a new policy" that affected US economic and defense relationships with other countries and therefore could not be applied in the same way in every circumstance.

Within the Department of State, this proved to be a contentious stance early in the Carter administration. In 1977, President Carter appointed human rights activist Patt Derian, who had fought for school desegregation in Mississippi, to be the Assistant Secretary of State for Human Rights and Humanitarian Affairs. Known for her passion and commitment to human rights, Patt was well prepared to confront brutal dictators—some of whom received US foreign aid—known for torturing their citizens, confiscating assets, and by suppressing citizens, including making them "disappear." A second Carter appointment of note was Roberta Cohen, who had previously served as executive director of the International League for Human Rights, and who would assist Patt Derian in elevating the tenacity of human rights work at the State Department.

Prior to Derian's arrival, the State Department's Cold War policy was one of forgiveness to countries that backed US policy. "We know these allies are dictators," Derian was told by her colleagues, "but they're our dictators." Trying to align President Carter's human rights pledge to ensure it would be priority in conducting foreign policy, she was faced with career State Department officials who were in denial, blocking such attempts to have a new official assert her idealism in what they felt was distracting and even counterproductive.

At every opportunity, the old-school at State would create roadblocks for her, and even plotted to have her removed. By raising the issue with Secretary of State Cyrus Vance and Deputy Secretary Warren Christopher, I was able to remedy some of the opposition. However, the resistance persisted. My subcommittee staff director, Fariborz S. Fatemi, who previously had been assistant to New Jersey governor, Brendan Byrne, was pressing me to raise the matter directly with the president. Patt Derian had a close friendship with Jimmy Carter and shared his strong commitment to making human rights integral to US foreign policy. She was known for her courage to address human rights issues whether or not they aligned with America's strategic and geopolitical positions. She did not hesitate to take on the Argentine Dirty War and helped save many, many dissidents whose lives would have been lost to torture and assassination. Married to Hodding Carter, Assistant Secretary of State Patt "spoke truth to power and never stopped," her husband would later say in an interview after her death in May 2016.

Fariborz was persistent about my personal outreach to President Carter. I was reluctant, saying, "Fariborz, no way can I tell the president how to run the State Department. That's Cy Vance's job, not mine. Besides, it's unlikely I could even get through to him."

He came back to me with this, "Congressman, you are the only one who can do this. You share the president's commitment to human rights, and you are head of the committee. Believe me, he will take your call."

Fariborz apparently had had a good contact at the White House, so I agreed, "Okay, go ahead, make the call, but I doubt if anything will happen."

Before going to New Jersey, Fatemi had served on the staff of Senator Frank Church of Idaho, and had also participated in the presidential campaigns of Robert F. Kennedy, Hubert Humphrey, Ed Muskie, and George McGovern. After leaving Governor Byrne's office, Fatemi had been staff director of the House Foreign Affairs Subcommittee on Human Rights and International Organizations, and special assistant to Senator Joseph R. Biden. Fariborz, an academic of Persian background, was greatly talented and he knew his way around Washington with great agility.

It eventually happened. A private call to the president was scheduled over the weekend. Carter was at Camp David. It was very brief, but I was able to express my concern about Patt Derian's treatment at State, and the ongoing efforts to undermine the human rights policy that he wanted to be the trademark of his presidency. He agreed with my concern, thanked me, and said he would take care of it. I put down the phone and felt pleased that my staff director had steered me in the right direction. That is what they are supposed to do.

One example of the difficulties Patt Derian experienced was how the State Department was handling its own report on human rights. Almost twenty years before the Carter presidency, the Foreign Assistance Act of 1961 mandated that the State Department prepare a report on human rights conditions in countries receiving US economic and security assistance. But it was treated as an internal matter with little significance beyond going through the procedures. The report should have been the public disclosure of human rights violations and improvements among countries we support.

Many of our embassies were reluctant to compile their respective reports—which presented a bureaucratic hurdle that made life more difficult for Patt Derian and her staff. Despite the obstacles, she succeeded in producing a complete report. With the help of Fariborz Fatemi, my subcommittee also passed legislation to include all countries, not just those receiving US aid, in the report. The human rights report, a thorough assessment of such conditions country by country, would be submitted to the House Foreign Affairs Committee. My subcommittee on Human Rights and International Organizations would conduct hearings at the end of February every year upon submission of the report to review findings and make new recommendations for continuing or cutting off support.

Our public hearings featured Patt Derian and Roberta Cohen from State, but it was also a rare occasion for human rights organizations such as Amnesty International, Human Rights Watch, Freedom House, and others to share their concerns, often outrage, about the egregious human rights conditions in a number of countries, some of which the US taxpayer was still funding.

The State Department identified many already under scrutiny in the foreign policy community for a variety of abuses, but I wanted to add more focus on cases of religious persecution. I conducted a series of ten hearings in 1982 on the theme of "Religious Persecution as a Violation of Human Rights." We raised awareness of the issue with a flood of articles and speeches, using the Scripps Howard News Service, which syndicated pieces into many newspapers including *The Seattle Times*. On December 29, 1982, a piece I sent to the Scripps Howard News Service was widely picked up. "During this holiday season, we tend to think of religious persecution in historical terms—Roman killings of Christians, the Inquisition, cruel religious wars, and more recently, the Holocaust. But most people are not familiar with the equally widespread but insidious religious persecution of today. In the contemporary world, thousands of innocent people are the victims of a special kind of human rights violations based solely on their religious beliefs or personal faith," I wrote.

"It is unlikely that the United States can end religious persecution, but we can make the issue an integral part of our foreign policy," I argued. "If America is to remain faithful to her past and values inherent in in those documents that formed this great democracy, then we must stand for religious freedom and human rights in the many countries that continue to abuse their citizens. Churches, synagogues, mosques, and pagodas often provide the last place of refuge for people to stand together for justice."

The sad truth is that few countries in the world enjoyed the religious freedom that is so treasured in the United States, a freedom rooted deeply in our constitution and supported by multiple court decisions over the decades. Few liberties in the country are as embedded as our freedom to worship as we wish.

Examining closely the State Department report. I concluded that there were three violations that stood out as meriting a more arduous and public campaign. These were somewhat obscure and otherwise ignored, but the more I learned about each, the greater my commitment grew to give them priority attention. Each had compelling stories that needed to be told to my subcommittee members and beyond—the Baha'is in Iran, the Copts in Egypt, and the Falashas in Ethiopia.

There are about 600,000 Baha'is in the United States, the second largest Baha'i community in the world after India. There are between five and six million Baha'is in the world. Their US representative came to see me in my office to share the dire situation of his people in Iran. The Baha'i community, he claimed, had been subjected to unwarranted arrests, false imprisonment, beatings, torture, unjustified executions, confiscation and destruction of property owned by individuals, denial of employment, denial of government benefits, denial of civil rights and liberties, and access to higher education. I listened carefully because this was a situation I hadn't heard about before.

The origins of persecution were embedded in a variety of Baha'i teachings that were deemed inconsistent with traditional Islamic belief, including the finality of Muhammad's prophethood, and the placement of the Baha'i religion outside the Islamic faith. Thus, the Baha'is were seen as apostates from Islam, and, according to some Islamists, must choose between repentance and death.

In the mid-1950s, the Iranian government orchestrated a national campaign intended to stir local opposition to Iranian Baha'is. They encouraged a range of activities to incite public passion against the Baha'is, including a propaganda campaign on national radio stations and in official newspapers. Members of the Muslim clergy used sermons to prompt mob violence against the Baha'is, resulting in properties to be destroyed. Baha'i educational centers were looted, cemeteries were desecrated, and many leaders were murdered. Baha'i women were abducted and forced to marry Muslims, others were expelled and dismissed from schools and places of employment.

I was astounded and upset by the reports I heard of systematic denial of religious choice and what seemed like blatant aggression. As the subcommittee received testimony from human rights and nonprofit organizations, it was clear that the Baha'i community in Iran had been subjected to persecution that was both political and cultural, and thus this should be a factor in the bilateral relationship between the US and the Islamic Republic of Iran.

Christians living in the Middle East have endured discrimination for centuries, but the situation in Egypt struck me as different. Coptic Christians are acknowledged as the remaining descendants of the civilization of the ancient Egypt with pharaonic origins. They are the largest ethno-religious minority in Egypt, constituting roughly ten percent of the country's ninety-five million people.

Not unlike Iran and the Baha'is, the persecution in Egypt has not been at the hands of the government, but the state did not do enough to discourage discriminatory action against the Coptic Church. The cultural prejudices against this community had led to the bombings of churches and other deliberate acts of violence. Egyptian prosecutors refused to investigate and the courts that needed to hold those accountable for committed acts of violence did not do their job. All this was well documented by various human rights organizations that appeared before the subcommittee. The evidence was prima facie.

Aside from the humanitarian concern, some ask why was this important to the US government. The historical context is important here. The Camp David Accords took place on September 17, 1978 following twelve days of secret negotiations between Israeli Prime Minister Menachem Begin and Egyptian President Anwar Sadat under the supervision of US President Jimmy Carter. This peace agreement reduced the intense hostility between the two countries in a volatile region. Begin and Sadat shared the 1979 Nobel Peace Prize for this work. The accord addressed the deep-rooted concerns held by both countries, but what sealed the deal was America's pledge of a huge financial commitment to both countries.

At the time, this represented about forty percent of the State Department's foreign assistance program. The succeeding Egyptian presidents had become dependent on America's billions in foreign aid, which Congress had to approve. The treatment of the Coptic Christians could not be ignored. During President Hosni Mubarak's reign, he faithfully met with congressional leaders to ensure the funding would continue.

In 1984, there was an official luncheon hosted by the House Foreign Affairs Committee, with the Speaker of the House scheduled to appear to extend warm greetings to the Egyptian president. Mubarak read an opening statement, which was followed with a few selected questions. As was customary, the Egyptian president was asked what his government was doing to protect the Coptic Christians in Egypt and ensure that those responsible for recent attacks were held accountable.

As I stood up to ask my question, President Mubarak interrupted quickly to say, "Congressman Bonker, I know your question is about the Coptic Christians, so please know my government is doing everything possible to give them the protection they deserve."

Not missing a beat, I responded, "Mr. President, I am now chairman of the Subcommittee on Trade, so my question this time is about our trade relationship." This way, I had answers to two questions while only asking one.

My response amused everyone in the room, but the takeaway was obvious. The Egyptian president was aware and sensitive to congressional concerns about the well-being of the Coptic Christians in his country. He was fully conscious that we were watching this, and that this and a lot of other points were directly related to our conditionality of continuing the very significant amount of aid the US provided to Egypt. Under the watch of my committee, the Copts were safer. This didn't last forever and religious violence in Egypt would later worsen, although the relationship between these conditions and US aid has largely not been written about.

The Falashas in Ethiopia were at a perilous crossroads historically and politically. This group of Ethiopians lived in the northwestern part of the country in an area that included more than 500 small villages across a wide territory. The Falashas were essentially a tributary of Jewish Ethiopians whose historical roots to Canaan go back to the biblical days when the Queen of Sheba journeyed to visit the Jewish King Solomon and returned to her homeland bearing Solomon's child. In present day Ethiopia, the Jewish Falashas live alongside neighbors and even family that are Muslim and Christian.

In my fact-finding trip to Ethiopia in 1977, I became familiar with Colonel Mengistu's systematic persecution of opponents and others who did not conform to his dictatorial demands. During the weeks surrounding his coup, an estimated 2,500 Jewish Ethiopians were killed and 7,000 became homeless. The communist-backed dictator ordered a policy of "villagization," relocating millions of peasant farmers onto state-run cooperatives which proved harmful to Ethiopian Jews called Beta Israel by forcing them to "share" their villages—though they were denied the right to own the land—with non-Jewish farmers. This resulted in increased levels of anti-Semitism throughout the Gondar province where the Falashas predominantly resided.

At the time my subcommittee was conducting hearings on religious persecution, Mengistu's government forbade the practice of Judaism and the teachings of Hebrew. Numerous members of the Beta Israel were imprisoned on fabricated charges of being "Zionist spies," and religious leaders were harassed and monitored by the government. Through forced conversion, dispersal, hunger, disease, and violence, the number of Falashas had been reduced to fewer than 10,000 from about 28,000 in 1975.

In August 1977, Israel Prime Minister Menachem brokered a secret deal with Mengistu to supply the Ethiopian military with weapons in exchange for allowing Falasha Jews to relocate in Israel. By the end of 2008, there were 119,300 people of Ethiopian descent in Israel, including 81,000 people born in Ethiopia and about 38,500 native-born with at least one parent born in Ethiopia. By an act of the Knesset, the Israeli government chartered El-Al airplanes to shuttle Falasha Jews from Ethiopia to Tel Aviv. The arriving Ethiopians were offered Israeli citizenship based on their historic ties as members of the Jewish people, although the rapid emigration from Gondar and the integration in Israel has posed numerous and ongoing complex sociological problems.

Our congressional hearings on religious persecution affirmed President Jimmy Carter's genuine commitment to advancing the cause of human rights. For the nonprofit organizations fully dedicated to religious persecution and human rights, it helped to give them a voice and vindicate their purpose and existence. For the embassies that closely tracked what was going on in Congress and reported back to their foreign ministries, it was a strong signal of what was important in these bilateral relationships.

On October 18, 1979, I published in the *Washington Post* a piece about disappearances in Central America. It began like this: "It is 7:00 a.m. Five men in civilian clothes burst into a home and seize a twenty-three-year-old man. The chief of the gang tells the young man's mother that her son has been named a subversive by a prisoner under custody and is being taken in for questioning. She is told that she can inquire about her son the following day. But the next day—and a thousand days later—the police deny knowing anything about him."

In the article, I intended to capture what had become a phenomenon at the time in the violation of human rights, the "disappeared person." This brutal and cynical practice was occurring almost daily in a significant number of countries. Most of the documentation came from South and Central America in the 1970s, but it was Argentina and Chile that stood out. At the time, Amnesty International estimated that in the previous decade, some 30,000 Latin Americans had disappeared as a matter of political repression. The era was characterized by military rule in these two nations where thousands had disappeared without any trace after being arrested by police, security forces, and paramilitary police forces. A pattern existed that had brutally removed people with no official accountability.

I kept as my mantra President Carter's words that human rights were to be the "soul of American foreign policy." As such, these horrendous acts of abuse in our hemisphere could not be ignored. As the new chairman of the Foreign Affairs Subcommittee on Human Rights, I was prepared to escalate these terrifying human rights violations as a national priority and conduct hearings on the "disappearances." Aside from the work of human rights organizations, the subject had been largely ignored at the time. The hearings highlighted the problem with emotional testimonies about how this abuse was, in fact, a rude reality in certain countries. Having President Carter's human rights appointees testify at the hearings certainly resonated with the embassies and authorities in the violating countries that we targeted. That *Washington Post* article in October 1979 concluded with a call for action: "We must let the word go forth to the relatives of the disappeared, to those locked in secret detention camps, and to the exiles around the world that 'if you are silenced, we will speak for you.'"

In 1982, filmmaker Costa-Gavras responded by making the historical drama *Missing*, with Jack Lemmon and Sissy Spacek, based on the true story of American journalist Charles Horman who disappeared in the Chilean coup of 1973. The film shared the Palme d'Or at the Cannes Film Festival with the Kurdish film *Yol* by Yilmaz Güney, also about political oppression. *Missing* was banned in Chile by dictator Augusto Pinochet, and I like to think that our work in the subcommittee helped elevate global awareness of systematic repression of people due to their beliefs, and advanced the cause for greater freedom of political and religious expression.

CHAPTER 26

TAXING ALL BUT GALL

Early in my tenure as the local congressman from Washington State's 3rd District, I had a scheduled a speech before the Rotary Club in Aberdeen, a lumber mill town in Grays Harbor County, where I would comment on national issues and address local concerns about the area's economic problems. This community was typical of many that were spread throughout Southwest Washington that had come to look more like ghost towns. Along main streets, retail outlets were posting "Closed" signs and the loss of lumber mill jobs had multiplied and was now very troubling. I had followed the lumber issue closely and was committed to helping on this, yet as a backbencher in those early days, I had not notched too many positive results yet as a newly elected Representative. It would take greater seniority and a higher committee position to deliver big time for my constituents.

When I entered the room, I was pulled aside to meet with a group of men who were not there to attend the Rotary meeting. As we assembled around a dining table, I spotted five men on the other side of the room who were obviously mill workers. They wore plaid shirts, suspenders, jeans, and heavy footwear. I was told that they represented family-owned companies that operated the shake and shingle plants, the wood that was largely used for roofing. These plants were located all around my district.

One of the men held a folder and he spoke first. "Congressman, we are here to get your help, otherwise we'll have to shut down our businesses." Their concern surprised me. It was not the logs being shipped to Japan that upset them but the imports from our neighboring Canada. The message resonated. "The Canadians are doing great harm to our companies." The Canadian provinces owned the timberlands and this made the valuable resources available free of charge to Canadian-owned timber companies. America's small shake and shingle plants had to pay market price for their timber from federal and state lands, whereas the Canadians got the wood at no cost and were able to process the wood and sell it at a handsome profit while undercutting the Washington State competitors who were hugely disadvantaged.

The guy with the folder reached out and handed it to me.

"Mr. Congressman, we've been informed that to stop this problem, it will take the federal government to do something. We've been informed to give this petition to you."

We had begun to work on an anti-dumping/countervailing (AD/CV) law that would impose an import tariff on incoming products that were subsidized by a foreign government. I knew what these guys were referring to and partly agreed with them. The issues, though, were far more complex. It would take a prestigious DC law firm specializing on the AD/CV tariff law and a long trial to get results. My speech at the Rotary went well and the mood was jovial, although the group of five guys and their petition made an impression. I needed to weigh in on this quickly. I couldn't let our communities become ghost towns. Driving back to the airport, I drove through several small cities like Hoquiam, where I saw trucks hauling logs to the Grays Harbor Port where they'd be shipped to Japan for processing into lumber. The reality was starting to sink in deep. I had understood the issue but I hadn't really felt its impact in my gut until just then. The lumber mills in my district had no chance of matching the egregious bids by the Japanese. The Japanese were getting our logs, and our jobs were going to Japan's twenty thousand lumber mills. Now our shake and shingle mills were threatened by subsidized lumber imports from Canada. My district's economy was under siege and suffering because of unfair trade practices that were not being addressed. Our local issues were tied deeply into the realm of international commerce, and I had to make some loud noise about this back in the other Washington.

Back at the capitol, the House Foreign Affairs Committee was meeting to reorganize and make assignments to the various subcommittees. I would now become chairman of the subcommittee on International Economic Policy and Trade. The jurisdiction covered a spectrum of issues including economic sanctions, export controls on technology, export promotion, and more, however, there had been little attention and no leadership on any of these issues. This was about to change. I knew what my calling had to be. Trade. It bridged my district with my interest in international affairs and joined economic growth with fairness. Trade would become my signature topic and it continues to be today, far beyond my days in Congress.

Trade is, was, and will be a two-way street, but since the Great Depression, the US Congress had been treating trade as primarily one-way traffic. Congress was obsessed with imports and quotas and other trade restrictions. The House Ways and Means Committee presided over these issues and had become a bumper crop on the Omnibus Trade Bill and bilateral trade deals for hundreds of law firms, lobbyists, and trade associations all savoring to deliver for their clients and members, all pushing Congress to limit imports of foreign products. Such efforts were intended to protect American companies which profits were threatened by cheaper products flowing into the US. When pushed to a more severe form, limiting the flow of goods into the US or imposing imports on these goods bordered on protectionism. The American system was not conceived to unfairly protect American companies. It was conceived to maintain open markets that enhanced the flow of goods and services based on the mechanisms of the marketplace.

Protectionism can and often does run amok, as the world clearly witnessed in 1928 when Congress passed legislation called the Smoot-Hawley Tariff Act, which promptly caused the world trading system to collapse, and thus precipitated the Great Depression. In 1988, I authored a book, *America's Trade Crisis,* which was published by Houghton-Mifflin. I described in a chapter called "Perils of Protectionism" the firestorm that occurred in a reckless Congress, a chaotic moment that also had its moments of levity. "By the late 1920s", I cited, "agrarian protectionism was on the rise. Farmers were resentful that they were not sharing in the general prosperity of the 1920s. If manufacturing could benefit from a little import relief, farmers reasoned, perhaps they, too, could prosper from some tariff protection."

In his 1928 campaign for president, and on taking office, Herbert Hoover's Clarion Call for higher tariffs led to a special session of Congress to consider the issue. Senators and congressmen seized the occasion and engaged in wholesale vote trading, that was rampant enough for elected leaders to jump on the bandwagon that was steaming through Congress. What began as a surgical treatment to assist a few ailing industries turned into free-for-all plundering that went on for a year.

"Hundreds of trade associations were formed that triggered an unbridled frenzy of logrolling," I wrote, "jockeying for maximum protection for commodity and industry producers, leading to enactment of the Smoot-Hawley Tariff Act that hiked import fees to 100 percent on over 20,000 imported products." As I reread these lines from 1988 and then read the front pages of today's *Washington Post* thirty years later, I shudder. " On the Senate side, another 1,200 amendments were added that proved so egregious, promoting Democrat Senator Thaedeus H. Caraway of Arkansas to declare that, 'I might suggest that we have taxed everything in this bill except gall,' to which Senator Carter Glass of Virginia responded, 'Yes, and a tax on that would bring considerable revenue.'"

What Congress sent to the president proved so alarming it prompted 1,000 of the nation's leading economists to sign a petition urging President Hoover to veto the bill.

The Smoot-Hawley Tariff Act tells of the folly and risks in how our political leaders have treated with parochial naivete the international trade. If there is a huge trade deficit, bilateral or globally, or if foreign suppliers are threatening a particular sector, then our response has been to erect barriers to block or limit those imports. But heaven forbid other nations act with the same reflex. The American Congress' idea of level playing field has often been shaped like the slopes of Mount Rainer, which would have any hiker huffing on the incline. There are serious consequences in going down that path erected with trade barriers.

Other countries reciprocate by imposing tariffs or quotas on US products, as we saw following the Smoot-Hawley Act. There is also harm inflicted on the US side, including trading companies, distributors, end users, and ultimately, retailers feeling the effects immediately. We help some Americans while sacrificing others. How many, which ones, to what degree—all need to be calculated. There is job loss, price hikes, shortages, and more to consider. A better alternative was to have a more robust program to expand our exports and deepen our competitive edge, which was the opportunity that awaited me as chairman of the International Economic Policy and Trade Committee.

But first, this was a rare opportunity to deliver on my campaign pledge to stop exporting logs and jobs to Japan. A key discovery for me was the trade provision in our laws that allowed the Department of Commerce to limit exports of any key resource if it were for economic security reasons. This, of course, presented the opportunity I'd been savoring. I inserted language in the authorizing bill to prohibit the exporting of any trees harvested from federal timberlands since these exports jeopardized the economic security of the country, which was both convenient and true.

Later that week, the full committee chairman, Lee Hamilton, a

Republican from the 9th District of Indiana who later went on to investigate covert arms transactions with Iran and served as the vice chairman of the 9/11 Commission, pulled me aside and said, "Don, I understand what's behind this amendment, but regret that I cannot allow it to pass." While maintaining a cordial discussion, it became obvious that his close friend, Representative Tom Foley, had weighed in on behalf of Weyerhaeuser, the Washington State company that had grown into one of the largest manufacturers of plywood, hardboard, particle board, and pulp, as well as other huge timber companies who were strongly opposed to it.

"Lee," I explained, "all these traditional family-owned businesses in the Northwest are up against the big timber companies that are bidding on behalf of the Japanese." I pleaded that this amendment will save those small family businesses. He said he agreed with me, but was in a difficult position. I had a backup plan. "Why don't we limit the ban to cedar logs?" That was what the shake and shingle plants in my district used.

He said, "Okay, rewrite the amendment to apply only to cedar logs." I did, and it was approved and it became the law of the land, and these family-owned companies still remain in business today!

The new subcommittee chairmanship not only enabled me to fulfill my primary campaign pledge, it also positioned me to be a national leader on international trade. I had my own budget and staff with jurisdiction over federal export-related programs, primarily the State and Commerce Departments.

At the helm of the new subcommittee, I contemplated, where should I start? My predecessors had done very little, and thus there was not too much to build on or continue with. A senior staffer who had been on my committee, and had just taken a position at the State Department, had showed up one day to talk about his new position. He was to be head the Trade and Development Agency (TDA), an agency that no one had ever heard of.

"Don, this idea has great potential," he started, "but it's a one-man shop—no budget, no staff, not much of a mandate." This was typical of how things worked out between the two branches of government. Back in 1961, someone had put a sentence in the State Department authorization bill to create the agency. Nothing else. The State Department, preoccupied with foreign policy and foreign aid, had no interest in economic and trade matters, so the TDA had been dormant for almost twenty years. But the staffer seized the opportunity, telling me, "It had been set up to help developing countries deal with their infrastructure and other major projects." He said the only way to get it up and running was if I put some teeth into the legislation.

"Okay," I responded with cautious hesitance, "but what do you need?"

He explained that banks were hesitant to finance these projects unless they had more information about the viability and risks associated with the projects. He continued, "What the agency can do is conduct feasibility studies that address the banks' concerns." I suggested he draft language that I could include as an amendment to the State Department authorization bill.

This was a bit of serendipity, but it was a first step. Over the next few years, I greatly expanded the TDA mandate and funding, and eventually passed a bill to move it out the Department of State to make it independent. Its mission was to help US companies enter highly competitive global markets. One example included bringing transportation ministers from the former Soviet Republics to Seattle where they'd be offered an impressive display of American capabilities and equipment needed to upgrade and expand the airport facilities in their respective countries. Indeed, the TDA ended up countering what our European competitors were already doing to get for themselves a good share of the post-Cold War market in Eastern Europe. We should have been doing that before, but at least now with the TDA, we were beginning.

Another innovation was the Inter-American Housing event, which also took place in Seattle. Invitations were sent to Ministers of Housing throughout South America to view firsthand the viability of using wood products to build housing. Traditionally, these countries avoided using wood products out of fear of fire, so their housing was mostly brick and mortar, which took longer to build and cost considerably more. At the Sheraton Hotel in downtown Seattle, a 1,000-square-foot house was constructed in the hotel lobby during the three-day event.

The 2016 TDA budget of $75 million generated an estimated $5.6 billion in exports for US companies, supporting 32,000 jobs across the country. It is illustrative of USTDA working with partner countries to modernize transportation infrastructure facilities, providing technical assistance in various sectors, energy renewal and innovation, training assistance, and the list goes on. Back in 1982, we started with nothing and built the program from scratch.

The USTDA had been idle for almost twenty years, and all it took was one entrepreneurial staffer to come on the scene, dare to sneak around State Department bureaucracy, and approach a new congressional committee chairman to launch an agency into fruition and generate wealth and jobs for the American people.

VII. Nature's Cathedral

CHAPTER 27

SONGS OF JOY

It is impossible to be alive and not be sensitive to the inspiring natural beauty of the environment. Being from the state of Washington only accentuates the connection to the extraordinary natural resources of our planet. Washington's Daniel Evans, who served as governor for three terms and then as US Senator from 1983 to 1989, said something that has always resonated within me: "When there is doubt, I hope we will always preserve wilderness. If ultimately we have too much, uses can be changed, but wilderness destroyed cannot be regained." That is a useful mantra as environment issues deepen and climate change grows as an increasingly menacing threat.

During my years in Congress, it was a privilege to represent an area so blessed with abundant natural resources—breathtaking scenic beauty, wilderness richness, an inspirational destination for many seeking to enjoy the planet's natural cathedral. Reverence with nature, for me, has been kin with godliness. The holiness of wonder and spiritual enlightenment comes while contemplating the glorious mystery and beauty of life itself. I have always felt a deep commitment to do whatever I could do to preserve the state's rich natural heritage as an enduring legacy for others to enjoy.

At the same time, much of this wilderness treasure was under assault as extractive industries and development strategies ramped up, and as a result, the state began to be marked by more and more scarred hillsides, fouled streams, and places where the beauty of yesteryear had fled. For me, the challenge was how to balance the economic well-being of my district's rural communities, which largely depended on sustainable harvesting and processing of timber and fish, with the value of preserving the remaining wild lands which would be forever cherished by both local residents, their offspring, and growing urban populations that needed nature for recreation, relaxation, and resourcing our inner life. For me, balance is the key and harmony.

An early challenge in my congressional career involved the eighty-mile Columbia River Gorge, carved through the Cascade Mountains by repeated catastrophic breakouts of mammoth glacial lakes at the end of the last Ice Age, and one of the most dramatic landscapes—and geologic stories—anywhere. In the early 1920s, Samuel Lancaster, noted for his elegant design of the highway paralleling the Columbia River, captured the exquisiteness of the Columbia River Gorge this way: "God shaped these great mountains round about us, and lifted up these mighty domes. He fashioned the Gorge of the Columbia, fixed the course of the broad river, and caused the crystal steams both small and great, to leap down from the crags and sing their never-ending songs of joy."

This description of the gorge continues to speak for all who cherish the awesome beauty and wonder of 3,000 basalt cliffs scoured out by the ancient Missoula floods—from the early preservationists a century ago to our present and future generations of concerned citizens. The gorge sheltered for eons our Native American peoples, provided the gateway to the Pacific for Lewis and Clark, and today, continues to bless the Earth with abundant natural resources, ranging from deep verdant forests in the west to the Columbia Plateau desert in the east. The gorge spans nine distinct ecosystems with sixteen species of wildflowers found nowhere else in the world and boasts the largest waterfalls in all of North America. Back in those early days as a young congressman driving along the scenic Columbia River Highway, now called the Samuel Lancaster Highway after the legendary landscape architect who planned the route, I loved that shared thrill of experiencing the overwhelming magnificence of this national treasure. Fifty years later, driving along Highway 84 on the Oregonian side of the river, people can still enjoy nature. But as they glance across the gorge to the north bank on the Washington side, the view is tarnished by large bare patches where timber had been clear-cut. Lumber mills with their wigwam burners filling the air with smoke unfold, and a pulp and paper mill lies a bit further west, while aluminum smelters burn on the east. While both Washington and Oregon states shared the Columbia River Gorge, their perspectives were quite different. For Oregonians, it only took a short drive from downtown Portland to enter the majestic gorge, which city folks often did, showing off to relatives and friends the natural splendor of Multnomah Falls, idyllic Hood River. The Oregonian side of the gorge had multiple locations for parks, campgrounds, hiking, bike paths, and boat landings. Portland's preservationists, including the Friends of the Columbia Gorge, partook in a campaign to save the gorge, which grew over the decades.

Oregonian voters took the problem of uncontrolled growth very seriously, and in 1973, their state legislature passed Senate Bill 100, which required every Oregon city and county to prepare a comprehensive land use plan which was aligned with the general state goals.

This was not the path that Washington State followed. A parallel drive from Vancouver eastward through Skamania and Klickitat counties, which had its own natural beauty along the river, revealed the scars of logging on the mountain side and lowlands. Lumber, paper, and aluminum mills transformed the once pristine landscapes into industrial sites, which also provided jobs and economic well-being to the local communities.

Two hundred miles to the northwest in the Seattle/Puget Sound area, I found it hard to muster much interest, let alone support, for the Columbia River Gorge. The political price of conservation was enormous for Senator Dan Evans and local Congressman Sid Morrison. Anyone daring to support legislation that would overlay federal and state land use controls on local gorge communities was committing political suicide.

Enactment of such legislation would simply not be possible in today's divisive political environment. Although "wedge politics" were coming into play in the 1980s, the Washington congressional delegation was still remarkably committed to the principle of nonpartisan teamwork for the state's interest. With senior statesman Senator Mark O. Hatfield serving as dean of the more unruly Oregon delegation, and Republicans Dan Evans and Sid Morrison leading the charge in the Washington delegation, there was hope that enactment of a conservation bill for the Columbia River Gorge has a chance. It was a small window of opportunity for the century-long effort to protect the gorge.

Oregon's various attempts to protect the gorge were building momentum with the launch of the Columbia Gorge Coalition in 1979 and its push for an Interior Department report that established the public interest in a national scenic area. Hearings were held in Washington, DC and in the Pacific Northwest, but differences among gorge protection activists over management with property and local rights organizations stymied progress. Because local officials on the Washington side of the gorge opposed federal and state protection, the only option for preserving the gorge was the US Congress. It would take federal legislation to define the boundary of a scenic area and establish a management structure to restrict development and overlay protective guidelines on the six counties and the many localities on both sides of the Columbia River.

The chances of federal legislation improved significantly when Senator Evans made "gorge protection" a top priority and charged his legislative counsel, Joe Mentor, with the task of reworking the gorge bill and hammering out a workable compromise. Although most Oregon delegation members were on board, there was jostling among members and staff over the management entity. Should it be the US Forest Service or the National Park Service? In addition, conservative House members, Bob Smith (R-NH) and Denny Smith (R-OR), were dead set against federal land use controls and infringement of private property rights.

The rising prospect of federal gorge legislation sparked outrage, especially in local areas along the Columbia River. Opposition quickly formed on the Washington side, headed by a 400-strong organization called Columbia Gorge United and other local opposition to any government control over private land. Bruce Stevenson, president of the SDS Lumber Company, which dominated much of the gorge and continues to manage 70,000 acres of wooded land, told *The Seattle Times* that "Everyone in the gorge except a few welfare hippies was against this legislation." Ed McLarney, a local newspaper editor for his weekly *Skamania County Pioneer,* stated that "the gorge-for-lunch bunch is threatening our way of life here. We are an endangered species, little counties like ours." In a memorable display of political courage and due process, Senator Evans endured repeated—and heated—public hearings in gorge communities where many of the residents let him know in no uncertain terms how opposed they were to the proposed gorge legislation. Local Congressman Sid Morrison, whose family ran a local fruit company, also got an earful from furious constituents. Opponents may not have liked the final compromise, but they could not say they hadn't been heard.

The Hatfield-Evans proposal was carefully crafted, striking the delicate balance of preserving the eighty-mile Columbia River Gorge while minimizing the impact on the local economies, and helping to boost them with visitor facilities on both sides of the river. Its main features were designating the boundaries of the scenic area and establishing a Gorge Commission of twelve local citizens, half appointed by the two governors and one from each of the six counties boarding the Columbia River, to be funded by the two states and supported by a professional staff.

Still, the odds of enacting a gorge bill in the final days of the 99th

Congress were slim. The Senate passed a version of the gorge bill on October 8th. But the House National Parks and Recreation subcommittee chairman, frustrated by procedural delaying tactics by Representative Denny Smith of Oregon and other Republicans on the subcommittee, ended consideration of the gorge bill. On October 15, 1986, just before the end of the congressional session, Senator Evans' aide, Joe Mentor, came by my office, which had become a base of operations for gorge supporters including Bowen Blair, executive director of the Friends of the Columbia Gorge. Joe had just walked out of a frustrating meeting with Oregon's Bob Smith, one of the bill's staunch opponents. He had thought that allowing the opponents an opportunity to offer several amendments might strike the right balance.

Based on that information, Joe Mentor and my legislative director, Dan Evans, marched over to the capitol office of Washington Representative Tom Foley, who was serving then as House Majority Whip. After a brief exchange, Foley led us across the hall to the Rules Committee, which allocated floor time for bills and just so happened to be meeting at that moment. At the Rules Committee, meeting Oregon representatives Ron Wyden and Jim Weaver were there working to get precious floor time scheduled before the end of the session for the gorge bill, which hadn't even been favorably reported from committee. Foley huddled with then Rules Committee Chairman Claude Pepper from Florida, known for his strong anti-Castro stance. Congressman Bob Smith arrived in time to hear Chairman Claude Pepper emerge from the closed-door session and tell him that he would be allowed to offer three amendments when the bill came up on the next day, literally the final hours of the 99th Congress.

On October 16, the gorge bill, HR 5705, which has been introduced by Jim Weaver the day before, was miraculously brought to the House floor with a modified closed rule allowing for several hours of debate and three amendments. One of the three amendments, requiring that at least one governor-appointed Gorge Commission member from each state be a resident of the scenic area, was adopted and the bill was approved on a vote of 290 to 91. But with only hours before adjournment, the Senate had to take up and adopt the House-passed bill as amended without change.

Senators Mark Hatfield and Dan Evans, both moderate Republicans and former governors, entered the room. Hatfield's staff had the House bill "held at the desk" of the Senate, meaning it could be called up for consideration by unanimous consent. After several unsuccessful attempts, Hatfield was able to bring the bill up for consideration. His position as chair of the powerful Senate Appropriations Committee was a serious

deterrent to any senator who might have objected. After several clarifi-
cations, the gorge bill was given full congressional approval in the final
hours of the 99th Congress.

With the gorge bill passed by both Houses of Congress, there was
still one more hurdle to clear, the signature by the president. President
Ronald Reagan's White House did not mince words in declaring that the
enacted bill was destined for a veto once it reached the president's desk in
the Oval Office.

It took Senator Mark Hatfield's experience and tactical skills to cleverly obtain President Reagan's signature on the Columbia River Gorge
National Scenic Area Act. Knowing that Reagan's top priority at the time
was funding of his Star Wars missile defense program, Senator Hatfield's
people graciously notified the White House that the Appropriations
Committee's busy schedule may have to delay any action on the Star Wars
project. Ah politics! Hatfield's message to the president was clear. And it
worked. The Columbia River Gorge National Scenic Area Act was signed
into law on November 17, 1986, the last day before a "pocket veto" would
have killed the measure for good.

How the two Northwest senators gathered bipartisan support among
House members in both states—overcoming insurmountable odds and
opposition and persuaded a reluctant president to sign a bill that was
contrary to his political and personal beliefs—made this a landmark
achievement? Senator Evans had to deal with his own constituent outrage
over the idea of a federal commission with authority to curb economic
development and even requiring permits to build a garage. While Senator
Hatfield garnered constituent support, his challenge had been getting it
passed in the Senate and signed by President Reagan. These two senators
working together, and with the Northwest House delegation, demonstrated the best of a political system that can work if there is bipartisan
will. These senators put the national interest, preserving the Columbia
River Gorge for future generations, above politics and displayed the leadership that was so essential to have made this happen.

After departing from Congress, I was appointed to the Gorge
Commission by Washington State's governors, Christine Gregoire and
Jay Inslee, and in January 2016, became its vice chairman. As one of
twelve commissioners, I worked closely with environmental groups, local
officials, Native American tribes, and other stakeholders to achieve the
Act's mission—preserving this cherished natural resource without disruption to the local economies. To have the federal government oversee
management of private land on this scale was unprecedented. Yet thirty

years later, the Gorge Commission and staff, headed by Bowen Blair, had proven successful, working closely with local officials and all the stakeholders, committed to achieving the mandates and goals in the National Scenic Area Act.

National Geographic magazine in December 2009 rated the Columbia River Gorge and scenic area as number six of 133 of the World's Great Places to visit. It noted "the incredible job of protecting the views and many towns with considerable charm," but also recognized "this is a federally managed scenic area that benefits from some of the best land-preservation programs in the nation." When I read that in this revered publication, I remembered just how proud I was to be the only congressman in the United States to have voted for the National Scenic Area Act and also to serve as a member of the Columbia River Gorge Commission.

CHAPTER 28

SHOREBIRDS SEEKING REFUGE

Bowerman Basin is one of only a handful of major migration refueling spots for shorebirds in the entire United States. Every spring, these mudflats become feeding grounds for more than a million shorebirds. Lying within the Grays Harbor National Wildlife Refuge, Bowerman Basin's 1,500 acres of salt marsh and mudflats play host each year to the massive influx of shorebirds that stop to rest and feed—some doubling their body weight in ten days after a thousand mile nonstop leg of their 7,000-mile journey from South America to nesting grounds in the Arctic.

Flocks of migrating shorebirds and waterfowl are present in smaller numbers in the fall, offering a rare opportunity to view shorebirds on their return migration, though nothing like the concentrated spring migration. In the winter, flocks of Canada geese may be found on the mudflats, while the lagoons offer birders a chance to see many types of waterfowl in the spring. All the usual ducks are there as well as gulls and a few wintering shorebirds. It is quite a gathering, and no humane individual would ever want to see this lost.

For bird lovers and advocates of preserving estuaries, Bowerman Basin was nature's crown jewel. But in the mid-1970s, it was about to be replaced with an industrial development project. That was the intention of the Grays Harbor port commission, the linchpin to the regional economy, and whose ownership of this estuary gave them the final say on such matters.

Port of Grays Harbor became the state's second public port with operations beginning back in 1922. From the outset, it was all about the timber sector. Lumber mills located on the shore enabled the rafting of their logs down diverse rivers from the logging camps only to be loaded on ships and hauled overseas. Over the decades, Port of Grays Harbor required large-scale harbor improvements, which included dredging channels—an expensive process which demanded significant funding from public and private sources. In the 1960s, the logging and lumber industry received a temporary boost from Mother Nature—the 1962 Columbus Day storm blew down thousands of trees, which resulted in the salvage of a huge quantity of timber. An unprecedented quantity of logs stacked up in the Port of Grays Harbor district.

Twenty years later, the decline in cutting and shipping prompted the port's general manager, Henry "Hank" Soike, to diversify and expand the area's industrial base. Soike's adroit lobbying outreach had him on my doorstep in Congress with the clear intent of securing federal funding for the dredging projects that he needed to deepen the inner harbor channels for ever larger ocean-going vessels. In essence, federal funding was needed to improve the infrastructure to accommodate foreign ships transporting Washington logs to overseas mills.

Soike was used to being shown royal treatment on Capitol Hill. Washington State's Senator Warren Magnuson was chairman of the Appropriations Committee. My predecessor, Julia Butler Hansen, had chaired a House Appropriation subcommittee, which had given Soike much needed access to federal funding. However, when I ran in the Democratic primary, Soike strongly supported my opponent. Now, the red carpet treatment that he had become accustomed would change. In fact, Soike got no carpet at all. Just my waiting room like anyone else. Yet Soike had sufficient experience and political savvy that he knew how to work around a freshman congressman to get what he wanted.

In the 1960s, specially allocated areas were established called Industrial Development Districts and Soike utilized loopholes in their regulations to enable the port to use its authority to lease land to companies which had located their manufacturing and related businesses in Grays Harbor County. Soike's ambitious plan was called the Grays Harbor Estuary Management Plan, and it was designed to convert this coveted estuary into an industrial park despite the opposition he and others encountered from environmentalists and public leaders statewide.

In early 1987, I met with Helen Engle, director of the National Audubon Society, and other environmentalists to discuss if Congress could pass legislation that would protect the shorebirds in this prime refuge area. As the local congressman, the Audubon Society was a first step, but I faced strident challenges. I had to confront Soike directly, navigate through the House committees, leverage favorable action on the Senate side, and finally, assume the likelihood of a veto if it reached the Reagan White House.

At the local level, my staff and I met with property owners potentially affected by the wildlife refuge proposal, city and county officials, a broad range of conservationists, and port officials. Back in Congress, we worked with the committees of jurisdiction on legislation and other Washington State delegation members who served with me on the House Committee on Merchant Marine and Fisheries, which had jurisdiction over National Wildlife Refuge designations. I then reached out to Senator Dan Evans, a Republican, who had been a governor of Washington State and who had a good environmental record. Evans was keen on the idea, but we shared differences over federal compensation on how to acquire property to preserve the refuge. Ultimately, we resolved these and my strategy advanced.

The Seattle Times ran a loud headline on December 10, 1987: "Evans and Bonker resolve wildlife refuge dispute." The article went on to report that "this year, Bonker crafted a refuge bill that won the support of both environmentalists and local landowners." The bill called for a 1,800-acre refuge and allowed the Port of Grays Harbor to accept compensation for its land either in cash or in "mitigation credits" to be used to pay compensation claims against the port "for environmental damage caused by the port's landfills elsewhere in the region."

The bill also ordered the US Fish and Wildlife Service to acquire sixty-five acres at the head of the bay to be used for a possible visitor center site and to pay the city of Hoquiam, which owned the land, $500,000. This was a clear win for everyone. I was pleased with the solution I had been instrumental in crafting.

Time, though, was running out and we only had days before the end of the year. My staff assumed a hectic pace of nonstop negotiations with Senator Evans' people and the House committee to resolve the remaining differences and get the bill signed and shipped off to the White House. Soike and other local officials accepted the reality that the bill would pass now that it included local economic benefits. On August 22, 1988, President Ronald Reagan signed the Bowerman Basin Wildlife Refuge legislation into law.

On April 22, 1989, the new legislation took effect and was officially recognized at the Grays Harbor National Wildlife Refuge Appreciation Day ceremony, which was sponsored by the National Audubon Society. By this time, I had announced that I was giving up my seat in the US House of Representatives and was running for the Senate. The Grays

Harbor National Wildlife Refuge would be my last of several major accomplishments. At the ceremony, Audubon Society director Helen Engle paid tribute to my efforts, and with a grace I deeply appreciated, recognized and noted my track record of environmental achievements during my seven terms in Congress.

"Few sites—a bare handful at most—compare to Bowerman Basin for its importance to shorebird migrations and no one compares to former Congressman Don Bonker in having made the difference in protecting this jewel of a site on the Washington coast. Because of his efforts, this critical place will provide safe haven for the migrations coursing northward to their nesting grounds in the Arctic."

Her citation went beyond Bowerman, noting the addition of Point of Arches to Olympia National Park in 1975, "Bonker's first achievement for his constituency." There was also the amending of a bill which stopped western red cedar exports and, of course, my attempts at passing an Olympic Peninsula wild and scenic rivers bill despite the political suicide it represented. I had contributed to Protection Island's being added to the National Wildlife Refuge System, and had succeeded in helping to add a quarter of a million acres of inventory to the 1984 Washington State Wilderness Act, followed by the creation of the precedent-setting Mount St. Helens Volcanic National Monument. in addition to the Grays Harbor National Wildlife Refuge, an ongoing sustainable resource, which was the reason for the ceremony in 1989.

Engle called the refuge "a well-deserved tribute to Don Bonker...the congressman dedicated to preserving Washington's natural heritage for all Americans." That was one of the most touching tributes I've ever received. I'm grateful for the support of Dan Evans, my senior staff assistant, and my staff who were so instrumental in spearheading this work, tirelessly interacting with the committees of jurisdiction, and Senator Evans' office under time pressure restraints to get the work done before I left Coess at the end of 1988. A lawmaker is only as good as his or her staff, and mine was remarkable.

Conservation and economic progress are often viewed as irreconcilable. From the outset, the enormous challenge I was faced with was characterized by the delicate balance of economic well-being of constituents with the indisputable need to preserve the area's natural resources. Balance is at the heart of justice, and justice embraces economic justice and social justice and moral justice and legal justice. Each concern needs to be addressed squarely and honesty, and the multiple needs of individuals and families and communities and companies all need to be satisfied. Lawmakers need to be judges and prophets and economists and priests. We need to be fair and wise as well as philosophical and politically astute. My district was heavily dependent on timber with logging and lumber mills providing the jobs that supported the local communities. Many towns in Southwest Washington were looking like ghost towns. To advocate saving large tracts of trees for the benefit of others was— as mentioned by Helen Engle—political suicide. In December 1988, weeks before the end of my term in office, Longview's *The Daily News*, published in the heart of timberland, wrote that when I had first taken office in 1975, "Southwest Washington was notably lacking in wilderness preserves. He is leaving office in January after helping achieve signifi- cant protection for the region's rich natural heritage. Bonker doesn't get exclusive credit for these achievements; none of them would have been possible without his commitment. Importantly, his accomplishments in natural resource conservation were made without sacrificing the timber and water-based industries of the region." What pleased me most, and what I care about sharing with policy makers and our next generation of leaders, is what the *Longview Daily News* went on to say. "Bonker's lead- ership has shown there is room for compromise and a surprising amount of common ground if competing groups cast aside their biases and mis- conceptions. Perhaps that lesson is as important a legacy as the majestic natural cathedral future generations will find in the Long Island Cedar Grove." If competing groups cast aside their biases, that is what Congress went on to forget and to ignore. Our government entered a long down- ward slide toward a partisanship that hurt the larger common interests of the republic, and rattled the very essence of a system designed to serve the greater good. My prayers today are for a return to the ethical stance that says well-intended, thoughtful leaders can cast aside their biases and create solutions to complex problems.

CHAPTER 29

VOLCANIC FURY

The postcard image of a graceful and symmetrical peak that reflected in the blue waters of the lake at its base all changed in an instant at 8:32 a.m. Sunday, May 18, 1980. The earth shook.

The north side of Mount St. Helens gave way. A firestorm of volcanic fury surged from the broken peak. What followed was a time of drama and determination for Southwest Washington residents—a time that few who lived through it will ever forget.

Anyone flying from San Francisco to Seattle and occupying a window seat on the right side of the aircraft could view the three magnificent mountains that defined the natural beauty of the Northwest. Mount Hood outside Portland, Oregon; followed by Mount St. Helens, which flanked my congressional district; and finally, Mount Rainer, which bordered the Puget Sound.

The same flight path in March 1980 revealed what was waiting to happen. From a gaping hole and a new crater spewed black volcanic ash into the winds. The summit looked as though it had been ravaged by a fire, which burned on the snow and rendered everything black. From the plane, one could see giant cracks and feel the great pressure pushing from within the mountain and causing the summit to swell and split.

After seven weeks of ominous suspense, on May 18th, the mountain exploded with a bang heard as far away as the Canadian border. The blast flattened thousands of acres of trees on the north flank of the mountain, unearthed the soil, and caused mudslides that choked the Toutle and Cowlitz rivers and spewed a 76,500-foot high cloud of hot ash that turned the day into night across all of Eastern Washington.

Apocalyptic.

Twenty-five years later, *The Washington Post* recaptured the essence of this catastrophic natural event, calling it "the most destructive eruption in US history," and reminding us that the event killed fifty-seven people, "incinerating a few, mummifying some, crushing, drowning or asphyxiating the rest. The summit of Mount St. Helens, named after an 18th century British nobleman, is now 1,314 feet lower, has become an icon of volcanic vulnerability in the Pacific Northwest."

I recall my disbelief of what was happening in my congressional district as I read in the *Seattle Post Intelligencer* the morning after the eruption. "Just before sunset," I read, "the 9,677-foot mountain belched out a dense cloud of smoke and debris in an eruption that continued with a drumbeat of explosions, blowing foul-smelling columns of steam, ash, and boulders high into the air over Mount St. Helens last night as molten lava from deep within the earth continued to breathe fire into the snow-covered volcano." As the news continued to pour in, I began to panic. The greatest natural disaster in America was happening in my district. The reporting confirmed many lives were in danger; ultimately, fifty-seven were killed directly. The eruption created a three billion cubic yard debris flow—filling the Toutle River valley an average of a mile wide and 10 feet deep for seventeen miles—the largest landslide ever recorded, choking the rivers that fed into the Columbia River, and closing the shipping lane to Portland. The multimegaton blast flattened thousands of acres of trees up to fifteen miles north of the mountain. And it spewed a 65,000-foot high cloud of hot ash that would spread eastward through the Northwest with the prevailing winds.

A few days later, President Carter would ask Senators Warren Magnuson and Mark Hatfield from Washington State and Oregon, respectively, along with Representative Tom Foley and myself to join him on Air Force One to tour the devastated area. Upon arrival at the Portland, Oregon airport and up to Longview, Washington, we were greeted by Governor Dixy Lee Ray, a renowned biologist and Washington's first woman governor, along with federal and state officials and began to discuss the damage and mounting problems. We proceeded by helicopter to view what was left of Mount St. Helens. When asked, President Carter called the destruction "the worst thing I ever saw."

I agreed with him. It was the worst sight I had even seen as well. Enough trees to build 300,000 two-bedroom homes lay jackstraw across an eerie and smoking land. The volcanic debris avalanche continued as an unstoppable flow of destruction that paralyzed traffic across the state, sweeping away twenty-seven bridges and burying 185 miles of road. The mudflows, squeezing out billions of gallons of melted ice water, had choked most of the Cowlitz River, spilling into the Columbia River and blocking shipping lanes. Then there was the thick black column of ash that swept across Eastern Washington, falling like snow that blanketed the landscape with up to ten inches of fine gray ash, drifting into dusty mounds. It was surreal.

This raised many serious questions that had no quick answers: Could a new forest be grown? Would the ash particles in the air damage lungs and human health? Would the fish populations return? And then there was the human agony—the lost lives and injuries, the thousands of homes destroyed, residents, many of whom were my constituents, were displaced. It would be my responsibility to respond to the urgent local needs that demanded government action.

On our return trip on Air Force One, Tom Foley requested a stopover in Spokane, the major city in his mostly agricultural district. When we landed and were rushed to the city hall, it became abundantly clear why Tom insisted on the stop. Five hundred farmers had gathered to complain about the volcanic ash that had covered and possibly destroyed their crops. They wanted the president and Senator Magnuson, who was chairman of the Senate Appropriations Committee, to hear their urgent pleas for federal funds to compensate them for the damage. As it turned out, we later learned the ash was a natural fertilizer that would produce bumper crops for the next dozen years.

There were even more urgent problems that my constituents faced in Castle Rock, Longview, and Kelso, which were on the Columbia River downstream of the volcano and were vulnerable to flooding and mudflows. A catastrophic outbreak of Spirit Lake was filling behind an unstable debris dam. We had to stabilize the largest debris avalanche on the planet or risk losing these Columbia River communities and their commerce.

The volcanic ash caused a broad assortment of problems that could not be ignored—transportation shut downs, air travel disruptions, compromised sewage disposal and water treatment systems, covered over farmlands and crops, power blackouts, respiratory illnesses on many people. One urgent problem was the huge amounts and high levels of ash that halted driving in communities near the mountain.

We returned to Washington, DC with a bold resolve to do as much as we could quickly to come to the rescue of those living and suffering on the front line. As soon as I reached my Capitol Hill office, I received a phone call from the mayor of Morton, the city closest to Mount St. Helens, a sleepy mill town twenty-two miles from the mountain which police chief, Jody Ulery, was the first to phone in the disaster to state officials in Olympia. "Congressman, we need a water truck to hose the ash from the streets. It's an emergency."

Anxious to help, I replied, "What can I do?" Someone told him that the Federal Highway Administration has such a truck. My staff quickly jumped on this and managed to secure a loner truck that was delivered to the Morton Fire Department within hours. It helped, and we were pleased to have been useful.

Curiously, our office received a call a few months later informing us that the truck was not returned, so I called the mayor myself. "Mister Mayor, this is Congressman Bonker, your streets should be cleared now, so when are you returning the truck?"

There was a long pause, and then he cautiously asked, "What do you mean, return? I thought you gave it to us."

I asked my assistant to work this out with the regional highway department, which he did, and the town was able to keep the truck. The following year, when Carolyn and I would be the grand marshals of the Volcanic Daze Parade, I had no idea that we would ride atop this truck. Some of the honored roles I got to play was judging the volcanic spitting contest and crowning Morton's Miss Ash.

The cost of the St. Helens eruption was best described in one newspaper headliner simply as an "avalanche of dollars." Senator Magnuson quickly asserted his authoritarian rule over the Appropriations Committee when he asked fellow senators to support his request for one billion dollars, which in the '80s was one heck of a lot of cash. This prompted Senator Daniel K. Inouye of Hawaii, who was the highest ranking Asian-American to date to hold office as the president pro tempore of the Senate, to pose this rhetorical question. "Mr. Chairman, I support your request for one billion dollars, but for the record, I want to say that, in Hawaii, we've had a number of volcanoes and never received any federal money."

Senator Magnuson had no idea how such a huge amount would be distributed, so most was designated for the Small Business Administration. As it turned out, the federal government picked up the tab for $1.06 billion to fund various projects, including the building of tunnels and sediment dams, the Corps of Engineers dredging of the Cowlitz, Toutle, and Columbia rivers, reforestation, highway, and roadway repair, repair of recreational facilities, which left a few federal dollars for small businesses losses.

My assistant, Dan Evans, established networking outreach involving local officials, federal agencies (USFS, Corps of Engineers), and Senate and House committees of jurisdiction. In an article featuring him in *The Daily News,* which received a Pulitzer Prize for its volcano coverage, noted: "Perhaps no one has been more critical to the successful teamwork on Mount St. Helens than Dan Evans, who had carte blanche to devote as much time to volcano needs as he saw fit." He was up against insurmountable odds, given the demands for ongoing funding during the Reagan "no increased spending" era, which kicked in in 1981.

There was also tightening of federal budget screws under the Gramm-Rudman-Hollings Balanced Budget and Emergency Deficit Control Act of 1985 and its amendment, demanding that state and local governments put up a quarter of the cost.

In *The Daily News* article "Coming of Age—flood battle gave young congressman chance to assert himself," I was quoted as saying, "We were coping with a very practical real-life, threatening problem while the administration was dealing with ideology."

The most complicated of our long menu of ongoing problems was dredging the rivers. The slow moving mudflow with a mortar-like consistency would continue to fill up the Toutle and Cowlitz rivers for the next ten years. Every year, I had to testify before the appropriations committees, requesting funds to continue the dredging. Fortunately, minor eruptions regularly occurred that grabbed headlines and helped make my case. But it was the Reagan administration that had to be convinced. *The Daily News* article on April 18, 1990 offered that "One of Reagan's budget writers was 'giving us this economic B.S.—this economic voodoo—and saying we were going to have to sit around for three years and wait,' Evans says. As he recalls, Bonker 'just went ballistic at that point,' dressing down the bureaucrat for his blind resistance to any federal spending on protection of lives and property in the shadow of Mount St. Helens. Bonker 'zinged in on this guy' and prevailed, Evans says. 'I think that was part of his maturation as an effective member of Congress.'"

The Mount St. Helens story had mostly had been about tragedy. But ultimately, another less reported dimension of the disaster emerged. There were positive lessons learned and long-term benefits that were reaped from this devastating volcanic eruption. Let me explain.

The year following the eruption, environmentalists announced their proposal to create a 21,600-acre monument that would protect everything of geological, scenic, recreational, and ecological interest around the mountain. It was a typically ambitious idea, drawing opposition from

Washington State agencies, the Forest Service, county officials, timber companies, and almost everyone else. A state committee consisting of timber company representatives and the Department of Natural Resources, but with no involvement of the conservation or scientific community, advanced their own proposal. It was insultingly small, recommending that just 50,000 acres be set aside for scientific study. The real issue was timber—the downed trees and the harvesting of old-growth timber. The US Forest Service's own proposal offered a compromise calling for an "interpretative area" of about 85,000 acres. Again, it was blatantly industry-friendly, and allowed for downed timber to be salvaged, permitted geothermal leasing and mineral prospecting, and invited open-pit mining operations.

All stakeholders were seeking my support, but I backed away from embracing any of these proposals. Six months later, the newly elected governor, John Spellman, a Republican and a committed environmentalist, cleverly combined elements from the US Forest Service (USFS) proposal with those from the environmental proposals into a neat and acceptable package. It was to my liking and in that it required congressional action, thus federal oversight, it was a serious step forward.

The one contentious issue in the governor's deal concerned the question of which federal agency would manage the protected area. The US Forest Service already presided over the Gifford Pinchot National Forest, but the environmentalists demanded that the National Park Service assume this responsibility. They feared that the USFS would build roads, promote logging, and just serve the timber industry just as they had prior to the eruption.

Susan Saul, a noted environmental activist in my district, and her colleagues organized a media tour of the Green River Valley to show how salvage logging was already occurring. Exposure to these operations were limited, though, since public access to the valley was not allowed. Susan called me with a request, "Congressman Bonker, can you help open up the Green River Valley to the public?" I reached out to the Forest Service and obtained permission. When I called Susan back with the good news, she asked if I could join them. I agreed, but I told her that I thought the Forest Service should be included as well. With reluctance, she consented.

Susan Saul and her group pulled up in their bus to the meeting spot, Spiffy's Restaurant where Highway 12 hits Interstate 5. I climbed aboard and looked around. "Where are the Forest Service people?" I asked.

"They're not coming," Susan replied.

"That can't be true," I said. I hoped that they would at least be at the ranger station in Randle where we were heading. Then I understood. The US Forest Service, if it were to manage the areas around Mount St. Helens, it would need to be mandated by law. It was naive of me to think that NGOs and government agencies would simply act accordingly. I had to formalize the relationship and assert myself far more proactively.

That spring, I introduced the Mount St. Helens Volcanic Area, a land mass of 110,000 acres, which was essentially the concept found in Governor Spellman's draft. To it, I added a provision that created the Mount St. Helens Visitor Center. In July of that year, the House of Representatives passed my proposal which protected 115,000 acres of lands around Mount St. Helens. A few days later, the Senate passed legislation that protected 105,000 acres. During a conference to reconcile the two bills, my staff remained constantly on the phone with Susan Saul and the Sierra Club's Charlie Raines, asking which acres were essential and which could be sacrificed. In August, a final bill emerged calling for a monument of 110,000 acres. The House approved the bill by a vote of 393 to 8. The Senate passed it without dissent.

The remaining difference came down to the single question of which federal agency would have jurisdiction and essentially manage the newly created monument area. The US Forest Service was awarded the mandate, but as a separate unit set up for this with its own planners and supervisor. The new law specified that "it shall manage the Monument to protect the geologic, ecologic, and cultural resources, allowing them to continue with their mission substantially unimpeded."

Once again, a Northwest land preservation bill, passed by both chambers of congress, was heading for a hostile White House. Ronald Reagan had not forgotten his promises to the Sagebrush Rebellion, a movement driven by supporters who wanted more state and local control over federal lands in thirteen Western states, where these lands ranged from 20% to 85% of the total surface. The rebellion took its name from the rampant desert plant of the same name that covers large patches of steppe in the American West. Ronald Reagan himself cause some stir by declaring himself a sagebrush rebel in an 1980 campaign speech in Salt Lake City. James Watt, Reagan's pick to head the Department of Interior, was dead set against any expansion of federal power over Western lands. The president's head of the US Forest Service, John Crowell, who was a former lobbyist for the timber industry, urged President Reagan to veto the bill.

Reagan knew, though, that the strong approval by the Senate and House would ensure that the veto he and his cabinet preferred would be overridden, and thus he opted for the least politically damaging option.

On August 26, 1982, with as little fanfare as possible, Reagan quietly signed the bill. The environmentalists and I had won.

A few weeks after the signing, I hosted a reception in my office to celebrate the Mount St. Helens National Volcanic Monument Act. Attending were prominent leaders representing the relevant groups including environmentalists, timber companies, railroads, chambers of commerce, other congressional staffers. There was a consensus that the land around Mount St. Helens should be saved for future generations. That was our moral authority.

The tributes started to flow in from across the spectrum, highlighting my work as we celebrated this rare achievement. Brock Evans, president of the Audubon Society, offered his thoughts in a letter to me that I cherish: "Without your original introduction of a bill, without your vigorous pursuit of a balanced formula that all parties could live with, and, above all, without your persistent gathering of support from our site delegation, we never could have protected this beautiful spot. I hope you will always carry with you in your heart a great pride in the knowledge that this place was your gift of love to this whole American people. Yes, many of us worked on it, but without you, it would have been nothing."

My colleague, Sid Morrison, a Republican whose congressional district was nearby, stated on the House floor, "If anybody worked to get us all together, the gentleman from Washington, Mr. Bonker, deserves that praise." Another colleague, John Seiberling, chairman of the House Interior Subcommittee on Public Works, commented that "Mr. Bonker, whose dedication leadership, effectiveness, and relentless energy on behalf of this legislation has been instrumental in helping bring about this remarkable achievement."

Finally, the *Longview Daily News*, in an editorial, stated, "Out of a logjam of competing proposals, Rep. Don Bonker has fashioned a compromise land management proposal.... From the start, Bonker announced he would act as a broker to forge a compromise between scientists, conservationists, and timber interests."

Afterwards, I paused long and hard to contemplate my two years of experience with the volcanic eruption, the natural disaster that caused so much heartbreaking damage and loss of lives. I thought about the extended struggles to gain government funding to repair and restore this pristine area. And now here we were celebrating its rebirth, the Mount St. Helens National Volcanic Monument. There was, in fact, new consciousness and new legal protection for our natural patrimony that found its birth with the eruption of a powerful and dangerous volcano.

During my time in the House, it was breathtaking in a political context to observe two Republican presidents sign into law two of the most important environmental initiatives of our times. For those keeping score, the Republicans in the White House not only approved these landmark wilderness areas, but went further by granting federal agencies the authority and mandates to manage these areas, which was contrary to party doctrine. At the time, there was a groundswell of opposition to all government designation of private land that would affect property rights or authorize public agencies to oversee or manage such areas. James Watt, Reagan's Interior Secretary from Lusk, Wyoming, wore the label of "anti-environmental." His mandate made history at the time by listing the fewest number of endangered species to the Endangered Species Act, and he actively campaigned to open the country's eighty million acres of undeveloped land to mining and drilling concerns by 2000. Watt leased a billion acres of coastal waters for potential drilling. That was the mindset we were working against.

CHAPTER 30

PROTECT AND PRESERVE

The largest designated wilderness area in the state of Washington, Olympic National Park, encompassed the upper part of my congressional district. This was a treasured resource appreciated by everyone who visited, but oddly, the national park had become a source of intense local resentment, hostility, and indigenous fury. Most of the anger was directed at the National Park Service, which had been granted authority over local entities and the so-called in-holders. This meant that, if you owned property within the confines of the area, you were subject to the policies and regulations of the National Park Service—in other words, the federal government—not the municipal or county authorities. As congressman, I had to deal with my constituents' outrage over having to obtain approval from a Park Service official whenever they contemplated physical changes on their personal property.

Back in the other Washington, the national interest in the Olympic Peninsula dated back to 1897 when President Grover Cleveland officially declared the national designation as Olympic Forest Reserve as a response to concern that the area's forest was disappearing. Eight years later in 1909, President Teddy Roosevelt set aside a part of the reserve as Mount Olympic National Monument to protect the habitat of the endemic Olympic elk which population was in sharp decline. This species was subsequently renamed the Roosevelt elk, the largest of the four species of elk found in North America.

In 1937, President Franklin Roosevelt personally visited the Olympic Peninsula and pledged his support for making this a national park, which led to his signing of the law that established the Olympic National Park.

The natural beauty and the majesty of the massive elk here inspired the president to protect the park as part of our national patrimony. Protection included regulation of Olympic Peninsula's natural and wildlife resources, its disappearing old-growth forests, and the grandeur of the Olympic Mountains themselves. In 1953, the rugged coastal area was added to the park, and thirty-five years later in 1988, Congress acted to further protect this remnant of wildlife of America by designating ninety-five percent of the park as the Olympic Wilderness.

The Olympic National Park is Washington's largest wilderness area and one of the most diverse in the US. The park spans the rugged Olympic Mountains and pristine old-growth forests and makes up for the third largest glacial system in the country. For beach lovers, it contains forty-eight miles of wilderness coast filled with beachheads, rugged headlands, tide pools, sea stacks, and coastal rainforests.

In the late 1970s, both the National Park Service and environmental activists approached me about partaking in a hiking expedition along the 600 miles of trails that led into the interior of the park. Hiking the trails myself would give me a greater appreciation of this magnificent natural resource. That, at least, was the thinking. The real reason for inviting me, however, was that the National Park Service wanted to secure my commitment to offset a local movement that wanted to dismantle the government's authority and its mandates, which were spawning the increased restrictions on land uses in the area.

I agreed to make the trek. Carolyn accompanied me, as did my district staff, and we embarked on a two-day sojourn into the ring of mountains which took us up steep slopes. We observed distant mountain goats scampering about, elk grazing in the expansive meadows, and unparalleled views of forests with the majestic Pacific Ocean in the distance. Our trekking then led us northward onto the High Divide Trail, and we enjoyed occasional sunlight and comforting quiet, disturbed only by exotic bird calls. The freshness of the mountain air made the whole experience seem like a blessing to life itself.

In the midst of all this bliss, something unexpected occurred. A park ranger approached me, pointing to his walkie-talkie, the only external communications we had. "Congressman, we just got a message. It's from the White House, the president wants to talk to you." Suddenly, our tranquil pace had turned into an urgent romp toward a landline. We had to speed up and goose step down the trails to the nearest ranger station. Along the way, we occasionally encountered other hikers who apparently sensed the urgency of our gait and rapid descent.

At the ranger station, I was seated next to the phone, collecting my thoughts on why President Jimmy Carter wanted urgently to talk to me, a low ranking member of Congress. I surmised it must have been about an important vote on an issue before one of my committees. Did he realize just how far into the wilderness I had trekked? The Foreign Affairs Committee had a scheduled vote on authorizing the sale of Boeing AWACS military security planes to Saudi Arabia, which the Jewish lobby strongly opposed. It must have been that that provoked this unscheduled emergency call.

Before I finished dialing the White House operator, I jotted down my talking points to explain my upcoming vote on the Boeing sale issue. It was a rare moment to be on a phone call with the president of the United States. I heard his voice crackle down the line. "Congressman, I know it was difficult to take this call and I appreciate that we can now talk." I braced myself for the rest. "You serve on the House Merchant Marine Committee, and I really need your vote on the Panama Canal resolution." I looked down at my useless notes on the AWACS planes, and quickly stumbled through my recollected thoughts on the Panama Canal. I gave assurance that he would have my vote. He replied, "Good, that's what I needed to hear." He wished me an excellent continued hike and hung up. That was that, the president of the United States. The contrast between the world in the Oval Office that I imagined and the thick canopy of trees here in the national park collided. I stepped out of the US ranger station and carried myself back up the trail.

In early 2016, Senator Maria Cantwell and Representative Derek Kilmer drafted and sponsored legislation to officially designate Olympic National Park as the Daniel J. Evans Wilderness Park. Our political system was at its best when politicians from both parties and all persuasions find the way to put the best interests of the country first. Two Democrats from Congress showed their commitment to honoring a Republican for a life-time of bipartisan accomplishments as a US Senator and a state governor whose work went beyond politics and protected the state's most beloved natural resources. It was moving. Of the many tributes at a dedication ceremony on August 17, 2017, *The Seattle Times* reported the next day: "For many, Evans is that rare thing—a beloved politician whose stature transcends party or generation. Naming the wilderness for Evans 'puts an iconic name next to an iconic place,' said Senator Maria Cantwell."

Within the bouquet of environmental actions I had taken in those days to protect my district and state, the work on another project, the Alpine Lakes Wilderness, although not in my district, continues to resonate as a source of pride as I relive those moments from early in my second term as congressman.

The time was dotted with exhausting debates, lively public meetings, and intense media coverage as Congress prepared to vote on the proposed Alpine Lakes Area Management Act which President Gerald Ford—yes, a Republican—signed into law on July 12, 1976. At the signing ceremony, Ford actually said, "Anywhere so beautiful should be preserved."

The wilderness was originally designated the Alpine Lakes Limited Area in 1946, but this did not offer protection from resource extraction and was exclusively regulated by the US Forest Service. The region and adjacent areas were being extensively used for mining, timber extraction, and fur trapping.

Swaths of tree were being clear-cut for roads and ecological degradation was eating away at the ecosystem. It was the USFS' policy to expand timber sales and road building briskly, which prompted a grassroots campaign to limit such activity and which made its way to Congress.

Alpine Lakes was the largest wilderness area near the population centers of Puget Sound, covering over 4,000 acres of the famously scenic Central Cascades. The area showcased some of the most astonishing terrain in the entire Cascade Range including saw tooth ridges, sharp summit spires, ice-scooped U-shaped valleys, and hundreds of glacially excavated lake basins. Small glaciers persisted in the Stuart Range and along the high crests between Chikamin Peak and Mount Daniels. A truly exceptional landscape.

Once again, Carolyn and I committed to a two-day hiking expedition. This time, it was organized by the US Forest Service, which was the major stakeholder in the pending legislation. Their regional office was fully supportive and gracious as they wanted Congressman and Mrs. Bonker to see firsthand this stunning yet fragile natural resource. Entry into the area by foot was a long and arduous hike, so they arranged for a helicopter to take Carolyn and me and my district assistant, Mike Murphy, and his wife to a particularly captivating destination deep in the area. I recall how hilarious it seemed then when our USFS hosts gently asked our wives their weight—necessary for the helicopter flight record. Carolyn cleverly teamed up with Mrs. Murphy and offered a combined pound number to avoid disclosure of their respective weights which amused everyone.

When we stepped off the helicopter, we hiked for several hours to a stunning meadow area alongside a sparkling crescent of cascading waterfalls, a picturesque site that would serve as our overnight stay. We were greeted by a trail guide who appeared with several mules loaded down with camping essentials, which included a metal shepherd's stove. In today's world, we'd be criticized for having the mules work for us, but in those days, the sight just affirmed that the outing had been well planned. As we sat by the fireside that evening savoring the outdoor scenery and a delicious meal, we felt the splendor of the Cascades as it was called, the trail that covered the entire spine of the mountain range north to south in Washington State. Our tents were pitched and Carolyn and I climbed into ours. As we were going to sleep we, could hear the falls cascading into the lake, and the magic of the place cast a spell. In the morning, we were greeted with the enticing sweet scent of the batter browning the thick pancakes in a wrought iron skillet on the shepherd's stove. We rose our coffee mugs to the mules in gratitude—and the US Forest Service, of course.

As we resumed our trek down the trail, we encountered other hikers coming up the same path but loaded down with heavy packs. Multiple times, we were asked the same question: "Where is all your gear?" A bit embarrassed by the VIP treatment the Forest Service was providing in this historic wilderness area, Alpine Lakes. Spared of a heavy pack, I was able to concentrate on why I was there, to help figure out how to preserve the state's natural resources by applying a shared commitment that effaced the differences between Republicans and Democrats. We worked closely to get the job done in Washington, DC, and shortly after our Cascades hiking tour, a Democratic Congress enacted the Alpine Lakes Area Management Act on July 12, 1976, which Republican President Gerald Ford signed. This was the foundation, and on March 26, 2009, thirty-three years later, Republican Representative Dave Reichert and Democrat Senator Patty Murray teamed up to expand the Alpine Lake Wilderness, a bipartisan effort that never reached the White House. Five years later, another bipartisan initiative ended with Congress approving legislation to add 22,000 acres and granting National Wild and Scenic River status to key sections of the Middle Fork Snoqualmie and Pratt rivers which President Barrack Obama finally signed into law on December 19, 2014, nearly forty years after our initial work, and those embarrassingly good campfire pancakes.

The examples of true legacy of bipartisanship and the occasionally achieved greatness in preserving the country's precious resources need to be remembered and repeated. They validate the best that our political system is capable of producing.

One final recollection from the environmental portfolio of my congressional years beckons to be shared. The southwestern portion of my district was noted for its natural terrain and stunning beauty.

Traveling on Highway 101 toward Seaview, one of the coastal communities, we would pass by Long Island, part of the Willapa Bay estuary, which was blessed abundantly with old-growth trees that we all assumed would be there a lifetime—theirs and ours. We couldn't imagine that these trees risked anything. Long Island was part of Willapa National Wildlife Refuge designated by President Franklin D. Roosevelt in 1937, the year I was born, and one of the most pristine estuaries in the United States. I had a personal sense of identity with the place, and in a sense, I am probably guilty of projecting my own wish for immortality on my attachment to Long Island. I felt privileged to represent this national treasure, a living heritage, conserving wildlife and habitat for future generations, hopefully forever. The Fish and Wildlife Service brochure describes it this way: "In this coastal environment, the incoming tides combine life-giving nourishment of the ocean with nutrient-laden fresh water of rivers and streams to create one of the most productive environments on the Pacific Coast."

I once arrived in Seaview for an overnight stay and registered at the Shelburne Inn, a historic landmark with massive charm and old-world comfort. It was a favorite retreat for our staff meetings as well as our family vacations. We loved the proprietors, David Campiche and Laura Anderson, who were known for their abundance of charm. David was a politically savvy Democrat, always prepared to engage in enlightened discourse on world and national issues, a great perk in addition to the lovely accommodations.

The next morning, I was having breakfast with David and he graciously offered to take us on his boat over to Long Island. "Fine," I replied, "but driving past Long Island coming down here, all we saw were just a lot of trees. Why go there?"

"That's the reason, the trees," he said. "On future trips when you drive past Long Island, those trees will be gone."

The federal government owned the land, he explained, but the giant timber company, Weyerhaeuser, had the harvesting rights. "Later this year, Don, I'm telling you, they are going bring in heavy equipment to chop down these historic cedar trees," he said. Dave painstakingly asked, "Is there any way we can stop this from happening?" That's what concerned congressmen are for!

Within a few hours, I was aboard his small boat on a very pleasant thirty-minute ride over to Long Island. I wanted to see the trees up close.

He was very familiar with the area, and after docking, we embarked on a short hike to the most magnificent collection of cedar trees on the planet. Many were over one thousand years old, four times older than the nation! Standing there, I was awed by the size and beauty of these giant cedars. And the thought also stunned me to think that Weyerhaeuser's powerful chainsaws would be ripping into these trunks and bringing down a millennium of growth. And then the logs would be shipped off to Japan where they'd be milled to the benefit of others. "David," I told him, "I will do my utmost to stop Weyerhaeuser and find a way to preserve this spectacular natural resource," I pledged.

Pledging to do something is good, but delivering a result on that pledge is something else. To hope for results, I needed to start by learning a lot more about the Long Island cedar grove, the last large remnant (274 acres) of the maritime cedar forest that once dominated coastal lowlands from Northern California to British Columbia. The rain-drenched forests on Long Island grow rapidly and densely, and have been naturally protected from mainland fires. The western red cedar trees have been there for more than one thousand years. To boot, the Long Island forests are home to black bears, Roosevelt elks, black-tailed deer, beavers, and river otters. Bald eagles and great blue herons also nest in large trees on the island. I had to make good on my pledge.

If something hadn't been done to block Weyerhaeuser's plan to make Long Island a clear-cut zone, all that would have been wiped out. Having conferred with my DC staff led by Dan Evans, I realized just how tough this task would be. Our objective was simply to get Weyerhaeuser to back off its harvesting plans. That's all. One idea was to have the US Forest Service negotiate a land exchange to guarantee the timber giant would have harvesting rights in another location. That would, at least, save Long Island.

We set the idea into motion and the USFS seemed game. As the negotiations deepened, it became clear that Weyerhaeuser required a buyout of $5 million payment. This monetary hurdle led to a meeting with Congressman Norm Dicks, a member of the House Appropriations Committee, who eventually agreed to add the amount to the House Appropriations bill for the next fiscal year. The deal went through and we saved the giant cedars on Long Island. On my future trips to the Pacific Coast, Dave Campiche and I would raise our wine glasses in gratitude and toast the preservation of the old-growth cedar trees.

Fifteen years later, I got a phone call from Brian Baird, who had been one of my successors in Congress. Calling from his Capitol Hill office,

"Don, I've been thinking about your environmental achievements and feel you deserve proper recognition," he said. I was flattered. "What would be your preference? What would you like to have your name associated with it?" he went on.

I thought for a minute and suggested the Mount St. Helens Visitors Center. My heavy involvement dealing with the volcanic eruption included obtaining funding for the center. The Don L. Bonker Mount St. Helens Visitor Center sounded good to me.

Baird said he would check with the US Forest Service and get back to me. A few weeks later, he called back to share that the Forest Service was grateful that I made the visitor center happen and they were supportive of having it renamed. "However," he explained, "their policy states clearly that this could only happen after you are deceased." Hmmm, that was really good news and bad news.

Brian found out that the US Fish and Wildlife Service did not have a deceased policy and inquired about the possibility of honoring me through them. I mentioned my attachment to Long Island.

Congressman Baird's due diligence led to a dedication ceremony on Long Island in 2005 in order to name—I'm pleased to report—the Don Bonker Cedar Grove Trail. The event happened and my dear friends, including Dave Campiche, his wife, Laurie; Congressmen Baird and Jay Inslee, who'd be elected governor the following year; Dan Evans, of course; and many others.

Every year since then, the Friends of Willapa National Wildlife Refuge make annual visits to the sentinels of Long Island. The current organization's president, Dr. Madeline Kalbach, reported in *The Observer* on July 20, 2017 that "Somewhere near the center of south Long Island stand ancient cedars, sentinels and guardians of the forest. While individual trees come and go, the Cedar Grove has existed for the past 4,000 years. The Cedar Grove is 274 acres of sheer beauty—together, the cedars contribute long-term stability to wildlife habitat. The trail to the ancient cedars is named after former US Rep. Don Bonker, who helped save the Long Island old-growth forest. We are honored to have him join the 100 members of the Friends of the Willapa National Wildlife Refuge, starting with a barge trip across the narrow channel that separates the island from the mainland." She went on to say that "the Cedar Grove is awe-inspiring and quiets the souls of all who go there." It quiets my soul thinking about the opportunity I had to help preserve refuges like Willapa.

Without Dave Campiche, proprietor of the Shelburne Inn, gifted at pottery and poetry, Willapa would not have been saved. His artful letter to me dated September 28, 2005, I will cherish for my remaining years. "Let's talk about the Grove and the implications of this gift you sagaciously arranged," he led with, "saving this stunning landscape for our grandchildren and theirs. When I visit Long Island, I am struck by the Presence that is bigger than you and me. Indeed, it is here where I find my God. This is my cathedral. How you included me in that dispensation of honors: How we drank coffee one morning years ago. How I might have influenced your decision to preserve that Grove, that entire island, from the chainsaw. If all that is true—and my mind has already forgotten those finer details—then I am the luckiest of purveyors, for I will have helped preserve a rare treasure. But the prize is yours, the accomplishment shaped in the hands of a dedicated, skilled, and honorable man. In a project so large, it is through the arduous and tangled machinations of government and applied skills that the clay is shaped. Isn't this ultimately how the prize is won?"

I read that out loud from time to time and recognize that if there is such thing as one's legacy, I wish mine to be remembered by the work of preserving the nation and state's natural resources. A congressman may receive attention and credit, but I was blessed with an exceptional staff whose commitment and hard work made all this happen—Mark Murray, Dan Evans, Nancy Parks, Scott Jackson, and Gretchen Sorensen.

In a book called *Washington Wilderness: The Unfinished Work*, I cite once more the inspiring words of former senator and governor Daniel J. Evans: "In today's technological, fast-paced, and sometimes transitory society, we are overwhelmed by electronic messages that create a jumble of chaotic and unfinished memories. We increasingly long for the simple, traditional, and natural experiences that will help steady us in an uncertain world."

VIII. A Fork in the Road

CHAPTER 31

PINSTRIPES AND PERRIER

The legendary baseball Hall of Famer Yogi Berra of the New York Yankees once said, "When you arrive at a fork in the road, take it." We all arrive at forks in our lives, and are faced with serious choices that determine the long-term future of ourselves and all things in our path. I arrived at that fork in the road in early 1987.

Usually, the fork has two prongs and one primarily consists of staying on the road you are already on, carrying forward, going straight, and not taking a risk of getting lost or losing time. There is a degree of safety in this choice, but with it often comes regret or doubt or wonder. What if I had taken the other prong in the fork? The other path? What might have I become or what changes might have I helped make in the world? There is the conservative route and there is the progressive one. There is low risk and low gain or more risk and the potential of great gain.

In 1987, I could have simply hung onto my secure congressional seat while moving up the seniority ladder with the prospect of one day becoming chairman of the House Foreign Affairs Committee. That would have been the top of the line, or the end of the line. With fourteen years in Congress and a solid reputation, the continuity of this path was pretty much assured and had genuine attractiveness. The other direction at the fork was admittedly riskier. For me, this was making a run for the US Senate from the state of Washington. Becoming a US Senator was the grand prize in American national politics. The only other elected office that commanded a greater voice and more authority was the presidency. I was attracted to the notion of becoming a senator and serving my state and my country as a member of the higher chamber of our legislature.

Speaker Tom Foley, whose wisdom I always cherished, cautioned me to stay put in the House. He advised me that I would one day be chairman of the House Foreign Affairs Committee, and that would be a great achievement and an influential place to serve the country. I considered his words carefully, but was troubled by only one problem—my colleague in the House, Steve Solarz, who ranked higher than me in seniority. He was also younger and came from a safe district in New York. At least, that was my appraisal at the time; several years later, he ended up losing his seat in Congress due to a redistricting, which upset the demographics of voters.

The political ambitions of our Class of '74 was not lacking, as John Lawrence astutely captures in his fastidious historic book *The Class of '74: Congress After Watergate and the Roots of Partisanship*. Twelve members attempted to run for the Senate. Half lost and were sent packing. Six succeeded. House members who opted to run for the Senate were obliged to sacrifice their House seats in order to run, so there was a heavy price to pay if you didn't succeed.

Much of the calculation regarding entering a political race comes down to timing. A pivotal factor to consider is simply whether there is an incumbent to run against or if the seat is open because the incumbent is not seeking reelection. Such was the case in 1987 when US Senator Dan Evans announced he would not seek reelection for senator of Washington, which sparked reporting and speculation around the state about who would be his successor. Linda Keene, the States News Service Washington, DC reporter, wrote about my situation at the time, and described my situation in her headline, "Don Bonker Ponders a Risky Race." "Don Bonker is thinking about saying good-bye to his secure seat and risking a long-shot run at the Senate. Republican Sen. Dan Evans' term expires this year, a situation that has caused considerable excitement among Bonker and three other Washington congressmen." She went on to ask whether the former county auditor have the name recognition, bankroll, and plain old energy to wage and win a statewide race next year. Should he risk his House seat and the chairmanship of a Foreign Affairs subcommittee that has made him a leader on trade issues? She put her finger on the nerve. Those were the questions.

This was deja vu. I thought back to 1974, struggling with a decision about entering a primary election against two powerful state senators. The odds were more stacked against me than in this race for the US Senate I was contemplating. Before that, in my first attempt at public office, going for Clark County auditor after being warned by the Clark County

Democratic chairman, that if I dared to enter the race, he would personally guarantee that "my career was over before it started." Yet, whether or not a foolish decision, I did go for both and ultimately was elected. In my early career, the big challenge was how to make it through the primary, knowing that I had a good shot at prevailing in the general election. This would be a third attempt. Despite the pundits and press predicting that it would be uphill to go against the Seattle congressman, I was the best choice to win the general election. I kept in mind and repeated to myself, "Okay, you've faced this challenge before and emerged victorious, you can do it again."

From July 1987 through the end of the year, the news coverage highlighted a primary showdown between Representative Mike Lowry and myself, with my Seattle-based potential opponent having a clear advantage. Profile pieces that appeared at the time were favorable, but the word on the street was that the primary would be a struggle for me. The Associated Press reporter, David Ammons, in his December 14, 1987 article, commented that it would be an "uphill battle" for the nomination and I would drop out of the race if my candidacy didn't "pick up steam." In an Associated Press release, Les Blumenthal reported in *The Oregonian* on November 16, 1987 that "when asked why he would risk a relatively secure House seat to enter a Senate race that polls already indicate he is twenty percentage points behind, he replied, 'It's not just an opportunity, it is an obligation.'" That was how I did see the fork in the road. I had to take the more ambitious but risky path. I had to test my limit if there were to be a higher calling.

One headline ran, "Bonker run for Senate riddled with guesses," and this was what it came down to given the high risks. Indeed, as I was constantly in flight, traveling between the two Washingtons, my mind was riddled with this momentous decision, coping with multiple questions. I had a solid record as congressman, but was I really up to the standards of being a US senator, especially considering our state's blessed past with highly regarded senators spanning over thirty years? How much money would I need to raise? Was I prepared to raise millions of dollars? What would be the tow on my family, especially my seven- and eight-year-old children? Carolyn and I discussed this in detail, of course, but it never came to that decisive moment. Instead, the decision evolved organically through the preparatory process of exploring the possible race and organizing a statewide campaign. The decision was inevitable. The sense of obligation was a major factor for many Democratic leaders who felt that, if Mike Lowry were the nominee, he would likely lose in the general election. So it was not just about my ambition to be senator, it was about our collective calculation that I was the only hope for a Democrat to recapture this coveted Senate seat. I found myself often reflecting about my first race for elective office—Clark County auditor and then for Congress in 1974. I had overcome insurmountable odds to win those elections, so why could this not happen again? I could do this, I told myself.

Mike Lowry, who curiously held a strong physical resemblance to Yasser Arafat, and even shaved his beard to minimize the comparison that the press enjoyed making, did have a huge advantage over me. Being a congressman from Seattle, he had name recognition that covered five Puget Sound congressional districts. He had previously been the Democratic nominee in a special election to replace Senator Henry Jackson, who died in office, challenging former governor Dan J. Evans, and so he already had a statewide campaign organization. Finally, Mike Lowry was the darling of the far-left, and noted as being one of the most liberal members of Congress. He had a network of liberal activists that he could tap into all around the state.

On the home front, I had assembled a highly competent team that was eager to launch a Senate campaign. The key people on my staff would transition to the campaign organization. That was the plan. All aspects of a statewide campaign were being considered, local operations, fund raising, strategy, etc., as we were approaching a deadline. A decision had to be made.

Mark Murray, my chief of staff, came into my office on one particular day in early July 1988 and tossed a piece of paper onto my desk.

"What's that?" I asked.

"It's your list of negatives," he replied.

"Is that really necessary?"

"Congressman, that's what this race will come down to—his negatives versus your negatives."

"Okay," I replied and sat up in my chair. "I'd look at it." I thought the exchange was over. But he stood there, did not budge. "What? Is there something else?"

His somber look was disturbing. "We don't know everything. Please complete the list." Then he turned and walked out of the office. There was an odd silence as I hesitated to look down, confront my flaws, and then continue to fill in the points that I recognized might be missing.

The state's political journalists were having fun characterizing the two Democrats who were about to get into the Senate race. But drawing up a list of contrasts was a limited activity, since we did not differ all that much when it came down to the issues. The real contrast was all about style and personality, and the journalists gleefully sketched the comparison in lively verbiage. "Lowry, effusive, demonstrative and 'hot' in media terms, is the stem-winder without parallel in Washington politics. Like a television evangelist, he can take a sedate roomful of people and whip them into foot-stomping, applauding frenzy. He's a backslapper, quipster, jovial and animated. He speaks from the gut with a 'take it or leave it.'" That was David Ammons' of the Associated Press' assessment of my opponent. As for me, he wrote "Bonker, stylish and cool, stands in rather stark contrast. He's cerebral and pragmatic, a button-down guy who likes to tinker with a problem like a kid with a broken clock. He's a team player, a low profile consensus builder. Bonker has a straight-laced, choirboy image, versus Lowry's rough-and-tumble irreverence. Lowry is the blue jeans and beer. Bonker is pinstripes and Perrier."

Ammons went on to say, "And physical appearance shouldn't count for anything in politics. But it does with Lowry, with his scraggly beard and his pop-eyes, and his rumpled appearance, looks like a shrunken Robert Bork. Bonker is Kennedyesque, a handsome, distinguished-looking man with his pinstripe suit always pressed and every hair in place."

The Lewiston Tribune in Idaho on November 5, 1987 added, "But this is no show horse. Bonker is one of the most scholarly and thoughtful members of the House, an expert on foreign affairs, and a man who interprets his Christian convictions in the literal, open-hearted way. Bonker is an open-minded liberal, less inclined than Lowry to cast knee-jerk votes in harmony with all the pet causes of the liberal establishment. Stripes always pressed and every hair in place."

They seemed to like my hair.

The fork in the road was leaning in one direction. From July through December 1987, the mood was about assessing my chances and about getting prepared, organizing statewide fundraising and staging press conferences, and these tasks put me solidly in candidate mode, making the run increasingly inevitable. Blessed as well with a stellar team led by Stephanie Solien, which included Mark Murray, Scott Jackson, and Gretchen Sorensen. My confidence grew as I got closer to announcing that I would indeed run.

And then a startling event had me back off.

The Washington State Young Democrat (YD) convention in Olympia, the state capital, was about to take place. That would be the first candidate endorsement event. Two days before the convention, Gretchen, my chief strategist, cornered me and said, "Don, I got word that Lowry is hiring a bus to bring in Seattle young Democrats to clinch his endorsement." Given the Bonker-Lowry rivalry, the YD endorsement would get media coverage and give a giant boost for the candidate who won the endorsement.

"What do you suggest we do, Gretchen?" I anxiously asked her.

Gretchen responded that I had some core supporters at Western Washington University where I had spoken earlier. "I will contact my sources and see if they can bring students to the YD convention."

"Do it," I told her.

As usual, Gretchen delivered big time. Several buses with about seventy students showed up and registered. I was pleasantly shocked, thinking that this will give me the upper hand. That was all it would take, the shift, the energy, to give me the endorsement. That seemed to be the good news, but the event turned out to be a nightmare, a fiasco.

My students from Western Washington University had enough votes to control the convention, and not only the endorsement but the policy platform as well. The big issue of the day, of course, was abortion. Pro-life versus pro-choice. My students were pressing to include anti-abortion language, which would have contrasted with Lowry's language on the subject but would have dire consequences on my candidacy. My position on abortion was far more nuanced. This is not a simple fork in the road— there are forks within forks. The anti-abortion language would alarm the Democrat Party leaders; media coverage would go what we came to call the contagion of sensationalism and gossip—viral. Gretchen nervously predicted a headline like "Bonker's evangelical supporters take over the Democratic Party." Politics is tricky. I may not believe that our tax dollars should subsidize programs that are morally objectionable to a large number of taxpayers, but that didn't mean that I opposed the right of each woman to make her own decisions concerning her own body.

This situation put me in an extremely awkward position, and one that was easily misrepresented. I met with the leaders of the students who supported me and explained the situation in careful detail. Finally, they relented and avowed that their coming to Olympia was solely to endorse me, not to do damage to my campaign. Yet the encounter was difficult for them and it was embarrassing too for me. In a private room surrounded by my key advisors, we had to do a quick assessment. Our goal, of course, was to get the state YD endorsement, and we now had the votes to do it. Yet there was concern that it would anger Mike Lowry who would fiercely go public that Bonker's young evangelicals were taking over the Democrat Party. To minimize the damage, we agreed to a resolution that the YDs would endorse both candidates. This was a glaring example of my fate of being a Christian and a Democrat. I also felt pain for those young supporters coming all the way to Olympia only to return conceding on the abortion issue and no endorsement of their candidate.

Later that evening, I was aboard the red-eye flight back to Washington, DC. It was my longest five-hour flight ever as I was contemplating what happened in Olympia. As the plane was landing at Dulles Airport, I had reached a decision about my candidacy. What I had put those students through was heartbreaking. They were enthusiastic about something they cared about and believed and I had to teach them to compromise and make political accommodations before they even got going in life. It was disheartening. I felt like I was not worthy to be a US senator. I would step out of the race.

Back at the Capitol, I made my way to the member's dining room to have breakfast with Carolyn who was waiting for me. As I approached the table to join her, the contrast must have been obvious to anyone who took notice. I was exhausted, having flown all night pondering the effects of the YD convention. The scene reminded me of another one fourteen years earlier, enduring a three-hour drive after a young man shared with me that he was carrying God's message for me not get into the race for Congress. I sat down across from Carolyn; she looked pristine and lovely with her shoulder-length hair and sparkling eyes, anxious to hear how things went in Olympia. I eagerly waited for the waiter to finish pouring us coffee before I spoke. I looked over to my wife with a reluctant smile. I was thinking, life would be so much better to have a pleasant breakfast and talk about our children and other matters on the home front than to have to share this. I sat down and put my elbows on the tablecloth. I was exhausted. Our coffee cups were filled. I looked over to my wife and smiled. She was filled with anticipation, wanting to hear how the convention went. How pretty she looked, and how supportive.

As I was about to share what had happened in Olympia, I was contemplating not entering the race for Senate. Only with Carolyn could I share my deepest thoughts about the situation that put these university students in such a compromising position. She knew me well enough to anticipate what was coming as I ended my sentence by saying that "I am going to the office to prepare a press release stating that I will not be running for the Senate." She listened with obvious sympathy for how I felt. I saw it in her eyes. I also saw how she honored my integrity but had a wise way of putting this into perspective. As we stood to depart, I asked her what she'd be doing today.

"I am going shopping for a nice suit to wear at the announcement of your candidacy next week."

Darn. How awkward I felt, ready to throw in the towel because I lamented a moment when compromise was needed. All of political gain necessitated compromise. That didn't mean I had lost integrity or had hid my convictions. The students had to see that, to gain a bigger victory, we needed to yield smaller things along the way. That was a positive lesson, not a moral defeat. Carolyn's elegance in listening, absorbing, and then letting me know that it is time to go back to the big picture continues to surprise and delight me.

On January 19, 1988, I officially announced my candidacy for the US Senate in Vancouver before a crowd of about 300 supporters. I acknowledged in my speech that it would not be an easy race, reciting that I knew full well the difficulty in running from Southwest Washington, especially against a candidate from the Puget Sound area. We were already twenty percent behind Mike Lowry in the polls. The climb would be steep, but we'd get there.

For the next ten months, I was consumed with fundraising, traveling around the state, seeking endorsements, anxiously evaluating the polls, preparing for debates, flying back and forth between the two Washingtons, and trying to preserve some time with family. Ross Anderson of *The Seattle Times* described a typical day in my life like this: "So there he is, zigzagging across the state in a small chartered jet from Vancouver to Bellingham, from Bremerton to Spokane, conducting press conferences in cold warehouses and processing plants, trying to interest voters in his not-so-sexy campaign sales pitch."

The Seattle Times continued to capture the frenetic pace of the campaign. "Rep. Don Bonker, campaigning for the Senate, was in a pickle last week. He needed to get from Tacoma to Olympia but I-5 was backed up for miles and he was going to be an hour late for his next speech. So he gladly accepted an admirer's offer to bypass the traffic jam, zipping him down the sound by speedboat." It went on to tell an unforgettable detail when "the sleek speedster sputtered to a stop—out of gas. Eventually, another boat came to the rescue, picked up the Vancouver Democrat, and promptly got lost somewhere in deepest, darkest South Puget Sound. Bonker, who is promoting a new seven-point plan for solving Puget Sound transportation problems, made it to his meeting—three hours late."

In a US Senate race, so much is about fundraising. You need cash to mount a campaign. Mike Lowry's advantage in name familiarity, particularly around Puget Sound where two-thirds of the state's voters resided, helped him collect contributions. I needed a hefty budget for television advertising. Where would it come from? I was always wondering. Of course, political action committees, lobbying firms in Washington, DC, local events, contributions from individuals…it all helped. A statewide campaign demanded that the candidate spent hours on the phone and meeting high-end donors.

My former aide, Scott Jackson, took the lead and arranged a series of meetings in Seattle with businessmen with deep pockets, not necessarily politically minded, and often with little idea who Don Bonker actually was. Sometimes it was awkward. A stranger walks in the door, introduces himself as a candidate for senator, then asks for $1,000. Many of the business owners and executives had little interest and asked few questions, other than one which stood out regularly: "Who else is supporting your campaign?"

Scott would set me down and talk me through the meetings. Who was who, who owned what, who was married to whose sister. What this one was hoping we'd support, what that one is obsessed with. What never to say. What always to say. What to say *if* he says this or that or nothing.

"Don, we got to get someone prestigious to write a check—that will be your reference when they ask who else supports you." He then wheeled me into a meeting with a prestigious real estate tycoon, known to be an active Democrat.

The guy was politically savvy and impressively familiar with my background and record. He asked outright, "What can I do to help?"

I looked over to Scott. He gave a slight nod. "I need a big budget for television advertisements in Seattle," I replied.

He reached for his checkbook, scribbled in a sum and signed it. He stood up and we shook hands and I walked out the door with a smile and a check bearing his name.

I walked out and looked down to see that the amount was relatively modest but it did the trick to give us bragging rights. When businessmen asked who was onboard, I happily claimed that Herb Z. was one of my strongest supporters. It worked. Indeed, it had a multiple effect and the checks kept coming in.

The larger reservoir for fundraising was the other Washington. Law and lobbying firms, corporate PACs, and trade associations eagerly poured dollars into campaign buckets of most campaigns for a variety of well-thought-out strategic reasons. Here, I had a serious advantage over Mike Lowry for reasons that were obvious when one considered my leadership role on trade, which had facilitated fundraising events and opportunities.

While Mike Lowry's feisty liberalism resonated in the Puget Sound area, he had little appeal among DC-based contributors and lobby groups.

One event that stood out in particular was hosted by the highly influential Pamela Harriman at her elaborate Georgetown residence. The English-born American political activist, socialite, and art collector had been married to Randolph Churchill, the son of Winston Churchill, with whom she had one son whom they named Winston Churchill. Following a long and famous affair to the man who, at the age of seventy-nine in 1971, became her third and last husband, W. Averell Harriman, Pamela set up house in Georgetown and organized parties of great envy. Old man Harriman had been active in the political world and an extremely wealthy business baron who served as US ambassador to Russia. Ms. Harriman had been instrumental in lining up both Democratic Party influencers and deep-pocketed funders for Bill Clinton's run for president, and thus in 1992, it wasn't surprising that President Clinton appointed Ms. Harriman to be ambassador to France, the crown jewel of diplomatic political appointments. The owner of a number of French masterpieces of art and with extensive European experience—as a seventeen-year-old student with aristocratic connection to British royalty, she was once introduced to Adolf Hitler, a fact I still find extraordinary. In Georgetown, she was a fundraising matriarch for Democrats, forming the PAM PAC—targeting nonincumbent Senate candidates. I was honored to be on her invitation list.

My first impression was how amazing to be among the select few invited, but as I observed the others in the dining room, I started to wonder how did these other guys get invited. Across the dinner table was a fellow called Joe Lieberman, who was Connecticut's attorney general. I mused, *Could this guy really be elected a US senator? Not that impressive.*

As it turned out, Joe Lieberman was elected and he rapidly became one of the most prominent members of the US Senate. He emerged as a national leader and remained prominent even after he left the Democratic Party and became an independent. Both Democrat and Republican presidential nominees seriously considered Joe Lieberman to be a vice presidential candidate. While I did not have a close relationship with the senator, I did become well acquainted with his wife, Hadassah Freilich Tucker, who joined APCO Worldwide as a consultant in the early 1990s. We had a weekly lunch that gave me more insight about this amazing couple. Her parents were Holocaust survivors, and she and the senator shared a deep Jewish faith and cultural identity. She told me once that young Joe had once called her in the early days for a date because he thought it would be interesting to go out with someone named Hadassah, the name of the Women's Zionist Organization of America and one of the largest volunteer international organizations. They first met while Joe, who had been married once before, was Connecticut's attorney general, and they married in 1982.

The PAM PAC did help, but by the end of the funding game, Mike Lowry and I had raised roughly the same amount. Equal funding, however, worked to his advantage in that I needed at least double the amount if I was going to be able to buy the ad space and television time needed to offset the familiarity of his name in the densely populated Puget Sound area.

I also came up short on endorsements. In primary elections, both political parties have pillars, organizations and special interests, which help ensure that they remain competitive in general elections. Yet obtaining these involved endorsements in primary elections can be contentious. With the Democrats, the three pillars are social/culture, environmentalists, and labor unions. Mike Lowry scored big with the first and third, and we split the middle group.

On the social agenda, Joel Connelly's article in the *Seattle Post-Intelligencer* properly described how this issue was playing out politically. "The difference between Mike Lowry and Don Bonker has brought the nation's abortion lobby forcefully into Washington's Senate race as Lowry backers. Bonker has not received money from anti-abortion groups. When New York philanthropist Robin Chandler Duke holds a fundraiser for Rep. Mike Lowry tonight in her Manhattan apartment, Lowry will be reaping the latest political rewards for his outspoken support of abortion rights. The Renton Democrat already has received the maximum legal donation of $5,000 from such groups as the National Abortion Rights Action League, Voters for Choice, and the Hollywood Women's Political Committee."

The article properly noted my dilemma. "While not an ally of the right-to-life movement, his (Bonker's) position has been to allow federal funding only in cases of rape, incest, and danger to the mother." This complicated issue continued to haunt my career as a Democrat, but in the Senate races, it was a veritable nightmare.

The environmental groups were less strident. Mike Lowry and I had high ratings at both the national and state environmental levels. It was more about politics than record. The most powerful organization, the Sierra Club, endorsed Mike Lowry on July 5, 1988. The media coverage did not ignore that the count was possibly rigged. The *Seattle*

Post-Intelligencer disclosed that "Local Sierra Club leaders insisted that their backing of Lowry over Rep. Don Bonker was unrelated to the fact that Lowry's campaign director, Rose Kapolczynski, was Sierra's national political director until two months ago."

What's puzzling is why the Sierra Club failed to recognize my record. *The Seattle Times* quoted Doug Pauley, president of the Washington Wilderness Coalition, saying that "the Sierra Club endorsement ignores Bonker's legislative record—12 successful bills protecting areas of the state such as the Columbia River Gorge, Protection Island, Mount St. Helens, Point of Arches, and Shi Shi Beach. If you are looking for an environmental champion," he said. "Bonker's got 12 trophies in his case."

He also recognized my difficulties as reported in *The Seattle Times*, stating that "Mike Lowry can vote for a wilderness bill and everybody cheers back home, while Bonker votes for wilderness and he has to go home to an angry group of timber people." Doug Pauley organized the "Conservationists for Bonker" to offset the Sierra Club endorsement.

Organized labor endorsement is of upmost critical importance in Democratic primaries. They can get fired up, and they have money and ground troops to commit which can make a difference. The Lowry and Bonker camps eagerly courted union leaders at the state and local levels, hoping these would lead to the Washington State Labor Council. But neither Lowry nor I could muster the two-thirds vote to win the endorsement. So each of us scrambled to pick up what we could, which worked to Lowry's advantage.

His spokesperson claimed they had twenty-seven unions with 225,000 members who pledged their support. My one big win was the Building and Construction Trades Council, but its 48,000 workers could not compare to Lowry's claim. The grand prize was Boeing's Aerospace Machinist union, by far the most significant in the primary election. Its 40,000 membership was politically active, which helped to block Lowry from receiving the Washington State Labor Council's endorsement.

The irony is blissful. Boeing and its workers were located in Lowry's district, so the expectation was they would bless his candidacy. Instead, I got their endorsement. The *why* is the important part. They were unhappy with Lowry because he opposed large government contracts to build military planes which would expand their workforce and membership roles. Lowry ignored their concerns, which further hardened the relationship.

I had good relations with the machinists' leadership, but they had questions about me as well, mostly regarding my pro-trade work in

Congress. In the late 1980s, labor unions were becoming more protectionists. So we decided to get together at a local pub and talk it through.

I tossed out my obvious question, "Why are you opposed to international trade when sixty-five percent of the airplanes you produce are destined for foreign markets, a fact that has everything to do with your members' livelihood?"

They were anxious to respond, saying, "Congressman, we've got to stand up for brothers in Pennsylvania, Ohio, Michigan.... Trade has mills shutting down and jobs going to other countries." It was a cordial discussion that ended with their formal endorsement of my candidacy on March 3, 1988. As reported in *The Seattle Times*, "What makes the action by the huge Boeing aeromechanics union significant is that it is one of the most politically active unions in the state. It is based in Lowry's 7th District, and it has endorsed his past campaigns."

The Boeing union had a typically strong presence two weeks later at the Raymond Crab Feed, one of the Democrats' premier events in the state. Best reported by Neil Modie, the *Post-Intelligencer* reporter from the oldest and most popular Democratic political livestock show in the state, he wrote that "Seattle's huge Aerospace Machinists Lodge 751, one of the few unions to endorse Bonker over Lowry, who is their own congressman—always sends a herd of members to the crab feed. About 70 of the Boeing workers and their spouses showed up, and most wore Bonker lapel stickers. That wasn't the only problem for Lowry, usually the darling of any partisan Democratic audience. The Renton congressman seemed to be having an off night. His standard partisan stump speech, usually a passionate, arm-waving, rabble-rouser showered with applause and cheers, seemed halting and awkward. A couple of times he asked his party-mood audience to listen better. He seemed to take a couple of pokes at the long table full of aeromechanics, scoffing at the 'the rap against me that I'm unelectable,' which was one of the reasons the machinists have given for endorsing Bonker. Bonker's speeches are sometimes jokingly prescribed for insomniacs, but he unleashed a Lowryesque stem-winder that whipped the audience into a happy lather. He told how proud he was to be endorsed by 'the biggest and most powerful union in the state,' and applause exploded. Later on, the aeromechanics presented Bonker with a bright red machinists union jacket, which he donned amid applause."

It was Mike Lowry's worst moment but it did little to curb his strong momentum statewide. Closer to primary election date, newspaper editorial endorsements begin to appear. These respectively bring smiles or angst to candidates and their supporters. I managed to pick up most of the endorsements in Seattle and statewide, which gave us bragging rights but little else as my opponent and I both vigorously maneuvered to lock down endorsements to capture the momentum heading to the September 20, 1988 primary election.

From the March 17 Crab Feed to the September 20, 1988 primary election, I was on the campaign trail nonstop, campaigning and making speeches stretching all over the state, making many daily calls in the pre-iPhone era to raise money, and then rushing back to the other Washington to cast votes on the floor of the House. I also had a family, which I could not ignore. Carolyn was terrific accompanying me, but she was also a mother with two eight-year-old children, an age that demanded steady attention.

Her parents, Major Kermit and Dorothy Ekern, dutiful grandparents, were there for us in full support. We all needed a break from the campaign and some time together as a family. As an English literature major, Carolyn had a keen eye for cultural classical things. She learned that the legendary *Les Miserables* musical performance was playing at Seattle's Fifth Avenue Theater. This seemed ideal for a three-generational family outing, so I splurged on the tickets, expecting to have good upfront seating. It was a great treat having special time off the campaign trail to enjoy this timeless French tale of ruin and redemption.

The Ekerns dressed up and ferried from Bainbridge Island over to Seattle, drove their deluxe Chrysler on a busy street, and parked in front of my campaign office. A bit rushed, the retired state patrolman and acting chauffeur that day quickly opened the driver's door and a speeding Metrobus rammed into the side of the car, leaving the car door barely hanging by its metal hinges. Fortunately, Major Kermit was not hurt, but was now trying to cope with the damage while figuring how he was going to get us to the theater on my one free evening.

Inspired by the 1984 low-tech hero, "Mac" MacGyver, Carolyn's father figured it out, somehow looping his own belt around the inside door handle and holding it in his right hand as he drove on with his left toward the theater. In awe, we succeeded in making it in time to the show, only to be ushered to our expensive seats in the very last row of the house. The joy of being free from campaigning, though, was ample pleasure for me, and my kids, Dawn and Jon, were so enthralled by the musical performance and the grand themes of *Les Miserables* that the lousy tickets and the mangled car door just wasn't able to ruin our great cultural night out.

On election night, the candidates and their enthusiastic supporters gathered in large halls to await election results.

The commanding lead that Lowry racked up had had me playing catch-up most of the year. Yet on election night, as the returns were being reported, it turned out to be nail-bitingly close. The newspaper headlines the following morning showed me as having a narrow lead. The *Post-Intelligencer* reported "underdog Rep. Don Bonker held a narrow lead over Rep. Mike Lowry last night in their race for the Democratic nomination and a chance to face former Republican Sen. Slade Gorton in November." Portland's *The Oregonian* similarly reported that "Don Bonker, the quiet, determined congressman from Vancouver, appeared late Tuesday night to be within reach of winning his uphill battle for the Democratic nomination to the US Senate. By late in the evening, a slim early lead in the race by Congressman Mike Lowry had turned around and Bonker took a 9,500 vote lead."

As the voting results poured in, the situation began to shift and I watched my lead as it was eaten away from voting stations that Lowry seemed to command. It was a nail-biting moment as I frantically checked the various postings of election results on the TV screen and got steady news from my campaign staff who were rushing to give me updates from precincts and counties around the state. As the clock was ticking and everyone eagerly awaited for a first television station to declare one of us as the winner, I kept feeling for the inside pocket of my blue blazer with the two prepared speeches for either a victory or a concession. In a few minutes, I'd be stepping up to the podium, viewing my loyal campaign staff, enthusiastic supporters, devoted family, and making the predictable announcement: "I am proud and thrilled to stand here and say I will be our state's next US senator," or "I am disappointed with the results, but ever so grateful for all your support."

It was a darn close election and I could have easily put off my concession speech until the next day, but I felt compelled to get on with it, and so, with reluctance, I headed over to Mike Lowry's HQ and dutifully declared my support of his candidacy against the Republican Slade Gorton in the general election.

This was the right thing to do. And I did it.

As I was walking back across the hotel ballroom, Stan Barer, a friend and supporter, pulled me aside and whispered in my ear. "Don, you are going to be a US senator before you know it." I was stunned by Stan's comment. Was he just being kind and supportive or did he really know something that I did not yet know. I did not break my gait, but my mind was turning. My sense of decorum and protocol and dignity and honor kept me moving across that dance floor like the old dance instructor I started out as. Somewhere deep inside me, I wanted to break into a cha-cha-cha and let the choreography of the dance propel me over to Lowry's place, but of course, our most secret moments of inner amusement cannot be played out in the real world—most of the time at least. Stan Barer, who aside from being my friend was also US Senator Brock Adams' advisor and lawyer, would never have made that remark if there wasn't something authentic within it. Stan had formerly served as Senator Magnuson's chief of staff, had founded a law firm, and had started a successful cargo shipping company. His intuition and his insider knowledge was not to be ignored.

In that delicate moment as I retreated across the ballroom, he had not elaborated his prediction, but what I learned later was that he had drafted Senator Brock Adams' press statement that the senator would be resigning from the US Senate. Since Adams' replacement would need to be appointed by Governor Booth Gardner, for Stan, it was obvious that I would be the pick. This scenario would have me in the Senate earlier than if I had won the primary and general elections. That was a wow moment.

The Adams affair turned out to be a sex scandal that had banner headlines on newspapers across the state. It was the senator's staff assistant, Kari Tupper, daughter of a longtime friend who made drug rape allegations that had been under investigation and about to be reported in a Washington, DC weekly magazine. In fact, eight women accused Adams of various acts of sexual harassment, and the senator chose to not seek reelection rather than not only dragging himself through the mud but hurting the chances of the Democrats retaining his seat.

His resignation was scheduled to be announced shortly after the primary election, which would draw media speculation about who would be appointed to replace him. However, Stan Barer got back to me, discreetly sharing that the senator's wife, Betty Adams, insisted he not resign, and that she would stand with him throughout the scandal. The controversy would not go away that easy, but the bottom line for me was that sublime fantasy moment when I just lost the Senate race only to imagine being appointed to the very same position, even before the general election. This, of course, would not happen.

Six months later, federal prosecutors made public why they declined to charge Senator Brock Adams with sexual assault in 1987. They determined the young woman involved acknowledged that she pursued him that night and did not leave after he made sexual advances, which would have meant that the encounter was consensual. *The Washington Post* reported about the drug allegations, quoting the federal prosecutor, "No objective evidence supports the supposition about drugging symptoms the morning after, which seemed equally consistent with excess consumption of alcohol over the course of an evening." A hospital test the day after showed no evidence of drugging.

While the senator was steadfast in his intention to remain in office and indeed run for reelection, *The Seattle Times* had a team of journalists investigating potential allegations among other women, notably former campaign and congressional staffers. On March 1, 1992, they reported on their finding which involved other women who alleged that the senator "sexually harassed and physically molested them," and signed statements attesting to the truth of their stories. This prompted Senator Adams to make an announcement the following day that he would not seek reelection in 1992.

This would open the door for another run for the US Senate. It was four years away and I had to get on with rebuilding my life, which most likely would be bound for the private sector. Another race for the US Senate was definitely a possibility, but the road was littered with unknowns. Since Mike Lowry ended up losing the general elections, which meant that we might have ended up squaring off again with a similar outcome. Our popular governor, Booth Gardner, would be finishing his second term and would be the preemptive favorite if he decided to get into the race. Yes, lots to think about, but the reality started to set in, and I had to start making the transition and finding a new job.

The day after the election, I was interviewed by Joel Connelly of the *Seattle Post-Intelligencer* about my post-election feelings. He noted that "Rep. Don Bonker and his wife, Carolyn, made a painful phone call to their two children in Washington, DC yesterday morning with the bad news that Bonker had lost his bid for the Democratic Senate nomination."

The article documented my wife's sentiments as well as mine. "Carolyn Bonker wiped a tear from her eye and said the couple's religious faith has provided 'stability and resolve' to accept an election defeat and the end of her husband's 14-year congressional career."

We decided to take a short break and spend time in Colorado with our children before returning to Washington, DC. I would remain a member of Congress for three more months, and this period was more about closing down my congressional office and helping my staff find new jobs than about attending hearings.

It was, frankly, a tough time personally. I not only lost the Senate race, but the sobering fact that my political career appeared to be over. Also, I faced an uncertain future. As I was coping with all of this, my assistant, Linda Sutter, entered my office with another batch of letters. They were from friends and supporters, naturally, but also others that were surprising.

One by one, I opened the envelopes and read them, pausing and reflecting as my eyes followed the lines across these pages. When I had won elections, I had received the typically ephemeral "congratulations" or "nice win" and "good luck." But this time, the letters were more personal, often handwritten, some were two pages. What surprised me were the many that came from adversaries, prominent Republicans, other elected officials, as well as, of course, my friends and supporters. Many came from leaders in the trade community. For them, this was more than an election lost, they would also lose their voice on trade in Congress.

Years later, as I reviewed these letters and contemplated what they meant in the context of my career, actually forty years later, I was touched in a fresh way by how people had shared in such a deep way. In defeat, I was offered far more personal and touching messages than I had in the case of victory. Was there a lesson to learn from this? I gave this some deep thought and decided, yes. In reviewing the letters, I observed that for some, my loss had reconnected others to their own experiences, their own setbacks or failed efforts or disappointments. We shared the pain that accompanies defeat, and in addition to paying tribute to my years in public office, they acknowledged the larger and deeper human commonality—empathy.

Although there are so many letters I could cite, there are two that continue to stand out and resonate with feeling for me as I revisit that moment of personal pain and loss; a road which fork led me to a place where there didn't seem to be a way ahead.

Sally Gordon, the wife of Slade Gordon, the Republican nominee who went on to defeat Mike Lowry in the general election and who had previously served in the US Senate and had been defeated by Brock Adams, had the kindness and character to write a letter addressed to Carolyn, my wife.

My Dear Carolyn,

We wanted you to know that we are thinking of you and Don. Believe me, we know and understand how you feel. You have my heartfelt sympathy. Our loss was the worst experience of my life. After saying that, I realized how fortunate we have been. Carolyn, it will hurt, for a long time. It is like a death in the family, except that instead of a private grief, it seems like a public humiliation. After the "debate," our Sarah said, "Mrs. Bonker is beautiful." And I told her, you were beautiful all the way through. Turn the page on this page of life and look forward to writing a new chapter. For me, each day that went by was easier than the day before and then life returned to normal. Normal is wonderful.

Fondly, Sally

The other letter I wish to share came from Chuck Colson, who many of us recall served in the Richard Nixon White House and was implicated in the Watergate scandal. Chuck served time in prison, became a man of faith, and founded the Prison Fellowship Ministries to which he devoted the rest of his life. He shared these heartfelt thoughts in his letter of October 3, 1988.

Dear Don, believe me, I have some idea on what you and Carolyn must be going through. I'm sure it's painful. You both are dear friends, and we are feeling the pain with you. We have thought of you often in our prayers, asking the Lord not only to heal and bind up the wounds but to give you a fresh sense of His direction for your life.

I'm sure you know from reading my books, Don, and from our many conversations that I view life to be a great paradox. At least, in my experience, God has used not my victories, but my defeats for His greatest glory—what He does through us is far greater than what we can do ourselves.

Knowing you as I do, I don't think you've ever had the problem of pride. But I can say that for me, the defeats turned out to be a blessing. I always seemed to be able to handle them better than I could the triumphs.

In any event, I'm sure there is a purpose in all of this for you. I hope and pray that you will seek God's will for your lives. I hope also that means further public service because there are too few men of deep Christian commitment and character willing to take on the rigors of public life. I would hate to think you were going to abandon it.

Grief and disappointment are normal emotions, so I'm sure this is a time in which you are hurting, and I just want you to know that we are sharing your hurts.

Yours in His service,
Charles W. Colson

On December 10, 1988, as I was about to exit from my political career, a so-called Toast and Roast event was scheduled to take place in Vancouver, my home base. *The Columbian*'s vice president and editor, Tom Koenninger, penned his take on the event with the opening line, "Don Bonker, exhibiting the grace of the statesman he has become, said goodbye to Clark County Wednesday night." His article, and others, covered the many tributes shared that evening, including one by Governor Booth Gardner "who gave Don Bonker one of the highest compliments any man could receive. If he could pick one elected official whom he would like his children to pattern their lives after, it would be Don Bonker, Gardner said." For six months, multiple interviews and articles highlighted that I would be back in politics sooner rather than later. Some of the headlines around the state stated, "Bonker says his political career is far from over," "Bonker: Politics may be in the future," "He still wants to be Sen. Bonker," "Bonker may run again," "Don Bonker enthusiastic about challenge of the future," and "Bonker will try a comeback." Those may have been the headlines, but the reality was something else. The fact was that there were no options for me in the near future. Republican Slade Gorton would become the next US senator from Washington. Senator Brock Adams, despite the sex scandal, felt confident enough to run for another term. Regardless of my appetite to run again, I knew it just wasn't going to happen.

On March 1, 1992, *The Seattle Times* unleashed its investigative report on the allegations by the eight women that Senator Brock Adams had allegedly harassed or abused them over the previous two decades. This time, his wife, Betty, did not discourage him from announcing he would not seek reelection. The pressure was too great and the charge too upsetting. *The Seattle Times*, in a follow-up article, "Who'll run for Adams' seat?" opened the gate for another shot at the Senate.

Mike Lowry and my name were highlighted in articles over the next few months as possible candidates for Brock Adams' replacement. However, our popular governor, Booth Gardner, announced he would not seek reelection for the governorship, thus propelling himself as the lead to be the Democrat nominee to run for Brock Adams' seat in 1992. Politics is a perpetual shuffle and reshuffle, and the nerve it takes to see the field ahead one way and then see it turn around completely is, well, not for everyone.

CHAPTER 32

THE MOM IN TENNIS SHOES

On May 7, 1992, I took a call that I hadn't imagined would occur. It was Joel Connelly, National Correspondent for the *Seattle Post-Intelligencer.* I was surprised he'd be calling me since I was no longer involved in politics. He wasted no time asking if I had heard the news that Governor Booth Gardner had just announced he would not, in fact, be a candidate for the US Senate. I had not heard this yet. Break news was fast but nowhere as instantaneous as it is today.

I was surprised, stupefied even, and wholly unprepared for his next question. "Don, will you now be a candidate?" As a good journalist, he was on top of the story and wanted to be the first to report this if this were to be the case.

"Joel, I can't give you an instant response, I must discuss this with Carolyn and others. It will take time."

He anticipated my response and shot back," I need an answer before my deadline in two hours." He then made a veiled offer, saying, "You let me know before my deadline, I personally guarantee you will not regret it." Media and politics, they make a potent libation!

Our relationship had dated back thirty years when Joel had shown up as a young reporter at the Young Democrats state convention in Port Townsend. As the youngest elected official in the state, I played a prominent role and we had some time together. Joel Connelly eventually became the most respected political reporter in Washington, and his fine reputation carried well beyond our state borders. He had turned down numerous offers from news publications in Washington, DC in order to continue covering state news. He was a pro. And still is, reporting regular stories in the *Seattle Post-Intelligencer.*

Joel Connelly covered me all those years so it is fair to say that we shared a close professional relationship that bonded us; not exactly friends because we needed to maintain the distance that kept us both credible and independent in our respective jobs. He was very professional, tough but fair, well informed and insightful, and became integral to reporting on the state's political history. He once described me as the "rising star" and when I ran a second time for Secretary of State in year 2000, his reference was the "fading star."

I had to take his offer seriously. But I needed some time.

"Joel, I will get right back to you." I put down the phone, already exhausted just thinking about another Senate race. There's so much to consider and I had only a few hours if I were to respect his deadline.

Foremost in my thoughts was Carolyn, but she was not reachable. She had a painting lesson with an artist in rural Virginia, so I could not discuss this with her. Our children, Dawn and Jonathan, were about to celebrate their twelfth birthdays, an age that demanded lots of attention and I would be an absentee dad. It was heartbreaking to think that I would be missing Jonathan's baseball games, something very special in the father-son relationship. Carolyn would have to cope with demands in both Washingtons, and I would want her next to me at high profile events, which was definitely an asset on the campaign trail. To make an instant decision to run without discussing with Carolyn was unthinkable, yet I was faced with that reality and had to act.

There was also my employer, APCO Worldwide. I'd be campaigning twenty-four seven away from my DC office while trying to hold onto my job. How was it possible that I could commit to a Senate race without coming to terms with my boss, Margery Kraus, who was traveling and was not available? It was hard to imagine that I could simply waltz into her office and say, "Hi Margery, here to inform you, I just decided to run for the US Senate so will be out of office for the next eight months. Oh, by the way, keep me on the payroll full-time." The worst case scenario would be that I would be away from my family and not have a job and salary for the rest of the year. I was sitting there glaring at the phone, coping with these factors, knowing that I had only a few hours to make a life-changing decision. Unlike the 1988 campaign, I had no team, no organization, no budget. But I also knew in the general election, it all tends to come together; it's the primary that begs the most serious questions. Who would the other Democrats be? Would I be facing off again with Mike Lowry? A repeat of the race I lost a few short years earlier? Possibly.

Maybe this was a godsent, a rare opportunity, my final shot of getting into the US Senate? Or would this be another campaign against the same Mike Lowry resulting in the same outcome? Another fork. Frankly, I asked myself, "Are you up to this?" I had begun to find a very pleasant life in the private sector and had more time with my children, and was liberated from the punishing demands of a statewide campaign. At fifty-five, I should be thinking ahead about a good paying job and retirement rather than restarting my political career.

I was a nervous wreck when I picked up the phone to call Joel Connelly.

"Joel?"

"Yes Don."

"I think I will go for it, and you are the first to know. I will get in the race to be the next US senator from the state of Washington."

It was like I could hear his smile and his pencil get down the exact words I had said into the receiver. He was pleased. "You won't regret it."

Indeed, his article was highly favorable—it covered half the front page and displayed two photographs, one of me on the ferry between Seattle and Bainbridge Island without a jacket and looking quite manly, if I can say so. The other photo was of me chairing a committee hearing. The piece was journalistically balanced and objective but bordered on full-blown praise with positive references to my record. Any candidate could only fantasize having an article like this as his opening piece of media to a senatorial race.

"Bonker made a reputation for standing up to special interests during a 14-year House career," the article stated. It then proceeded to recount four key examples: 1) my opposition to the exportation of logs from public lands, a position anathema to my district's powerful ports and not popular with such major employers as Weyerhaeuser; 2) anti-log export stand which was cheered by small mill owners. He added that I had made them mad by backing the creation of a large Mount St. Helens National Volcanic Area; 3) he cited that I was the first lawmaker to call for preservation of Bowerman Basin, a Grays Harbor estuary that is an annual stopover point for up to one million migratory birds. At the same time, the Port of Grays Harbor wanted to use the marsh as a landfill; 4) he said my finest hour may have come in 1979 when I "called for shut down of two nuclear plants under construction in Grays Harbor County, citing the plants' out of control costs and chaotic management. "The stand infuriated public utility districts in Bonker's district. Two years and billions of dollars later, the partially finished plants were forced to shut down."

The lengthy article covered all aspects of my public career, including my religious beliefs, how I dealt with abortion and related issues, my centrist position on economic issues, my national leadership on trade, and my few years in the private sector. It was positive and affirming, which gave me some needed solace to offset my fears about launching another statewide campaign.

Two days later, I got a call from Karen Marchioro, state Democratic Party chairman, saying, "Don, great you are in and this time we will get you elected."

I thanked her, then she quickly got to the point.

"You have to get someone to run your campaign, and I have the right person," she said.

"Karen, I don't want someone I don't know. A campaign chairman has to know all about the candidate, his whims, positions, support base," I told her.

Her response was, "Don, Trust me, she's the right one."

Within two weeks, my new campaign manager arrived on the scene. Her first words in a rather strident tone were, "Congressman, I am here to get you elected; it's your job to raise money. Do you understand what I am saying?" Her message to the candidate was don't interfere with running the campaign. Off to a rough start with the person who was selected to be in charge of my campaign.

As I was dutifully "raising money," my headache continued to be Mike Lowry getting into the race. He would again have a huge advantage, but I felt it could play out differently this time. The first big event was on my turf, the legendary Pacific County Crab Feed, drawing all the Democratic leaders and elected officials from around the state. On my way down to Raymond, I got word that Mike Lowry had decided to run for governor, not US senator. Hallelujah! That was the big roadblock removed from my path to securing the Democratic nomination.

As I entered the labor union hall, the aroma was more than the fresh crab that was spread across the decorated tables in the room. I could smell victory for the first time. Included among the speakers gathering at the podium was a woman I did not recognize. I turned to a local legislator and asked, "Who is that person?"

He responded, "Patty Murray, a state senator from Seattle."

As she spoke, it was obvious she may also be a candidate for the US

Senate. At the moment, I was jubilant about Lowry opting out I gave little attention to Ms. Murray's possible candidacy.

In July 1992, according to a prominent pollster Elway Research, I was leading the pack with 19%, Murray with 14%, and the lead Republican Representative Rod Chandler trailing at 10%. One month later, the results were: Bonker 20%, Murray 11%, and the leading Republican Rod Chandler at 16%. These results were posted one month before the primary election. I was leading two-to-one over Patty Murray.

But there was a lot more going on beyond the polls that would affect the election. Patty Murray committed early on to challenging Brock Adams, recognizing that the incumbent senator would be vulnerable because of the alleged sex revelations. She hesitated until Governor Booth Gardner opted out before aiming for what she then saw as a clear shot. She had already lined up endorsements from the Washington State Labor Council, the Sierra Club, and women's organizations nationally. She was dead serious.

That was all done in the conventional sense but there were other less conventional developments that worked in her favor. In October 1991, Senate Judiciary Committee shocked the nation as a calm and credible law professor, Anita Hill, testified against the nomination of Clarence Thomas to the Supreme Court, alleging sexual misconduct when both worked at the Equal Employment Opportunities Commission.

Thomas, a George H. W. Bush nominee, and the judge's former female employee—both African-American—were grilled by senators about the graphic details of the sexual harassment allegations. The live television broadcasting of the Senate Judiciary Committee hearings was mesmerizing. The charges of a stunning collision of issues of race and gender involving an appointee to the Supreme Court was polarizing. Both the nominee and his accuser were viewed as having credibility problems, creating a deep divide in the US Senate and across the nation.

I was fascinated watching the hearings, having no idea how they would ultimately impact me personally. The Anita Hill testimony unleashed a political tsunami that carried across the country. Women were motivated to get more involved in politics, a trend which had a significant impact on the primary and general elections. The first big hit was in Illinois where a little known woman, Carol Moseley Braun, angered by Democratic Senator Alan Dixon's vote to confirm Clarence Thomas, stepped up out of nowhere to oppose the incumbent. She scored a major upset, defeating Dixon in the primary and carrying on to win the general election. The wave carried to California where, on rare occasion, both

Senate seats were on the ballot. Two women defeated their white male opponents. Diane Feinstein and Barbra Boxer would go on to serve with distinction for many years in the US Senate. Washington State, my home, would be next.

The Olympia AP reporter, David Ammons, characterized the Anita Hill phenomenon and its probable effect on our state. "A Mother's Day note: this is turning out to be the Year of the Woman in Washington State politics. This comes in the springtime of discontent, following the Anita Hill-Clarence Thomas hearings by an all-male Senate panel, several celebrated rape trials, accusations of sexual harassment levied against the state's senior senator, Brock Adams, the resignation of Sen. Stan Johnson after an aide charged the same thing. Senate hopeful Patty Murray, who proudly calls herself 'a mom in tennis shoes,' is riding that mighty wave and may find herself washed into the male-dominated Senate. She says her meteoric rise in politics—she has been in the state legislature only one term—is partly due to the backlash against the Thomas hearings and out-of-touch incumbents she calls 'those guys in blue suits and red ties.'"

The "guys in red ties" was part Patty Murray's rhetorical appeal to supporters, a subtle reference to Al Gore's standard attire. My thought was to shoot it down at our first debate before the Capitol Press Corps in Olympia. When introduced, I stood up and removed my red tie, tossed it onto the table, then made my point: "This campaign is about more than red ties. Let's now discuss the serious issues in this race."

I scored the first punch. But Patty Murray had the last word, wrapping up her remarks, glancing at my wrist and began to chuckle. "I'm laughing because my opponent's watch is at 4:30, on DC time." She said. Her point was that Bonker was more about the establishment in the "other" Washington than the reality here in this Washington.

Patty Murray stumbled onto a message that greatly enhanced her candidacy statewide and nationally. She called herself "the mom in tennis shoes." The coinage came from a colleague in the legislature who said, "Patty, you are just a mom in tennis shoes, no way can you have a political career." Few political strategists could have matched what became a slogan that all but ensured her election victory.

The mom in tennis shoes seemed to speak to thousands of women voters.

The media reporting got their teeth into the slogan and rode with it. The deeper issues were lost in the noise, not unlike the Bonker-Lowry race in 1988.

The headlines screamed and the public lapped it up. "Scripts don't fit notions about Murray, Bonker"; "Murray and Bonker, a study in contrasts"; "Same concerns, different angles"; "Senate primary is a contest of styles." The journalists had fun with the jousting match.

In our several debates and joint appearances, I came across as thoughtful and substantive, but Patty Murray had a more riveting effect. Mark Matassa of *The Seattle Times* wrote on August 3, 1992 that "Don Bonker, the former Vancouver congressman with 20 years of political experience, came off as the uncharismatic bumbler on the radio, while Patty Murray, the self-styled 'mom in tennis shoes,' was the ultra-prepared slicker."

More than anything, it was the EMILY's List that fueled the Patty Murray campaign. Founded in 1985, this organization captured the passion women were feeling across the country, tapping into wealthy donors, raising tens of millions to support women candidates for the US Senate and House of Representatives. Their interest specifically focused on pro-choice women, and pivoted on the point that "women couldn't be equal until they had control over their bodies." Patty Murray was a top priority, in part, because her opponent, Don Bonker, had a nebulous position on an issue near and dear to their hearts.

Ellen Malcom, president of EMILY's List, said "Women will be the face of change in 1992." She was right!

And I simply wasn't a woman.

With all this playing out weeks before the primary election, the national trend was a wake-up call for me. Our election was all about Patty Murray; I was simply a bystander. Of course, we debated, I raised money, a good statewide organization, and my campaign manager did an excellent job. But the national mood was stronger than anything I could do or say. It was an unusual year, not unlike my first race for Congress in 1974—a national mood that would influence election results across the country. This time, it was all about women, and of the thirteen names on the ballot for US Senate, Patty Murray was the only woman candidate.

On the primary election night in Seattle, I watched the posting of election results come in county by county. What struck me early on were the votes pouring in from the state's rural counties, which were traditionally very Republican and conservative. The results even here were all favorable to a liberal woman candidate. It was obvious—independent and Republican women were making a statement in the voting booths. Anita Hill may not have blocked the confirmation of Clarence Thomas as Supreme Court Justice, but she definitely changed the results of the 1992 national elections. It made sense, but for me, it was a political tsunami in tennis shoes that ended my political career.

IX. Oligarchs Reign Amok

CHAPTER 33

RUSSIA'S MEDIA CZAR

My transitioning from twenty-two years in public service to the private sector put me in unchartered waters. Still reeling from election defeat, a campaign debt, shutting down my congressional offices, I had to put my focus on next steps.

What do former congressmen do? Where do they reside? Do they remain in DC or head back to the district? Do I get a trade position in the Clinton administration? Do I run for office again? Senator Warren Magnuson advised that I had millions invested in my political career. "Don't abandon it," he advised me.

My international trade mantra prompted several new offers from law firms, but without a law degree, these ultimately were not my best options. I also wanted to avoid being a lobbyist, a field that is often a big temptation to former congressmen and women. I didn't like the idea of peddling influence in this way. Suddenly, I was faced with a new reality of finding a job after twenty-two years in public service. There were other offers, but what stood out was one that was spearheaded by a woman who appeared in my office one day. Her name was Margery Kraus and she headed a firm called APCO, a consulting arm of Arnold & Porter, the largest law firm in Washington, DC at the time. Arnold & Porter was founded by Thurman Arnold, a Yale Law School professor; Paul Porter, who had chaired the Federal Communications Commission; and Abe Fortas, whose name was removed when Fortas was nominated and confirmed to serve on the United States Supreme Court. The consulting branch, APCO, had grabbed the initials from the partners. They had a strong and viable international trade practice, so the fit for me was natural.

Kraus quickly caught my attention and I welcomed her into my empty office. I observed later that when Margery Kraus, an inductee of the PR Hall of Fame, entered into a room full of notable people, her presence had a captivating effect on others and they'd gather around her. From that first encounter, I saw the personal and professional skills that ultimately served to escalate her startup company to an award-winning global public affairs firms. As we were talking, I was drawn to her vision and the possibilities it held for me personally. Following that conversation, and as Margery left my office, I realized that something real was on the table. I was anxious to tell Carolyn about this meeting with Margery Kraus and the possibility of a new job in the private sector. When Carolyn smiled, I knew this would be the route to take.

I joined APCO—which soon became APCO Worldwide—when the consulting arm of Arnold & Porter was only in its fourth year, still modest in size but with ambition far beyond the scope of its parent law firm. Margery had ambitions to take the project globally, and although the law firm partners had been dabbling in debate over the question for years, Margery had already laid out the groundwork.

The global vision was ignited with her meeting with a certain Vladimir Gusinsky, a Russian startup entrepreneur who was eager to take advantage of both the risks and opportunities now emerging in the post-Soviet Union market. She had established the first foreign office of APCO in Moscow in 1989.

Just a few days after that first meeting, Margery invited Carolyn and me to a small dinner party with Mr. Gusinsky. Carolyn, in her lovely green silk dress, was seated next to the guest of honor who was gracious and attentive. Everyone was asking Mrs. Bonker about the Senate race. Gusinsky was not yet conversant in English, but he listened carefully. Carolyn mentioned to me later that while referring to my election loss, he said to her that "days ahead may be more better." I had no idea the Gusinsky dinner would be my entrée to the private sector. And I have never forgotten the elegance of his grammatical error. If better can be more, I knew I'd want some of that!

One month later, I left my Capitol Hill office and twenty-two years of public service to become part of Margery Kraus' team. The expectation had everything to do with my international trade expertise, but ultimately, it had limited value to the law firm that APCO was part of. My arrival was timely. It synchronized with the dissolution of the Soviet Union and Margery's connection to Vladimir Gusinsky.

The door to multiple opportunities during the 1990s swung wide open.

Russia was going through an arduous transformation from a highly centralized form of socialism to what could best be described as the Wild West. This post-Soviet era would span more than a decade and a half—from the dawn of Mikhail Gorbachev's 1985 *perestroika* and *glasnost* reforms to the aftermath of Boris Yeltsin's resignation on December 31, 1992. Russia was on the edge of a new horizon—what would be the new alignment of power and property? Or, as Russians have been asking for centuries, *"Ktokogo?"*—"Who beats whom? "Who benefits?"

These new business elites foresaw that the collapse of the Communist Party and its imperial control over the economy—prices, production, wages, investments—would lead to an economic free-for-all, unprecedented in modern history. But they also recognized that in chaos, there would be possibilities. Some referred to the "thieves in law" that had grown wildly competitive and brutal. Vladimir Gusinsky was one of six so-called oligarchs who became Russia's ruling elite known as the apostles of a new order—or disorder. This new gang of businessmen was aptly described in David Hoffman's book, *The Oligarchs: Wealth and Power in the New Russia*, like this: "They amassed and lost fortunes, took over the crown jewels of Russian industry, commanded private armies, played kingmaker in elections, and ruled the country and its citadel of finance. They bought up the Russian mass media, especially television, and they seized not only factories but also the assets of the state itself, including the budget, the law enforcement system, and the Kremlin leadership. In their swaggering domination of the early Russian capitalism, they were secretive deceptive, and, at times, ruthlessly violent."

True, there was moral ambiguity in this new environment, given the vagaries of would-be legitimate business trying to operate in a wild landscape. But not all were mafia types or corrupt. The two that stood out were Vladimir Gusinsky and Mikhail Khodorkovsky—both amazingly entrepreneurial, even visionaries, as they built their respective empires. Khodorkovsky was the wealthiest, acquiring a defunct oil company and making into the second largest in the world. Gusinsky was the most powerful given his political savvy and media holdings. What they had in common was the courage to confront and challenge the newly installed President Vladimir Putin, which they did, but at a high cost. Both were sent off to prison, and the Russian state confiscated their huge business enterprises.

Russia in those days was vast and unruly and filled with unmanaged or mismanaged assets, companies, funds, resources, talent, and crudely ambitious characters. With the fall of the Berlin Wall and the dismantling of the Communist Bloc, Gorbachev had ushered in a new era of openness and Russia, with its former bloc of satellite countries, represented the Wild West of capitalist opportunity. Boris Yeltsin became the first elected president of the new Russia and despite his well-known liking to vodka, loosely held the reins of power. The scramble was on for leadership and management in the ownership of the nation's valuable assets. Margery Kraus saw the huge potential for new global clients needing to know how to join the global economy, especially wealthy Russians as they gobbled up voraciously what was there for the taking, crafting deals that transitioned a mammoth public sector into the avarice paws of the new private sector, some showing respect for law and others without.

Margery Kraus joined a group of American businesspeople pursuing these investment opportunities in Moscow, and she promptly met for the first time a spirited Russian who was gaining attention named Vladimir Gusinsky. They quickly bonded, thanks in part to their shared Jewish faith, but mostly due to their common vision that there were lots of new businesses to harness between Moscow and Washington. The contact resulted in a joint venture partnership that would, at first, bring American business prospects to Moscow. It made sense and Margery, like a natural running back, was quick at spotting holes in the defense and sprinted to the open spaces. Inviting her Russian counterpart to the US, Gusinsky swiftly accepted.

At the time, Russia was going through an arduous transformation—from its highly centralized form of socialism to a new political and economic environment, which could be best described as the Gold Rush of '48. Vladimir Gusinsky, from the start, was not lacking in ambition, even when at those initial, lowly jobs like driving a Moscow taxi and working as a deputy manager at a local theater house. But he quickly got his act together and emerged in record time as the most colorful of Russia's self-made oligarchs, building a media and financial empire literary overnight. Hoffman described Gusinsky's early career like this: "The dawn of perestroika found Vladimir Gusinsky at a dead end. An easily insulted young man with outsized emotions, Gusinsky had trained as a stage director but failed to find a place in the world of Moscow theater. He was a Jew, and he believed that anti-Semitism was the unspoken reason why doors slammed in his face. He drove his car as an unofficial taxi and dabbled in a number of ventures, but in the 1980s, Gusinsky was going nowhere."

In 1988, Gusinsky opened a cooperative named Infeks as a consulting company to help Western investors fathom the complexity of doing business in Russia. He was still a skinny young man wearing outsized eyeglasses and a big smile. For a fee, Gusinsky served as a fixer based on his growing legion of connections and savvy sidestepping and supported by some crude marketing data.

On that early visit to Washington accompanied by Margery Kraus, needing some quick cash, Margery motioned him to a nearby bank's automatic teller machine. It was his first time pulling out cash from the wall. Gusinsky was blown away, having never seen cash appear so quickly. The ATM outlet was part of the electronic banking network called MOST, which was written on the ATM itself. That moment was a game-changer for the Russian magnate as he had one of those lightbulb moments; he quickly embraced the word "most" which meant *bridge* in Russian, and he expropriated it as the corporate identity of his new joint venture—returning to Moscow and naming the bank he would establish "Most."

Gusinsky learned early on the importance of well-placed connections and befriended Yury Luzhkov, a stout, strong-willed deputy head of the Moscow City executive committee. They were in sync on many fronts as a journalist who knew them both well told David Hoffman, "Luzhkov is a workaholic. He likes to have a result. Gusinsky is very energetic too. They complimented each other very well."

Luzhkov became the powerful mayor of Moscow, a connection which paid big dividends to Gusinsky. His newly formed Most Bank was little more than an accounting department without funds until Mayor Luzhkov allowed the city's substantial cash deposits to flow into Most Bank, enabling Gusinsky to preside over huge sums while expanding his operations including branches and, of course, his own ATM machines throughout Russia.

In the early 1990s, Gusinsky was unstoppable, and his impatience to acquire fueled his build of an empire that included financial institutions and major construction and real estate properties. As Gusinsky and the other oligarchs were becoming more established, they expanded sectors and acquired media outlets which they saw would not only drive new revenue but would give them the control of the tools to garner positive public attention for themselves while punishing enemies or competitors. Indeed, Gusinsky had known the feeling of been upset by newspapers that criticized his business activities. Now he found a way to protect and defend himself, his public image, and his commercial interests. A group of prominent journalists, who formerly worked for the reform paper *Nezavisimaya Gazeta* convinced Gusinsky to raise $6 million for the startup publication *Segodnya*, which quickly earned a niche among Moscow's elite.

This was the first building block in Gusinsky's media empire. When *Segodnya* began publishing, another group of disgruntled journalists at the state-run Ostankino TV station took notice. Until then, no one had associated Gusinsky with the news media, but his new paper which was smart, progressive, and privately owned changed that. It was a signpost. And the media atmosphere of the new Russia took on a new élan.

Russia's most popular television newscaster, Yevgeny Kiselyov, sensing the shift in media culture in the nation, approached Gusinsky. According to Hoffman, the scene when Kiselyov entered Gusinsky's office was a tipping point for the business leader. "When Kiselyov walked in, Gusinsky was enormously excited. He had never met Kiselyov before but admired the newsman greatly. He was a household name, the Russian Walter Cronkite. 'Imagine!' Gusinsky recalled. 'Kiselyov in the flesh, at my office. How can this be?'"

What Kiselyov proposed was that Gusinsky finance the production of *Itogi*, a popular program on the state-owned TV station. Gusinsky quickly agreed but responded with "This is a small project, I think the big project is to start an independent television company, broadcasting twenty-four hours a day." It would be called NTV, *Novoe Televidenie* or New Television, and it went live on the air on October 10, 1993, eventually becoming the largest television station in Russia. Gusinsky understood that cash could drive fame, and fame drove influence.

While Gusinsky held onto his Most Bank, his new passion would be media. It fulfilled the needs of his ego, grabbed everyone's attention including the Kremlin's, it gave him political clout inside and outside Russia, and it just so happened to be profitable. By Western standards, Gusinsky did everything right, made the right moves, and crafted a truly independent media, daring event to criticize government leaders and their policies. That tends to be the American hallmark. A country is free if it tolerates its press to openly criticize its political leaders without reprisal. He hired the highly regarded Igor Malashenko to head the new NTV station and the enterprise became an overnight magnet that fetched professional journalists eager to be associated with the new press freedoms in Russia.

When Vladimir Putin, former KGB intelligence operative, succeeded Yeltsin and became president in 2000, NTV's top-rated satirical puppet show *Kukly* was wildly popular and the object of Putin's growing annoyance. The show depicted Putin as small, squeaky, and dependent on his staff. In one episode, he was portrayed as a prostitute on a street corner, following which the Kremlin threatening to shut down the TV station. Gusinsky's reply was "The Putin puppet will be back. And if *Kukly* disappears, you will know what's happening to the country."

The APCO-Gusinsky partnership had shifted to be more about representing the Russian media tycoon's interest in the US. Margery maintained a close business and personal relationship with Vladimir, whom she now called Volodya as did his closest friends. She asked me to take the lead in overseeing Gusinsky's expanding US activities. For the next several years, it was my task to set up and accompany Gusinsky on all his visits in the US. I became familiar with his persona, his ambitions, and his faults. My job at APCO, put bluntly, was to meet his expectations, which were often vague and unrealistic, which kept the mission a continuous challenge.

At the outset, Gusinsky's two top priorities were financial—engage Wall Street firms to build relationships and cough up more money, and deepen the empire's media reach, which was a natural role and one that I would help him exploit. A third concern was his contact with the American Jewish community. He ultimately founded the Russian Congress in January 1996 and, a few years later, became vice president of the World Jewish Congress.

This assignment turned out to be far more fascinating than most during my days as a congressman. The meetings were high level to be sure, but it was the body language on both sides of the boardroom table that I found most captivating, the cultural divide that needed to be interpreted and translated into action. Volodya had not lost or grown out of his pre-Soviet demeanor. He wore the same smudged wire rims and peered through the lens with the diffident eyes of an office clerk. He was chronically impatient with the interpreter, and would interject with his sparse but forceful English.

On the other side, newspaper publishers and editors and Wall Street executives were dazzled by what they saw in this guy, and wondered if he was the face of a new Russia. Is this what the survivors of our old enemy now looked like? Gusinsky was buoyant and anxious to cut deals. The impression he left was, on the whole, favorable. As we were departing the conference room after a long session, the journalists and American business leaders pulled me aside and uttered, "We want to meet with him again; let us know the next time he is here." They smelled the size of opportunity that Gusinsky represented.

On Friday, April 7, 1995, the *Washington Post* ran an exceptional piece on Gusinsky's visit to Washington, DC. What I found odd was the scale—the oversized photo and half-page article that ran on the front page of the "Style" section, the page normally reserved for celebrities and inside-the-beltway gossip. The headline was cute and brash, "Russky Business, The Mogul in Exile Who's Got Moscow Up in Arms." The reporter, Lloyd Grove, who edited the section and had often shown interest in Russia and the unspoken intrigue that characterized the shadows of US-Russian relations, tantalized readers with his portrayal of Gusinsky. "One could barely believe he had flown in from New York that morning on his very own private jet, a richly leathered British Aerospace 700; that he is the czar of a Russian real estate, banking, and media empire known as the Most Group; and that over the past three months he has found it prudent to stay out of Moscow and his corporate headquarters, lest he be assassinated by Mafiosi or possibly even the henchmen of his one-time ally, President Boris Yeltsin. Gusinsky has been described in the international press as everything from robber baron to freedom fighter."

Gusinsky's ambitious plans in the America were significantly boosted by a feature in the February 28, 1994 issue of The New Yorker. The headline and tagline alone set the tone: "The Tycoon and the Kremlin–Vladimir Gusinsky is sometimes referred to as Russia's Citizen Kane." The author, David Remnick, who had been former Moscow Bureau Chief for the Washington Post and was fluent in Russian, captured the essence of the man, writing that Gusinsky was "a kind of robber baron—a forty-two-year-old-first generation capitalist. He is also Russia's first and biggest media mogul and, as a result, is deeply embroiled in Kremlin politics. Gusinsky collects art, bankrolls a few charities, flies in his own plane. Since he travels in a business world rife with Mafiosi (fifty executives were assassinated in Moscow alone last year), he protects himself as if he were a head of state. Of fourteen thousand people his companies employ, more than a thousand are members of a privately trained security force."

It was Hoffman's The Oligarchs, though, that expanded public curiosity with Gusinsky beyond those who held previous interest in Russia. He accurately situated the Russian media baron in a rare moment of history, while bringing the high drama of Moscow's private clubs and street life in the mid1990s to American readers. "Known as the apostles of a new order," he wrote, "they amassed and lost fortunes, took over the crown jewels of Russian industry, commanded private armies, played kingmaker in elections, and ruled the country and its citadel of finance, Moscow."

Gusinsky, who had built his empire on political networking in Moscow, now had his sights on Washington, DC with APCO's help and his own recent congressman orchestrating the moves. By portraying himself as the symbol of Russia's new class of business elites, Gusinsky was positioned as newly empowered in both national capitals. That was my task, as it was his expectation. The end of the Cold War was a riveting moment among the policy community and on Capitol Hill, and this greatly facilitated my work in staging Gusinsky's grand entrance. He had become something of a celebrity, and of course, the *Washington Post* article helped, and I was catapulted from legislator into a new role that felt at times more like a Hollywood agent than a policy specialist or trade negotiator.

The meetings I set up for Gusinsky went far way those that most APCO clients commanded. One memorable encounter was with the United States Librarian of Congress Emeritus, Dr. James Billington. Highly regarded with impeccable credentials—Rhodes Scholar, former university professor at both Harvard and Princeton—Billington was also noteworthy as a scholar on Russian history and culture, and had authored numerous books including the celebrated *The Icon and the Axe*. Having run the Library of Congress for thirty years, he had been closely aligned with Congress and an A-list of business leaders.

Dr. Billington called me one day at APCO. "Congressman, I understand you handle Vladimir Gusinsky's visits to DC. If so, I'd like to host a luncheon for him and invite special guests whom I'm sure he'd enjoy meeting. Is that possible?"

I knew in an instant that Volodya would savor this opportunity, so I quickly confirmed. Billington's royal treatment was on display as he set up a VIP conference room near his private office at the Library of Congress. The former librarian had partnered with PBS on *The Face of Russia*, a three-part television series on an interpretive history of Russian culture and how it had been shaped by its Christian heritage and forms of artistic expression. Dr. Billington not only wrote and narrated the TV series, but had tackled the fundraising for the project as well. Bringing Gusinsky along attracted the deep-pocketed sponsors and patrons of culture. That was how the American culture machine worked, reliant on private sector and wealthy individuals who took tax deductions, enjoyed having their names in programs and on billboards, and being called out at luncheons and receptions. This, too, is how licensing of rights for contents works. People put on bowties and elegant dresses and write checks.

Entering the room, I could sense Gusinsky was impressed with the DC elites seated around the table, most notably Sharon Rockefeller, bearing the legendary name and whose husband was then serving in the US Senate. She was also president of the Public Broadcasting Station and partner in the project for which we were meeting. Billington hoped to impress his Russian guest of honor as he had the distinguished list of guests, and he succeeded in both directions. The evening event helped broker the Billington-Rockefeller pitch to get Gusinsky's check for $100,000. The Russian mogul obtained the rights to the PBS series for his television station back in Russia.

Jack Valenti, the president of Motion Pictures Association of America (MPAA), was there too. Previously, Valenti, a close friend of President Lyndon Johnson, had served as a top advisor to the president. In 1966, with Johnson's consent, he resigned his White House position and became the president of the MPAA. A Clinton administration official, who worked closely with Valenti, observed that Valenti's "personal passion and extreme comfort around politicians gave him credibility that others lacked. With the build of a miniature bulldog and his fondness for a wildly ornate, orotund oratory, he was a throwback character and may have raised winces on the faces of the new breed, laidback moguls. 'Mr. Valenti, he continued 'was a consummate salesman, who, like all great salesmen…worked himself up into believing the truth of his message. He was a great actor working on the stage of Washington, DC (sometimes globally) on behalf of an industry that appreciated his craft, but that never let him forget that the message was theirs, not his.'"

All this was a backdrop to what happened next. As Gusinsky was boarding his private jet, he said to me, "Don, get me connected to the movie industry."

I gave this comment a thought. "You know, I think Jack Valenti is their person in Washington," I answered. The more I learned about Jack Valenti, the more I thought the relationship would be a good fit.

Both men had an agenda. For Gusinsky, it was all about his new television station, NTV, that was struggling to fill a lot of empty space. Russians relished the Hollywood-made movies that were highly restricted during the Soviet era, but now, a more open society gave Gusinsky a rare opportunity not only for his TV station, but to become the designated main distributor of American movies in Russia and other former-Soviet republics. The business opportunity was beyond imagination.

Valenti's big headache, on the other hand, was movie piracy, which was rampant in countries that had no enforcement mechanism or simply ignored concerns about illegal and criminal appropriation of intellectual property. Most of films had been released in formats that were easy to copy, and in countries where they thrived, American law enforcement agencies had little cooperation and no jurisdiction, especially Russia. Hollywood producers were putting enormous pressure on Valenti to get the US government to take action. It was natural for me to get Gusinsky and Valenti together for a meeting, which exceeded Gusinsky's expectation. Another point on the scorecard for our Russian client! Valenti readily agreed to set up a series of meetings in the media industry, mostly in Hollywood, testing Gusinsky's entrepreneurial skills and ambitious plans to become a media mogul in Russia. He readily agreed that the movie piracy issue needed to be halted and pledged outreach to the Kremlin to clamp down on this problem. In exchange, he hoped to walk away with commitments to designate his Most Media to be the distributor of American movies in Russia and beyond. I was in the meetings and observed the interest on both sides, but despite the enthusiasm and pledges, there would be no immediate results.

Gusinsky was also committed to cutting deals on Wall Street. He was seeking huge investments in his media empire, bragging his NTV would be the next NBC. I remember his pitch well—invest $300 million and you will reap handsome returns, which got everyone's attention, but no one was buying into it. He wanted to launch a private satellite, to greatly expand his media outreach. The investors insisted the NTV station be the collateral as insurance, but Gusinsky was not prepared to sign off on such a deal. He thought he was the collateral. His word, his reputation, his wealth, and the size of his potential market was all he planned to put up. He did not want to mitigate Wall Street's risk with his own, a reflex that didn't fly with American financiers. Despite multiple trips and meetings in New York's financial district, my Russian-Jewish dealmaker client came up short.

Gusinsky had another idea which drew us to New York. The idea started in Washington when I arranged for him to meet with the *Washington Post* management and editors. They were fascinated with Gusinsky's media cartel, which was unprecedented in Russia. Gusinsky had in his bouquet of media outlets a major TV station and a major newspaper, but he didn't have a weekly magazine like *Newsweek*, which the *Washington Post* owned. At that time, the reputation of the weekly news magazine was powerful, both for the owners and for those who got their photos on the cover. Being the cover story on *Time* magazine, *Newsweek*, or *US News and World Report* was as good as it got in media prestige. Gusinsky wanted to own one of those, so I proceeded to set up a meeting with the *Newsweek* president, Howard Smith, in New York.

Gusinsky and I arrived at the *Newsweek* building in Manhattan. As the elevator was climbing up to the thirtieth floor, I observed Gusinsky closely. His head was pitched downward and he was either in prayer or in deep consultation with himself, contemplating the possible deal with this American icon in the publishing field. This was the elevator to the New York big leagues. Doing a Russian version of *Newsweek* would be another cornerstone in building his media empire. This was neither Hollywood nor Wall Street, which was about ramping up dollars—an activity he was already good at—but world-class journalism, a respected news publication which he saw as a safeguard to reputation. People still viewed Russian media as being state-owned or state-controlled, and so Gusinsky knew that he had to be more cautious in assuring his commitment to independent media in the meeting that was about to take place.

Once in *Newsweek's* executive suites, we were quickly escorted to the president's office. Following the typical greeting and exchange of polite formalities, we were led to a conference room and joined by the publication's international director. The conversation was highly animated with lots of questions for Mr. Gusinsky about the tumultuous political scene in Russia. The old Soviet Union was being replaced by what? *Newsweek* wanted to know from an informed source. Gusinsky happily responded, offering assurances that the country was going through transitions but moving in the right direction, with an independent press leading the way. I was pleased; the conversation was also moving in the right direction, and the two top executives agreed to move forward and launch a startup version of *Newsweek* in Russia, and in Russian. Much remained to be done, but there was a clear agreement of principles.

What was particularly noteworthy was what happened after the meeting. The three of us moved to a comfortable lounge to have a drink and a less formal chat. The conversation was highly animated with lots of questions while Gusinsky exchanged with the *Newsweek* president. They sat down for a drink and a chat. In an affable if not mentoring tone, Smith challenged Gusinsky to be a pioneer in creating a truly private, independent, and free press at this rare moment in Russian history. However the *Newsweek's* president came out, they managed to reach Gusinsky. The speech resonated with the ambitious Russian, and as we walked out of the building into the brisk wind tunnel that New York streets produce, I could tell the *Newsweek* meeting had changed his way of thinking.

Gusinsky took this media mantel back to Moscow and began building with fury, a choice that added to his global reputation but one for which he would eventually pay a heavy price. Newsweek International and Gusinsky's company agreed to form a partnership and jointly publish the new Russian weekly, *Itogi*, in Moscow to begin in early 1996. This publication became one of the rare examples of Russian investigative journalism in the 1990s, and stood out for its critical reporting of the Chechen War and disclosures of official corruption that led right to the Kremlin. It is often overlooked that *Washington Post*-owned *Newsweek* played its part in helping to establish *Itogi* magazine in Moscow. President Putin would soon after have Gusinsky thrown in jail and his media assets seized. Although he would be released after only a few weeks in prison, the warning was clear—once again, the Kremlin had reclaimed the levers of power, including control of the media.

On his many stopovers in New York, Vladimir Gusinsky faithfully met with Rabbi Arthur Schneider, whose prominence and influence stretched around the globe at the highest levels. As the senior rabbi at Park East Synagogue in New York City and founder of the Appeal of Conscience Foundation, Rabbi Schneider was the ideal matchup for Gusinsky who was seeking recognition in the United States as the founder, and funder, of the Russian Jewish Congress, an organization that could be seen as a ray of hope in a country with a long history of both vibrant Jewry and daunting anti-Semitism. Again, here was a relationship that proved mutually beneficial. Gusinsky relished being on the world stage along-side the internationally renowned New York rabbi, which helped him to secure the prominent title of vice president of the World Jewish Congress. It was Gusinsky's outreach which set him apart from the other oligarchs who had little or no standing outside of Russia. The US networking that we set up for him had Gusinsky swirling around Hollywood, enjoying a privileged dalliance with financiers on Wall Street, and then strutting through the halls of the Congress. That was Gusinsky's distinction. I set up one meeting with six US senators, Jewish senators who were keenly interested in how the new Russia would handle Russian Jews.

Vladimir Gusinsky relished the attention, and back in Russia, his dominance grew in the media arena. His Media-Most company had become the largest in terms of viewers and readers in Russia, and possibly one of the largest in Europe. Local media hailed him as the "Rupert Murdoch" of Russia, which may, in the minds of readers today, seem paltry, but at the time was a reference of colossal proportion. He managed to get himself entangled as well in the volatile political arena during the 1990s—which was in a dramatic free fall from a highly centralized and controlled system to an open and treacherous one that invited great quick gain but also put Gusinsky and others at high risk. Boris Yeltsin's presidency, which began on July 10, 1991, marked an era of escalating corruption, economic deterioration, as well as the start of the contentious Chechen War.

Risk to Gusinsky went well beyond Most Media's critical reporting on Kremlin corruption and the Chechen War. At the core of the magnate's problems was a bizarre political episode, a fierce rivalry between Yeltsin's inner circle headed by the commander of the presidential guard, General Alexander Korzhakov, and Gusinsky's base of support inside Moscow's City Hall. Within the Kremlin, Korzhakov, who had been a close friend and advisor to Boris Yeltsin, was a powerful force who despised Gusinsky, accusing him of corruption and being a political threat to Yeltsin's bid for reelection.

Gusinsky's close relationship with Yury Luzhkov, the mayor of Moscow, served both men. Gusinsky's Most Bank prospered on the city's huge deposits and significant advantage in a booming, city-dominated real estate market. Luzhkov needed Gusinsky's political and financial support in a possible run for president. The situation was escalating. And the power brokers were all dealing.

On December 2, 1991, Gusinsky's security people were driving back from their boss' *dacha* in the secluded Uspenskoye region outside the city and heading to company headquarters at the city hall when they were confronted by what David Remnick had described in *The New Yorker* as paramilitaries. "At around 5:00 p.m., the mysterious troops turned aggressive. Armed with Kalashnikov assault rifles, they ordered several of Gusinsky's drivers and guards to lie face down in the snow-covered parking lot and made them stay there for nearly two hours. The soldiers roughed up the leader of the Most security team and Gusinsky's driver badly enough to send them to the hospital with broken ribs and other injuries."

General Korzhakov, head of the so-called "party of war," continued to be a force to be reckoned with. Having urged Yeltsin to abandon democratic niceties and use an "iron hand," he continued his aggressive campaign against Gusinsky. Shortly after the raid, he issued a statement, claiming that his men had gone to Most to investigate the possibility that the bank had helped engineer a temporary collapse of the Russian ruble in October—an event the world has come to know as Black Tuesday. Gusinsky's own media assets—NTV, *Segodnya*, and Ekho Moskvy— offered critical reports of the raid, declaring that such actions "could bring on a police state." As this played out, the rising signs of a mounting police state had turned into what Russians popularly call *bespredel*, meaning anarchy, lawlessness, limitless greed. The temptations were enormous and unchecked, and independent media was in the middle of the wild volleys of live ammo.

On my several trips to Moscow, my association with Gusinsky had me at various scenes that were mindful of Chicago in the 1920s. On my visits to his Most headquarters located at the city hall, what I observed entering the building, Remnick also captured in his reporting. "There is something unnatural and unnerving, walking through the lobby—dozens of guards in fatigues, rifles slung over their arms, slumped on couches, watching cartoons on television."

I recall being at a dinner cohosted by Gusinsky, which involved a half dozen of Russia's wealthiest oligarchs. Entering the hotel lobby, what I confronted was nothing short of terrifying. Each businessman had his own security protection, which collectively added up to around twenty paramilitary types, armed with assault weapons positioned in combat-ready standing guard position. One would have assumed we were in a war zone. Trying to absorb the absurdity of what I was witnessing, I recall asking myself the core question: "Did all this armed security make me more or less safe?" In any case, wherever I traveled with Gusinsky, this military style overkill typified the scene.

The Yeltsin-Gusinsky rivalry began to change shape as it became increasingly clear that Moscow Mayor Yury Luzhkov would not challenge Yeltsin in the upcoming election for the Russian presidency, and that Gusinsky, an ever pragmatic operative, would shift his loyalty toward the incumbent. Yeltsin was eager to accept the media mogul's support publically as he was struggling with the memory of his 1996 campaign given that his poll numbers were plummeting despite having a week opponent, the uncharismatic Gennady Zyuganov, the head of the revived Communist Party.

At the World Economic Forum in Davos, Switzerland in January 1996, Vladimir Gusinsky mobilized Russia's elite businessmen who were out in force at the annual powerbrokers' event. His objective was to muster support for Yeltsin's presidential campaign, and to block former Communists from returning to power. Yeltsin, who was ever grateful to Gusinsky, won the June 1996 election by a healthy 13.7% margin, and understood in no uncertain terms that he was indebted to the media giant. This was the precise the dynamic that Gusinsky loved, and the stage was set for new rounds of typical Gusinsky dealmaking. His top assistant, Sergey Zverev, ascended to the position of one of the president's chief of staff, and over the next two or three years, Media-Most secured two large state loans for approximately $300 million each from the Russia Central Bank and the state-owned Gazprom.

The honeymoon was soon over as only six months later, Yeltsin was pushed out of office in December 1996 and everything changed. In a succession arranged by Yeltsin's own daughter and another oligarch named Boris Berezovsky—known as a member of the "Family"—former high-ranking KGB agent Vladimir Putin took over.

While Yeltsin had been gregarious, careless, and often hopelessly inebriated, Putin was a highly disciplined control freak determined to return the country to order using authoritarian rule. During the Yeltsin reign, most of the state enterprises were allowed to be put up for private sector grabs, and Putin's initial mission was to renationalize private companies and bring these assets back into state control. Oil company Yukos, for one, was in his sights, and guaranteed state control over the national media would be next.

Vladimir Putin wasted no time. He ordered Russia's six top mega-oligarchs to the Kremlin for an urgent meeting where he put them on notice: "I am in charge, you play by my rules. Do you understand?" The Putin diatribe had a stinging effect and no one dared to object, except Mikhail Khodorkovsky, who headed Yukos and who dared confront the new president about known corruption within his ranks.

Khodorkovsky actually had the audacity to have prepared a power point presentation that highlighted how Putin's inner circle was ripping off the Russian state. He is quoted as having said, "It must end."

A haughty Gusinsky, emboldened by his young media power, approached the new Russian president a bit later in a defiant tone, and read his own riot act. "Vladimir, I can either make or break you; it's your call."

Putin's reaction was predictable. He did not tolerate such insults, nor was he pleased with Media-Most's harsh coverage of him. In early June 2000, the prosecutor general raided Gusinsky's office and had him arrested. The lesson for Gusinsky, the other oligarchs, and everyone else was clear, "You don't mess with Vladimir Putin."

Shortly after Gusinsky's arrest, the Kremlin officials came to see him with an offer. The fraudulent charges could have him in prison for some time, which would be worrisome for anyone. The proposal? Gusinsky owed the Central Bank of Russia and Gazprom hundreds of millions, so his choice was either to pay off the debt immediately, which he could not do, or sign over Media Most's assets in return for his freedom.

After three days and a lot of public pressure, scandal, and speculation,

Gusinsky was released from prison on June 16 and placed under a milder house arrest. Several weeks later in early July, he signed the agreement that was prepared for him, and the case was closed.

Gusinsky immediately left the country and would never return. Gazprom, Russia's largest energy company, took full ownership of Gusinsky's NTV station, news and magazine publications, and the Echo of Moscow radio station. The state-owned company would ensure that future media coverage of Vladimir Putin and his policies would be noticeably more favorable. Gazprom conceded that Media-Most's assets were fairly valued in excess of $1.1 billion. In a matter of just a few days, Gusinsky had lost it all. Putin's no-nonsense practices were no joke; you didn't mess with the former KGB agent.

Gusinsky's sizeable public following in the United States and throughout Europe was shocked by what was unfolding in Moscow. This independent startup media company, which had been employing professional journalists and dared to criticize Putin and the Kremlin, was being confiscated by a government which agenda did not include a robust free press. Throwing its entrepreneurial founder in jail captured front-page headlines in major newspapers in the United States and around the world.

On August 3, 2000, the *New York Times* ran on its front page, "Russia Trying to Get Assets of Top Critic—A Battle for Control of Gusinsky Empire." *The Washington Post* printed on the same day, "Russian Faces Battle to Save TV Station, Kremlin Could Gain Control of Last Independent Channel." *US News & World Report* followed with, "Is the new Kremlin up to old Tricks? Tycoon's arrest stirs fears for press freedoms." Five months later, the *Wall Street Journal* plastered, "Russia Media Mogul Battles to Hold on to a Besieged Empire Under Villa Arrest in Spain." The subhead read: "He Looks to Ted Turner for an Investment Deal."

Upon Gusinsky's loss of his Media-Most media empire and his forced departure from his homeland, he faced multiple challenges. Even in exile, Putin didn't let up since Gusinsky continued to garner international media attention. The Russian leader brought new charges and had Gusinsky put on the Interpol list for extradition back to Russia, which led to subsequent arrests in Greece and Spain and a series of legal actions which Gusinsky used to remain free from the grip of Moscow's vengeance. He ultimately resettled in Israel, where he acquired a prominent media company and entered the local political environment yielding a not so insignificant amount of influence. And Gusinsky continued to maintain his home in Greenwich, Connecticut.

I recall a vivid conversation with Volodya in 2008, at which time we discussed the US presidential election. I asked him pointblank, "What candidate do you favor?"

He smiled, and blurted something that caught me by surprise. "Bill Richardson."

As a close friend of Bill's, an idea instantly came to mind and I didn't hesitate to ask. "Volodya, would you do a fundraiser for him?"

He quickly replied, "Absolutely."

A few months later, he agreed to host a Richardson event at his lovely Greenwich residence. I arrived early, walking out to the patio. I loved the scene, a grand poolside setting, bowtie attendants, delicious servings. But I was worried. No one but Gusinsky and two or three friends were present. "Volodya," I told him, "usually fifty to 100 people turn out for these kinds of things. They listen, drink a few glasses of white wine, and then reach for their checkbooks. Where are the people? I think Richardson will be disappointed."

He responded with his usual gregarious manner. "You said raise $50,000. I did. Here are the checks I will give to him."

We didn't need the guests. I smiled and chuckled. He had saved time, Bill's voice, and a case of good wine.

Upon arrival, Richardson seized the moment. He would be sparred working the crowd and the usual donation pitch. Instead, it was a welcoming moment and he didn't mind being given the chance to simply relax. He removed his suit coat and tie, asked his assistant to bring a cigar from the car, reached for a glass of wine, sat down next to Gusinsky, and asked point blank, "Tell me, what the heck is going on in Russia these days?"

I learned later that Richardson told his assistant as they drove out of Greenwich that he so enjoyed his time there that "he wanted to turn the vehicle around and come back." This was "Vintage Volodya"—always making a good impression with everyone, except Vladimir Putin, a glitch, which cost him dearly. My dealings with Vladimir Gusinsky also included an interesting encounter with founder of the National Prayer Breakfast, Doug Coe, and his Fellowship Foundation. It started back in the early '90s when I accompanied Gusinsky to the Cedars for a private meeting with Doug. I had had no idea how this would play out—Vladimir being a secular Jew and Doug being, of course, a devout follower of Jesus. Despite Gusinsky's flawed English, the connection between these two men seemed to generate its own power. Gusinsky stopped me as we were walking toward his limo. "This is an amazing man," the oligarch said to me. "I want to come back here and see him again."

Gusinsky attended the National Prayer Breakfast the next year and

Doug had him seated at the best table—next to the podium. One day, months later, I get a call from Doug. "Don, is it possible you can contact Vladimir for me?"

"Of course, anything in particular?"

Doug said, "I know he has a private airplane, so is it possible he could take a few of us to visit all twelve of the Soviet Republics?"

It was a big request, I was thinking. This was not just a bitsy favor. But coming from the precious Doug Coe, I said, "Sure."

I made the call, and without hesitation, Gusinsky responded favorably. "I'll do that."

A few months later, I joined the delegation of Doug Coe, his son-in-law, Doug Burleigh, who spoke Russian, and Congressman Joe Pitts (R-PA) and we flew to Moscow as the first step on this whirlwind journey. Upon arrival at Moscow's second airport, there was no sight of Gusinsky and no signs of his airplane. Just a bit stressed, I tried all my numbers for the man but could not get through to him. I began to worry that he forgot what he had promised or simply could not deliver for some unexplained reason. It was an awkward moment to say the least as Doug Coe and his friends, including Congressman Pitts were standing idly by, wondering if the trip was going to happen. Finally, I'm paged. I have a call and given instructions where to proceed to at the airport. I'll never forget the feeling of being blown away as we were directed to board a private Boeing 727. There were more crew members, pilots, and flight attendants than the number of our entire small group. It was Gusinsky's nature to make a favorable impression, which he certainly did with us. But he was also touched by Doug Coe's faith and wanted to be supportive, especially involving former Soviet Republics. No better way than to roll out his Boeing 727 to usher us into thirteen countries in as many days. .

Gusinsky did not join us, he just sent his plane along with a first-class crew of eight or nine stewards and stewardesses trained in the finest elegant service.

For the next two weeks, we visited all twelve former Soviet Republics, one country each day. The journey was extraordinary, but for me at least, a bit weird. Our small group would fly into the capital city of a nation in the confederation of Russian states, often without any preparation or any scheduled meetings. If needed, the US Embassy would come to our rescue and help facilitate our presence. In several countries, we met with the respective heads of state, who were often the former communist leaders. What stood out was our visit to Azerbaijan in the South Caucasus along the Caspian Sea. At the time, Azerbaijan was at war with neighboring Armenia, which was supported by the United States, so having Congressman Pitt in our group assured us easy access into President Heydar Aliyev's residence, which was much closer to a royal palace than a house. We were invited to dinner, a memorable meal that lasted for six hours. Led into a formal and elaborate dining room, our delegation was seated on one side of the fully set table adorned with large white dinner plates and heavy silverware and crystal glasses and gaudy salt and pepper shakers. The Azerbaijan leader sat opposite us with his son to his left and an aide to his right. The son, I'd guess, was in his early thirties and sat there with his playboy Joe Namath hairstyle, looked around in great boredom as his father greeted us with a booming sermon on the American wrongheadedness on the issue of former Communist Albania. I have never boasted about my astuteness on Albanian politics, but I did note that this was not exactly a style of diplomacy or etiquette that I approved of. You don't bash your guests on the politics of their country before you serve them the appetizers. I watched the son as he grew progressively bored with the dinner and the conversation topic. It was obvious his father had obliged him to attend, and he was being groomed for an eventual transfer of power. The son downed several glasses of red wine far too quickly for anyone with manners, finished his slab of steak like a caged lion, and pushed away from the table, waving as he left the party with clearly something better to do. We politely nodded, thinking how odd it was for this boy to just leave like that.

After the dessert, President Aliyev rose and we all took his cue and rose too. It was time for his tour of his palatial house. We turned down a wide stone stairway and entered a dark medieval-feeling cellar. The light rose from behind iron sconces and lit a massive stone reception hall, and as we walked deeper into the castle, we passed a room to our right. I peeked in and there he was, the same son, conducting official business with a pool cue in his grip, playing snooker at a large and obviously world-class pool table with cherry red wooden sides. A noted playboy, this young upstart would go on to assume the reins of power of his country in 2003, and occupies still today what they call the Presidential Apparatus on Istiglaliyyat Street in Baku, where we shared that memorable dinner and verbal whipping on our faulty position on Albania.

Doug wanted to talk about faith, about the life of Jesus, while the president was looking to get us to speak about Washington's stance and why Armenia should be sanctioned. More than once, we heard the reproach or resentment that we were there proselytizing on their soil.

As for Vladimir Gusinsky, his commitment to Doug Coe and the

National Prayer Breakfast continued for the next twenty-five years. His only ask was for VIP seating each year at the Thursday morning breakfast. It is noteworthy how he used the opportunity to organize delegations of parliamentarians and business leaders to accompany him to the event. He brought strategic leaders from Israel some years, and also from the Ukraine and Spain and others. Following the philosophy of Doug's "the way," he wanted the delegations to be representatives of opposition parties, so they could see firsthand how faith and reconciliation could make the difference. He always picked up the tab for the travel, often offering transportation on one of his private planes, and covering the related costs including hosting dinners and other activities. Did this make the difference? Doug was thrilled that many of these Gusinsky-sponsored delegations returned to their countries and set up parliamentary-sponsored prayer breakfasts in their respective capitals. Coe's influence was contagious.

He even convinced the Ukrainian oligarch Hryhoriy Surkis, whose considerable wealth included the popular national soccer club, and who had engaged APCO to represent him to convert a shutdown soccer stadium in Kiev into a center for the needy.

I arranged for Surkis' invitation to the National Prayer Breakfast in 2002. He had grown up in a country that was devoid of religion, marked by suppression and fear. On the personal front, he was relatively young and good-looking, but also noted for his arrogance and toughness. That's how they got to be oligarchs, I suppose. I escorted him that Thursday morning into the grand ballroom with 3,500 people gathering around the tables. As Surkis was taking his seat, I could see he was enthralled. Later, I asked his assistant, Barry Blufer, a former CIA agent, to get back to me on how Surkis felt about the breakfast. He reported that Surkis' excitement related not so much from the speakers, even the president, but the people in the room. He saw in their faces joy. There was hugging everywhere and a sense of the love flowing all around the ballroom. He contrasted this with his own country, the Ukraine, and said he could see why America was such a great nation.

CHAPTER 34

THE SAINT BEHIND BARS

The second oligarch also prominent on the APCO roster was one who would shine like a star in the global arena—Mikhail Borisovich Khodorkovsky (MBK), the wealthiest and most prominent of all the Russian oligarchs at the time, and who had emerged as an increasingly vocal critic of Vladimir Putin. Indeed, among the six powerful oligarchs that dominated the Russian economic landscape, Khodorkovsky stood out for his courage and convictions, which did not settle well with Russia's new president.

I had an early encounter with him in February 2001, having arranged for him to attend the National Prayer Breakfast (NPB) in Washington. Conscious about how delicate relationships are, especially when they concerned the scheduling of sensitive meetings, my colleague, Ariuna Namsrai, a Mongolian citizen who spoke Russian, joined me as we escorted Khodorkovsky to a private gathering of the head table speakers and foreign heads of state in the nearby Cabinet Room. The NPB founder, Doug Coe, helped arrange for Khodorkovsky to meet the US Senate Majority Leader, Bill Frist.

This was a "big deliverable" for APCO, so as Ariuna and I approached the roped-off area, I whispered, "Ariuna, as translator, you're at the center, we have just five minutes—please, it's got to go well." Once we sat down, I handled the introductions, including Ariuna, and I mentioned that "she's from Mongolia."

Senator Bill Frist quickly turned to Ariuna and said, "Really? Mongolia? I can't believe this. My wife is going there next month—tell me something about Mongolia." That led to four minutes with Senator Bill

Frist's attention focused on Ariuna and Mongolia, while our client, the billionaire global star, was seated alone and feeling ignored. I anxiously tried to steer the conversation to him thinking, *This is not going well.* We proceeded to escort Khodorkovsky to a VIP table at the breakfast, within only a few feet where the president of the United States, Ronald Reagan, was seated. After the breakfast, we escorted him to Doug Coe's hideaway office on the tenth floor, where he met with select heads of state and other notables.

The four of us sat around a coffee table, making introductions and chatting about the breakfast speakers. Doug always began by asking a series of mostly personal questions about family, personal priorities, etc., but this time, it was Khodorkovsky who had taken charge of the conversation with a host of his own questions. Usually, Doug was clear and persuasive about his mission and questions of faith, but not this time. I was intently observing this dialogue and was puzzled with Doug's uncharacteristic ramblings, making little sense, as Ariuna, who was Mongolian and a nonbeliever, struggled to interpret the entire scene. I remember thinking that this was not Doug's finest moment, and an embarrassment for me. My big concern was that my client, Khodorkovsky, would be upset that I had arranged such a useless meeting. But instead, as we were heading to the elevator, Khodorkovsky pulled me aside and said something that pleasantly surprised me. "This man is very special; is it possible I can meet with him again?" He was pleased, and I was so relieved. That moment reminded me of something that I have always believed profoundly. Experiences often go beyond words. Sometimes the decisive thing is the "spirit" in the room.

Something nonverbal about Coe had connected with the richest, and maybe bravest, man in the room.

For the next ten years, and all throughout Khodorkovsky's ultimate imprisonment, Doug Coe and Khodorkovsky corresponded regularly. Doug also extended to Khodorkovsky's mother and son invitations to attend the National Prayer Breakfast. This was a few years before he confronted Vladimir Putin on the issue of Russian top-level corruption, which resulted in his arrest and imprisonment.

The backdrop of Khodorkovsky's story is fascinating. Only in his mid-thirties, he had built the world's second largest oil company. But what was truly noteworthy was that he ultimately spent ten years in prison and gained notoriety internationally as a human rights symbol. "Where human rights will no longer be contingent on the whim of the czar, whether he be kind or mean," he stated during his second trial sentencing in Moscow, "where government will be accountable to the people and the courts will be accountable only to God and the law. Call it having a conscience, if you wish."

MBK's intelligence and entrepreneurial skills propelled his early career that included his venturing into state and business deals, including importing personal computers. It was his startup company, though— Bank Menatep, among the first privately owned banks in Russia—that garnered state deposits to finance many of his business initiatives. He abandoned the Communist doctrine in the posting of his "capitalist manifesto" entitled the "Man with the Ruble," and stated, "It is time to stop living according to Lenin…. Our guiding light is Profit, acquired in a strictly legal way. Our Lord is His Majesty, Money, for it is only He who can lead us to wealth as the norm in life." MBK would later abandon his wealth doctrine and embrace social and political reforms as his mission in life.

What happened to bringing Russia's most powerful private sector businessman to his arrest at gunpoint on a snowy Siberian runway on October 25, 2003? There were three contributing factors: Putin's personal push to renationalize Yukos Oil Company, MBK's daring to stand up to Vladimir Putin and openly confronting him on corruption, and MBK's political activities that were perceived as threatening to the Kremlin.

The Yukos Oil Company fiasco started when Khodorkovsky was appointed Deputy Minister of the Fuel and Energy of Russia in 1993. At the same time, his bank, Menatep, acquired Yukos which had debts exceeding $3.5 billion. Menatep paid $309 million for the company. Known as the "loans for shares initiative," the elite private sector oligarchs were flagrantly taking over oil, gas, minerals, and other resources during the Yeltsin presidency. And MBK walked away with the biggest prize of all of the state enterprises.

MBK turned Yukos Oil, a near defunct Soviet company, into a world-class corporate giant nearly overnight. Early on, he retained McKinsey & Company to overhaul and upgrade its management structure, and Price Waterhouse to establish a western accounting system and ensure transparency. Khodorkovsky was also in preliminary negotiations with Exxon and Chevron and was planning to expand his company globally.

By 2003, Khodorkovsky was the richest man in Russia, and potentially on his way to being among the wealthiest in the world. In 2004, Forbes placed him sixteenth on its list of the world's richest people, with a fortune estimated at $16 billion. To keep a perspective, the author, Masha Gessen, wrote that "Khodorkovsky was the most reticent among the oligarchs, choosing not to buy yachts or villas on the Cote d' Azur or to become a fixture of the 'Moscow playboy scene.'" Indeed, his social life consisted mostly of "barbecuing for fellow Yukos managers and staying up nights and reading until two."

The second factor that led to his downfall was his daring to take on the Russian president. In February 2003, Putin summoned Russia's wealthiest businessmen to the Kremlin for a stare down meeting. Khodorkovsky arrived with a power point presentation entitled "Corruption Costs the Russian Economy over $30 billion a Year." He strongly felt that Putin needed to be confronted about the corruption that had gone viral inside the Kremlin. People who knew Putin acknowledged that it was clear from the characteristic smirk on his face that Khodorkovsky's audacity turned him livid with rage. The results were Putin's counter attack including allegations that Yukos Oil may have been involved in bribing tax inspectors. His thuggish smile, insiders agreed, was a clear sign that Putin was making a threat, implying that the Russian state was considering a takeover of Russia's largest oil company.

Another side of Mikhail Khodorkovsky began to emerge in 2002–2003. Captured in the April 2012 edition of *Vanity Fair*, the magazine reported that "Khodorkovsky swore off his absolute faith in wealth just as he had sworn off his absolute faith in communism. When the price of oil began to recover, he formed a foundation and called it Open Russia. He funded Internet cafes in the provinces to get people to talk to one another. He funded training sessions for journalists all over the country. He established a boarding school for disadvantaged children and pulled his own parents out of retirement to run it." The article went on to state that by estimates, the Russian billionaire was supporting between 50% and 80% of all nongovernment organizations in Russia." In 2003, Yukos pledged $100 million over ten years to the Russian State Humanities University, the best liberal arts school in the country.

It was not only his humanitarianism that drove such philanthropy, there was clearly undisguised political aspiration as well. Against the advice of his inner circle, Khodorkovsky went on a barnstorming tour with a message that resembled a campaign stump speech: "Russia must join the modern world—stop running its companies like fiefdoms at best and prisons at worst. Russia must transform its economy into one based on the export of knowledge and expertise rather than just oil and gas. Russia must value its educated workers and pay them well."

MBK was not a great public speaker. He tended to be stiff, and his voice was soft and incongruously high. But he could leverage the force of conviction and the weight of his reputation. While his message was resonating around the country, it had a piercing effect inside the Kremlin. For Putin, Khodorkovsky's voice had to be silenced.

Based on Vladimir Gusinsky's recommendation, MBK reached out to Margery Kraus and APCO in Washington, DC. Like Volodya and other Russian oligarchs, the oil tycoon and political aspirant wanted to position himself and his Yukos Oil Company securely in the US and other western countries. Beginning in 2003, Kraus pulled together a team at APCO to meet his expectations and asked me to be an integral part of APCO's attention to MBK's needs while on his North American visits. His style and ambitions did not match those of Vladimir Gusinsky, but Khodorkovsky came across as credible and reliable. For Volodya, it was about media and political networking compared to MBK's focus on business and the research of think tanks.

I arranged for Khodorkovsky to attend the National Prayer Breakfast in February 2001, a few years before he confronted Vladimir Putin (about corruption) that resulted in his arrest and imprisonment, and his company and other assets being seized by the Russian government.

MBK and Congressman Tom Lantos, with the help of Margery Kraus, formed a friendship that would prove mutually beneficial. As chairman of the House Foreign Affairs Committee and a champion of human rights, Lantos was an outspoken critic of Vladimir Putin. He had information that the Kremlin was preparing to renationalize the Yukos Oil Company, mostly to stunt MBK's political activities.

In the summer of that year, Congressman Lantos invited the Krauses and Bonkers to join him in Budapest, Hungary to celebrate his seventy-fifth birthday. The occasion was particularly special for two distinct reasons. Born in Budapest, Lantos endured the Nazi Holocaust as a young man before departing to the United States, and this return thus had a strong emotional meaning. His two daughters, Katrina Swett and Annette Tillemann-Dick, and his twelve grandchildren would be in tow, and so the trip to the old country was his way of completing a circle with the next generations as witnesses.

It was a trip to treasure. The celebration took place outside Budapest— in a rural area that revealed the natural beauty of the eastern European landscape. The evening was clear and the air was lovely. We were all blessed with a full moon. The venue included an outdoor stage, which was perfectly suited for the Lantos family to perform their rendition of the legendary musical, *The Sound of Music*. What a magnificent performance it was involving all of the Lantos grandchildren, who had rehearsed this as a special gift to their grandfather.

Mikhail Khodorkovsky, on a convenient stopover on his return trip to Russia, arrived on a private jet. He absolutely wanted to join in celebrating Lantos' birthday. There was something larger than life that evening as the legendary MBK huddled with us in a small circle to chat privately about the US-Russian bilateral relationship. The birthday boy, Tom Lantos, US congressman, chose that moment to bring up the situation in Russia. "Mikhail," he said, as we all listened closely. "I am worried about your safety. Your partner, Platon Lebedev, was just arrested, I believe, on tax returns filed by your company. If they arrest him, are you next?"

There was a long pause. An uncomfortable chuckle. The question haunted each of us. We all knew the peril ahead if MBK returned to Russia. We were genuinely worried. He responded, "Congressman, your concern is shared by many. My other partner, Leonid Nevzlin, reminded me that they in the Kremlin are thugs, that we should leave the country, take our money out and start a new business and a new life." He continued, "Leaving the country I love would be immoral, especially if my other partner is already in jail."

We heard him clearly. He was principled. He'd not flee.

Despite Tom Lantos' plea that he reconsider and do more to save himself, Khodorkovsky simply hugged him, wished him a happy birthday, and boarded his private aircraft, knowing in no uncertain terms the risks that returning to Russia entailed.

Leonid Nevzlin once described his friend and partner as possessing an iron will. "He has strong emotions, but when it comes to making decisions, he can just turn them off. His thinking runs perpendicular to his feelings."

On October 25, 2003, Khodorkovsky made a stopover visit in the city of Saratov on the Volga River, where he was apprehended by officials and arrested at gunpoint on a snowy Siberian runway. Under custody, he was promptly escorted to Moscow, where he was charged with fraud and tax evasion. The Russian authorities gave him a stark choice—sign over all his Yukos assets and promptly leave the country, or remain in detention and face possible imprisonment. Unlike Gusinsky, Khodorkovsky refused the offer, unwilling to acknowledge that any crimes had been committed.

The trial lasted for ten months. The prosecutor's case was described as flimsy, but the state had undeniable clout in the court proceedings and the power of intimidation. It limited Khodorkovsky's defense witnesses since the risk for anyone who dared to testify in behalf of the defendant was intense. In Russia, when Putin is involved, the rule of law cannot be counted on, nor can the judiciary count on secure independence. In no uncertain terms, the case was stacked against MBK at the outset, which he knew and nonetheless accepted. "Give me liberty or give me death" could have been MBK's motto. President Putin ordered a large black metal birdcage to be prominently placed inside the courtroom in which the defendant was prominently put on display. This agitprop of solitary confinement throughout the trial and within the context of a Russian court of law captured the perversity of Putin's clever hoax and served as a message to the other oligarchs and opponents. "Cross me and you will see the fate that awaits you." Paradoxically, Putin's antics had the opposite effect on the global scene. Viewing Khodorkovsky behind bars in that cage, he looked more like a saint than a criminal. His righteousness was amplified. It was even weird, this precious soul locked up inside that oversized birdcage. Photos of the scene went viral worldwide, prompting sympathy and support for Khodorkovsky at this perilous moment in his life. Beyond MBK and Yukos Oil, Russia was on trial.

The verdict was, of course, inevitable. Khodorkovsky was sentenced to nine years in prison, shipped off to a remote colony (a nine-hour flight and fifteen-hour train ride from Moscow), working in a mitten factory, often housed in an unheated solitary cell. One night, another inmate— who later admitted that he had been forced to do this—attacked him, slicing his face with a knife. Such was the fate of one of the new Russia's most visionary business leaders.

Those who wondered what happened to his Yukos Oil, Russia's largest company, were not surprised. Putin's top assistant, Igor Sechin, was charged with a manipulated government takeover of the company assets, taking steps that ensured Yukos was placed in his own hands. Sechin became the new president of the state-owned Rosneft, a makeover of Khodorkovsky's now stripped Yukos Oil.

Throughout Khodorkovsky's prison term and beyond, APCO Worldwide worked with his London-based attorney on a strategy and outreach to keep the business leader and freedom fighter in the public eye as a symbol of human rights and the face of opposition to the injustice that reigned in Putin's Russia. Led by APCO's founder and chairman, Margery Kraus, both the US and European offices lined up their commitment to three main strategic axes: media awareness, support from political and government leaders, and engagement from human rights organizations. Media awareness included stroking continuous press coverage and commentary that went beyond MBK's horrifying imprisonment, but how Putin's actions raised questions about doing business in Russia. As world leaders were assessing the country's direction under Putin's rule, MBK became a symbol of Russia going in the wrong direction. The strongest messages were the result of verbal support from political heads of state, presidents, prime ministers, and parliamentary resolutions, which expressed concern for MBK's well-being and demanded that he be released. Lastly, with support for a Russian oligarch and nouveau billionaire charged with tax evasion hard to garner at first, APCO found that human rights organizations were extremely useful in building MBK's credibility. Working closely with Amnesty International, Human Rights Watch, and other organizations, APCO familiarized them with the politically motivated sabotage of MBK and how Russian injustice was mounting as a major human rights problem domestically and across the former Soviet republics.

During his nine-year imprisonment, no Russian received more worldwide attention than Mikhail Khodorkovsky. Other than Vladimir Putin, of course. The difference is that media coverage of MBK was favorable while Putin's reputation was caving in. My own personal archives from this work includes nearly a hundred articles, many of which we were involved with fostering that featured MBK. Most of these included front-page headline stories, which went on to recount or update the imprisoned business leader's situation. As incredible as it was, Khodorkovsky sitting in an obscure gulag, so remote and unreachable from any center of attention, was repeatedly treated as heroic in the *New York Times*, the *Wall Street Journal*, and many other major news publications.

Khodorkovsky was an inspiration for authors and artists. A dozen artists attended his trial and put together an exhibition of courtroom drawings. Three of Russia's best-selling writers published their correspondences with Khodorkovsky. Composers dedicated symphonies to him. A group of Soviet-born classical musicians traveled to the European Union capital of Strasbourg in France to mount a concert in honor of Khodorkovsky. Several documentaries were made and widely distributed, including a production by Vlast (Power), which played on Capitol Hill in the attendance of a number of senators and House Members. Cyril Tuschi made a documentary film called *Khodorkovsky*, which enthralled and appalled viewers. The *Financial Times* film critic Nigel Andrews wrote that "Tuschi collates the evidence masterfully—TV footage, documents, interviews—to substantiate what much of the world is already convinced of. Khodorkovsky crossed swords (or worse, words) with Vladimir Putin and took the toll. He rebuked him on public television; he campaigned for the political opposition. Before that, Khodorkovsky himself had turned from Russia's leading oil tycoon to a brave, even reckless do-gooder. Next, he found himself living 4,000-odd miles from Moscow in a snow-girt fortress prowled around, in one sequence, by Tusch's cameras. It is an old documentarist's trick: when you cannot get in, gawp helplessly."

While in confinement, MBK published six books and numerous articles. He managed to conduct interviews and issue statements that were widely distributed. His article, "Notes From a Russian Penal Colony," featured in the *Wall Street Journal*, opens with "I am writing these notes because I want to convey to caring people what I have experienced in prison."

Khodorkovsky's arrest and imprisonment became a sticking point in Putin's dealings with other world leaders. It went beyond injustice; it conveyed a disturbing message to Western corporations and investors: conducting business in Russia came with high risk. Khodorkovsky's story was a prime example. That was our strategy at APCO, keep the Khodorkovsky issue on the agenda whenever Putin met with foreign leaders. Our offices in Washington, DC and throughout Europe worked closely with government officials and parliamentarians, urging various actions that called for the release or pardon Mikhail Khodorkovsky.

That was my role in the Washington, DC office. Throughout MBK's time at the prison camp in the Chita region of Siberia, I prepared a number of congressional resolutions with respect to the trial and sentencing of Mikhail Khodorkovsky and the seizing of assets and state-directed takeover of the Yukos Oil Company. The sponsors in both the Senate and House of Representatives were the respective chairmen and ranking members of the Senate Foreign Relations Committee and House Foreign Affairs Committee. The resolution that stood out for me was introduced in the 109th Congress and was sponsored by Senators Lugar, Biden, McCain, and Obama, and was eventually approved by the Senate Foreign Relations Committee and adopted by the US Senate.

APCO's commitment to MBK was witnessed on many fronts. We had many of his well-crafted statements included in the *Congressional Record*, which helped ensure that he was prominently mentioned at congressional hearings. We maintained regular contact with the Department of State and the US Embassy in Moscow. We engaged human rights and media organizations, monitored and reported on all related matters. Our mission was singular and clear—Khodorkovsky was a symbol of what was just and right compared to what was coming from the Kremlin. Our client should be released.

A trickle of legal procedures complicated MBK's final years in prison, and which threatened an extended time in prison or the parole or pardon we anticipated. Vladimir Putin had the final say, and the situation was not hopeful. At one point, President Barack Obama, German Chancellor Angela Merkel, and British Foreign Secretary William Hague condemned and expressed concern over the extension of MBK's sentence.

On December 19, 2013, Russian President Vladimir Putin stated publicly in a surprise announcement that he intended to pardon Khodorkovsky in the near future. He did so on the following day, stating that Khodorkovsky's mother was ill and for that reason, he recommended clemency. Putin also expressed that ten years in jail was still "a significant punishment." The 2014 Winter Olympics in Sochi, no doubt, was a possible factor in his granting of the pardon, and an indication that the leader thought a display of the "gracious" side of his thuggish persona would be beneficial.

The story did not end, though, with Khodorkovsky's leaving the gulag and his homeland.

Putin's state takeover of Yukos Oil Company had prompted a number of legal actions, based on the claim of improper expropriation of private assets, the violations of human rights and due process, a lack of adherence to international treaties, inappropriate government interference in private markets, and the political pressure on Russia's judiciary. Prominent were several cases before the European Convention on Human Rights (ECHR), citing violations of human rights and due process involving the Khodorkovsky-Lebedev trials and sentencing.

The most significant case was filed by Khodorkovsky's London-based company GML, Ltd., which represented majority of investors and shareholders who brought the affair up before an ad hoc arbitral tribunal, which ended up recommending $100 billion in damages in December 2009. After five years of intense litigation, the tribunal in The Hague ruled that the Russian government deliberately bankrupted Yukos Oil in order to seize its assets for itself and thus ordered Russia to repay Yukos shareholders a sum of roughly $50 billion. Not surprisingly, Russia refused to honor the court ruling, which served to splinter legal reactions into multiple legal cases based on the New York Convention, which allowed plaintiffs to seize state assets to make compensation. APCO's Washington and European offices, on behalf of GML during the five years of litigation, continued to inform government officials about the status of these cases, recognizing that seizing assets would become a hot political issue in most of the countries involved.

I like to imagine Khodorkovsky and Gusinsky seated together in their respective prison cells, contemplating, "Why am I here? What did I do wrong? What is my fate?" Both had taken on the Russian president, but had no clue of the severity that their opposition would provoke the man to impose. Should they have acted differently? I recall that Vladimir Putin had summoned a meeting with Russia's top six oligarchs and put them on notice that he was in charge, warning, "Play by my rules, or else." Four of them reluctantly agreed and ended up wealthy and thriving. Gusinsky and Khodorkovsky, my clients, were the exceptions. Whatever motivated them—conscience, pride, foolishness—they dared to put everything at risk by taking on one man's iron-fisted insistence on control of a system.

As chairman of the House Subcommittee on Human Rights, I had earlier defined democracy as having three pillars: a viable political opposition, a free and independent press, and rule of law and independent judiciary. During his presidency, Boris Yeltsin was making progress toward a true democracy. However, Putin swiftly reversed it and both Gusinsky and Khodorkovsky, wisely or not, put conscience above self-interest.

Vladimir Gusinsky had championed an independent and free press. When his newspaper *Segodnya*, first appeared in February 1992, it was a respected liberal organ that soon attracted many of Moscow's most talented journalists. The following year, Gusinsky, together with several leading TV journalists and media experts, notably Igor Malashenko and Yevgeny Kiselyov, founded the first private television channel in Russia—NTV. This privately owned TV station was independent and featured uncensored news and unbiased political shows, their slogan was "News Is Our Profession." It was NTV's puppet show *Kukly*, which depicted the Russian president in a satirical way, that ultimately upset Putin. His personality would not tolerate being depicted as ridiculous. He was a hard-liner and threatened to shut it down. Gusinsky did not back off and realized what to expect when he said, "The Putin puppet will be back. And if *Kukly* disappears, you will know what's happening in this country." Shortly thereafter, *Kukly* disappeared, Gusinsky went to prison, and his Media-Most empire was repossessed and ownership and operations were taken over by a state company.

For Mikhail Khodorkovsky, the other two pillars were central. He was fully committed to promoting a true democracy in the post-Soviet Russia, funding a number of initiatives in support of political parties and their related activities. It was not just political, but also his philanthropic initiatives that included MBK contributing computers to schools in remote areas, founding Internet training centers for teachers, launching a forum for the discussion by journalists of reform and democracy, and many other activities. This is what alarmed President Putin—MBK's political, social, and cultural outreach that was benefiting citizens far more than what the government was doing, and thus positioned the private sector leader as a potential contender for his job.

Of the three democratic pillars, the most important in my thinking has always been the rule of law, an independent judicial system. That has not taken root in the Russia of today. The system there is commonly referred to as "telephone justice," whereby direct orders from the Kremlin replace the rule of law. It was clear that Mr. Khodorkovsky's imprisonment was politically motivated from the start. Seeing Khodorkovsky as a direct threat, calling him out on national television "a thief should sit in jail." Freedom House Director Jennifer Windsor stated on May 31, 2005 that the "lack of judicial independence poses a distinct threat, not only to the Russia's business community, but to the country's overall political and social development."

Khodorkovsky's major contribution was the worldwide attention on his arrest, trial, and imprisonment as he became a symbol of fundamental rights in all societies. The narrative about these two Russian individuals, who stood for something beyond self-interest for the common good, touched a more universal meaning and highlighted a deeper message especially poignant to those in public life. Is there a higher calling, a greater purpose above self-interest? Is moral authority a factor in making decisions? As Khodorkovsky asked in his memoir from prison, how do we "deal with one's conscience?"

X. A Higher Calling

Since my first election to Congress in November 1974, I have flown across America's heartland, between the two Washingtons hundreds of times, millions of miles—for over forty-five years. For the first ten years, I transited via Minneapolis on the Northwest flight, tagged in those days—I'm sorry to say—as "Northworst Airlines." After the first decade, the nonstop to Seattle opened up and I flew the friendly skies of United Airlines. Aboard those endless hours in the air, I was often seated alongside lovely strangers with whom I quickly learned to avoid conversing if I wanted to get any work done. Sitting next to a congressman triggered all sorts of sharing and opposing views, questions about my positions and votes, and embarrassing comments that you never know how to respond to. The best thing is to say hello, smile, put on your reading glasses and keep your head on the page, sip your drinks, and look busy. No one wants to interrupt a member of Congress drafting a bill.

Some of those flying neighbors were on lobbying missions to Capitol Hill, and the prospect of having a captured congressman all to yourself as we crossed the nation at 30,000 feet was a fantasy come true. So, I had to learn by nature how to be less friendly than I naturally was.

For most West Coast members of Congress, the lengthy cross-country flights were built-in work sessions. Staffers on both ends saddled you with briefing papers, special reports, speech preparations that had you so indulged in work that no one dared to distract you. Regardless of where you were stepping off the plane, DC or the congressional district, you hit the ground running, with full schedules, and surrounded by staffers and others who'd rush you from one meeting to another. There was no time to think. Just ask the essentials: "Who am I seeing?" "What's her husband's name?" "Do we know what they want?" "Oh yes, I remember now, they have a son in the Air Force." The office of an elected official relentlessly asks you to campaign, to raise millions of dollars, to cope with the political attacks and media scrutiny, to abandon your family for much of the time. They are doing their job. There is more stress than comfort. But you are doing your job too.

In flight, I always preferred sitting next to the window, which allowed me the joy of viewing America's vast heartland, of remembering the vast scope of the real estate. I'd stare as we glided over the Appalachians, across the massive plains, and the majestic Rockies as we approached the scenic Northwest. There was always a private moment of inner thrill as the plane descended over the district that I represented in Congress. A congressman flying over his district makes for a great feeling. And then I'd also have moments of existential questioning. As a congressman, was I being me or was I trying to be someone I wasn't? Yes, I was striving for accomplishments, but was I always focused on the values within those achievements? Is this how I wanted to be remembered? Or was it another way? Flying brought on those pangs of creative self-doubt. Being detached from the land, halfway to Heaven but still very much connected to land culture, I could think and reflect and wonder and hope. Sometimes I'd even preach. Glancing out the window, viewing the ever-changing terrain, I was often overtaken by the thoughtful question: "What if?" What if I had continued as a dance instructor, with the enjoyment of twists and turns that led to nowhere in particular?" "What if I had succumbed to the odds stacked against my first shot at public office? Would my political career have been over before it started?" What if Carolyn's rejections of my first two proposals had prevailed? How would that have altered my life? Would I have had the courage to forge ahead on the national scene?" "What if I remained in the House of Representatives instead of giving up a sure place in exchange for a Senate position?" I would have ended up a national leader on foreign policy and trade issues. If one of my two Senate races had succeeded in propelling me into the upper chamber, who knows where that would have taken me. "What if?" was a popular game on those United flights.

Moving on to the private sector after the days in Congress, the stimulating years at APCO Worldwide have kept me active internationally at the top of my game even in the gray period of life. Counseling Russia's most prominent oligarchs during the post-Cold War era, representing two of China's largest global companies; jetting through the clouds, you get the perspective to see the whole path, your lifeline as a singular narrative. For fifteen years, I had also served as president of IMDI, where I organized and moderated Transatlantic Roundtables with Europe's top corporate leaders. There was stress, of course, on the home front. Yes, I had given up my seat in the Congress, lost two Senate races, I still think about that. But the outcome Carolyn and I have come to agreement on is one that we have come to cherish. Our dear friend, Chuck Colson, once said to us, "I view life to be a great paradox. God has used not my victories but my defeats for his greatest glory. What he does through us is far greater than what we can do for ourselves." The path of a life is a sacred journey. Flying home in either direction, I am constantly reminded of that. As long as I keep my head down and stay clear of lobbyists!

Almost a half century later, I am still taking the same flights, but today, I am viewing the national landscape down below differently. The "what if" game seems to have lost its kick and has been replaced with the tragic rhetorical yelp, "What the heck happened?" During Donald Trump's extended moment, there has been a harvesting of many books on how our political system has deteriorated, the erosion of the fundamentals of our democracy, and worse, how the beacon light of our model has been a worldwide standard for two centuries. And how the underpinnings of that model have been rattled. The civility I experienced and contributed to had been replaced by political tribalism. Today, the ambiance is more about fear and anger which is wrapped firmly around a form of nationalism and which is far from the core values of our origins. How did this happen?

Yes, maybe a glass of red wine before dinner.

Far more complicated this moment in both domestic and world affairs than in the days in which I first danced around the halls of the US Capitol. Far more complicated and sinister. I'm reminded of the dangers on the steps of the Roman colosseum. Mixed in with the fright of leaders who have lost touch with their former interest in civility, I share now the sensation of spinning dizzy in a helix of technological advancement, digital invasions, and social media mischief driven by greed and lust for power. Without blaming technological advances and the acceleration of scientific invention, the mesmerizing presence of artificial intelligence which is overtaking not only our means of production but our mechanisms for communicating with each other as humans, well, behooves. How to integrate into our humanity the state of overwhelming perpetual connectedness and the painful reality of profound disconnectedness all at once? Disruption, I think, as we bank now over Indiana or Southern Michigan, is so pervasive that the word itself has become banal. Disruption is supposed to disrupt; now we are tame in its guise. New levels of disruption continue to lay just beyond our ability to grasp their implications. Old time alienation seems quaint these days. How will both citizenship and governance act and respond at the hands of new controls?

I started out writing that this would not be a memoir. Hopefully, it would be an appreciation, a historical and personal inventory of not only what I have done with my life, but a review of what might be worth sharing. Legacy, to have meaning beyond the ego, has to mean something to someone else. Worthiness is mostly a matter of what someone else can make us of, can benefit from, can turn into her or his own. That's the only way to measure if what you did really made a difference.

I'll have the fish this evening. In those days, United offered choices for meals, no charge. Today, we get box lunches and need to reach for our credit card.

Today, I continue to fly west but without the demands that once accompanied me as a member of Congress. I am heading to my origins, to my personal self, the other half of me. Still a few solid hours and I look forward to landing, heading to the ferry that delivers me to my treasured place on Bainbridge Island, an outpost of delight that we popularly refer to as Journey's End. Carolyn will dutifully take a break from her daily routine yard work, the pruning and planting tasks that are unending, and will motor over to pick me up at the ferry dock. It has been forty years since our wedding, and she is as elegant and lovely as she was in her wedding dress back in 1971—even in yard attire. That's love.

The country sure has changed. The leadership has changed. The intolerable is being tolerated. The level of shame that would have ended a political career now is emboldening one. And the battle for sane existence has become a confused, agonizing process of keeping the issues straight and the facts accurate. The moral issues need to be kept uncontaminated by the cruelty of influence and greed. There always is hope, I tell myself. And I hope now that there will be healing. I hope that the nation as it had been conceived will recover from the viruses it has contracted. Hope that our collective sense of public service and our deeper spiritual belief in humanity will guide those who have been lost to the trance of unsustainable possession and wrong wealth. Hope for a new wave of integrity.

America no longer is the beacon light that once shined globally, setting an example of democracy at its best. In Washington, DC, most US senators and congressmen cannot avoid being entangled in a highly politicized culture that often draws them into an uneasy dilemma. Either bend to self-interests which have metastasized into greedy reflexes, or recognize the higher calling that not only brings out the best in you but also enables the possibility of achieving what is best for our nation. If we can forego the first flighty sensations of pleasure when serving our material interests, we are almost always assured and served a deeper and more enduring joy of being on the right side of decency and morality. Just show others how to resist the false attraction of greed.

During my fourteen years in Congress, I observed up close various House Speakers who brought their unique personal and political traits to the Speaker's chair. Upon arrival in 1975, the so-called "Little Giant," Carl Albert, led with his placebo-like strength. Indeed, during his tenure, he left a vacuum that gave rise to the so-called committee barons. Tip O'Neil followed, the typical savvy Boston political who restored respect to the position. Then Jim Wright from the 12th District in Texas, who had claims to Southern charm and intellect but could not compare to another Texan, the powerful Sam Rayburn who was Speaker in the 1950s.

It was in January 1995 when the revolutionary Newt Gingrich replaced the traditionalist Tom Foley as Speaker of the House of Representatives that everything changed. Governance was no longer about respect for the institution in the transition of one political party to the other. Newt Gingrich's clear intention was to blow up the bipartisan coalitions that were essential to legislating, and then seize on the resulting dysfunction to wage a populist crusade against the Congress itself. Look around and take stock in where we are. Today's malaise finds roots in Newt's socks.

Two extraordinary leaders representing both the "best" and "worst" in our political system since the origins of time—Congressman Foley and Newt Gingrich. As I look down on the rolling hills below, I recall when I first met Tom Foley. I was in Eastern Washington campaigning for Secretary of State in 1972. I had some knowledge of him but was awed when I saw him up close. Foley, in every respect, was a true gentleman—tall at six feet and four inches, impeccably dressed, gracious, warmhearted. When I was elected to Congress two years later, he quickly became my mentor, helping to guide those early years in the House. His beginning in that first election win in 1964, a shocking upset over an eleven-year-term Republican incumbent, Walt Horan. Foley had been a moderate Democrat going up against a secure Republican incumbent in a mostly rural, conservative district. Graciously praising his opponent, Foley did not opt for the typical prescription for winning elections. His harshest comment about his opponent hadn't exceeded his hinting that "maybe it was time for change." Typically, candidates ran TV ads attacking their opponents, but Foley's campaign strategists must have been dumfounded by their candidate who never hesitated to say nice things about the incumbent he wanted to replace. It got him elected to represent the 5th Congressional District, and it impressed me as the way to treat opponents. Martin Luther King often said of his enemies that we'll love them to death and, of course, Jesus' other cheek would never stop instructing me and many others.

Often, flying over Foley's district, scattered with ranches and seasonal rodeos, I would think of the same funny story that Tom enjoyed sharing with colleagues and friends. The Omak Stampede was a local rodeo that occasionally featured the congressman riding a horse. He had little or no equestrian experience, he'd remind listeners, and thus he mounted cautiously a feisty horse to join the grand processional, but the waving flags and excitement caused the horse to bolt and suddenly reverse course. Congressman Foley found himself galloping in the opposite direction, quickly exiting the rodeo as fans were hooting and howling at the bizarre scene, prompting the nimble announcer to shout out gloriously, "We can all agree, our good congressman is not wasting our tax dollars and his time in DC on riding lessons!" He was mortified, but an aide assured him that the incident was perfect; there was nothing locals hated more than a city slicker showing off on a horse. Perfect political choreography.

Upon being elected Speaker of the House of Representatives on June 6, 1989, Tom Foley immediately appealed to "our friends on the Republican side to come together and put away bitterness and division and hostility," to counter what had become a rising tide of partisanship. For a short time, he succeeded in restoring comity and civility in the House of Representatives, the core of an enduring legacy and a style sorely missed.

Aside from being a leader on a ruckus political battlefield, Tom Foley was respected by both sides for his congeniality and civility, wisdom, and affable demeanor. Indeed, the trust he enjoyed from Republican presidents and congressional leaders was testimony to bringing out the very best in our political system. A subsequent GOP speaker, John Boehner, said, "Forthright and warmhearted, Tom Foley endeared himself not only to the wheat farmers back in his district, but also colleagues on both sides of the aisle. That had a lot to do with his sense of fairness, which remains a model for any speaker." The GOP congressman from Illinois, Henry Hyde, gave Tom Foley the ultimate compliment when he proclaimed, "I wish he were a Republican."

Despite the Republicans favorable view of Tom Foley, there were unintended consequences. As speaker, and thus top Democrat in Congress, he was expected to lead the charge against the other party, raise millions for campaign funds, recruit strong candidates to run in Republican districts, and launch attacks—sometimes calculated cheap shots against the other side that was not Tom Foley's good-hearted nature, and often, he'd simply not do what others wanted him to do as the leader of the majority party in the House of Representatives. In the November 1994 elections, the Democrats suffered a huge loss in House seats, including Tom Foley—the nation's top Democrat was among the casualties. He went on to become US ambassador to Japan.

A national leader known for his fairness, these very traits led to his demise and his party's failure in the 1994 elections, allowing the Republican Newt Gingrich to grab the speaker's gavel, which became his weapon of political destruction and the beginning of a long descent into indecency. In *The Atlantic Monthly* November 2018 edition, McKay Coppins captured what everyone knew about Newt Gingrich, that "few figures in modern history have done more than Gingrich to lay the groundwork for Trump's rise. During his two decades in Congress, he pioneered a style of partisan combat—replete with name-calling, conspiracy theories, and strategic obstructionism—that poisoned America's political culture and plunged Washington into permanent dysfunction...to strip American politics of the civilizing traits it had developed over time."

What a contrast not only to his predecessor, Speaker Tom Foley, but also his Republican colleague, the Minority Leader Robert Michel, widely recognized for his ethical behavior and committed to trust relationships with Democrat leaders to advance, not obstruct, legislation intended to serve the nation's best interest. Indeed, Newt Gingrich's political revolution tarnished the image of the Republican leadership in Congress.

Many scholars have come to credit Gingrich as the lynchpin in undermining democratic norms, ushering in an era of polarization, partisan, and prejudice which had never been seen before. For Republicans in Congress, his prescribed strategy was to take a "combative" approach where hateful language and hyperpartisanship became common, and where democratic norms were abandoned. Unlike his predecessors who reached over the aisle to build consensus on national issues, Gingrich called his Democrat colleagues corrupt, traitors, pathetic, and often compared them to fascists. If this is his legacy, Newt Gingrich must be very proud about how he changed the course of our political history and continues to have the ear of Donald Trump. "Gingrich has found the apotheosis of the primate politics he has been practicing his entire life—mostly vicious and unconcerned with those pesky 'Boy Scouts words' as he fights in the Darwinian struggle that has redefined America's life today," McKay Coppins rightly states. Gingrich himself predicted "Trump's America and the post-America society that the anti-Trump coalition represents are incapable of coexisting…. One will simply defeat the other." There is no room for compromise.

My wine glass is empty and I reach for the salted almonds. The country has changed.

At age eighty-two, I am still enduring these five-hour flights between the two Washingtons. And yes, I continue to book my seating next to the window so I can still relish the incredible landscape across America's heartland that, despite all the changes, has not really changed. There is still a lot of space. A lot of farmland. A lot of unspoiled beauty. What has changed is the other landscape, the political one, and my thinking. I have recently stopped reflecting so much on the past, certain that psychic energy must focus seriously on the future given the havoc that threatens today's political system. It is no longer the days that inspired the "best." The Gingrich-inspired Trump moment strokes the "worst" and the mounting fears about our country's future.

Although I'm not a sentimentalist, I look back at our Founding Fathers and wonder about the likes of Thomas Jefferson, Alexander Hamilton, James Madison, John Adams—if they had a cozy relationship with the "best" of their day as they crafted the US constitution and built the foundation of the greatest political system ever conceived.

My viewing of the immensely popular hip-hop Broadway musical, *Hamilton*, was a shocking reminder that there was also the "worst," as Paul Aron in *Founding Feuds* portrayed the interactions "screaming, spitting, and occasionally shooting each other; their politics every bit as polarized as a modern-day version."

Legendary feuds driven by ideological differences may have outsized personal ambitions, and relentless attacks on opponents, the spreading of scandalous stories, both true and untrue, prying on voters' emotions, and manipulating an electoral system seems to be close to the soul of the American republic. We traverse the wide state of Montana now, I see it on the screen, and the slim chimney of Idaho as we nose our way toward Spokane. I beam down from the oval window. It's all green. I'm worried about the climate, and the trees, and the protracting ice at the top and bottom of the planet. And the main tenant of our constitution, the three branches of government. The populist movements that rebel against government institutions don't seem to understand what it took to get here, and what's coming if we weaken the pillars. That's why Alexander Hamilton pressed hard for those checks and balances, cautioning that "Someday, we may elect a demagogue who could become a tyrant." He actually said that.

Despite their political and philosophical differences, our Founding Fathers "believed in genuine deliberation and compromise...and they had institutional loyalty," the congressional scholar, Thomas Mann, wrote. They fiercely engaged in debate that was divisive, yet they maintained a deep respect for one another. They understood that debate was not division, it was a stronger form of unity. Upon learning of Hamilton's death by Aaron Burr's bullet, Jefferson purchased an elegantly sculpted bust of Hamilton that was placed on a pedestal in the entrance hall of his home, opposite a bust of himself. On display at Jefferson's home in Monticello, these busts of political foes stare at each other. The rivalry may continue in the afterlife. As a gift, Carolyn bought me a pair of socks at the Monticello store. Jefferson on one foot faces Hamilton on the other. Privately, I've walked through the chambers of our legislature embodying on my very feet the deep debate that captured both the vehemence and balance of modern democracy. When I get home, I promise myself, I'll put them on tonight.

In today's public square, those who are elected to represent others, regardless of our political beliefs, must rise to a higher calling to put the national interest above our political and self-interest. We need to remind each school pupil that politics is how we achieve the common good, not the end.

What's important is who we are as individuals. Only individuals can follow a moral beacon that guides our attitudes and actions. Song of myself, as our national poet, Walt Whitman, yelped. Once I moved beyond the dance studio through college and my first election to the US Congress, I realized that I had to be guided by something beyond lofty pursuits and politically driven ambitions. Careers should be guided by values. Without values, an ambitious journey has no purpose or real reward.

Carolyn's face, I can picture now, and that look that led me to embrace a faith I didn't start out with, and the inspired teachings that would guide me and help shape who I would become and the purpose I'd give to my life. I feel the landing gears drop into place. Out to the right of the wide-bodied Boeing, I see the Olympic National Park with fond memories and recall like yesterday that hiking expedition when President Jimmy Carter unexpectant dialed me up. That call reminded me of our 39th president, "He who walks with integrity and works righteousness, and speaks the truth in his heart." It just comes to me like that, the fifteenth Psalm of King David The United flight is now descending with Redmond off to the right and Bellevue to the left.

Upon landing at the SEATAC airport, I was ushered off to the ferry dock, anxious to see Carolyn and head back to Journey's End, our cherished place on Bainbridge Island. Now at home, pulling up my laptop to resume working on my book, I am mindful of a favorite passage, found in Micah 6:8, "He has shown you O man, what is good; And what does the Lord require of you, But to do justly, To love mercy, and to walk humbly with your God?"

My life's journey had little purpose until I met Carolyn and embraced the Christian faith that made the difference—the title of this book, A Higher Calling.

— Don Bonker
Bainbridge, Washington State,
January 2019

And, at Journey's End, we're still dancing....

ACKNOWLEDGEMENTS

Authoring a book has proven to be an arduous journey. It truly represents a lifetime of experiences and memories—a journey which meaning for me comes from my family, dear friends, and those who became role models that helped to shape my public persona.

From the outset, it has been my wife, Carolyn, who profoundly influenced my life. From the moment she showed up at my courthouse office to how she had me embrace the faith and values that made such an indelible difference in my personal and public life. What is not featured in the book are Carolyn's many artistic gifts, which may be the subject of my next book.

Also, my children made a significant contribution. Despite living worlds apart (Dawn in Seattle, Jonathan in Bangladesh), early on, they teamed up to design a book cover and offered insights only family members can do.

A special recognition to my former congressional staff. They not only served me well on Capitol Hill, but went on to highly successful careers and remain dear friends these past thirty years. They have graciously reviewed the various chapters to make sure I got it right. A special thanks to Scott Jackson, Dan and Terri Evans, Mark Murray, Gretchen Sorensen, Stephanie Solien, Nancy Parkes, Linda Suter, and Megan Bowmen.

Other former congressmen have authored books that were insightful about how Congress works (or doesn't work), and pressing for the reform agenda. My attempt at the genre may have added another such work to the cannon had I not met an international journalist, David Applefield, at a media forum in Astana, Kazakhstan. As we hang out at this former Soviet Republic, his interest turned to commitment that encouraged me to delve deeper into the narratives and sparked the episodes that have been crucial to my personal and political life. Thanks to David's involvement, *A Higher*

Calling became far more captivating and hopefully of greater interest to the reading public.

David Applefield later shared that he was so inspired by the book, he discussed with his wife and decided they would relocate (based in Paris at the time) to his previous home in New Jersey and run for Congress.

David was indeed a godsend, given his background and skill at nurturing authors, and now as a candidate for Congress, has allowed *A Higher Calling*, well, to dance in another congressional district!

— *Don Bonker*

PHOTOS

Bonker with Senator Henry Jackson at Olympia Port District in 1983. Log exports to Japan a major issue in 1974.

Lumber mill workers sharing concerns over the escalating shipment of logs to Japan, rather than being processed locally.

President Jimmy Carter with Congressman Bonker near Mt. Saint Helens on May 19, 1980, shortly after the volcanic eruption that left much of the area devastated and took 57 lives.

Portrayal of Washington Congressman, being led by Speaker Tom Foley. David Horsey, Seattle Post-Intelligencer, 1987

Cartoon jab at Congressman Paul Tsongas and Don Bonker, on their Official fact-finding trip to the Horn of Africa.
Lowell Sun newspaper.

Congressmen Bonker & Paul Tsongas in the oval office reporting on their fact finding mission to the Horn of Africa.

Accomplishments during one's lifetime are worthy of attention.
The true legacy are the children.

Three generations of Bonker males on the
beach in Southwest Washington.

Dawn Elyse accompanying her Daddy at a
Congressional event in the Capitol.

The Bonkers on the campaign trail at a typical 4th of July parade with robot volunteers
at a park in the 1988 U.S. Senate race.

Political Soulmates. A bipartisan group who met faithfully for 12 years in the U.S. Capitol. Paul & Rosemary Trible, Bill & Grace Nelson, and the Bonkers

Same couples, thirty-five years later at the Trible residence in Virginia

Private luncheon at the White House with President Jimmy and Roselyn Carter. What's interesting—the appearance of Ms. Carter and Bonker, attire in coordination, her arm around his... (who is that stranger standing next to them?)

Don And Carolyn wedding photo
at the Stanger property on
July 10, 1971

At a White Houlse Christmas
party hosted by Ronald Reagan

Bonker family at the Long Island Cedar Grove Trail twelve years after it was
designated as "Don Bonker Cedar Grove Trail" by the Fish and Wildlife
Service in June, 2005.

PROFILES OF CHARACTER

by Don Bonker

John F. Kennedy's profiles in courage portrayed eight US senators who had the courage and integrity to take great political and personal risk to put the national interest above the personal and political gain. During my years in Congress, I witnessed similar individuals, whose character and integrity not only represented the best in our political system but helped to shape my sense of public duty, highlighted in my book.

As Speaker of the House of Representatives, Tom Foley's congeniality and civility drew respect and admiration across the political spectrum. Our Founder Fathers would simmer with pride - a Speaker who bridged the differences, which is solely missed these days. His trust relationship with Republicans prompted a common musing among its leaders, "I wish he were a Republican." But his rising above the political and self interest came at a cost. As the de-facto leader of the Democratic Party, he failed to raise millions and launch attacks to

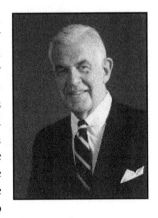

defeat Republican House members. In the 1996 election, the Democrats lost enough seats to give the Republicans the the majority, ushering in the Newt Gingrich era of combativeness and obstructionism. Tom Foley himself lost the election. He also served as ambassador to Japan.

His two book titles speak volumes about Mark Hatfield's political courage: *Between a Rock and Hard Place* and *Against the Grain: Reflections of a Rebel Republican*. Most notable was his opposition to the Vietnam War that had him at odds with the Republican Party, at a time when he was Richard Nixon's top choice as vice president. His conscience would not have him alter his position, the ultimate sacrifice for doing what's right. He was highly regarded in the US Senate and renowned nationally as a leader with a deep faith. Carolyn and I were in a small prayer group with the Hatfields during our years in Congress and since.

The former US Senator and presidential candidate Paul Tsongas, at the time of his death at age fifty-seven, was described by the Massachusetts newspaper, *Independence*, "as the country's most straightforward, farsighted and utterly honest...setting an unparalleled example of integrity, candor and commitment."

We came to Congress, part of the Watergate Class of '74, and were closely associated, including being on a fact-finding trip to Ethiopia in 1976. We had an unexpected meeting with the so-called "butcher of Addis Ababa" whom Paul confronted about human rights abuses—that was courageous but risky. His campaign for president is noted for adopting a pro-business doctrine at odds with his party and organized labor, not catering to his primary base but rising to a higher calling.

It is rare that someone in the House of Representatives becomes a legend in his own time—this was Tom Lantos, the only Holocaust survivor to serve in Congress. It was a cause deeply imbedded in his early life at age sixteen when he was sent to a labor camp in Hungary. He eventually escaped and joined a resistance movement headed by Raoul Wallenberg who helped to usher thousands of Jewish citizens to safety. We had a shared interest in human rights. At the time, I chaired the Foreign Affairs  Subcommittee on Human Rights, but Tom Lantos was the authentic voice and beacon light that was reflected in capitols around the world. He was the conscience of our foreign policy, an advocate who confronted suppressive regimes, and he provided the moral authority unmatched during his service to our country.

It has been a century since a president's cabinet secretary was also a cowboy celebrity. Malcom Baldrige's hobby was steer roping that set him up to win prize money at rodeos, but ultimately, he succumbed to internal injuries from riding a horse in competition on July 25, 1987. Secretary Baldrige's vision and managerial style was way beyond what we generally see at the bureaucratic Department of Commerce. Surprisingly, I received an invitation to have breakfast at the secretary's office to discuss international trade. We were  entirely in sync which led to meeting monthly. A Republican cabinet member outreached to a young congressman that led to many accomplishments—a contrast to today's Trump administration and the House Democrats who are hardly in communication on any issue.

A former Republican governor and US senator, Daniel J. Evans' legacy is preserving Washington State's precious natural resources. A rare moment of bipartisanship, bringing together the Northwest senators and congressmen, then persuading committee chairmen and the Senate leadership to send the most landmark environmental legislation to President Ronald Reagan's desk. At a time, local hostility to passing such legislation made his task all the more daunting. Yet, thanks to Daniel Evans, future generations can enjoy his accomplishments: The Columbia Gorge National Scenic Area, the Mount St. Helens National Volcanic Monument Act, the Washington Park Wilderness Act, Bowerman Basin Wildlife National Refuge Act, and much more.

No one had more influence on my life than Doug Coe. He had no position, no title, never became a household name, yet Doug was well known and highly regarded by ten US presidents, congressional leaders, foreign dignitaries, and prominent American and international businessmen. A worthy glimpse of Doug Coe, who presided over the National Prayer Breakfast for fifty years, appeared in a *New Yorker* article by Peter J. Boyer: "his admirers describe him in terms that suggest a near-mystical visionary with a powerful personal magnetism." Doug's focus was on the teachings and principles of Jesus Christ, which he felt transcended all faiths, writing, "Peace between nations depends on goodwill between individuals."

Mikhail Khodorkovsky was among a group of oligarchs who acquired state assets and immense wealth during the Boris Yeltsin era in Russia. In his mid-thirties, Khodorkovsky was head of Russia's largest oil company and listed among its wealthiest, but he had a higher calling. In 2012, *Vanity Fair* magazine reported, "Khodorkovsky  swore off his absolute faith in wealth, just as he had sworn off his absolute faith in Communism." Devoted to social justice and democratic norms, he dared to confront Vladimir Putin about corruption in the Kremlin, who then had him arrested, put into a courtroom cage, and sent to prison for ten years. At APCO Worldwide, I represented this man as he became a symbol of human rights and moral courage worldwide.

Another Russian oligarch, Vladimir Gusinsky acquired a media empire overnight and became a champion of free and independent reporting in the post-Communist era. Featured in *The New Yorker* (February 2b8, 1994) by David Remnick, who referred to Gusinsky as "Citizen Kane, Russia's first and biggest media mogul and, as a result, is deeply embroiled in Kremlin politics." That is what got him  in trouble with Russia's Vladimir Putin, who had no tolerance for objective reporting and criticism. He had Gusinsky arrested, put in prison, seized his media assets, and forced to leave the country. I accompanied Gusinsky's meetings with *Washington Post*, *Newsweek*, the Newseum, observing his embracing Western values, which he stood up for and paid a heavy price.

Women have been dominant in my political life. It began when I served as an intern to Senator Maurine Neuberger (D-OR), one of two women in the US Senate at the time. A few years later, elected to Congress to succeed the legendary Julia Butler Hansen, then replaced by the exuberant Jolene Unsoeld. In 1992, the "Little Mom in Tennis Shoes," Patty Murray ended my political career. But what stands out is Margery Kraus, founder of APCO Worldwide, who led a startup consulting firm to become a global leader in public affairs and strategic communication. At APCO Worldwide for thirty years, I saw up close Margery's phenomenal business skills and many accomplishments, but also how she treated everyone like family—a rare blend that led to APCO receiving numerous awards for the best place to work.

WORKS CITED

Bisnow, Mark. 1990. *In the Shadow of the Dome: Chronicles of a Capitol Hill Aide*. New York, New York: William Morrow & Co.

Bonker, Don. 1988. *America's Trade Crisis: The Making of the U.S. Trade Deficit*. Boston, Massachusetts: Houghton Mifflin Harcourt.

Hatfield, Mark. 2001. *Against the Grain: Reflections of a Rebel Republican*. Ashland, Oregon: White Cloud Press.

Hatfield, Mark. 2003. "Introduction." In *Real Christianity: Discerning True and False Faith*, by William Wilberforce, edited by James M. Houston. Vancouver, British Columbia: Regent College Publishing.

Hoffman, David E. 2001. *The Oligarchs: Wealth and Power in the New Russia*. New York, New York: PublicAffairs Books.

Manning, Harvey. 1984. *Washington Wilderness: The Unfinished Work*. Seattle, Washington: Mountaineers Books.

CPSIA information can be obtained
at www.ICGtesting.com
Printed in the USA
LVHW042016100320
649649LV00001B/1